DAUGHTER OF THE EMPEROR

1

RINO

Original story by **YUNSUL**

DAUGHTER OF THE EMPEROR

1

RINO

Original story by YUNSUL

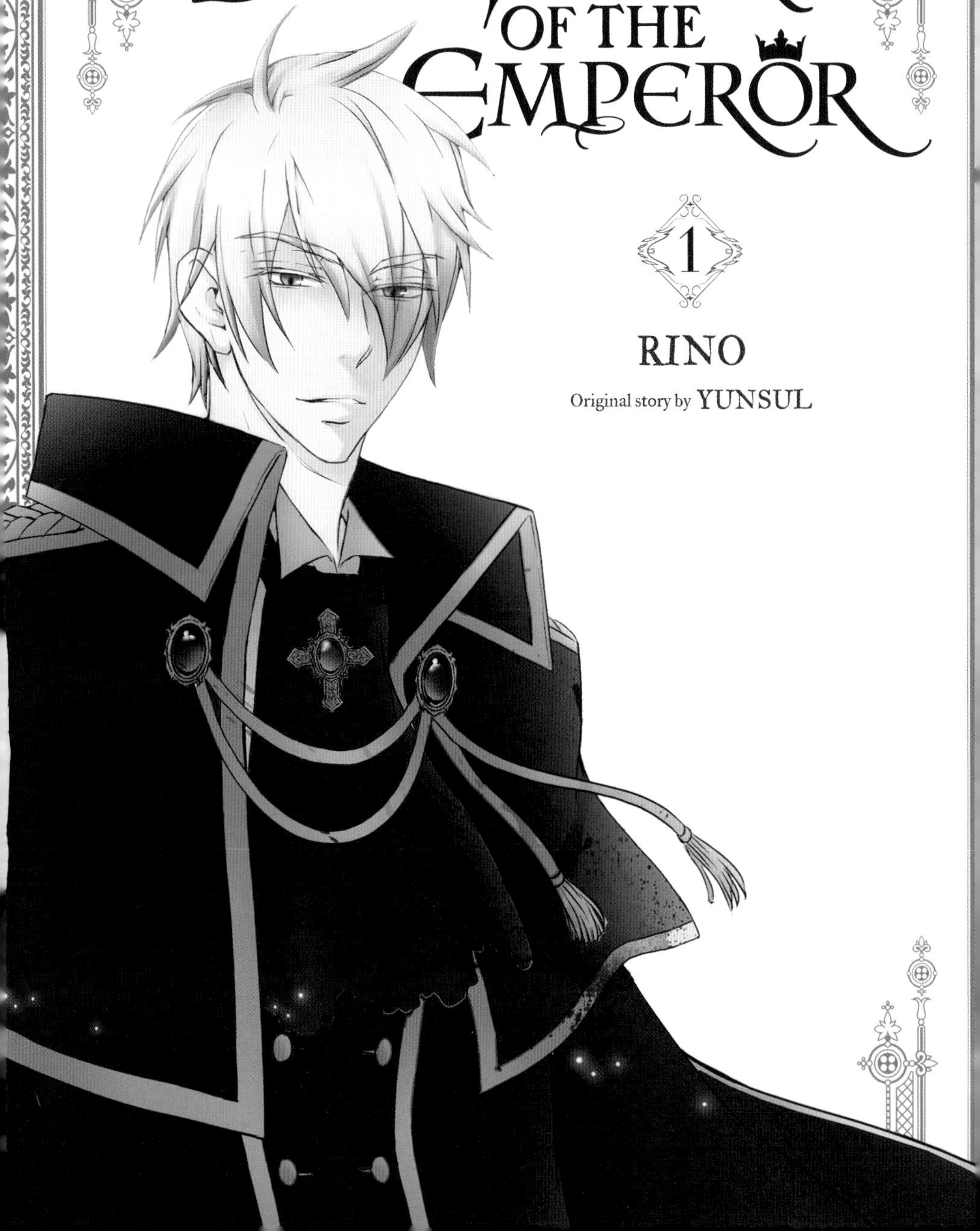

CONTENTS ✦ 1

DAUGHTER OF THE EMPEROR

Prologue

DAUGHTER
OF THE
EMPEROR

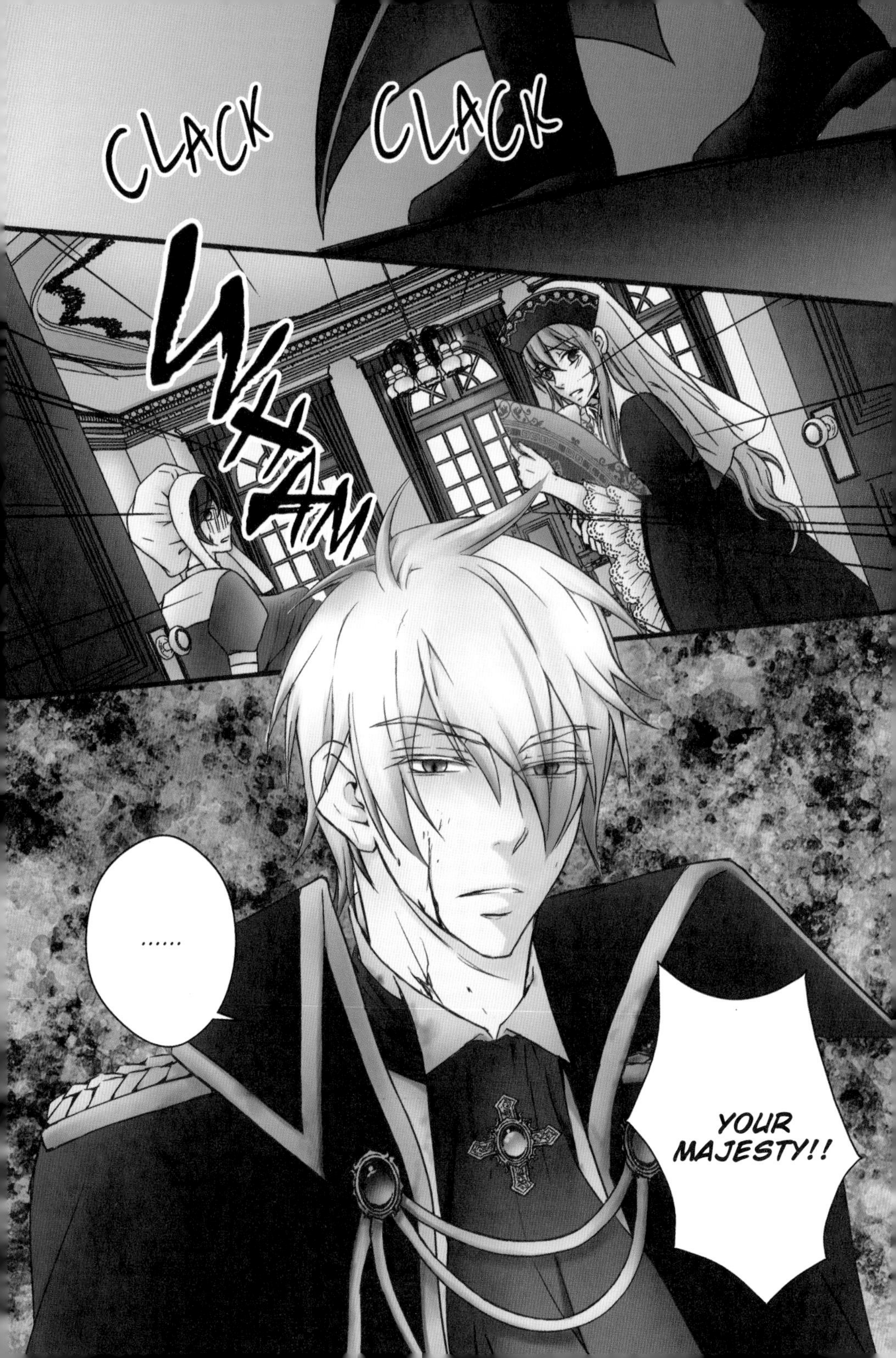
CLACK CLACK
WHAM
......
YOUR MAJESTY!!

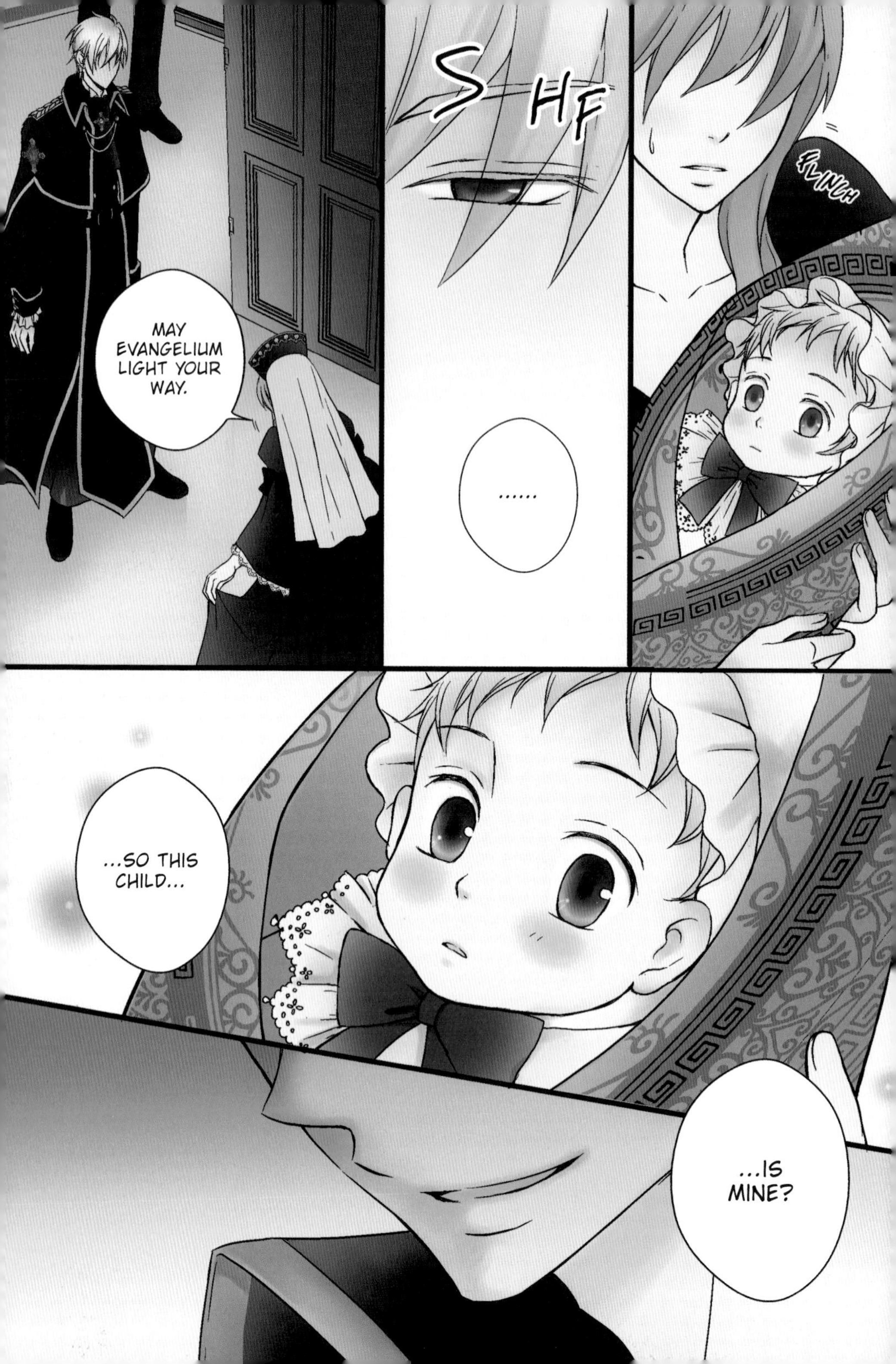
MAY EVANGELIUM LIGHT YOUR WAY.
SHF
......
FLINCH
...SO THIS CHILD...
...IS MINE?

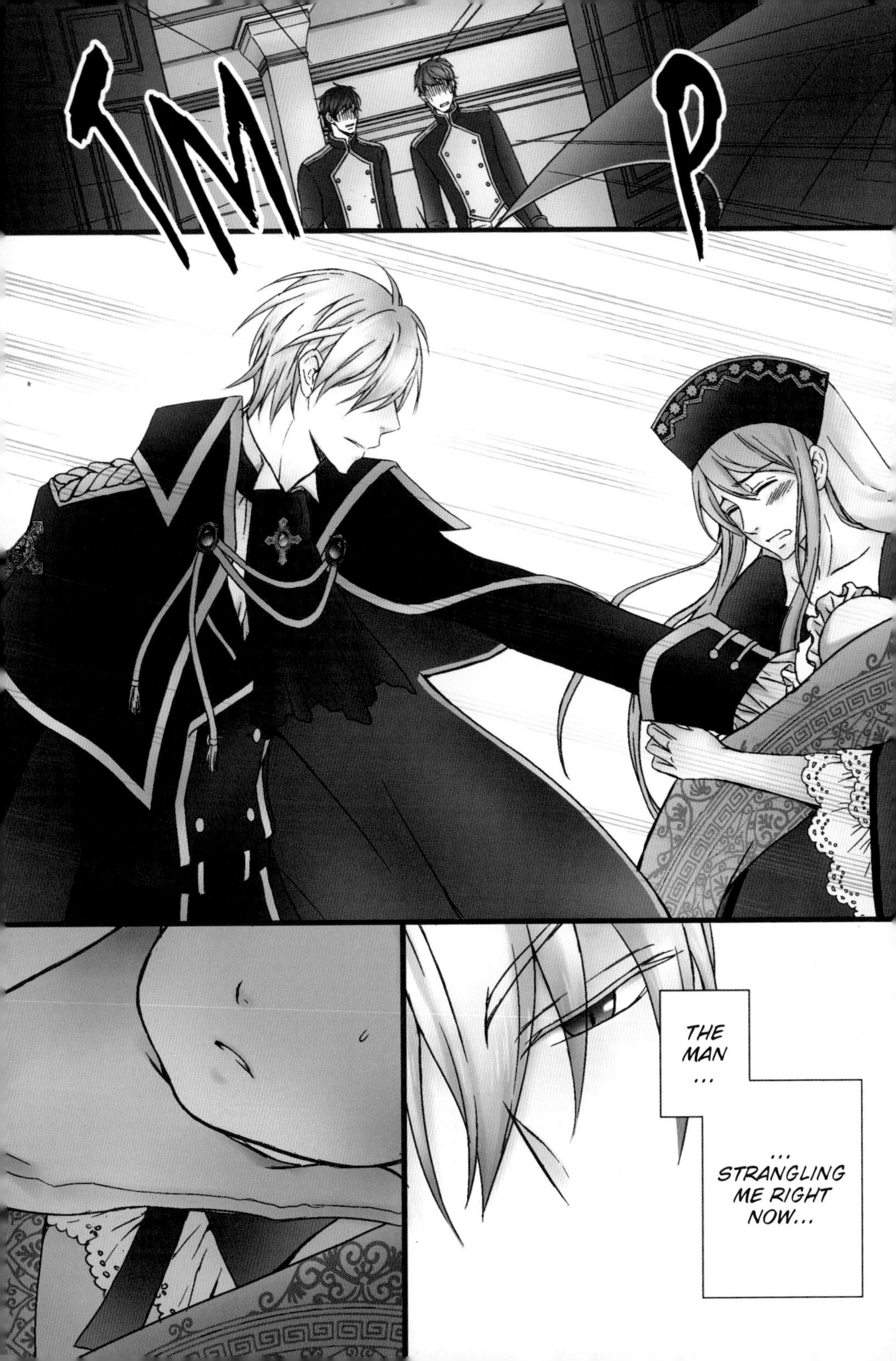
TMP
THE MAN...
...STRANGLING ME RIGHT NOW...

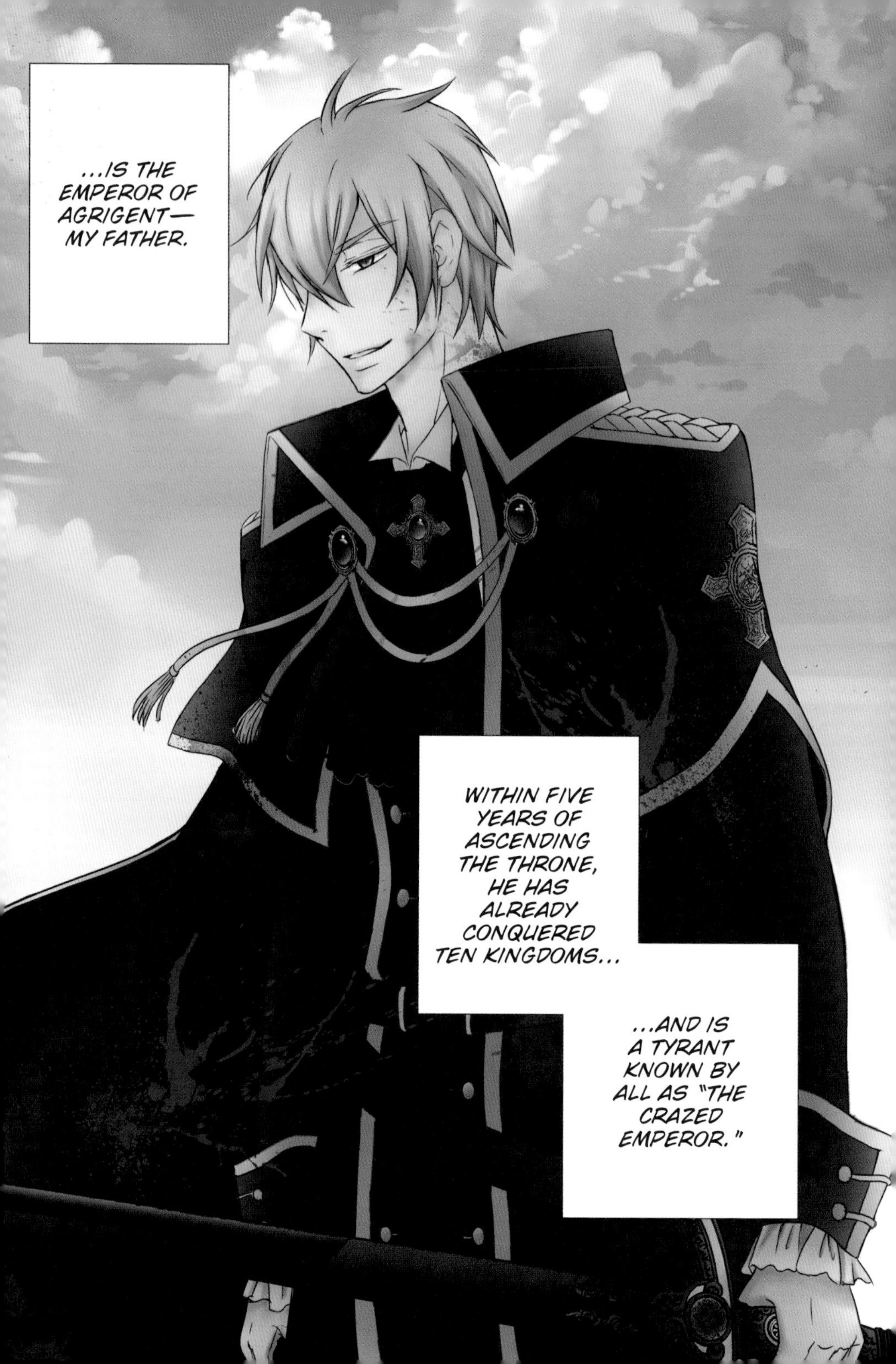
...IS THE EMPEROR OF AGRIGENT—MY FATHER.
WITHIN FIVE YEARS OF ASCENDING THE THRONE, HE HAS ALREADY CONQUERED TEN KINGDOMS...
...AND IS A TYRANT KNOWN BY ALL AS "THE CRAZED EMPEROR."

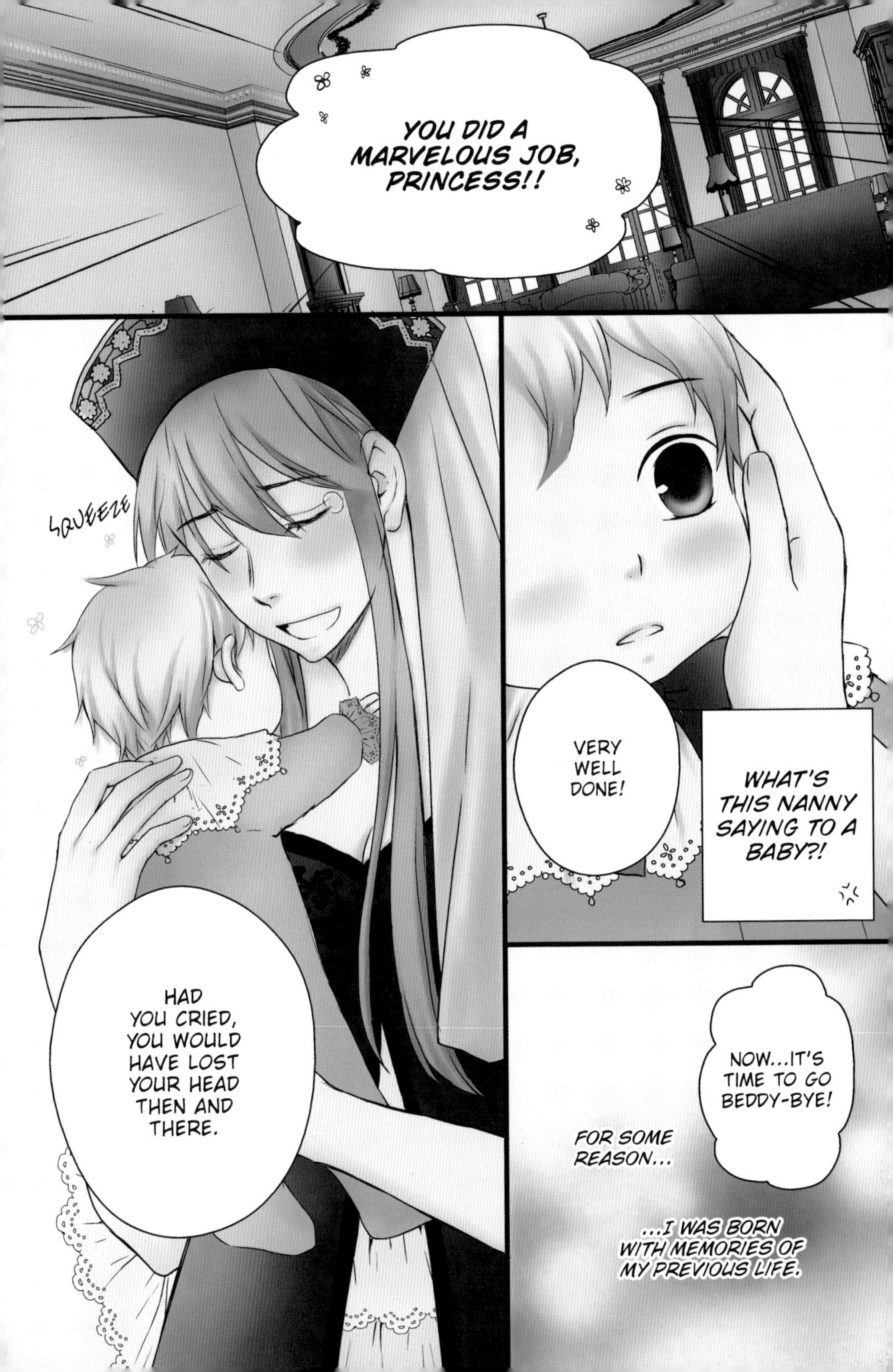
YOU DID A MARVELOUS JOB, PRINCESS!!
SQUEEZE
HAD YOU CRIED, YOU WOULD HAVE LOST YOUR HEAD THEN AND THERE.
VERY WELL DONE!
WHAT'S THIS NANNY SAYING TO A BABY?!
NOW...IT'S TIME TO GO BEDDY-BYE!
FOR SOME REASON...
...I WAS BORN WITH MEMORIES OF MY PREVIOUS LIFE.

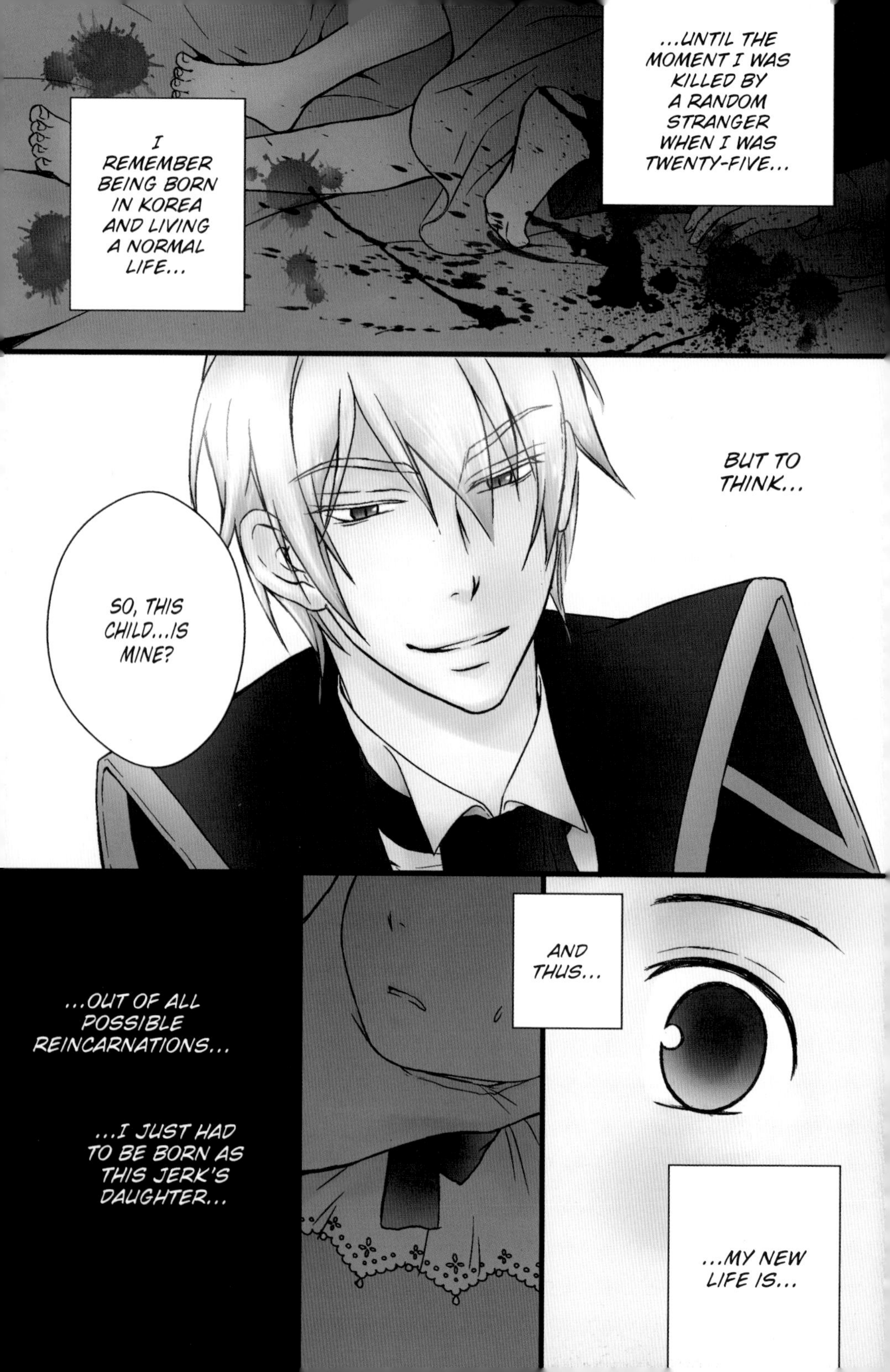

I REMEMBER BEING BORN IN KOREA AND LIVING A NORMAL LIFE...
...UNTIL THE MOMENT I WAS KILLED BY A RANDOM STRANGER WHEN I WAS TWENTY-FIVE...
SO, THIS CHILD...IS MINE?
BUT TO THINK...
...OUT OF ALL POSSIBLE REINCARNATIONS...
...I JUST HAD TO BE BORN AS THIS JERK'S DAUGHTER...
AND THUS...
...MY NEW LIFE IS...

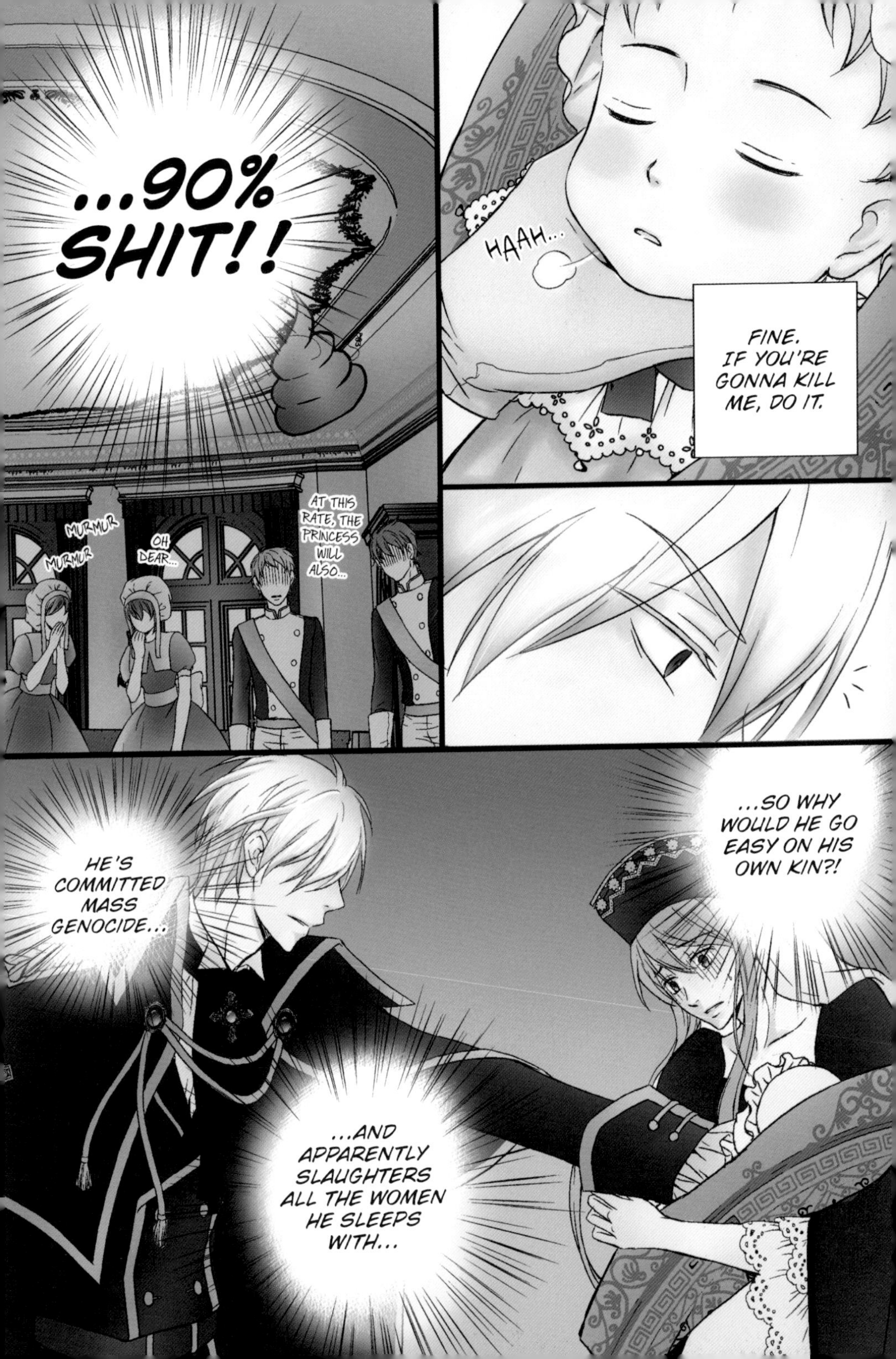

...90% SHIT!!
MURMUR
MURMUR
OH DEAR...
AT THIS RATE, THE PRINCESS WILL ALSO...
HAAH...
FINE. IF YOU'RE GONNA KILL ME, DO IT.
HE'S COMMITTED MASS GENOCIDE...
...SO WHY WOULD HE GO EASY ON HIS OWN KIN?!
...AND APPARENTLY SLAUGHTERS ALL THE WOMEN HE SLEEPS WITH...

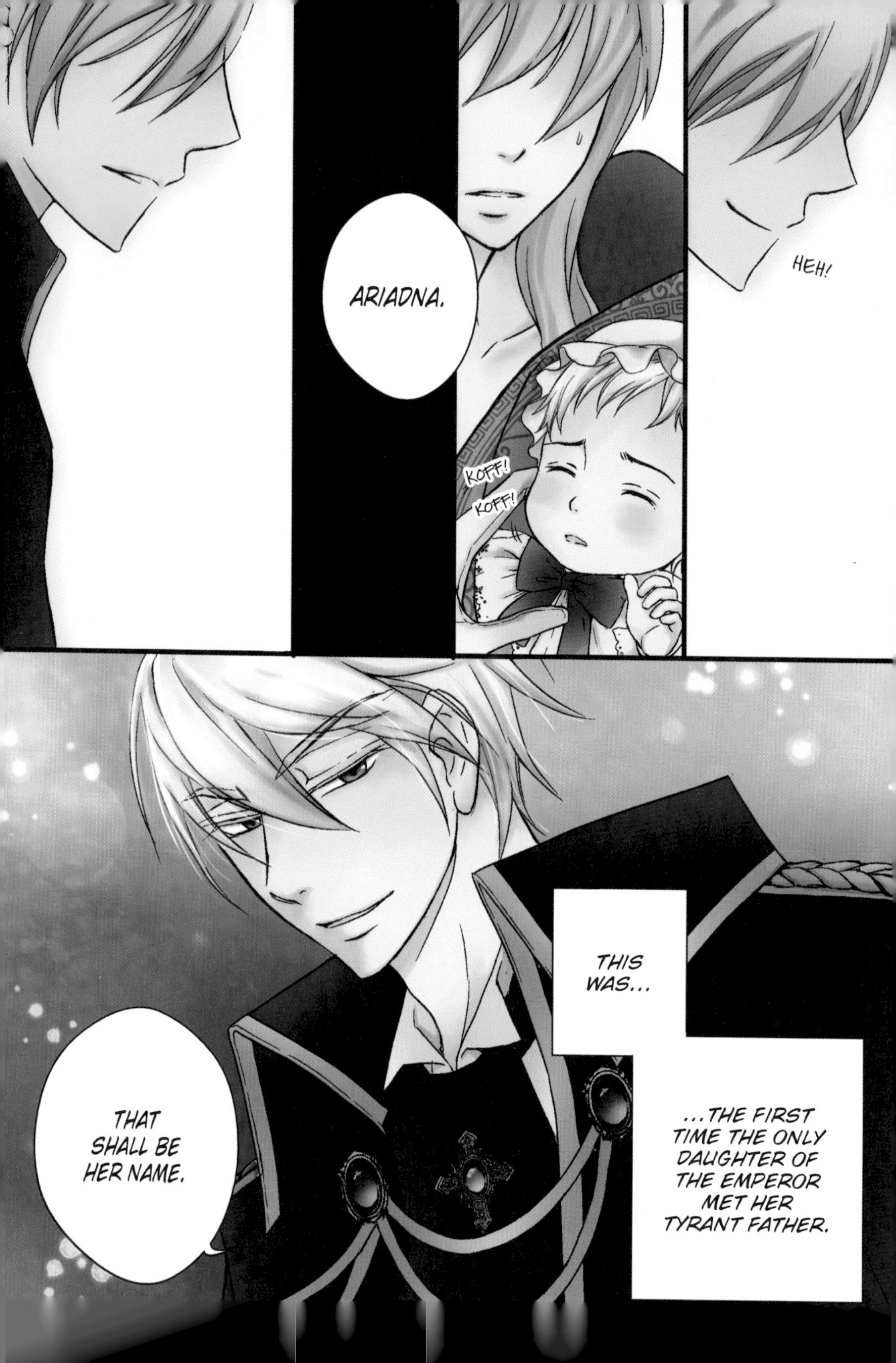

ARIADNA.
KOFF!
KOFF!
HEH!
THAT SHALL BE HER NAME.
THIS WAS...
...THE FIRST TIME THE ONLY DAUGHTER OF THE EMPEROR MET HER TYRANT FATHER.

Hello, I'm Your Baby (1)

DAUGHTER
OF THE
EMPEROR

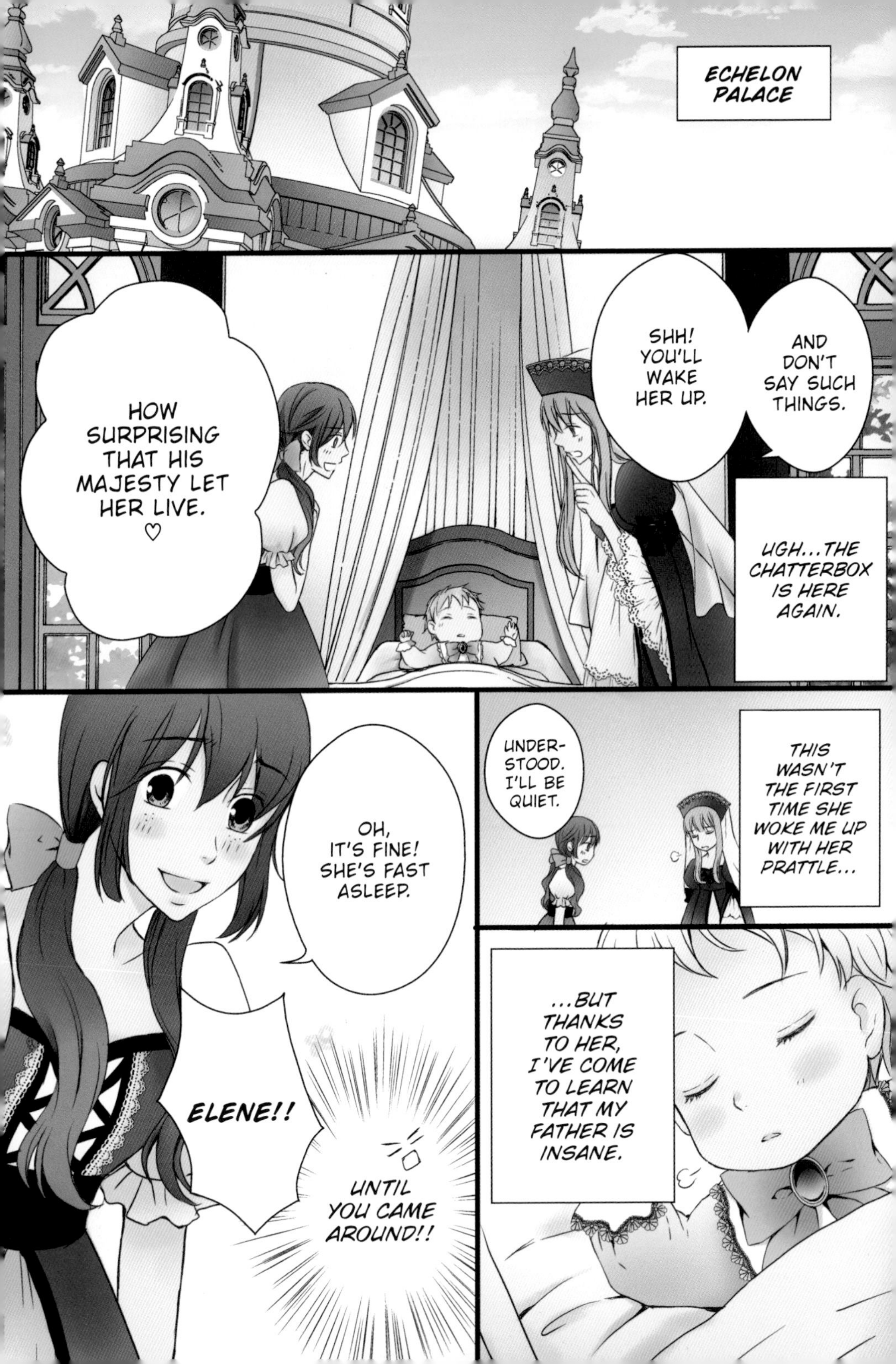
ECHELON PALACE
HOW SURPRISING THAT HIS MAJESTY LET HER LIVE. ♡
SHH! YOU'LL WAKE HER UP.
AND DON'T SAY SUCH THINGS.
UGH...THE CHATTERBOX IS HERE AGAIN.
OH, IT'S FINE! SHE'S FAST ASLEEP.
ELENE!!
UNTIL YOU CAME AROUND!!
UNDER-STOOD. I'LL BE QUIET.
THIS WASN'T THE FIRST TIME SHE WOKE ME UP WITH HER PRATTLE...
...BUT THANKS TO HER, I'VE COME TO LEARN THAT MY FATHER IS INSANE.

COUNTLESS WOMEN HAVE BEEN ENTICED BY HIS LOOKS AND POSITION...

...AND HAVE GOTTEN PREGNANT AFTER SEDUCING HIM, BUT...

SINCE YOU BEAR MY CHILD, YOU WISH TO BE THE EMPRESS, YOU SAY?

...APPARENTLY, NONE OF THEM SUCCESSFULLY GAVE BIRTH.

IN THE FACE OF THE CRAZED EMPEROR, WHO HELD NOT A SHRED OF AFFECTION FOR HIS OWN BLOOD...

...THE DEMANDS OF THE WOMEN USING THEIR UNBORN BABIES AS WEAPONS...

...WERE MET WITH GRUESOME ENDS.

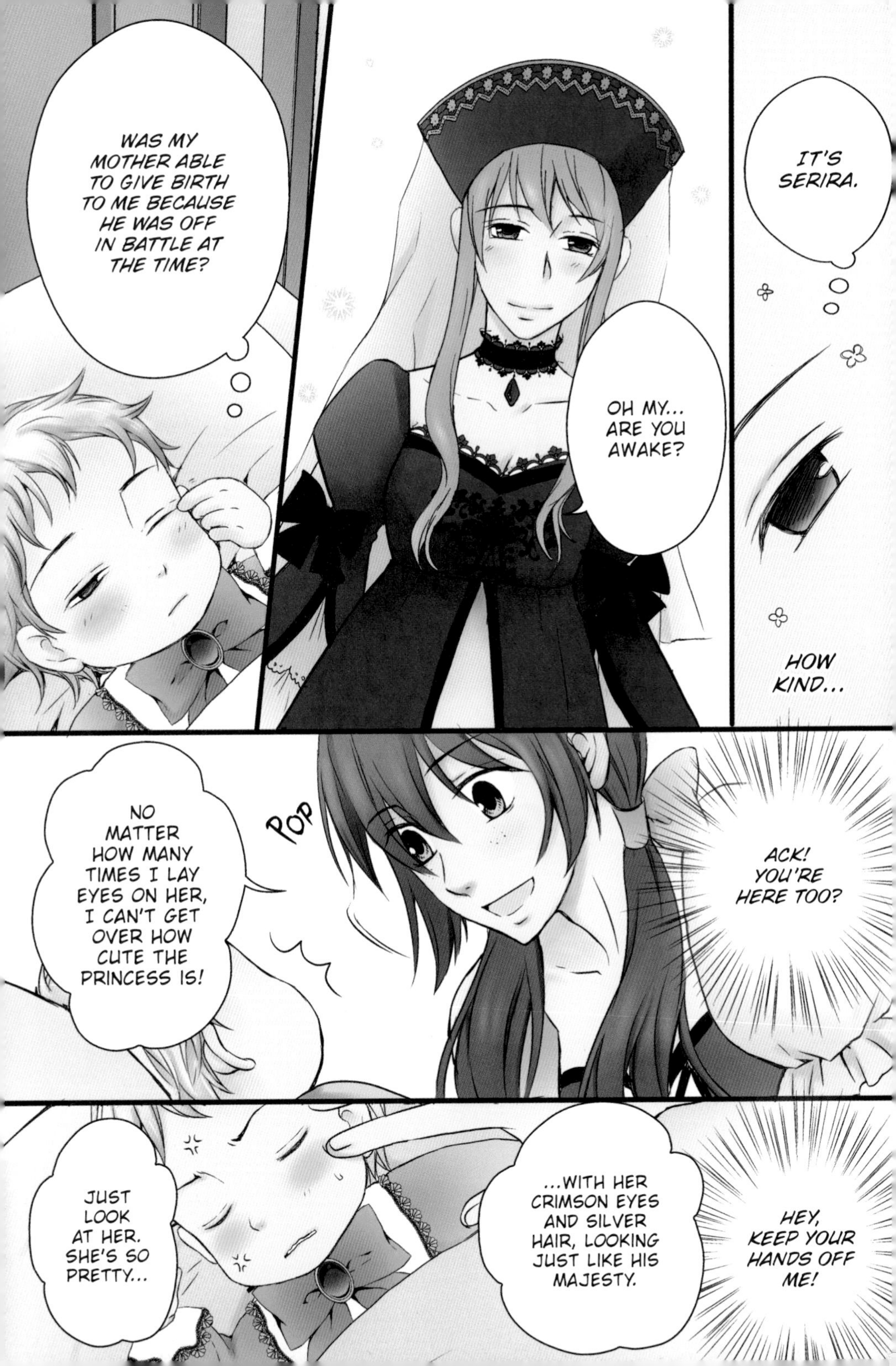
WAS MY MOTHER ABLE TO GIVE BIRTH TO ME BECAUSE HE WAS OFF IN BATTLE AT THE TIME?
OH MY... ARE YOU AWAKE?
IT'S SERIRA.
HOW KIND...
NO MATTER HOW MANY TIMES I LAY EYES ON HER, I CAN'T GET OVER HOW CUTE THE PRINCESS IS!
POP
ACK! YOU'RE HERE TOO?
JUST LOOK AT HER. SHE'S SO PRETTY...
...WITH HER CRIMSON EYES AND SILVER HAIR, LOOKING JUST LIKE HIS MAJESTY.
HEY, KEEP YOUR HANDS OFF ME!

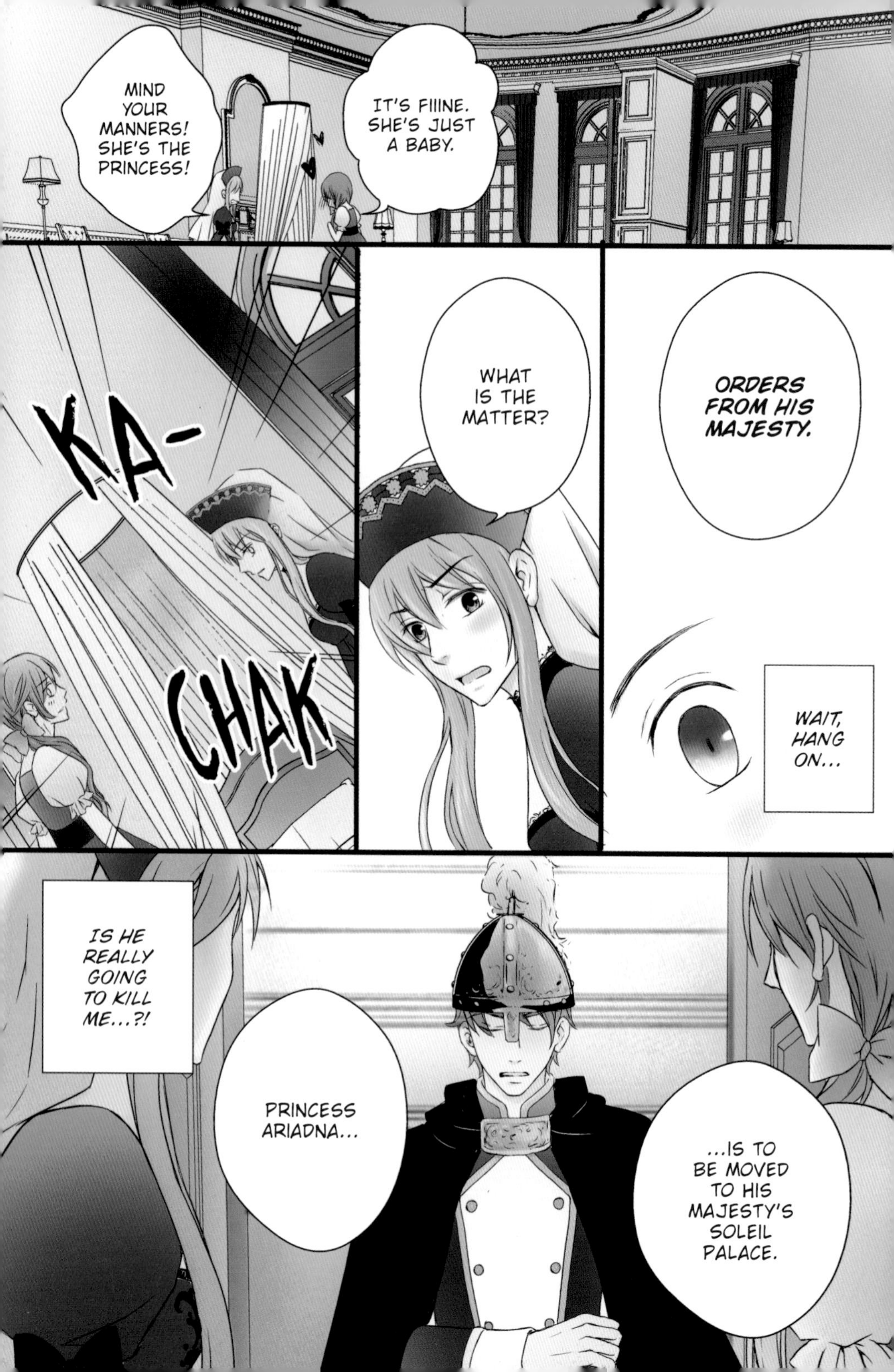
MIND YOUR MANNERS! SHE'S THE PRINCESS!
IT'S FIIINE. SHE'S JUST A BABY.
KA-
CHAK
WHAT IS THE MATTER?
ORDERS FROM HIS MAJESTY.
WAIT, HANG ON...
IS HE REALLY GOING TO KILL ME...?!
PRINCESS ARIADNA...
...IS TO BE MOVED TO HIS MAJESTY'S SOLEIL PALACE.

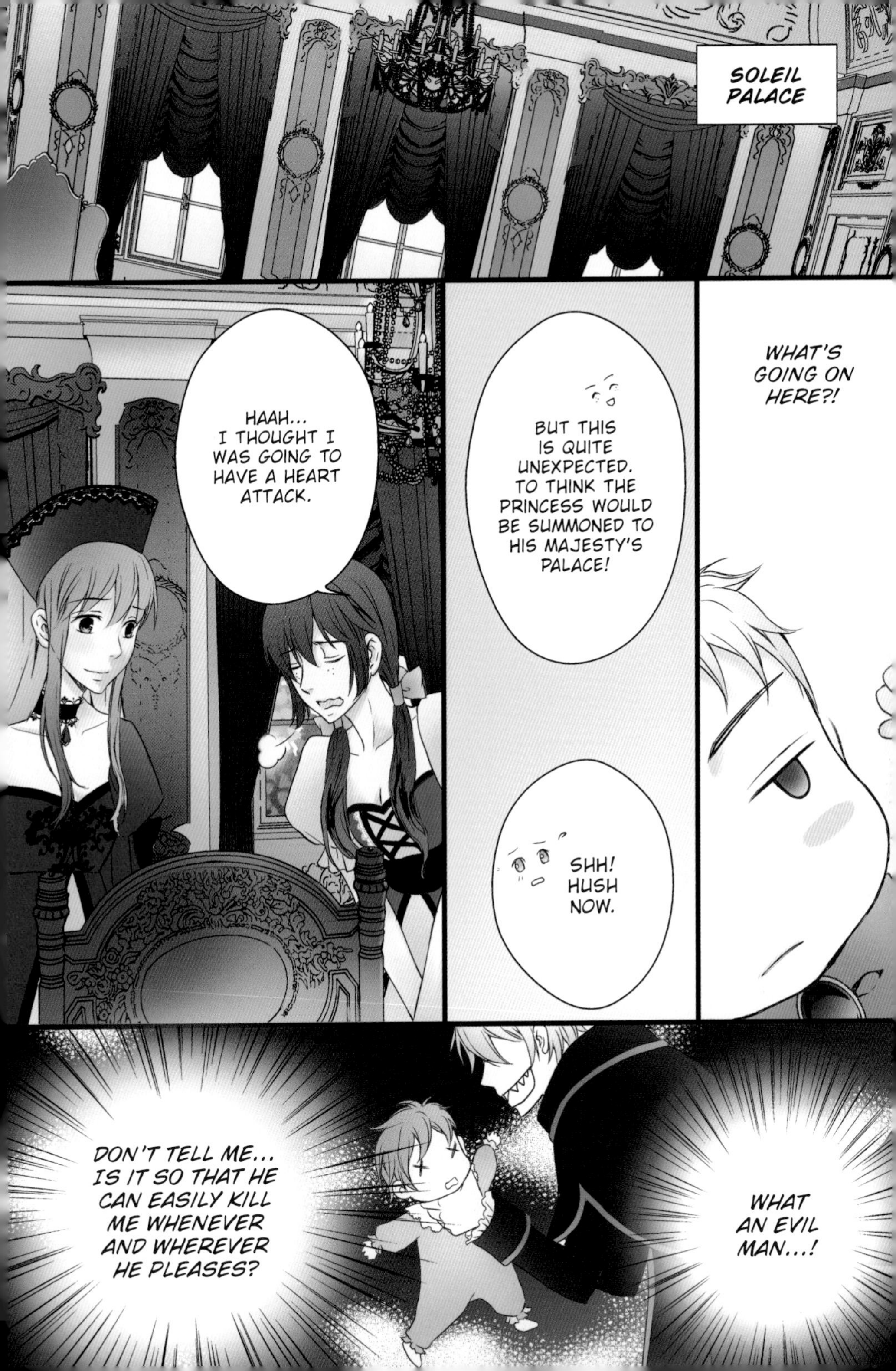
SOLEIL PALACE
HAAH... I THOUGHT I WAS GOING TO HAVE A HEART ATTACK.
BUT THIS IS QUITE UNEXPECTED. TO THINK THE PRINCESS WOULD BE SUMMONED TO HIS MAJESTY'S PALACE!
SHH! HUSH NOW.
WHAT'S GOING ON HERE?!
DON'T TELL ME... IS IT SO THAT HE CAN EASILY KILL ME WHENEVER AND WHEREVER HE PLEASES?
WHAT AN EVIL MAN...!

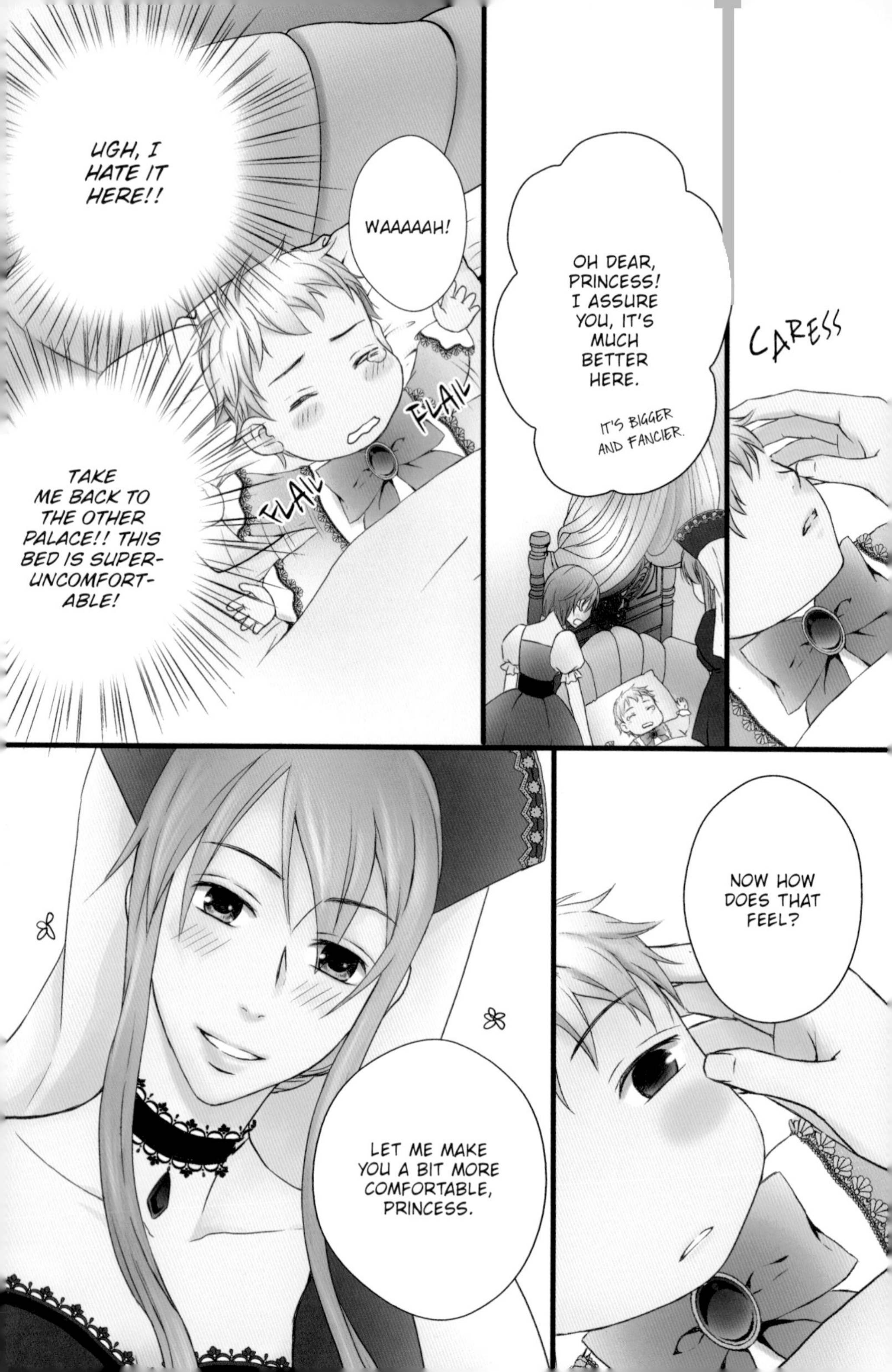
UGH, I HATE IT HERE!!
WAAAAAH!
FLAIL
FLAIL
TAKE ME BACK TO THE OTHER PALACE!! THIS BED IS SUPER-UNCOMFORTABLE!
OH DEAR, PRINCESS! I ASSURE YOU, IT'S MUCH BETTER HERE.
IT'S BIGGER AND FANCIER.
CARESS
LET ME MAKE YOU A BIT MORE COMFORTABLE, PRINCESS.
NOW HOW DOES THAT FEEL?

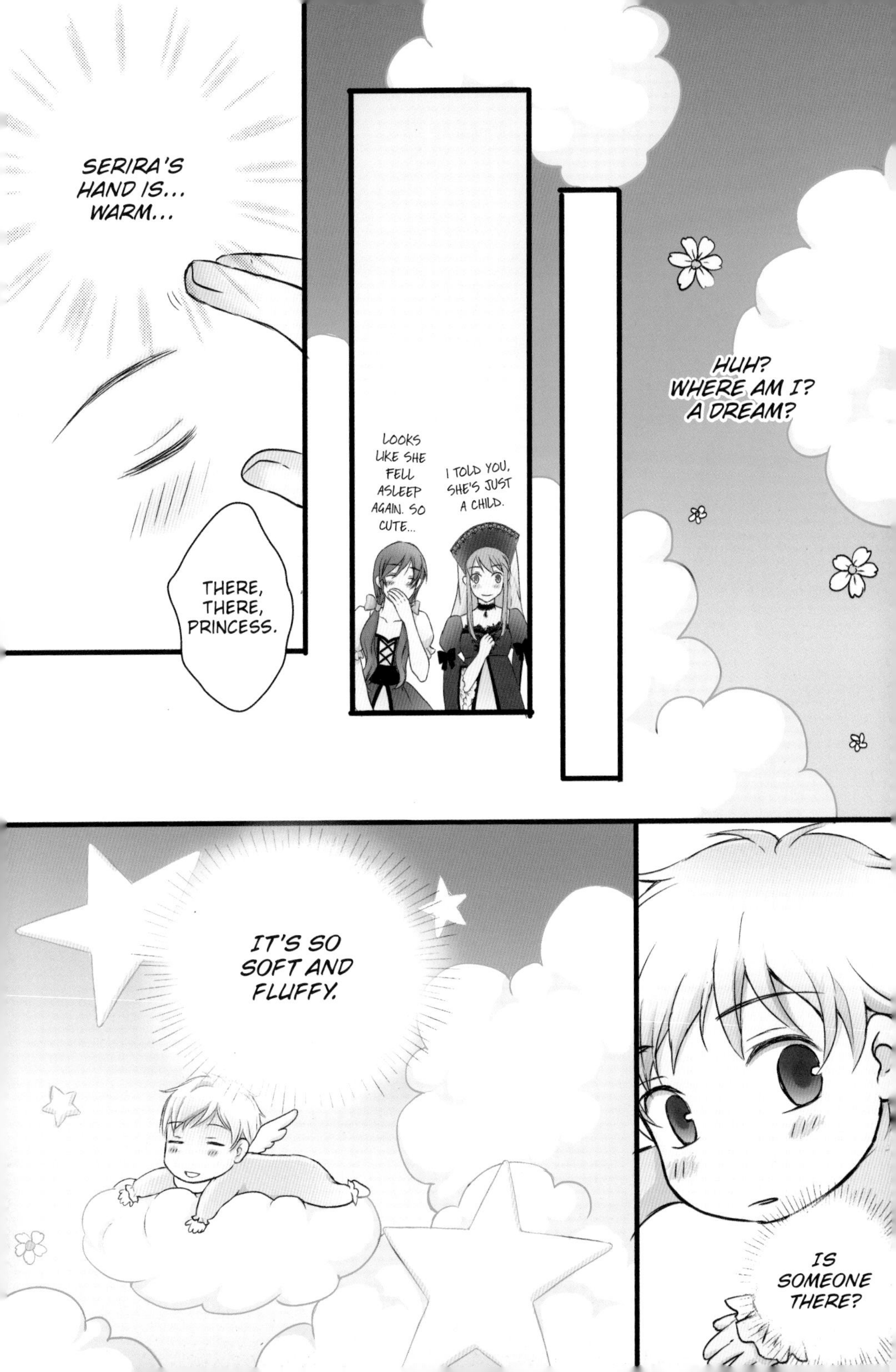
SERIRA'S HAND IS... WARM...
THERE, THERE, PRINCESS.
LOOKS LIKE SHE FELL ASLEEP AGAIN. SO CUTE...
I TOLD YOU, SHE'S JUST A CHILD.
HUH? WHERE AM I? A DREAM?
IT'S SO SOFT AND FLUFFY.
IS SOMEONE THERE?

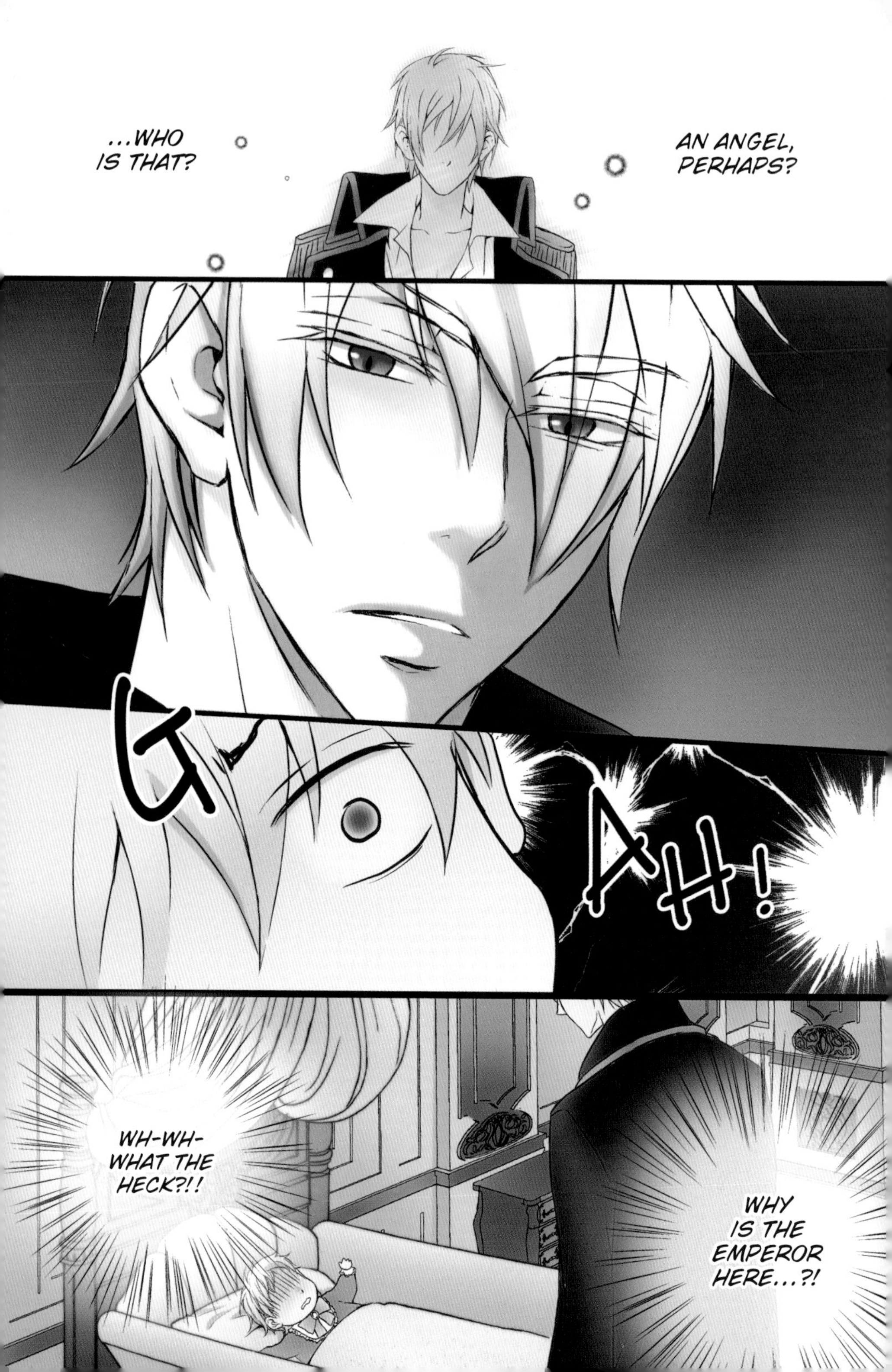
...WHO IS THAT?
AN ANGEL, PERHAPS?
GASP!
WH-WH-WHAT THE HECK?!!
WHY IS THE EMPEROR HERE...?!

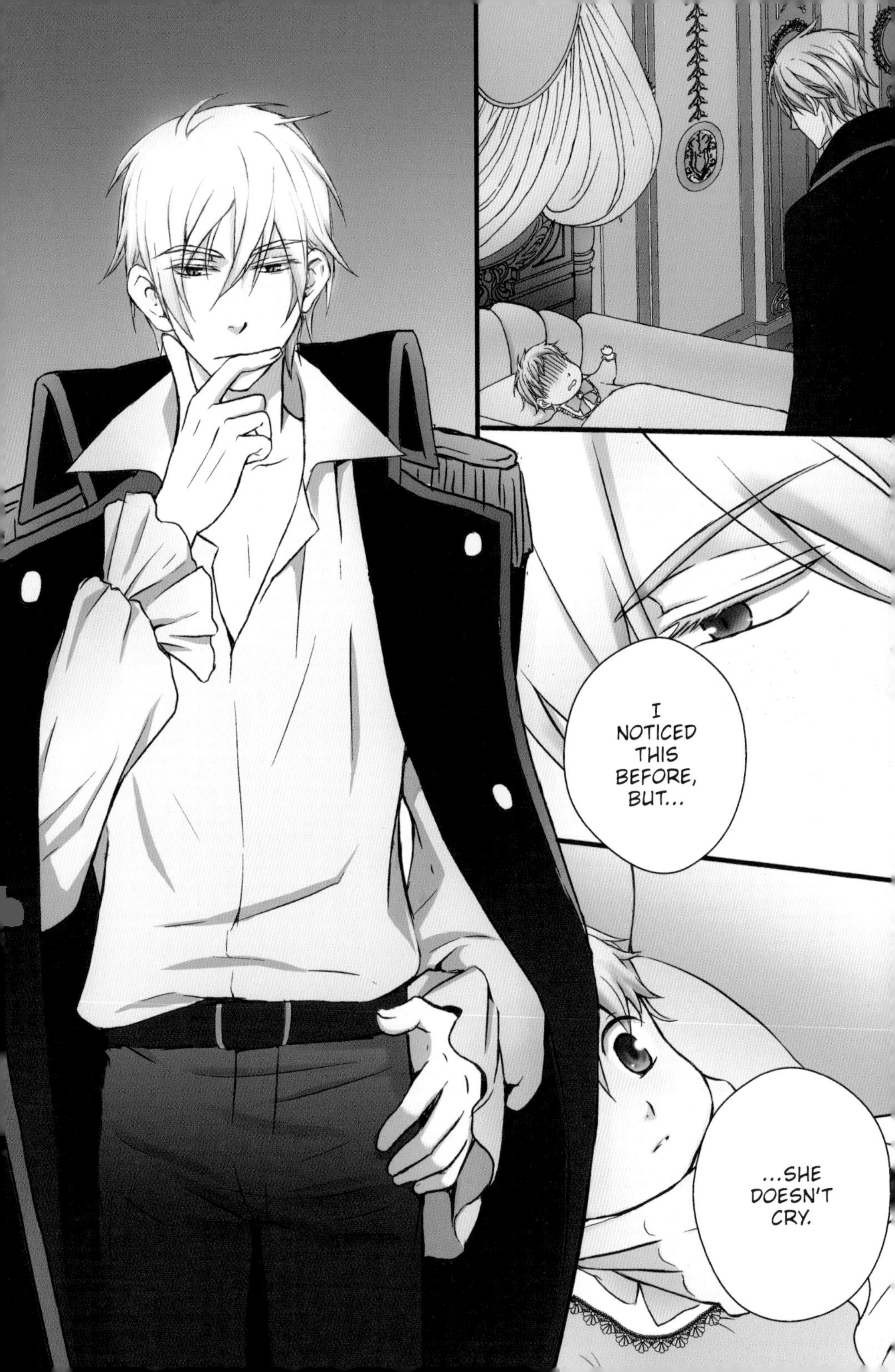
I NOTICED THIS BEFORE, BUT...
...SHE DOESN'T CRY.

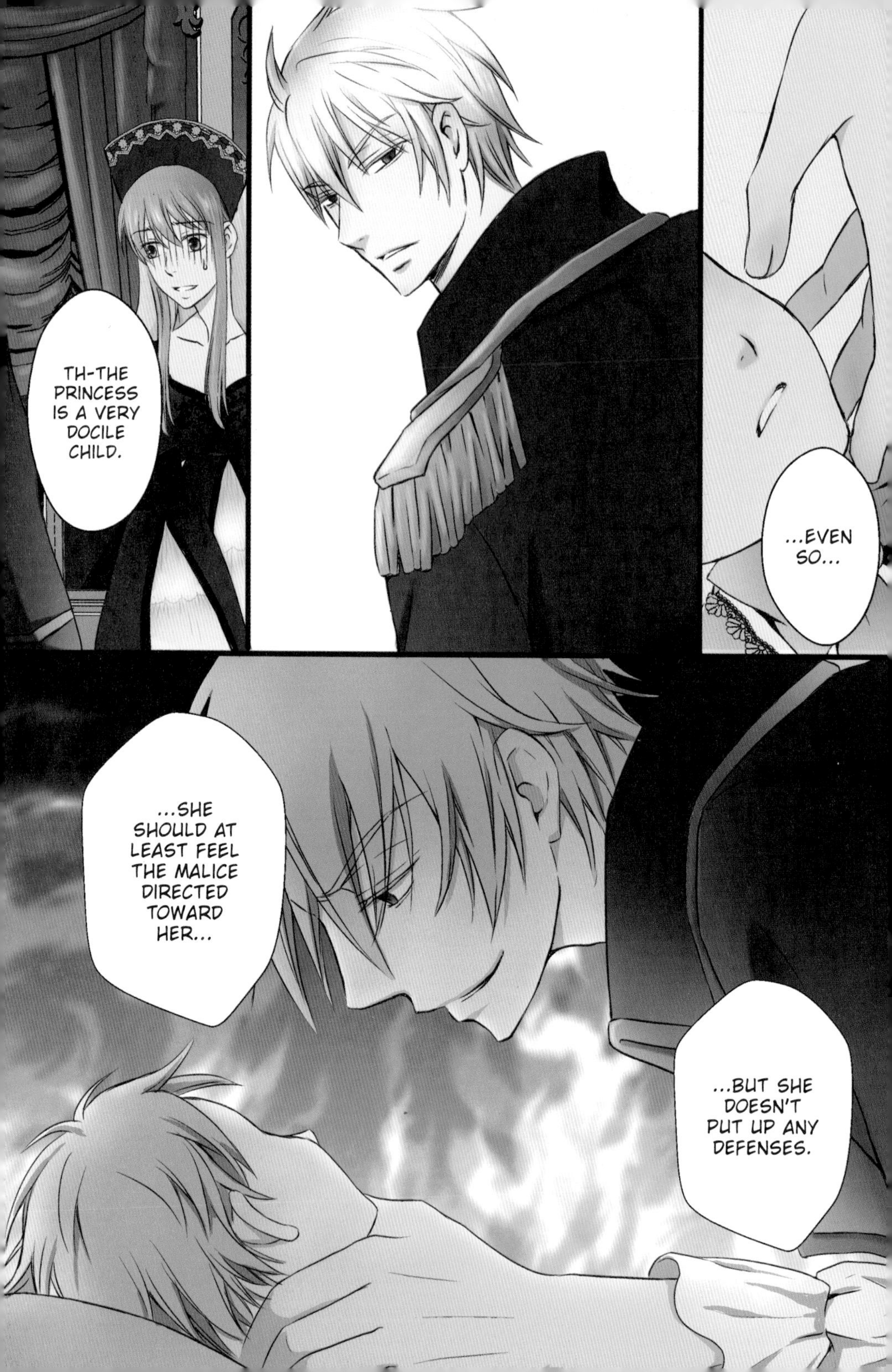
TH-THE PRINCESS IS A VERY DOCILE CHILD.
...EVEN SO...
...SHE SHOULD AT LEAST FEEL THE MALICE DIRECTED TOWARD HER...
...BUT SHE DOESN'T PUT UP ANY DEFENSES.

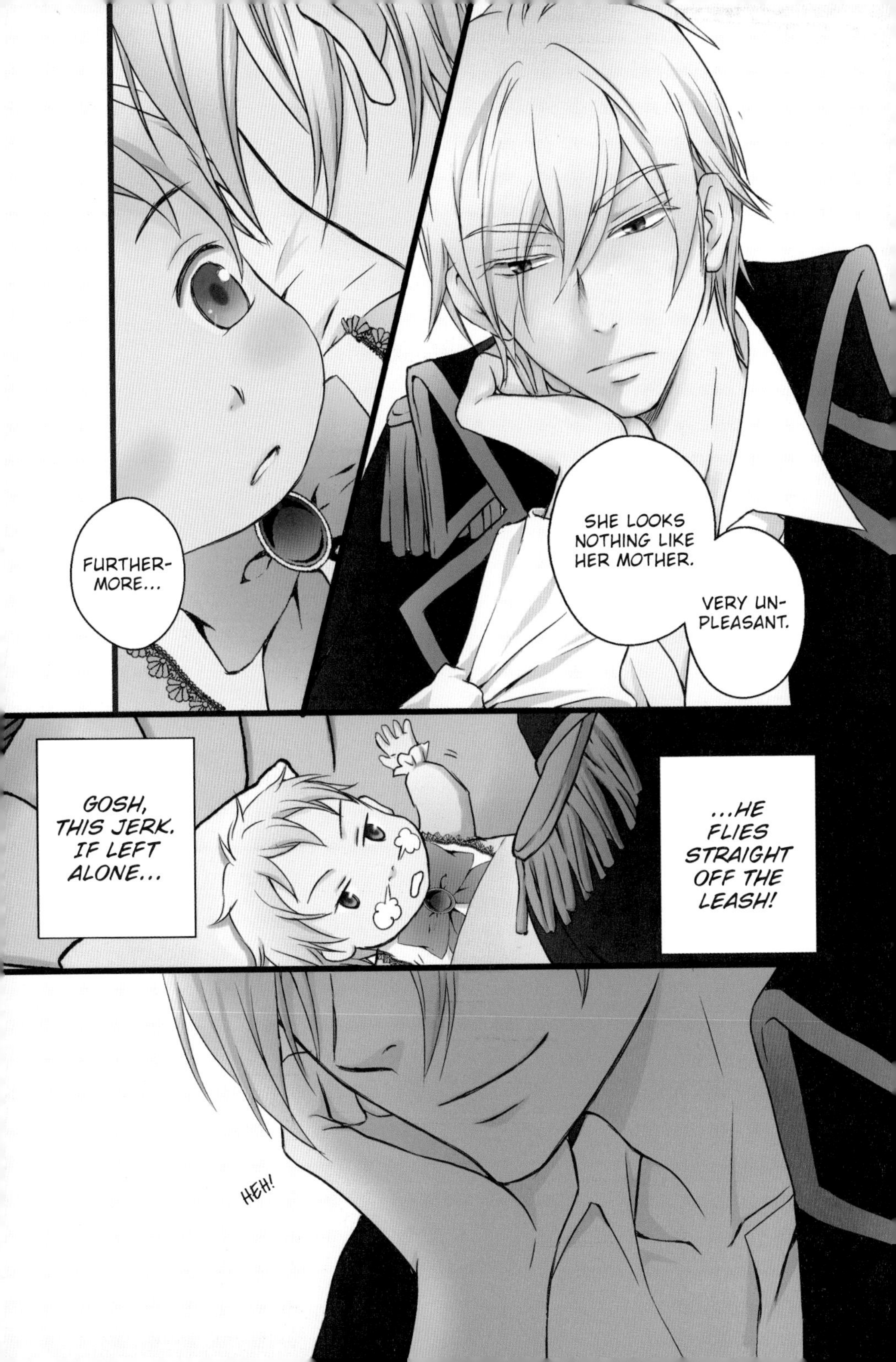
FURTHER-MORE...
SHE LOOKS NOTHING LIKE HER MOTHER.
VERY UN-PLEASANT.
GOSH, THIS JERK. IF LEFT ALONE...
...HE FLIES STRAIGHT OFF THE LEASH!
HEH!

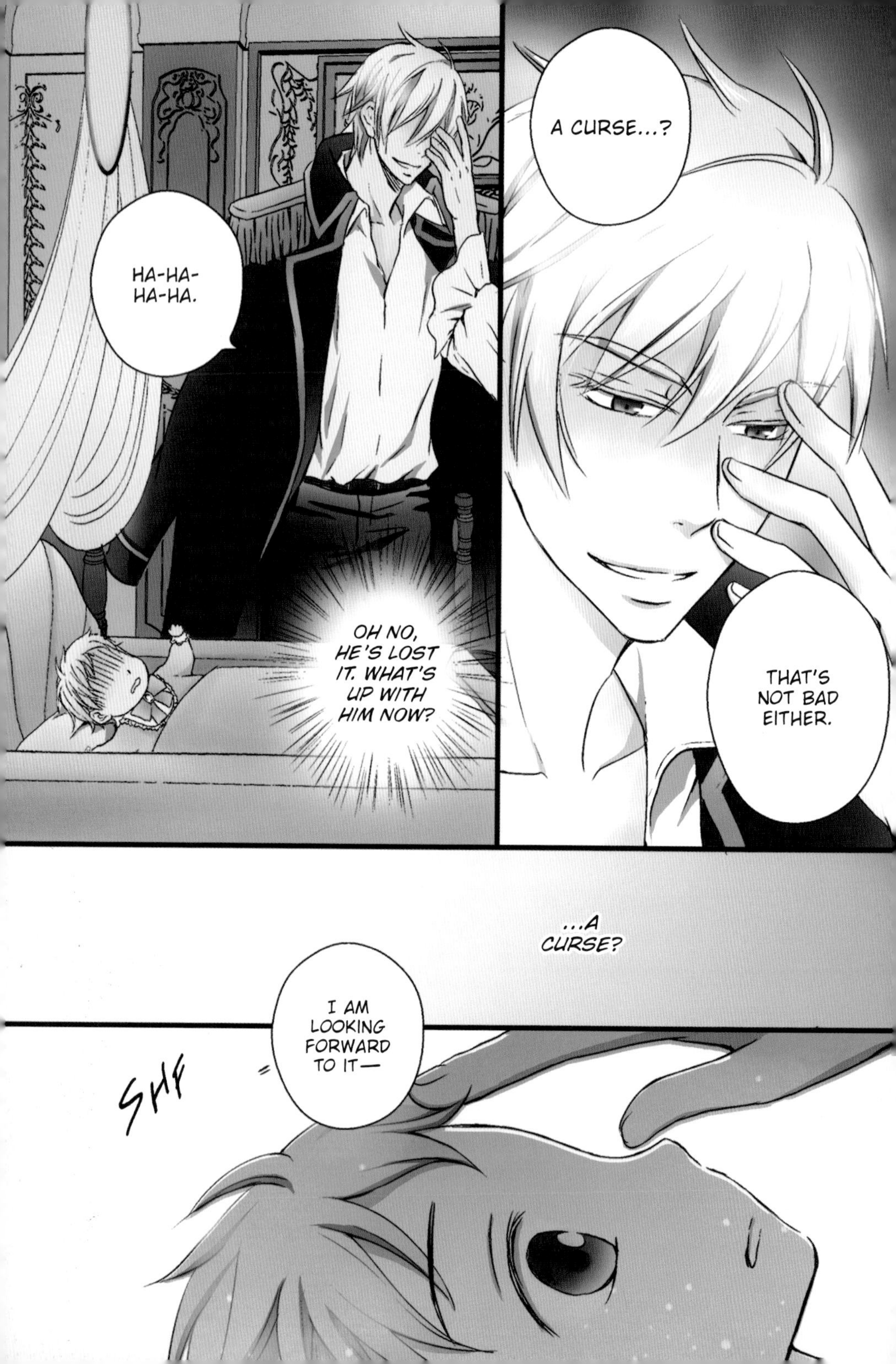
HA-HA-
HA-HA.
OH NO, HE'S LOST IT. WHAT'S UP WITH HIM NOW?
A CURSE...?
THAT'S NOT BAD EITHER.
...A CURSE?
SHF
I AM LOOKING FORWARD TO IT—

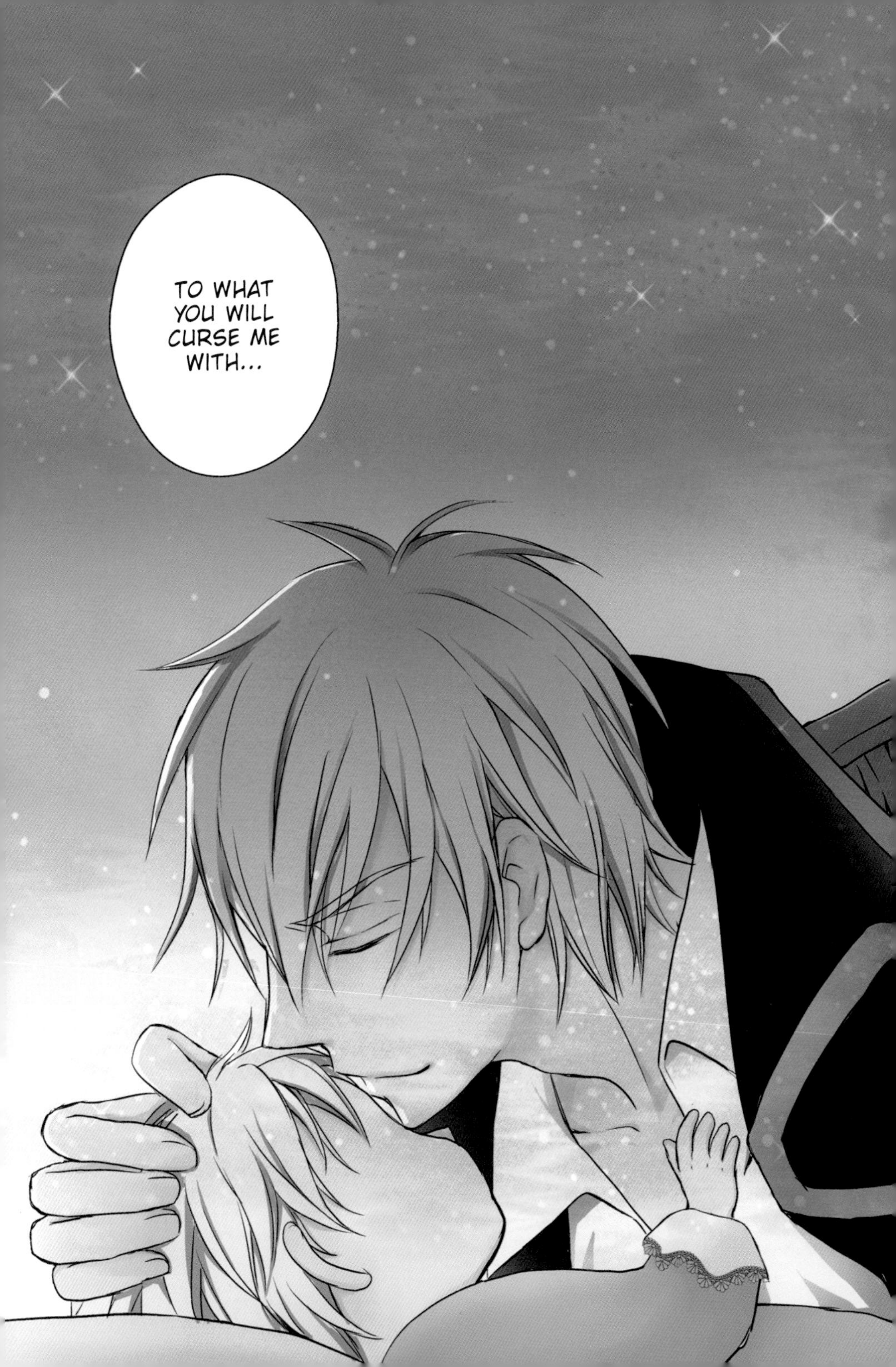
TO WHAT YOU WILL CURSE ME WITH...

DAUGHTER
OF THE
EMPEROR

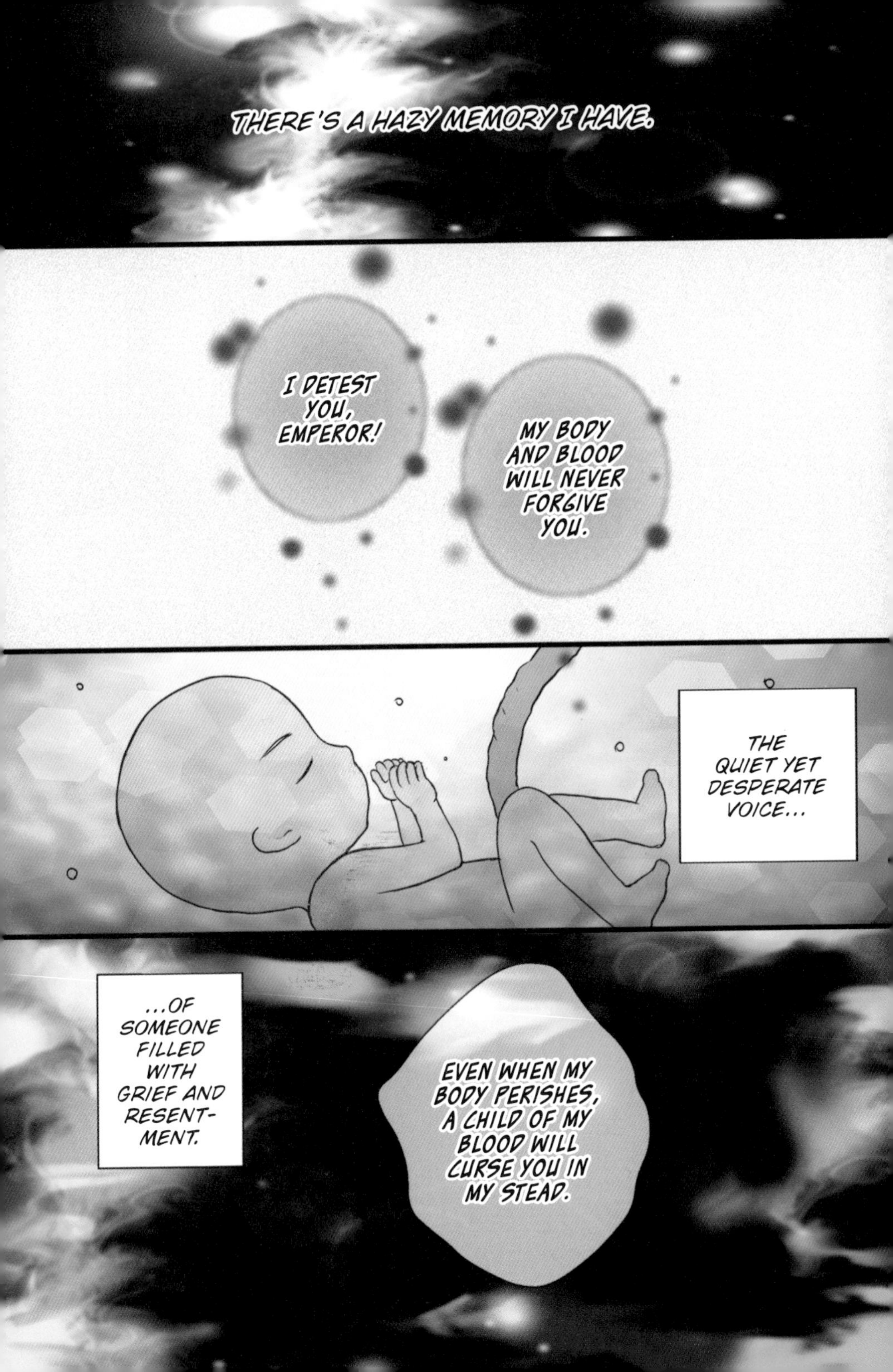
THERE'S A HAZY MEMORY I HAVE.
I DETEST YOU, EMPEROR!
MY BODY AND BLOOD WILL NEVER FORGIVE YOU.
THE QUIET YET DESPERATE VOICE...
...OF SOMEONE FILLED WITH GRIEF AND RESENT-MENT.
EVEN WHEN MY BODY PERISHES, A CHILD OF MY BLOOD WILL CURSE YOU IN MY STEAD.

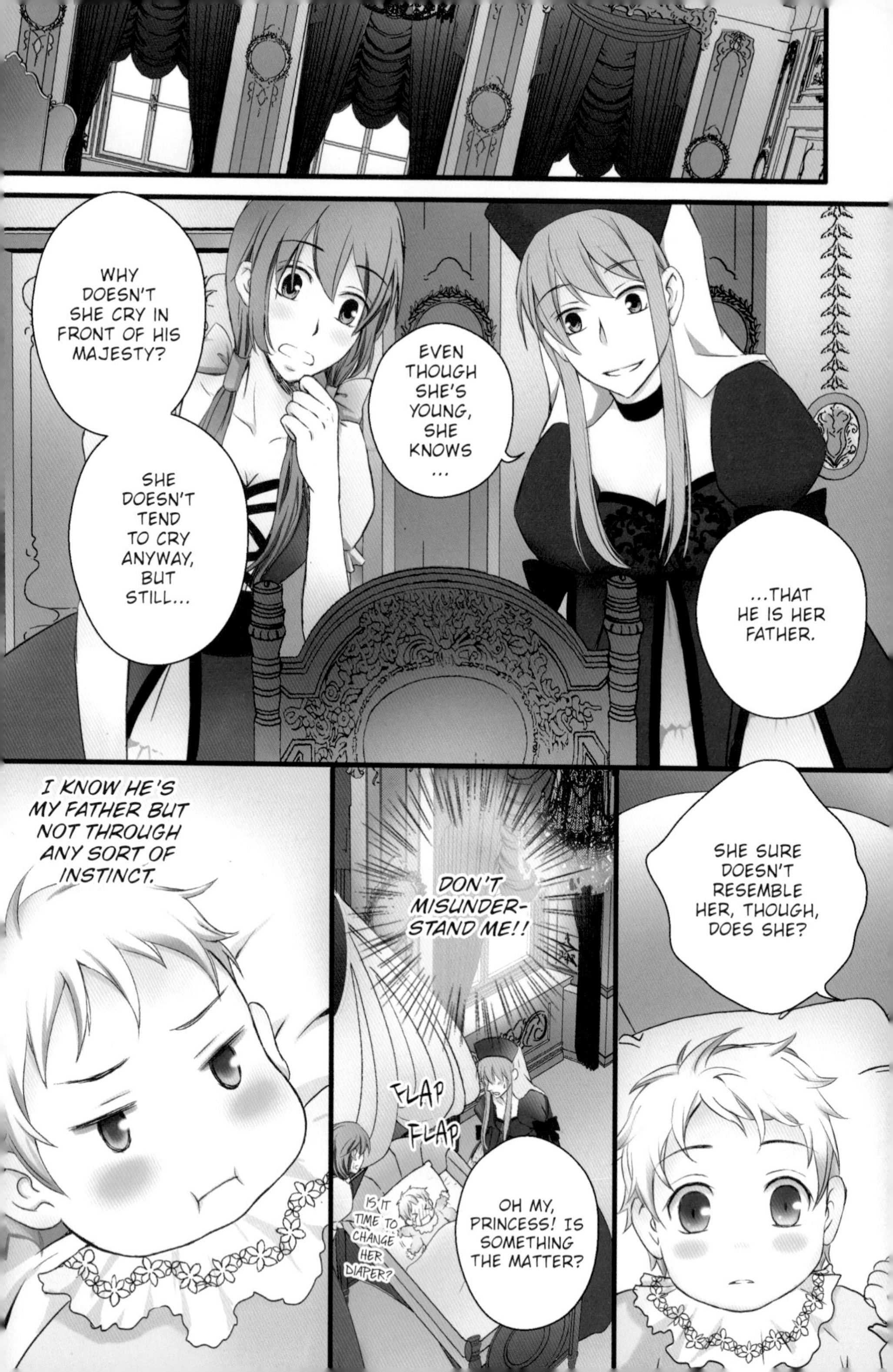
WHY DOESN'T SHE CRY IN FRONT OF HIS MAJESTY?
SHE DOESN'T TEND TO CRY ANYWAY, BUT STILL...
EVEN THOUGH SHE'S YOUNG, SHE KNOWS ...
...THAT HE IS HER FATHER.
I KNOW HE'S MY FATHER BUT NOT THROUGH ANY SORT OF INSTINCT.
DON'T MISUNDER-STAND ME!!
FLAP
FLAP
IS IT TIME TO CHANGE HER DIAPER?
OH MY, PRINCESS! IS SOMETHING THE MATTER?
SHE SURE DOESN'T RESEMBLE HER, THOUGH, DOES SHE?

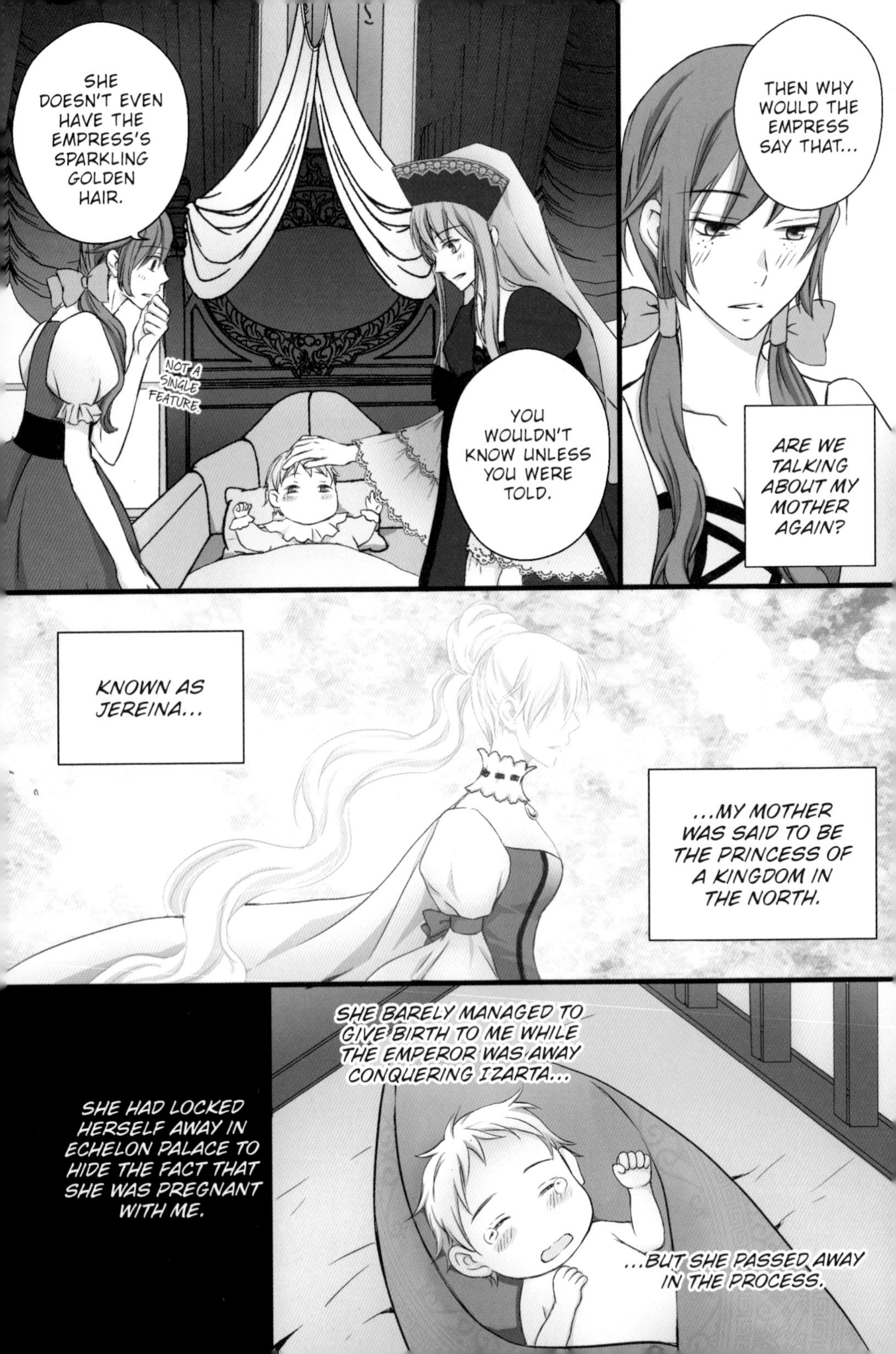
SHE DOESN'T EVEN HAVE THE EMPRESS'S SPARKLING GOLDEN HAIR.
NOT A SINGLE FEATURE.
YOU WOULDN'T KNOW UNLESS YOU WERE TOLD.
THEN WHY WOULD THE EMPRESS SAY THAT...
ARE WE TALKING ABOUT MY MOTHER AGAIN?
KNOWN AS JEREINA...
...MY MOTHER WAS SAID TO BE THE PRINCESS OF A KINGDOM IN THE NORTH.
SHE HAD LOCKED HERSELF AWAY IN ECHELON PALACE TO HIDE THE FACT THAT SHE WAS PREGNANT WITH ME.
SHE BARELY MANAGED TO GIVE BIRTH TO ME WHILE THE EMPEROR WAS AWAY CONQUERING IZARTA...
...BUT SHE PASSED AWAY IN THE PROCESS.

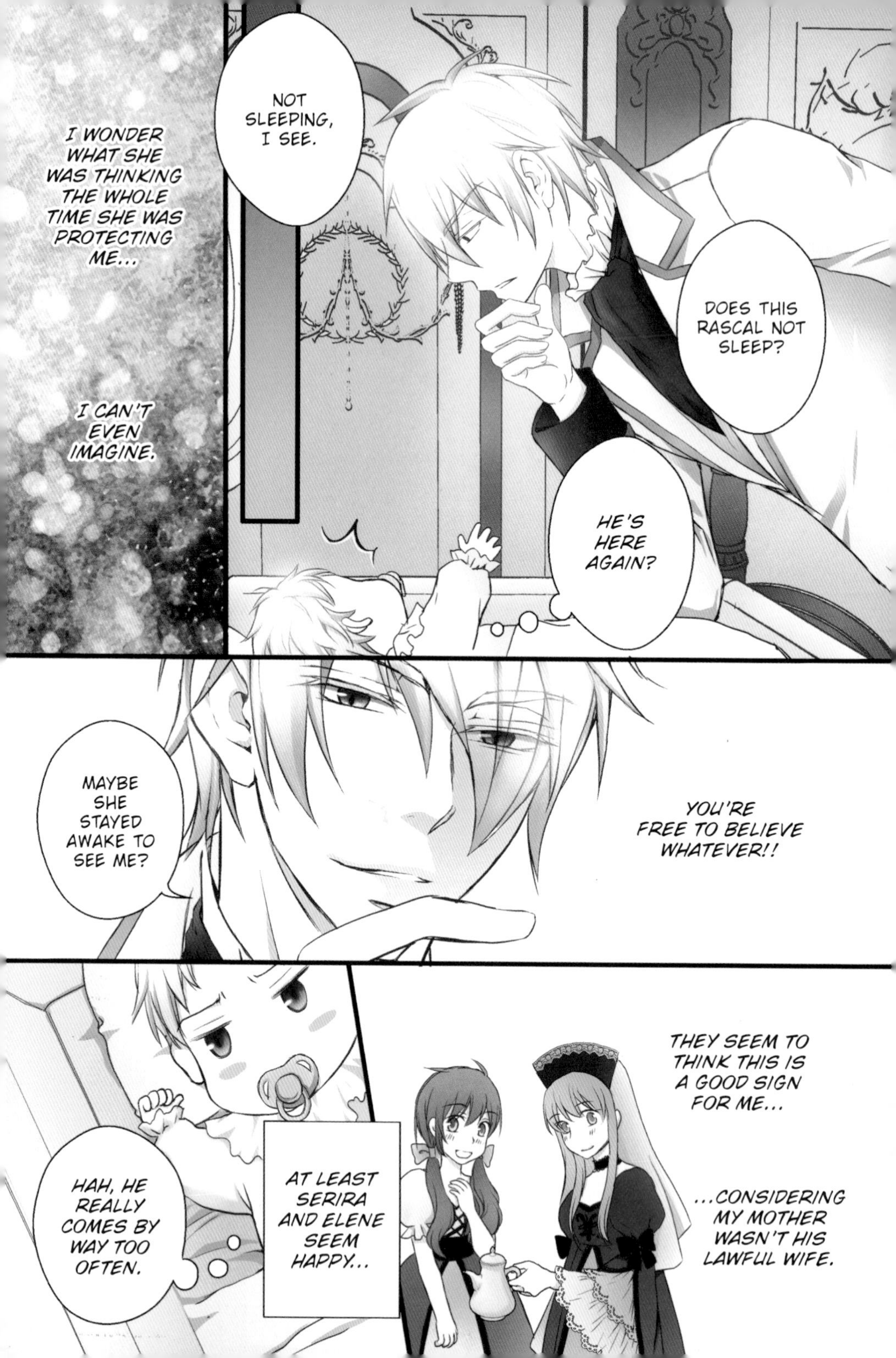
I WONDER WHAT SHE WAS THINKING THE WHOLE TIME SHE WAS PROTECTING ME...
I CAN'T EVEN IMAGINE.
NOT SLEEPING, I SEE.
DOES THIS RASCAL NOT SLEEP?
HE'S HERE AGAIN?
MAYBE SHE STAYED AWAKE TO SEE ME?
YOU'RE FREE TO BELIEVE WHATEVER!!
HAH, HE REALLY COMES BY WAY TOO OFTEN.
AT LEAST SERIRA AND ELENE SEEM HAPPY...
THEY SEEM TO THINK THIS IS A GOOD SIGN FOR ME...
...CONSIDERING MY MOTHER WASN'T HIS LAWFUL WIFE.

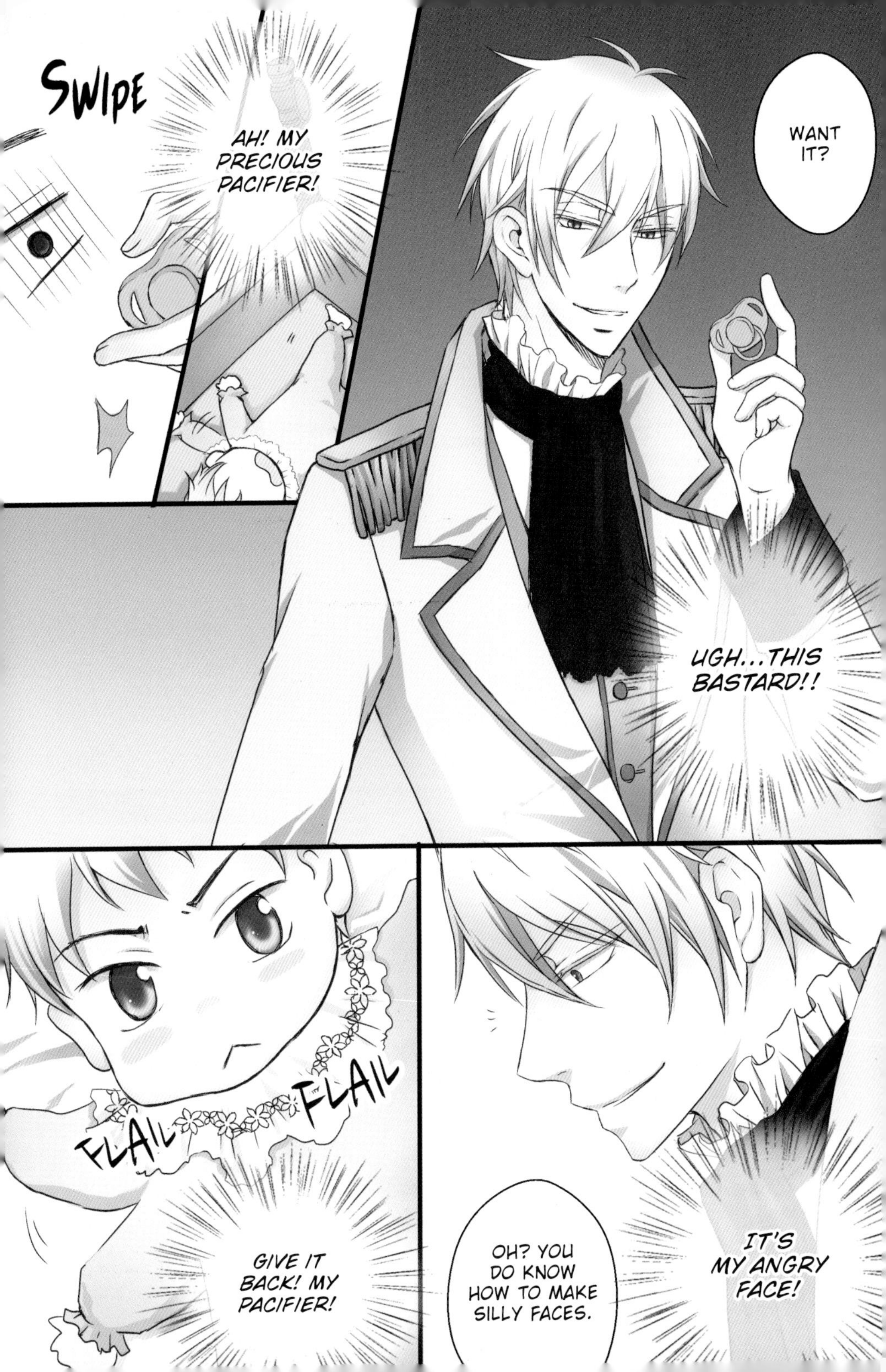
SWIPE
AH! MY PRECIOUS PACIFIER!
WANT IT?
UGH...THIS BASTARD!!
FLAIL FLAIL
GIVE IT BACK! MY PACIFIER!
OH? YOU DO KNOW HOW TO MAKE SILLY FACES.
IT'S MY ANGRY FACE!

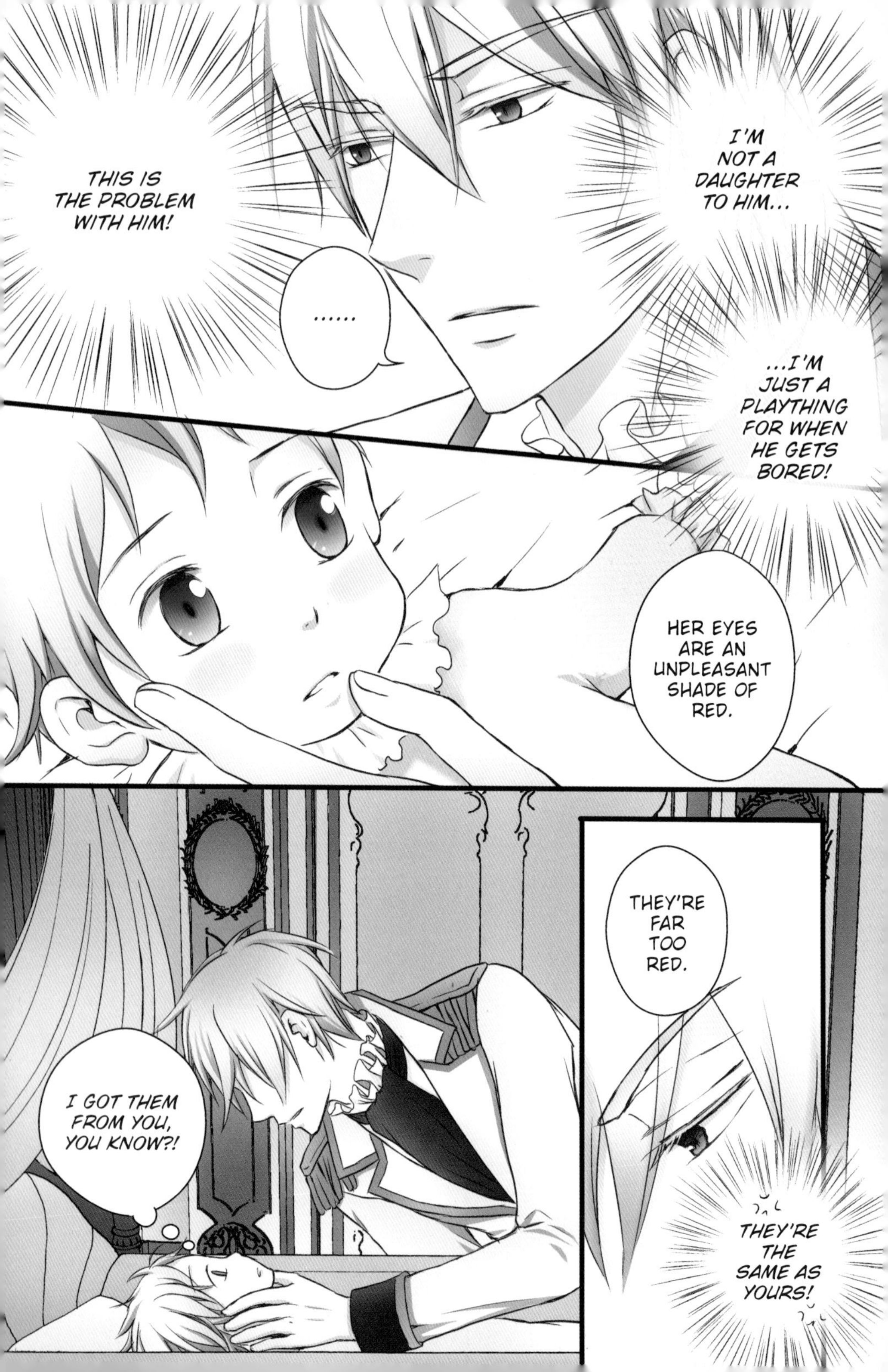
THIS IS THE PROBLEM WITH HIM!
......
I'M NOT A DAUGHTER TO HIM...
...I'M JUST A PLAYTHING FOR WHEN HE GETS BORED!
HER EYES ARE AN UNPLEASANT SHADE OF RED.
I GOT THEM FROM YOU, YOU KNOW?!
THEY'RE FAR TOO RED.
THEY'RE THE SAME AS YOURS!

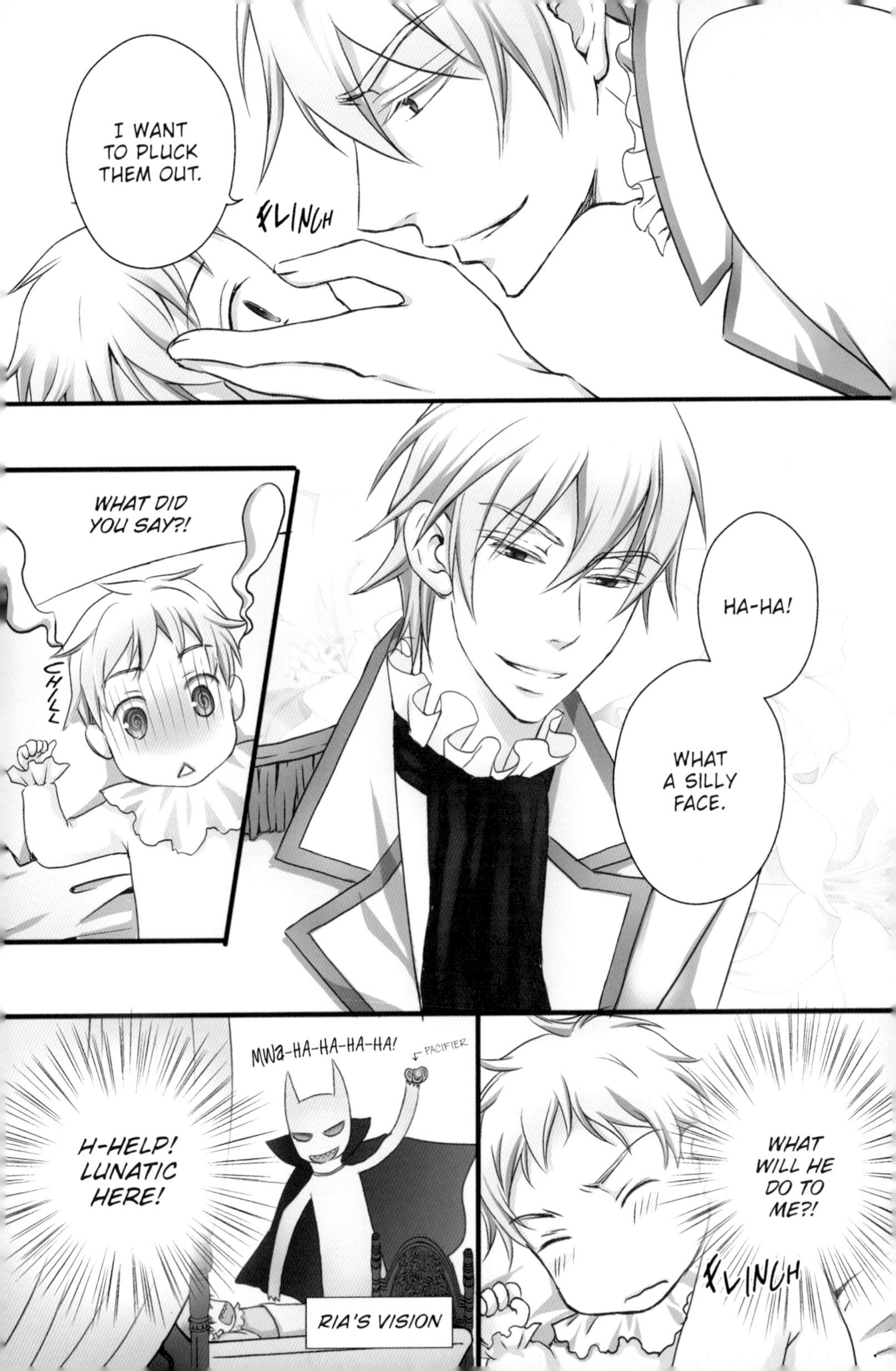
I WANT TO PLUCK THEM OUT.
FLINCH
WHAT DID YOU SAY?!
CHILL
HA-HA!
WHAT A SILLY FACE.
H-HELP! LUNATIC HERE!
MWA-HA-HA-HA-HA!
PACIFIER
RIA'S VISION
WHAT WILL HE DO TO ME?!
FLINCH

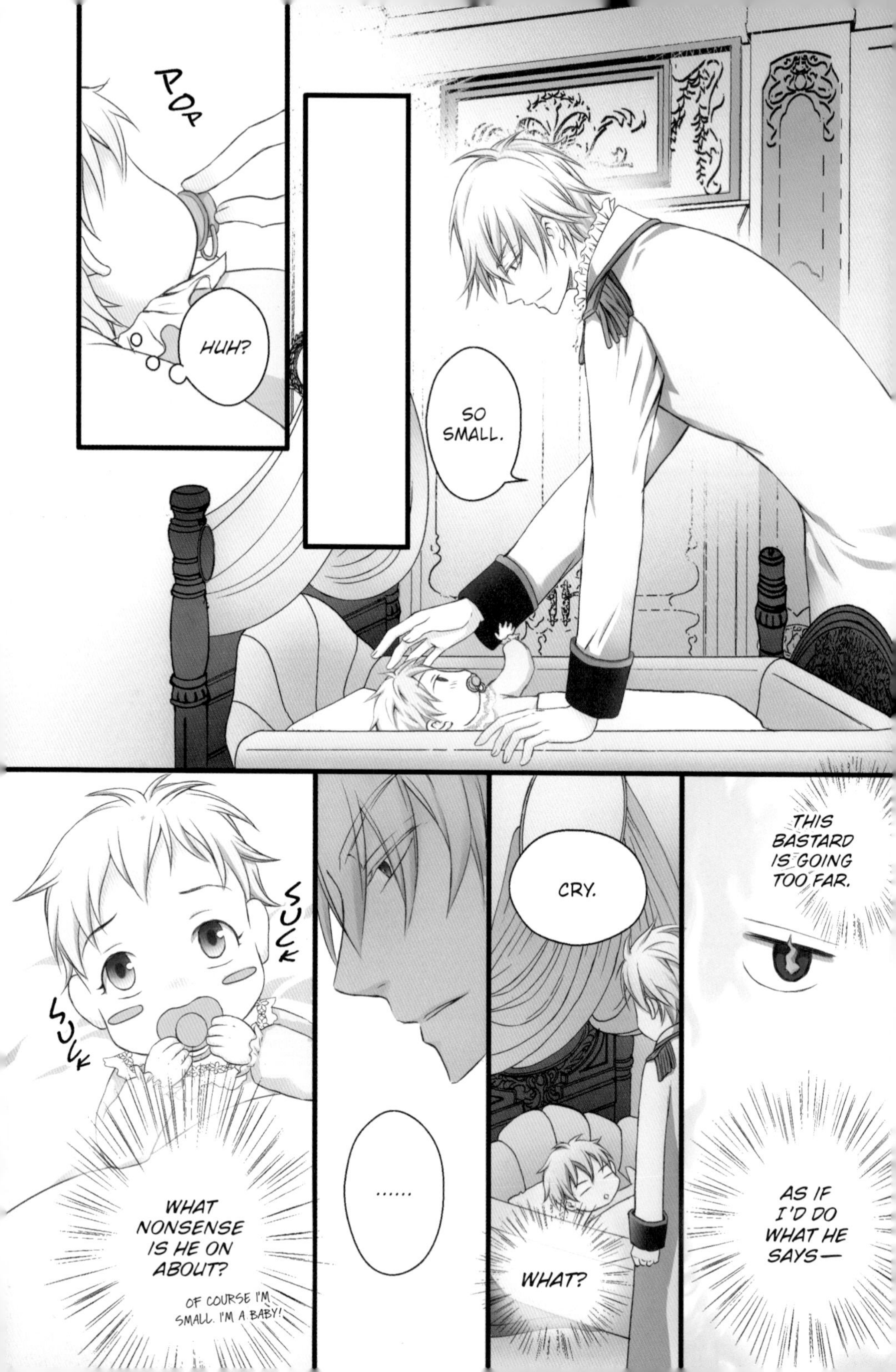
POP
HUH?
SO SMALL.
SUCK
SUCK
WHAT NONSENSE IS HE ON ABOUT?
OF COURSE I'M SMALL. I'M A BABY!
......
CRY.
WHAT?
THIS BASTARD IS GOING TOO FAR.
AS IF I'D DO WHAT HE SAYS—

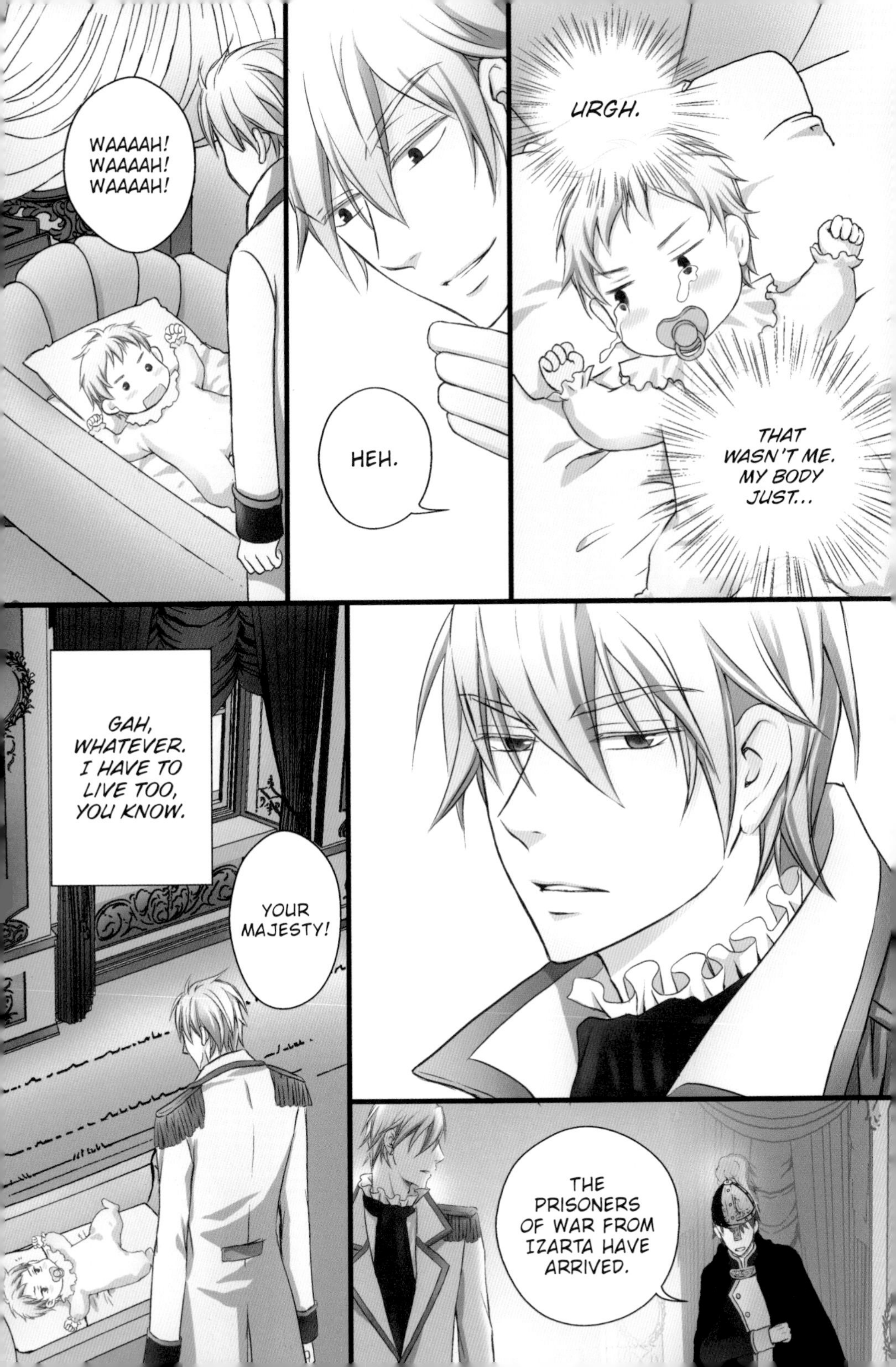
WAAAAH! WAAAAH! WAAAAH!
HEH.
URGH.
THAT WASN'T ME. MY BODY JUST...
GAH, WHATEVER. I HAVE TO LIVE TOO, YOU KNOW.
YOUR MAJESTY!
THE PRISONERS OF WAR FROM IZARTA HAVE ARRIVED.

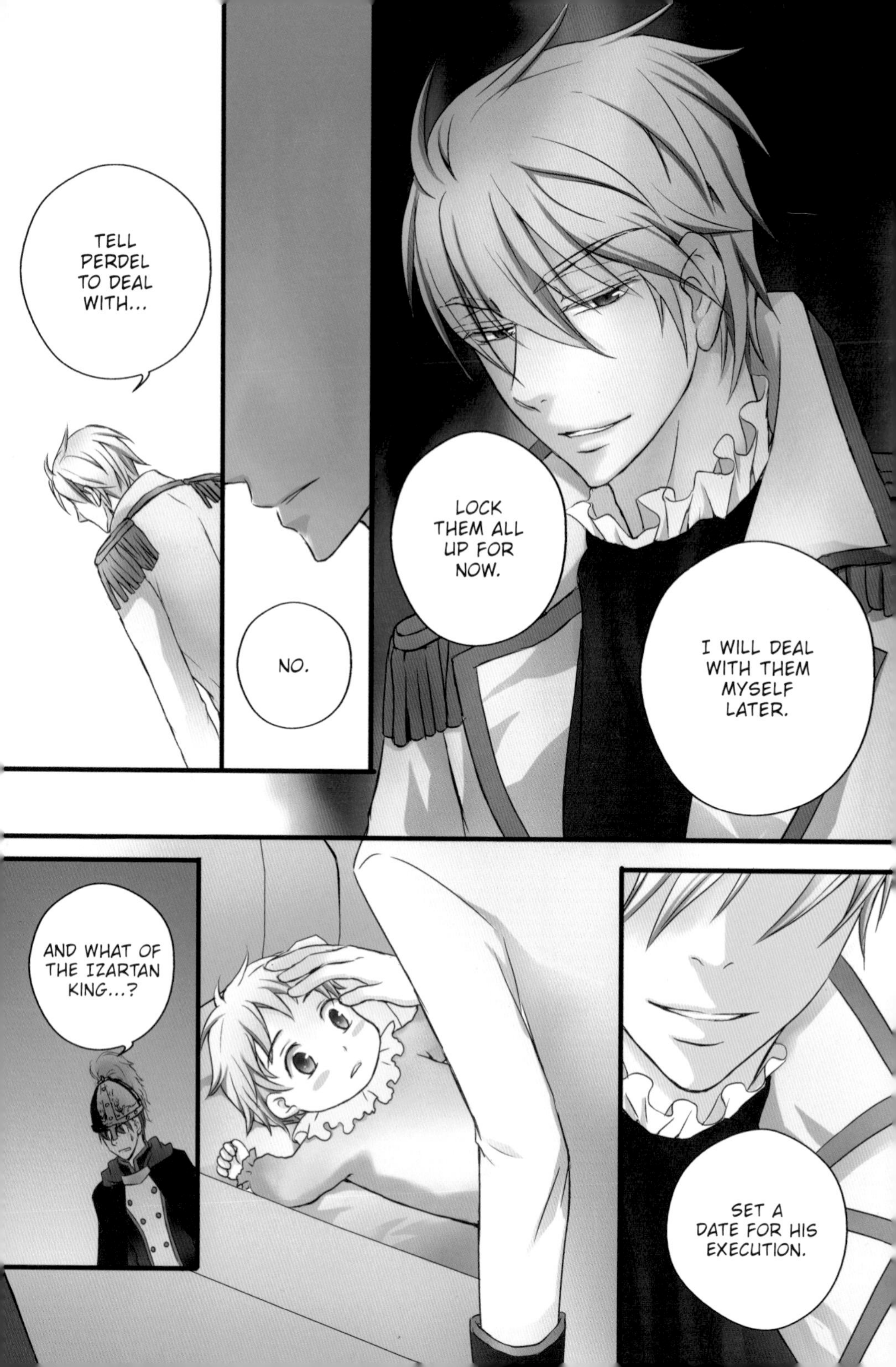
TELL PERDEL TO DEAL WITH...
NO.
LOCK THEM ALL UP FOR NOW.
I WILL DEAL WITH THEM MYSELF LATER.
AND WHAT OF THE IZARTAN KING...?
SET A DATE FOR HIS EXECUTION.

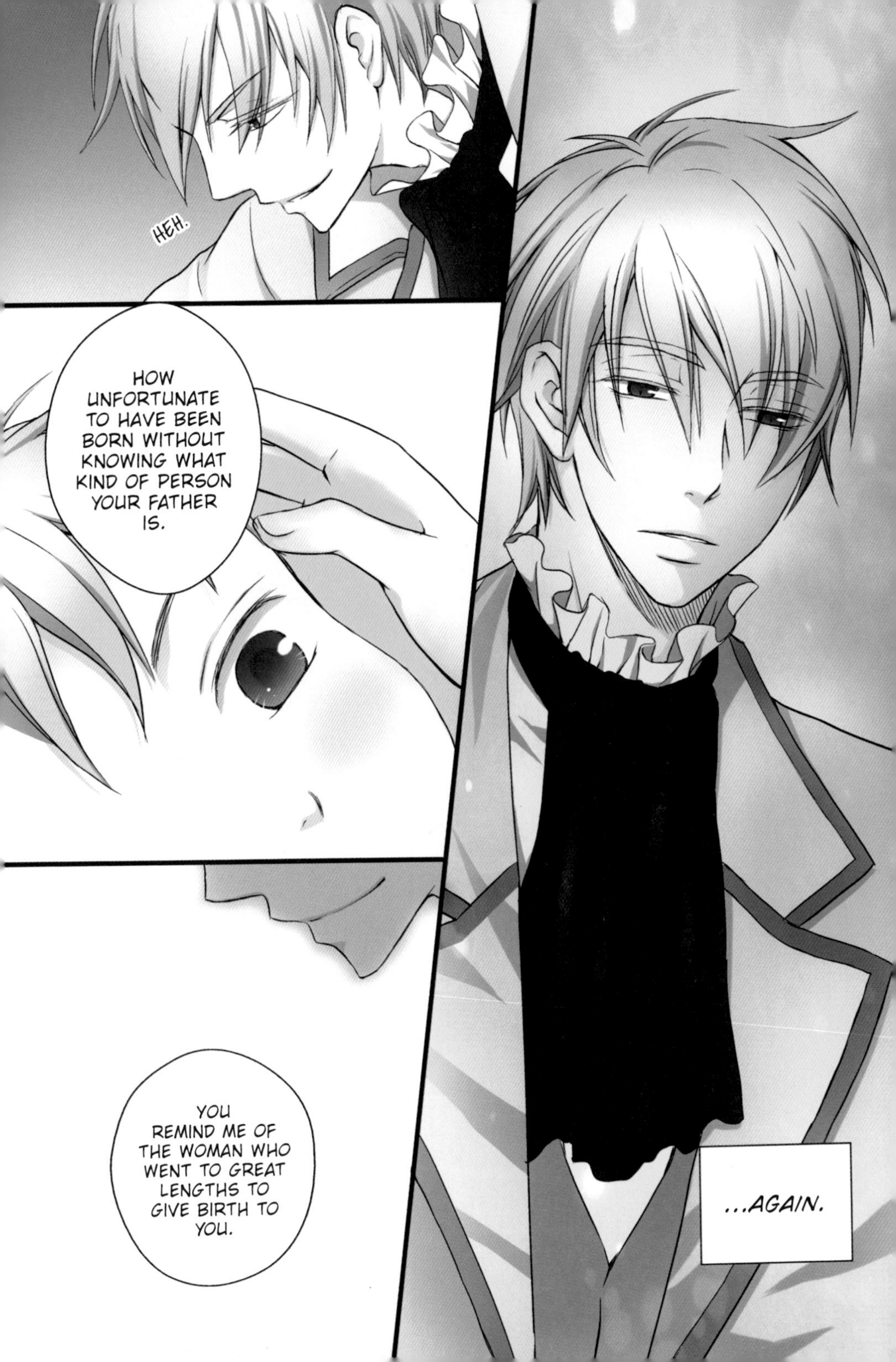
HEH.
HOW UNFORTUNATE TO HAVE BEEN BORN WITHOUT KNOWING WHAT KIND OF PERSON YOUR FATHER IS.
YOU REMIND ME OF THE WOMAN WHO WENT TO GREAT LENGTHS TO GIVE BIRTH TO YOU.
...AGAIN.

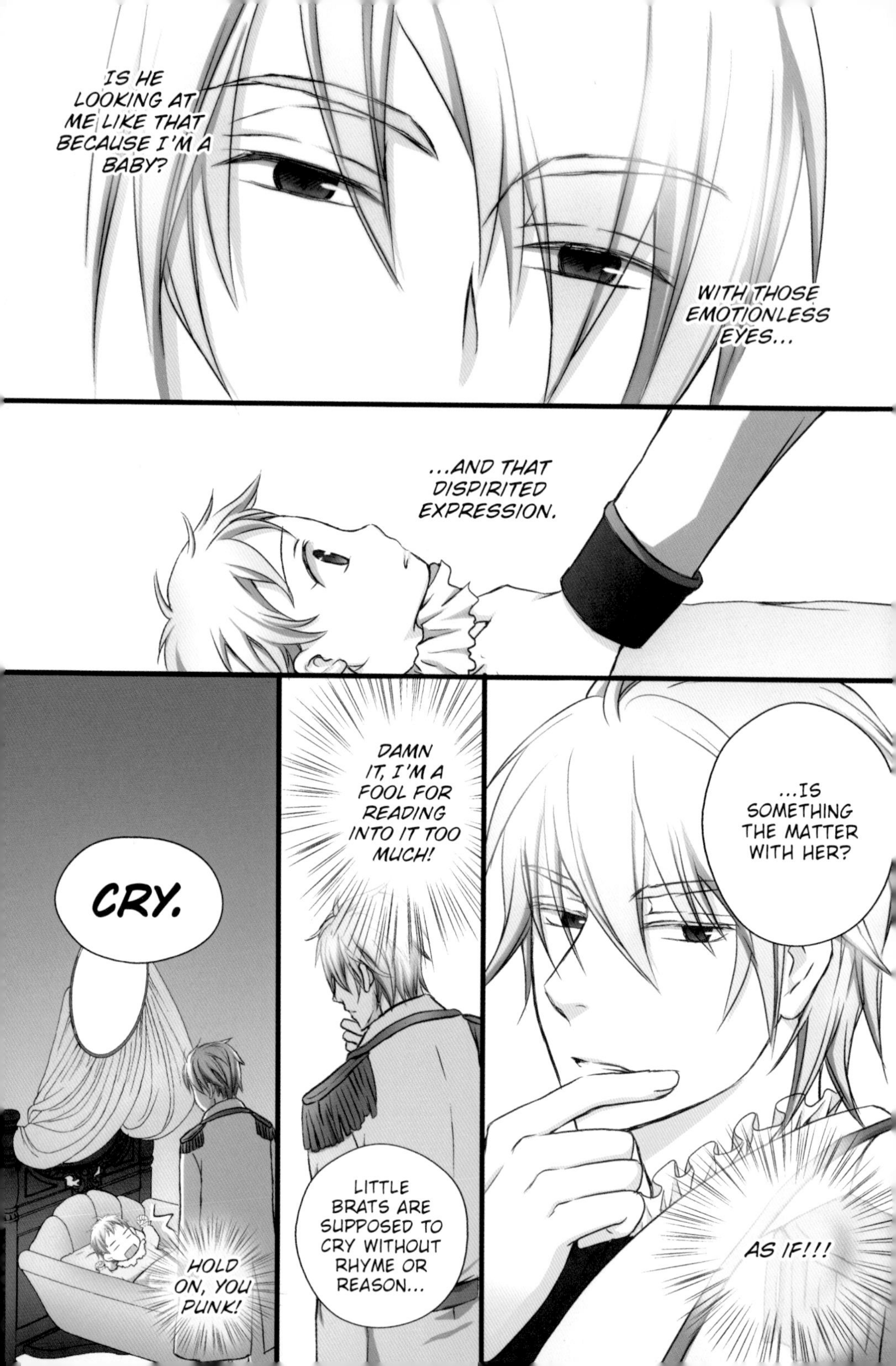
IS HE LOOKING AT ME LIKE THAT BECAUSE I'M A BABY?
WITH THOSE EMOTIONLESS EYES...
...AND THAT DISPIRITED EXPRESSION.
CRY.
HOLD ON, YOU PUNK!
DAMN IT, I'M A FOOL FOR READING INTO IT TOO MUCH!
LITTLE BRATS ARE SUPPOSED TO CRY WITHOUT RHYME OR REASON...
...IS SOMETHING THE MATTER WITH HER?
AS IF!!!

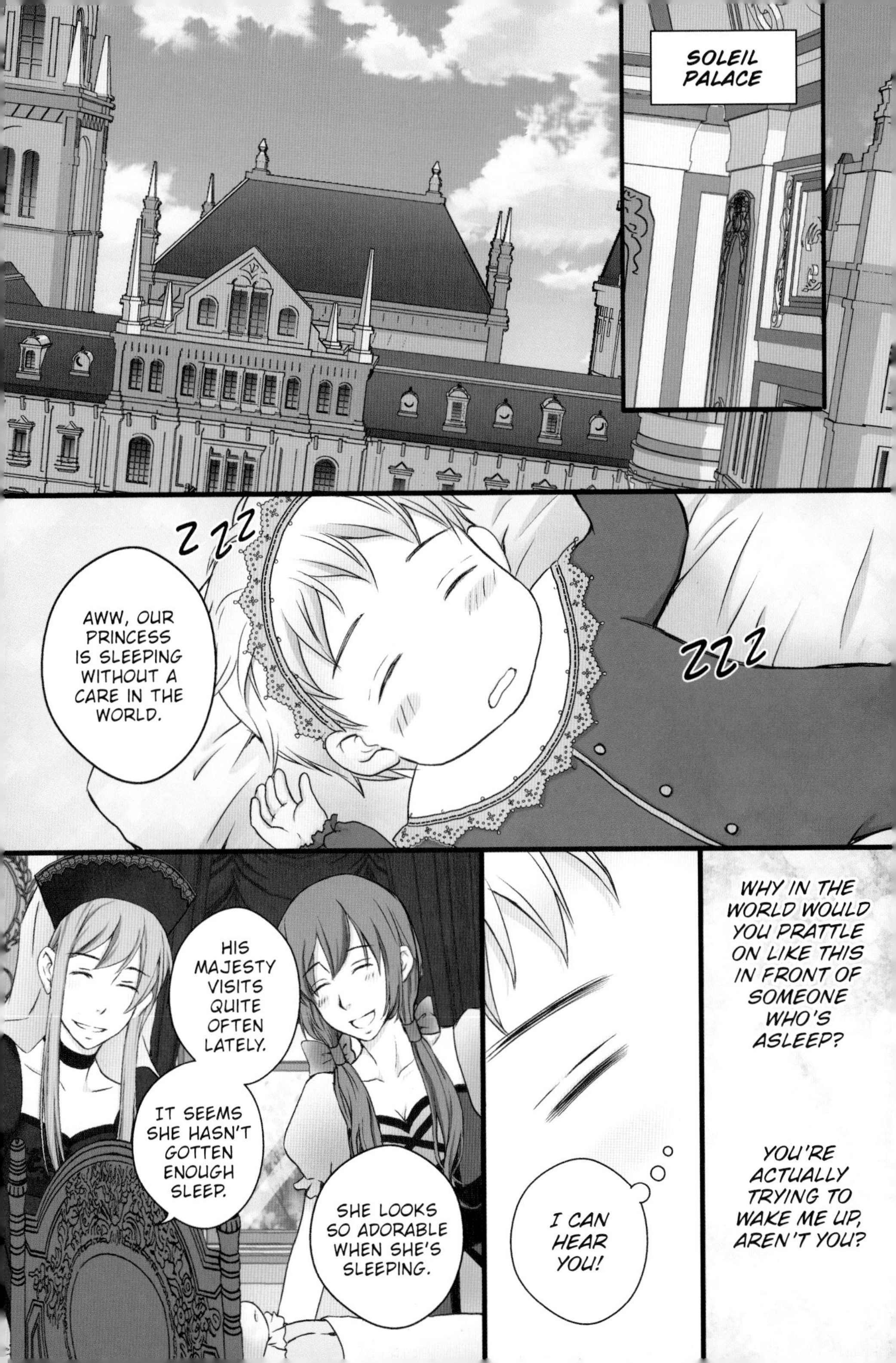
SOLEIL PALACE
ZZZ
AWW, OUR PRINCESS IS SLEEPING WITHOUT A CARE IN THE WORLD.
ZZZ
HIS MAJESTY VISITS QUITE OFTEN LATELY.
IT SEEMS SHE HASN'T GOTTEN ENOUGH SLEEP.
SHE LOOKS SO ADORABLE WHEN SHE'S SLEEPING.
I CAN HEAR YOU!
WHY IN THE WORLD WOULD YOU PRATTLE ON LIKE THIS IN FRONT OF SOMEONE WHO'S ASLEEP?
YOU'RE ACTUALLY TRYING TO WAKE ME UP, AREN'T YOU?

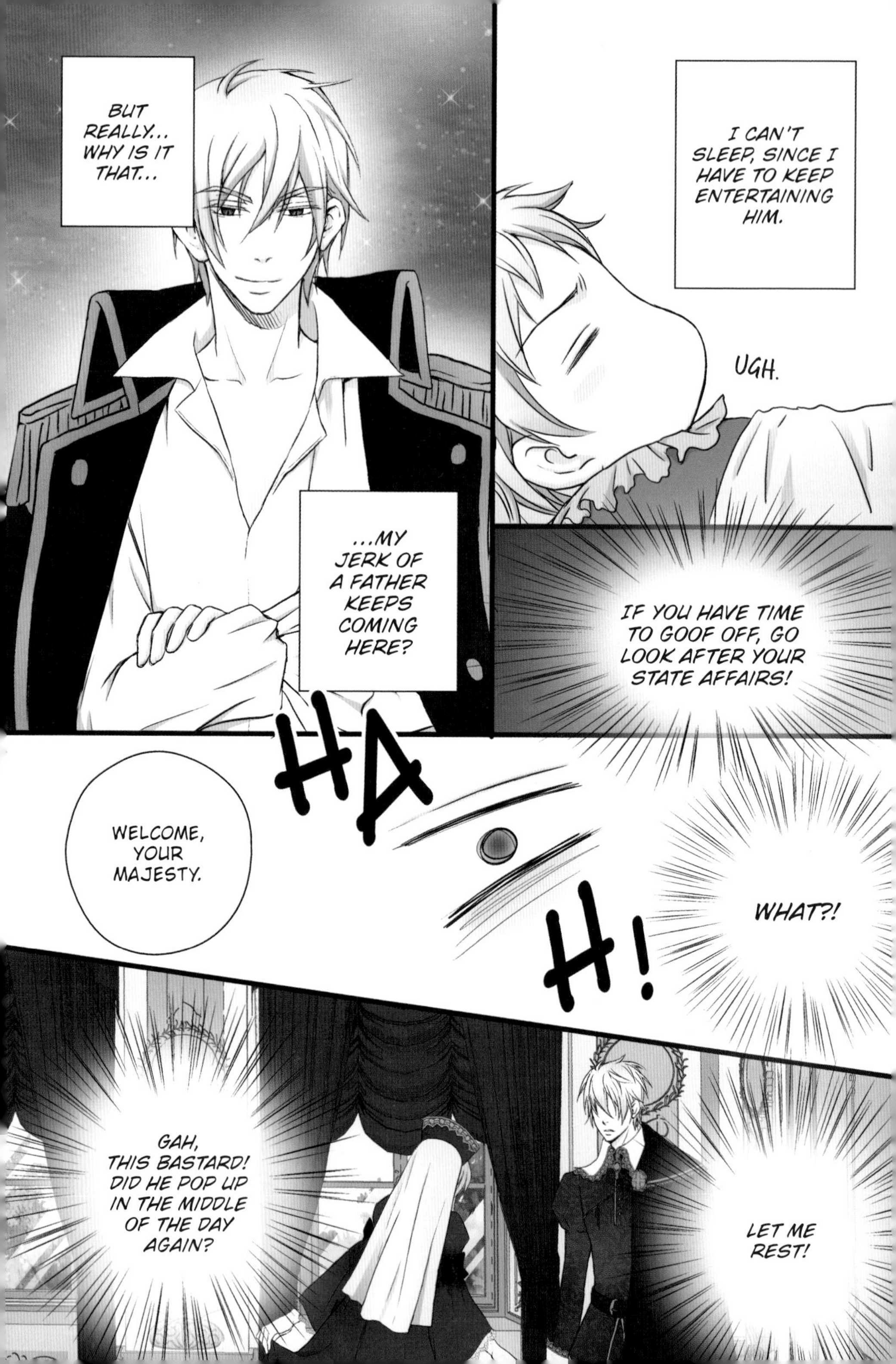
BUT REALLY... WHY IS IT THAT...
...MY JERK OF A FATHER KEEPS COMING HERE?
I CAN'T SLEEP, SINCE I HAVE TO KEEP ENTERTAINING HIM.
UGH.
IF YOU HAVE TIME TO GOOF OFF, GO LOOK AFTER YOUR STATE AFFAIRS!
WELCOME, YOUR MAJESTY.
HAH!
WHAT?!
GAH, THIS BASTARD! DID HE POP UP IN THE MIDDLE OF THE DAY AGAIN?
LET ME REST!

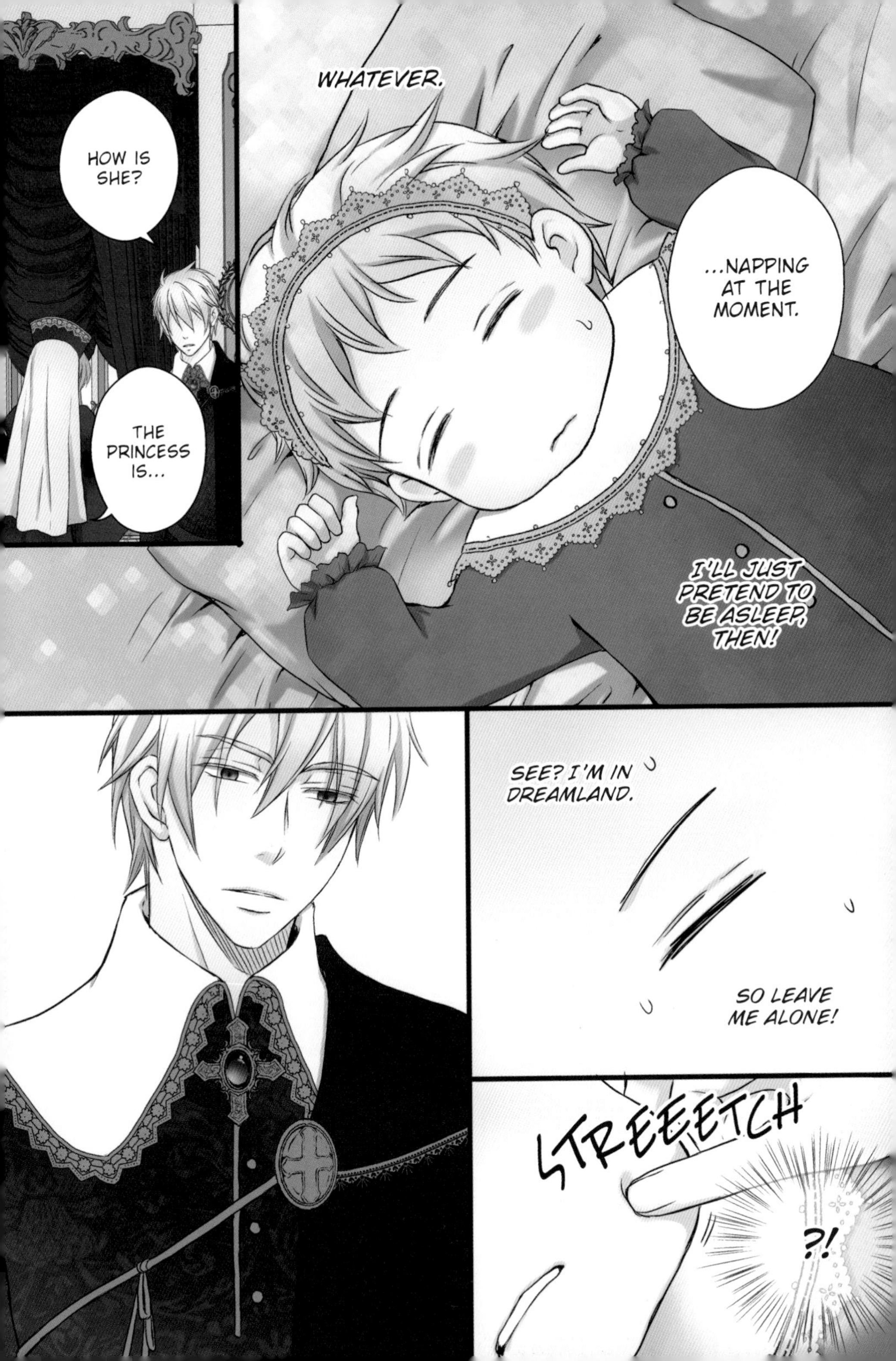
HOW IS SHE?
THE PRINCESS IS...
WHATEVER.
...NAPPING AT THE MOMENT.
I'LL JUST PRETEND TO BE ASLEEP, THEN!
SEE? I'M IN DREAMLAND.
SO LEAVE ME ALONE!
STREEETCH
?!

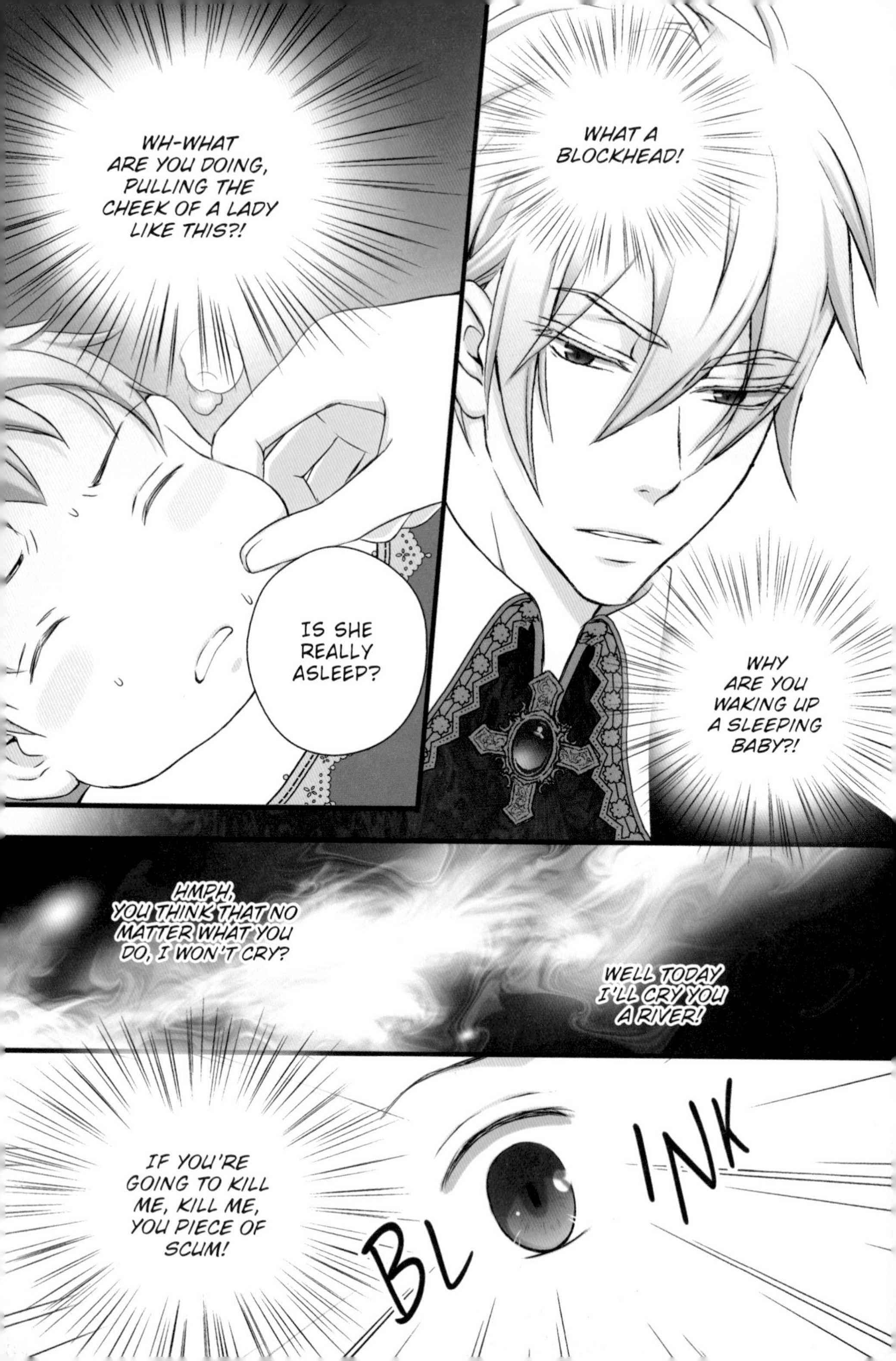
WH-WHAT ARE YOU DOING, PULLING THE CHEEK OF A LADY LIKE THIS?!
IS SHE REALLY ASLEEP?
WHAT A BLOCKHEAD!
WHY ARE YOU WAKING UP A SLEEPING BABY?!
HMPH, YOU THINK THAT NO MATTER WHAT YOU DO, I WON'T CRY?
WELL TODAY I'LL CRY YOU A RIVER!
IF YOU'RE GOING TO KILL ME, KILL ME, YOU PIECE OF SCUM!
BLINK

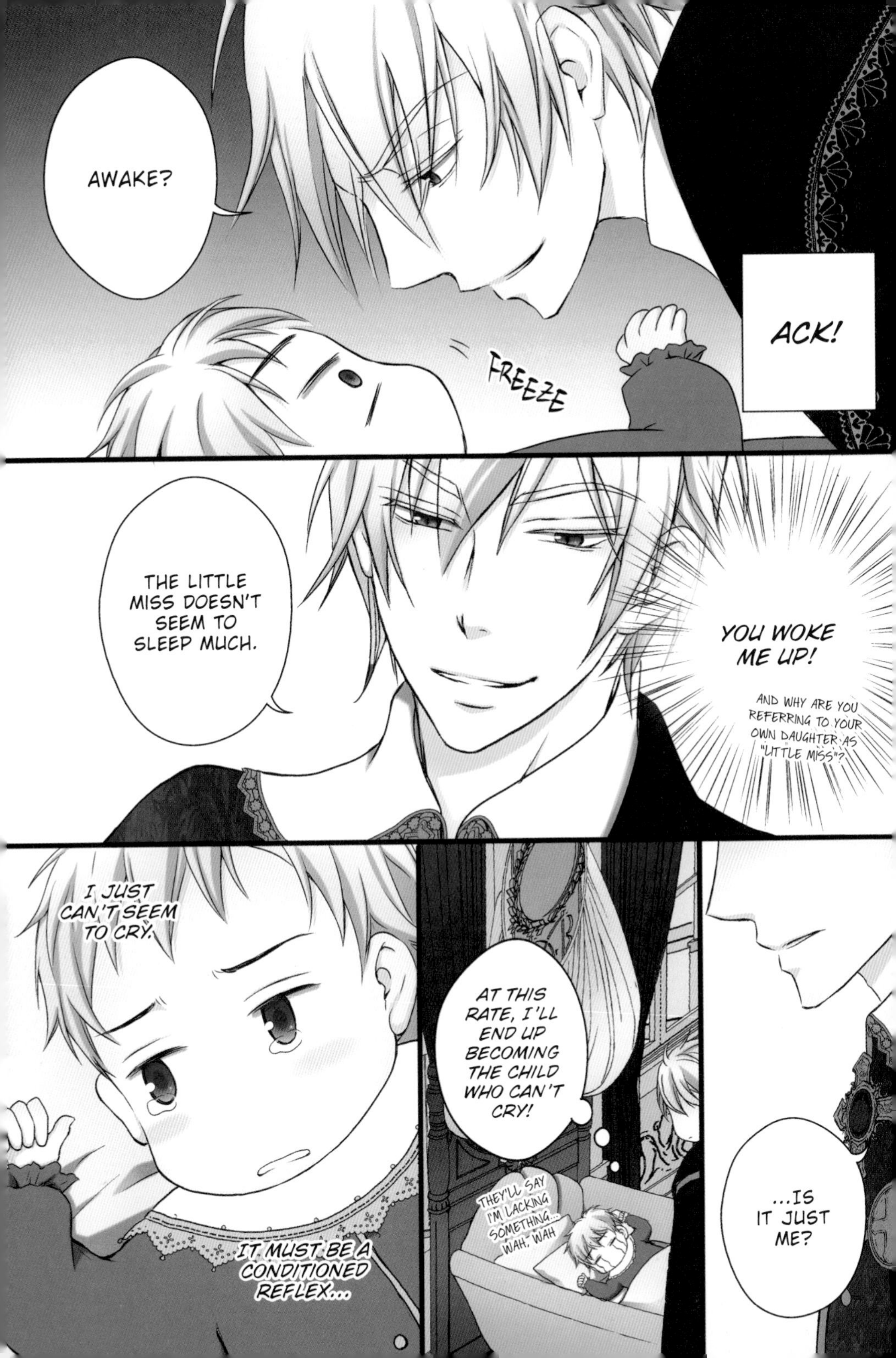
AWAKE?
FREEZE
ACK!
THE LITTLE MISS DOESN'T SEEM TO SLEEP MUCH.
YOU WOKE ME UP!
AND WHY ARE YOU REFERRING TO YOUR OWN DAUGHTER AS "LITTLE MISS"?
I JUST CAN'T SEEM TO CRY.
IT MUST BE A CONDITIONED REFLEX...
AT THIS RATE, I'LL END UP BECOMING THE CHILD WHO CAN'T CRY!
THEY'LL SAY I'M LACKING SOMETHING... WAH, WAH
...IS IT JUST ME?

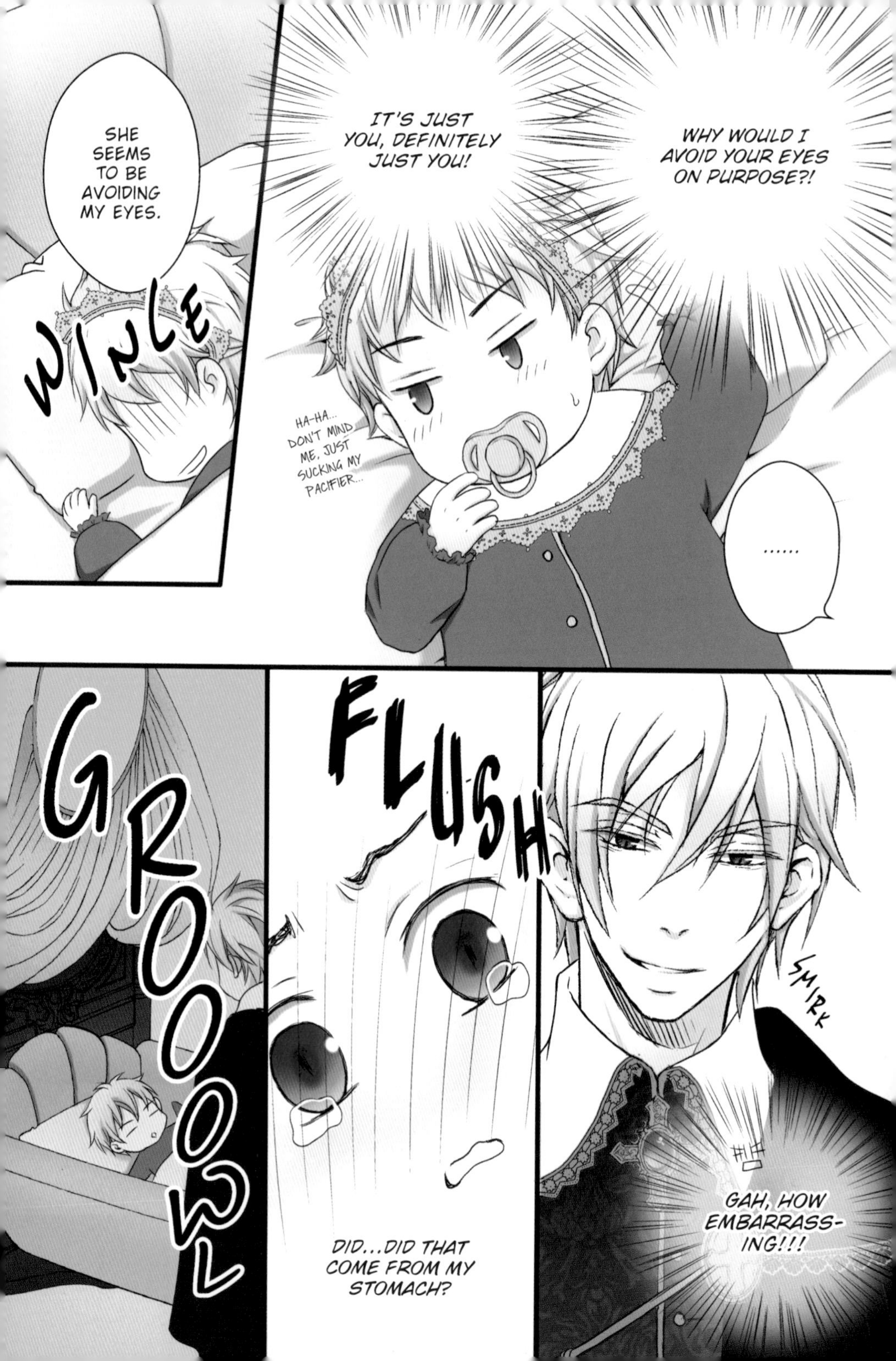
SHE SEEMS TO BE AVOIDING MY EYES.
WINCE
IT'S JUST YOU, DEFINITELY JUST YOU!
WHY WOULD I AVOID YOUR EYES ON PURPOSE?!
HA-HA... DON'T MIND ME, JUST SUCKING MY PACIFIER...
......
GROOOOWL
FLUSH
DID...DID THAT COME FROM MY STOMACH?
SMIRK
GAH, HOW EMBARRASS-ING!!!

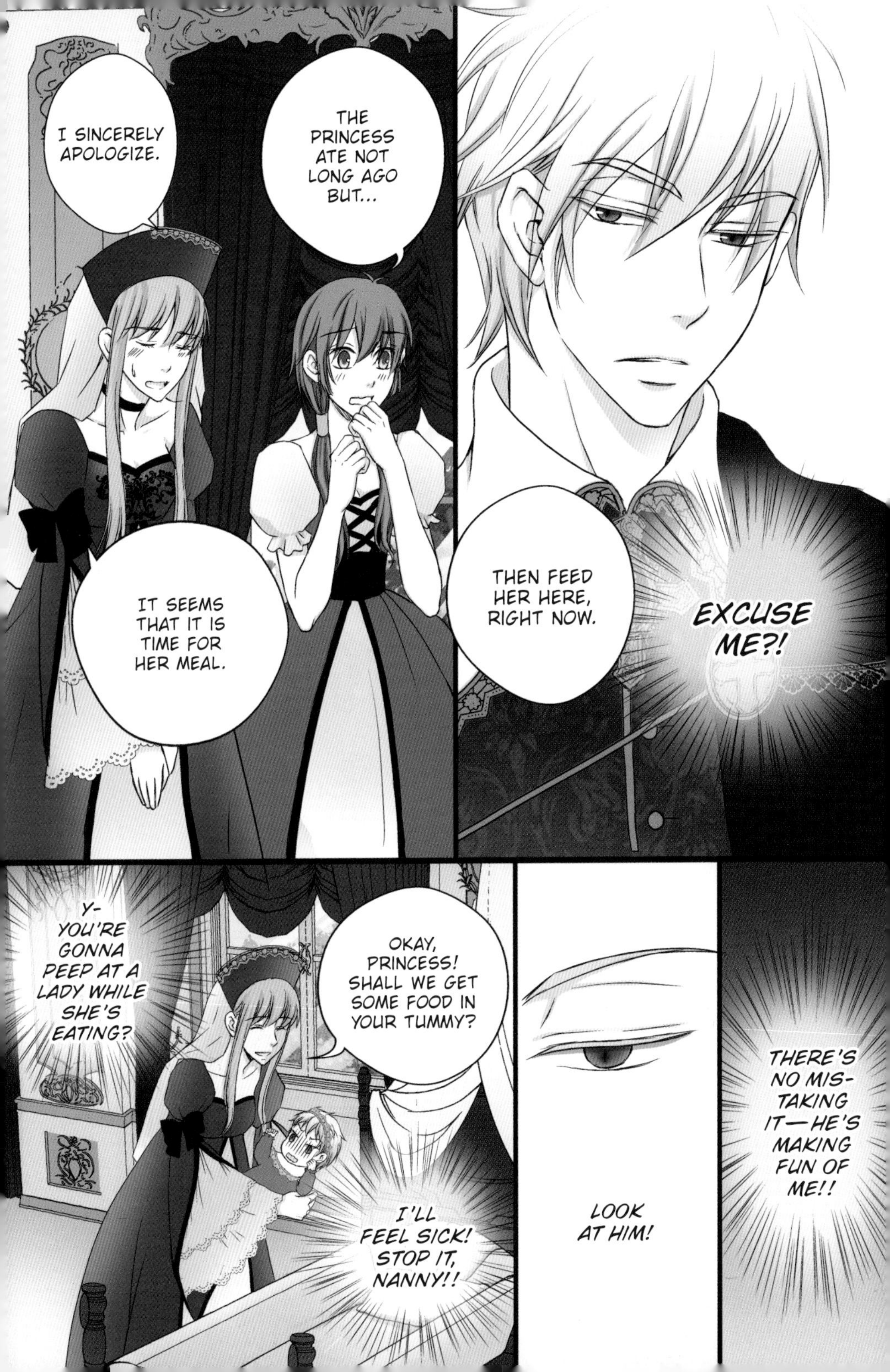
I SINCERELY APOLOGIZE.
THE PRINCESS ATE NOT LONG AGO BUT...
IT SEEMS THAT IT IS TIME FOR HER MEAL.
THEN FEED HER HERE, RIGHT NOW.
EXCUSE ME?!
Y- YOU'RE GONNA PEEP AT A LADY WHILE SHE'S EATING?
OKAY, PRINCESS! SHALL WE GET SOME FOOD IN YOUR TUMMY?
I'LL FEEL SICK! STOP IT, NANNY!!
LOOK AT HIM!
THERE'S NO MIS-TAKING IT—HE'S MAKING FUN OF ME!!

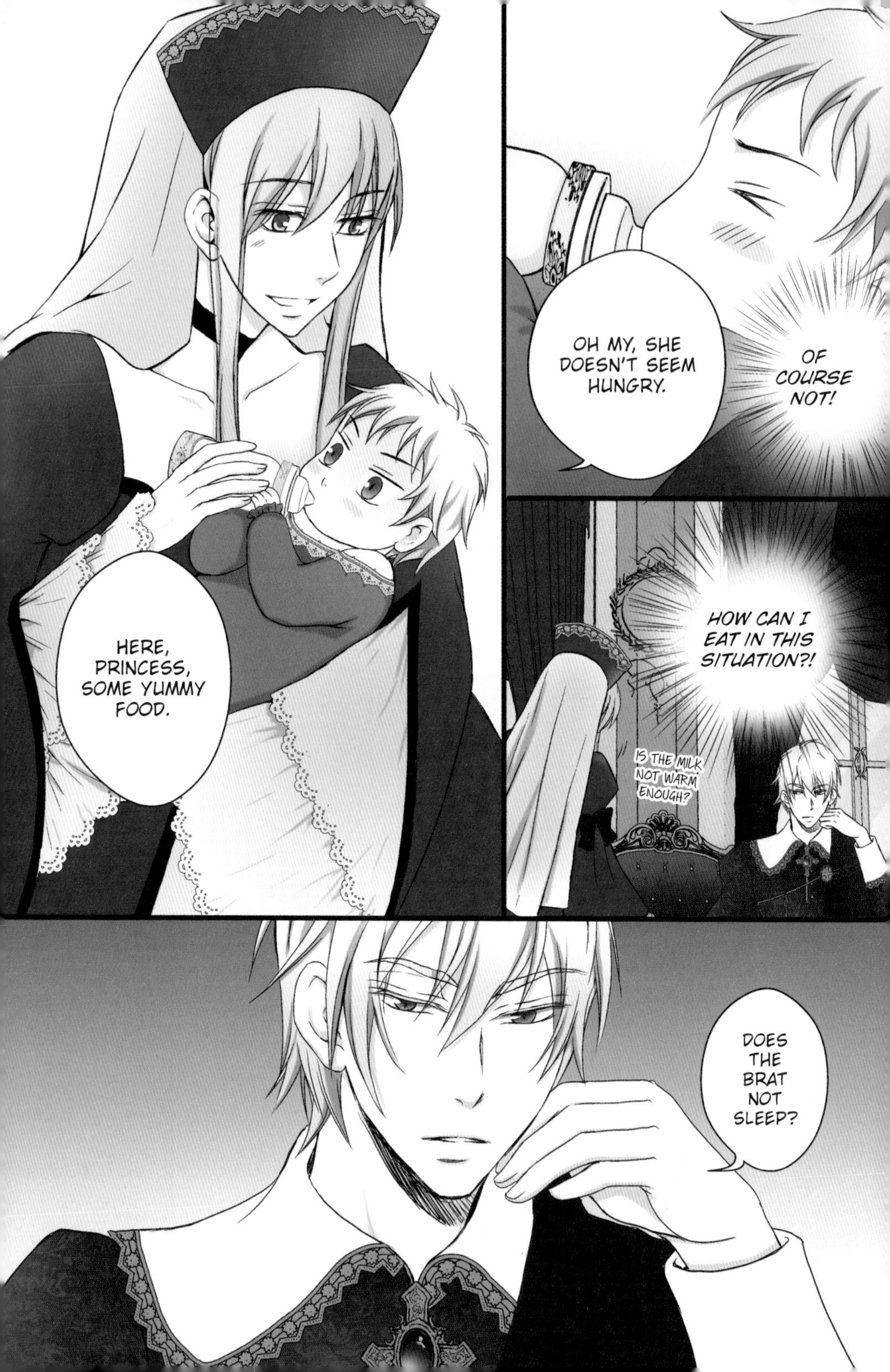
HERE, PRINCESS, SOME YUMMY FOOD.
OH MY, SHE DOESN'T SEEM HUNGRY.
OF COURSE NOT!
HOW CAN I EAT IN THIS SITUATION?!
IS THE MILK NOT WARM ENOUGH?
DOES THE BRAT NOT SLEEP?

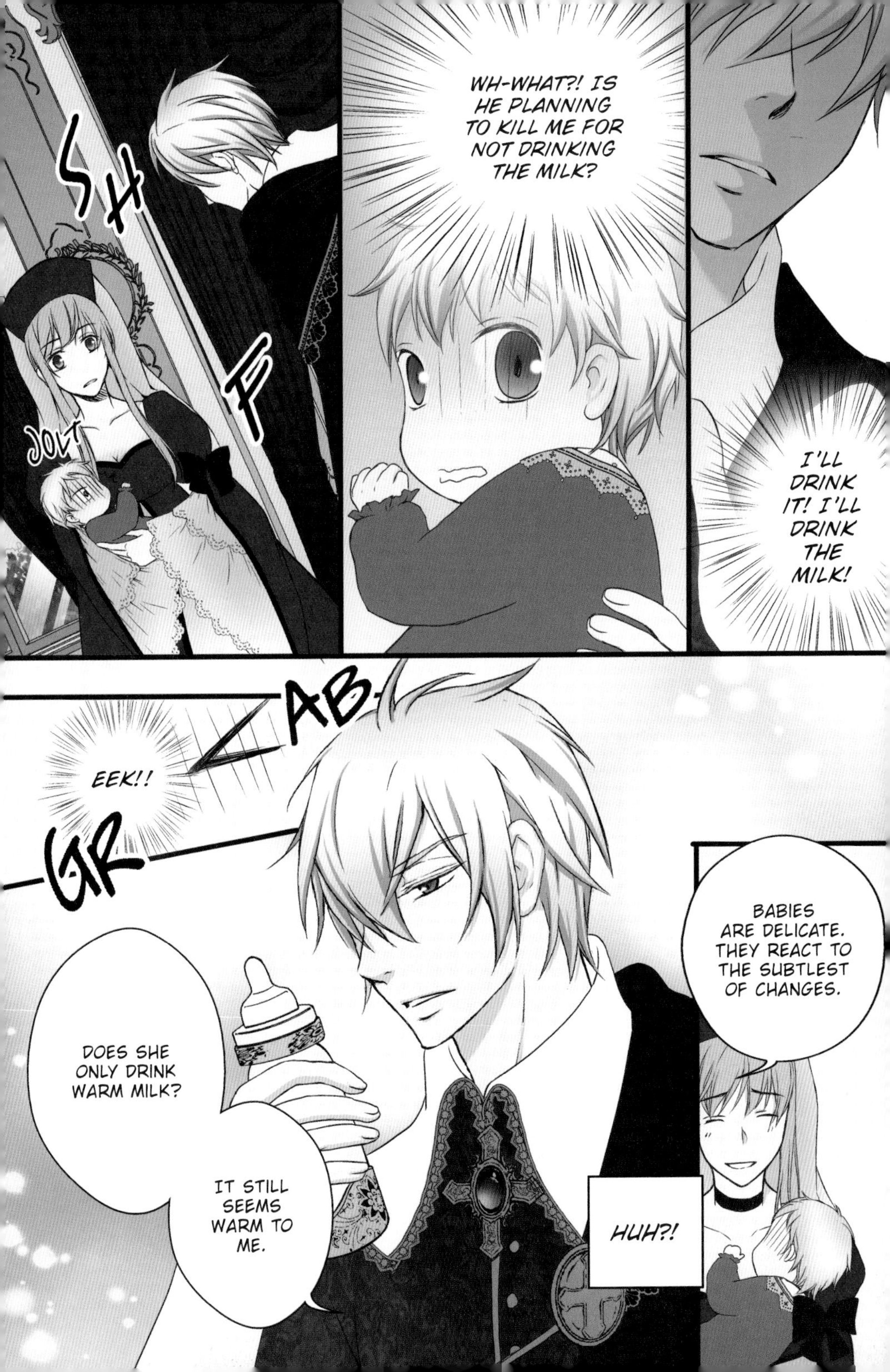
SH
F
JOLT
WH-WHAT?! IS HE PLANNING TO KILL ME FOR NOT DRINKING THE MILK?
I'LL DRINK IT! I'LL DRINK THE MILK!
GR
ZAB
EEK!!
DOES SHE ONLY DRINK WARM MILK?
IT STILL SEEMS WARM TO ME.
HUH?!
BABIES ARE DELICATE. THEY REACT TO THE SUBTLEST OF CHANGES.

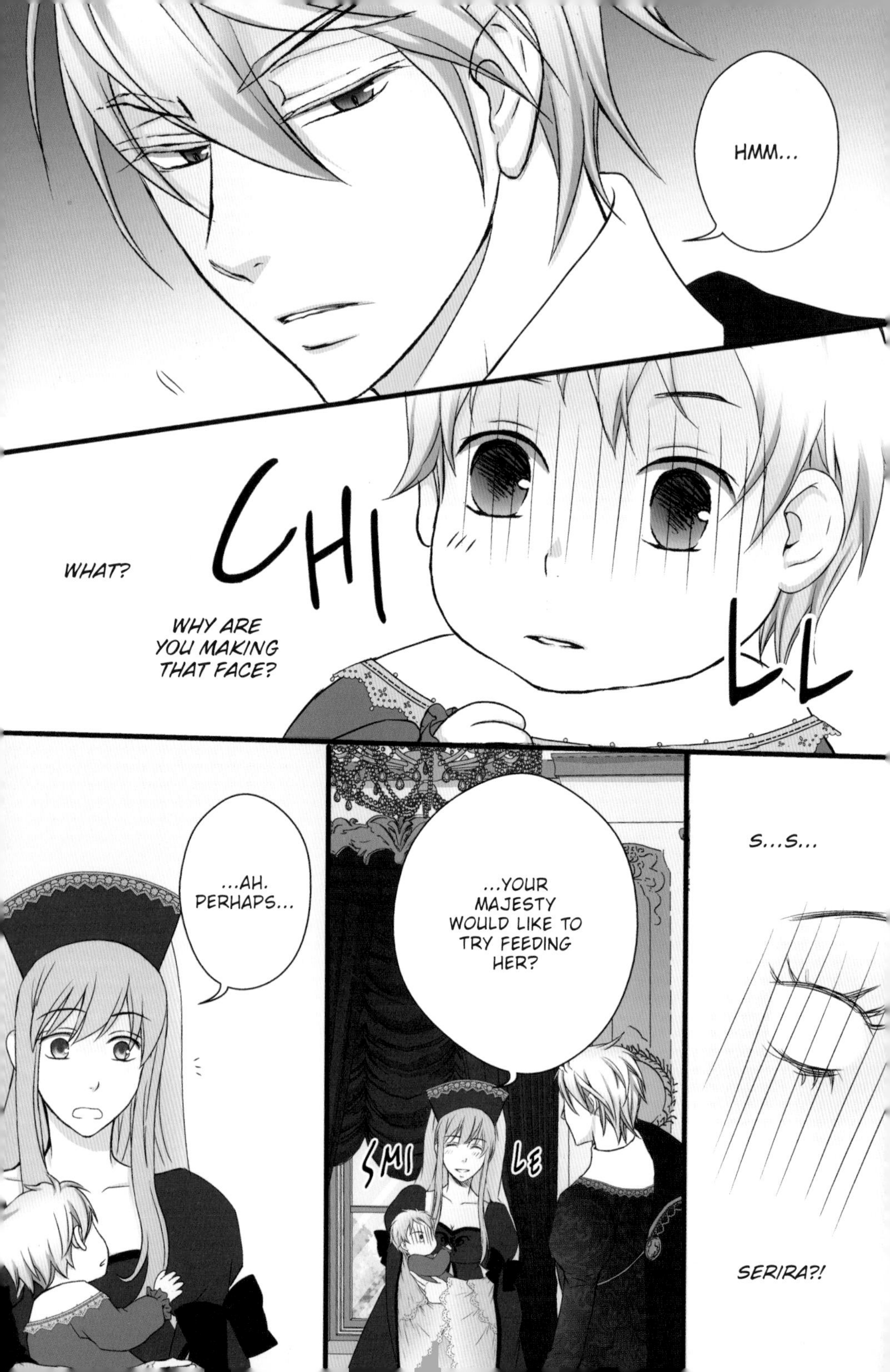
HMM...
WHAT?
WHY ARE YOU MAKING THAT FACE?
CHI
LL
...AH. PERHAPS...
...YOUR MAJESTY WOULD LIKE TO TRY FEEDING HER?
SMI
LE
S...S...
SERIRA?!

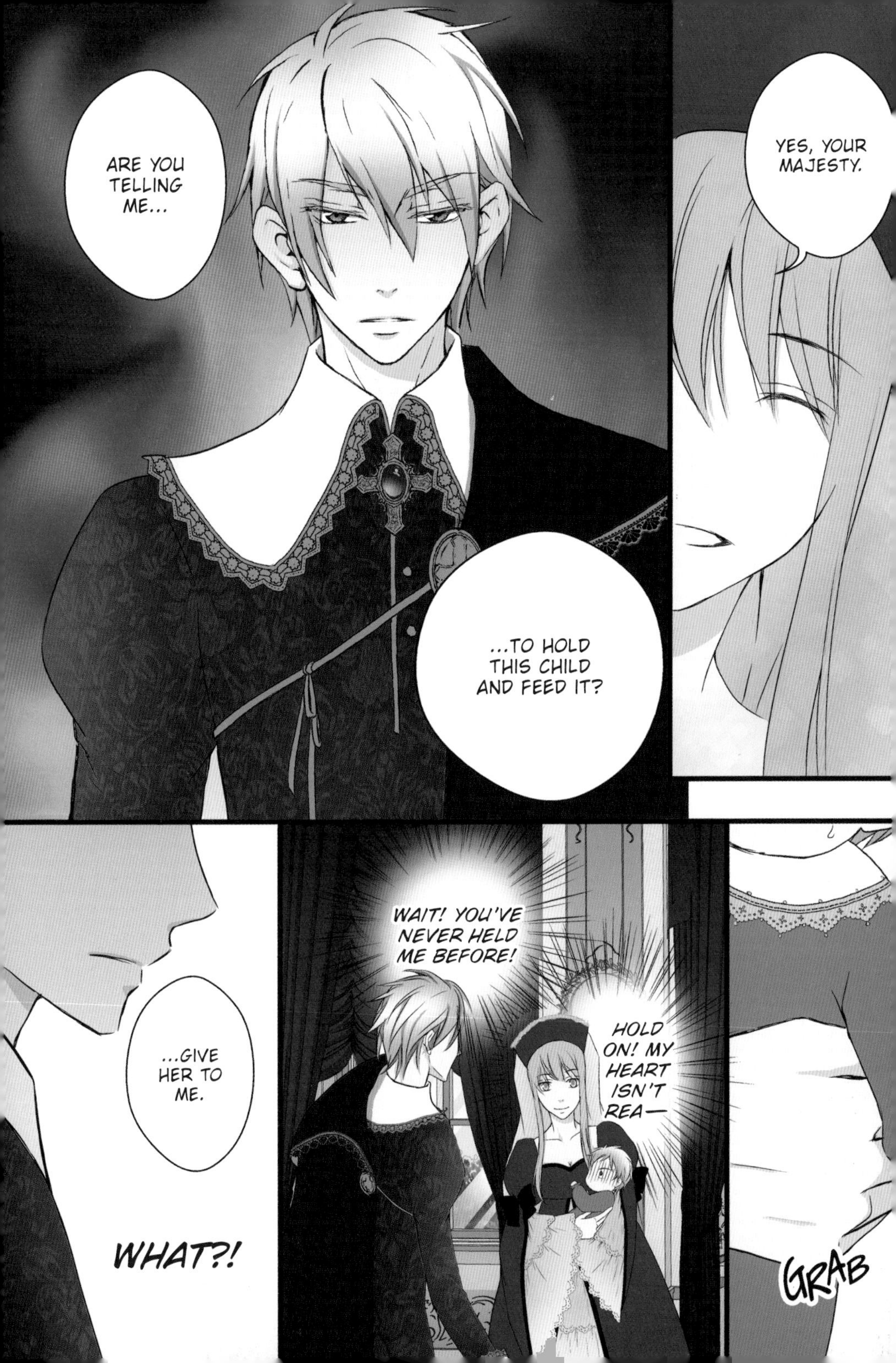
ARE YOU TELLING ME...
...TO HOLD THIS CHILD AND FEED IT?
YES, YOUR MAJESTY.
...GIVE HER TO ME.
WHAT?!
WAIT! YOU'VE NEVER HELD ME BEFORE!
HOLD ON! MY HEART ISN'T REA—
GRAB

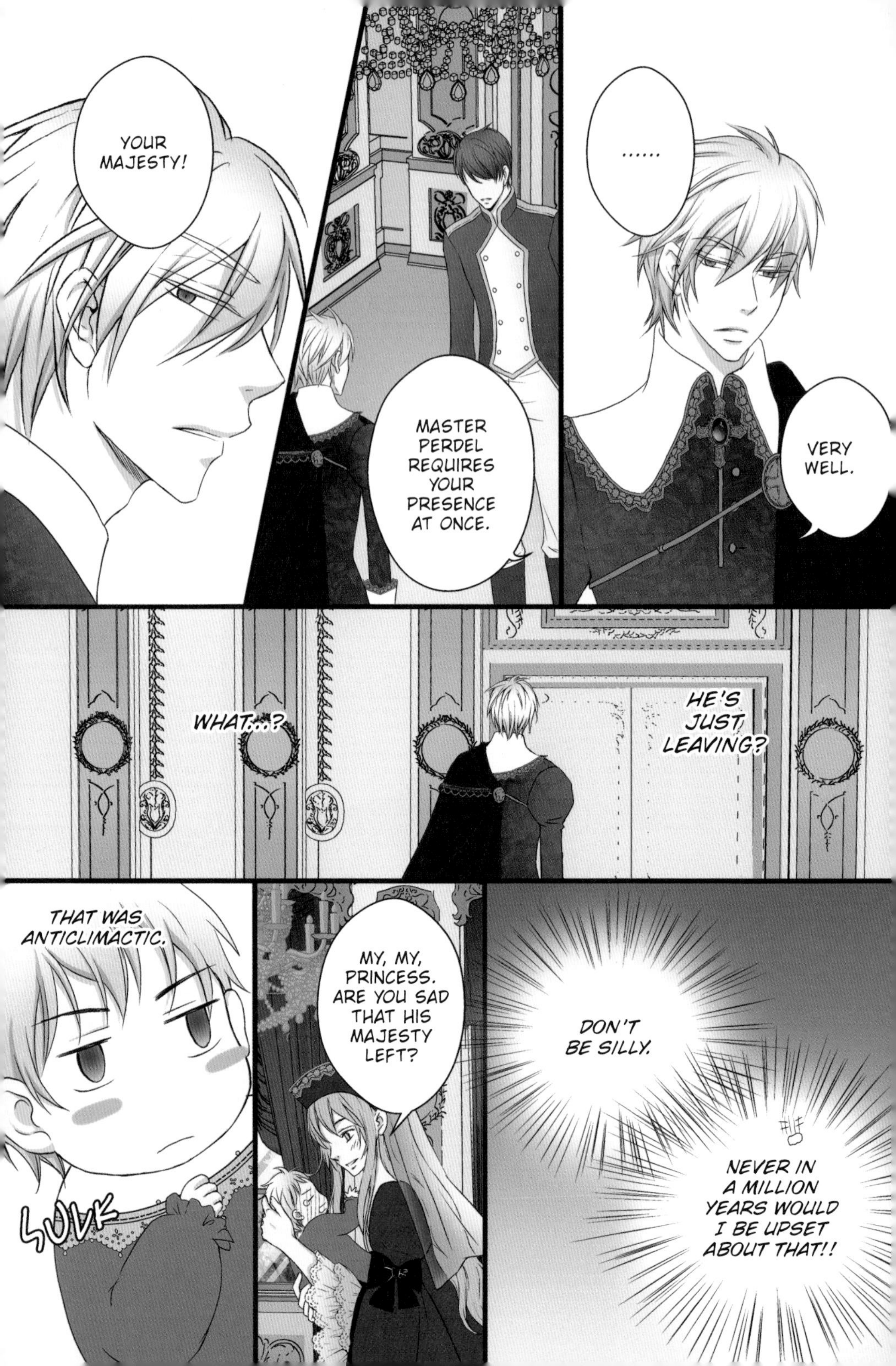
YOUR MAJESTY!
MASTER PERDEL REQUIRES YOUR PRESENCE AT ONCE.
......
VERY WELL.
WHAT...?
HE'S JUST LEAVING?
THAT WAS ANTICLIMACTIC.
SULK
MY, MY, PRINCESS. ARE YOU SAD THAT HIS MAJESTY LEFT?
DON'T BE SILLY.
NEVER IN A MILLION YEARS WOULD I BE UPSET ABOUT THAT!!

Hello, I'm Your Baby (2)

DAUGHTER
OF THE
EMPEROR

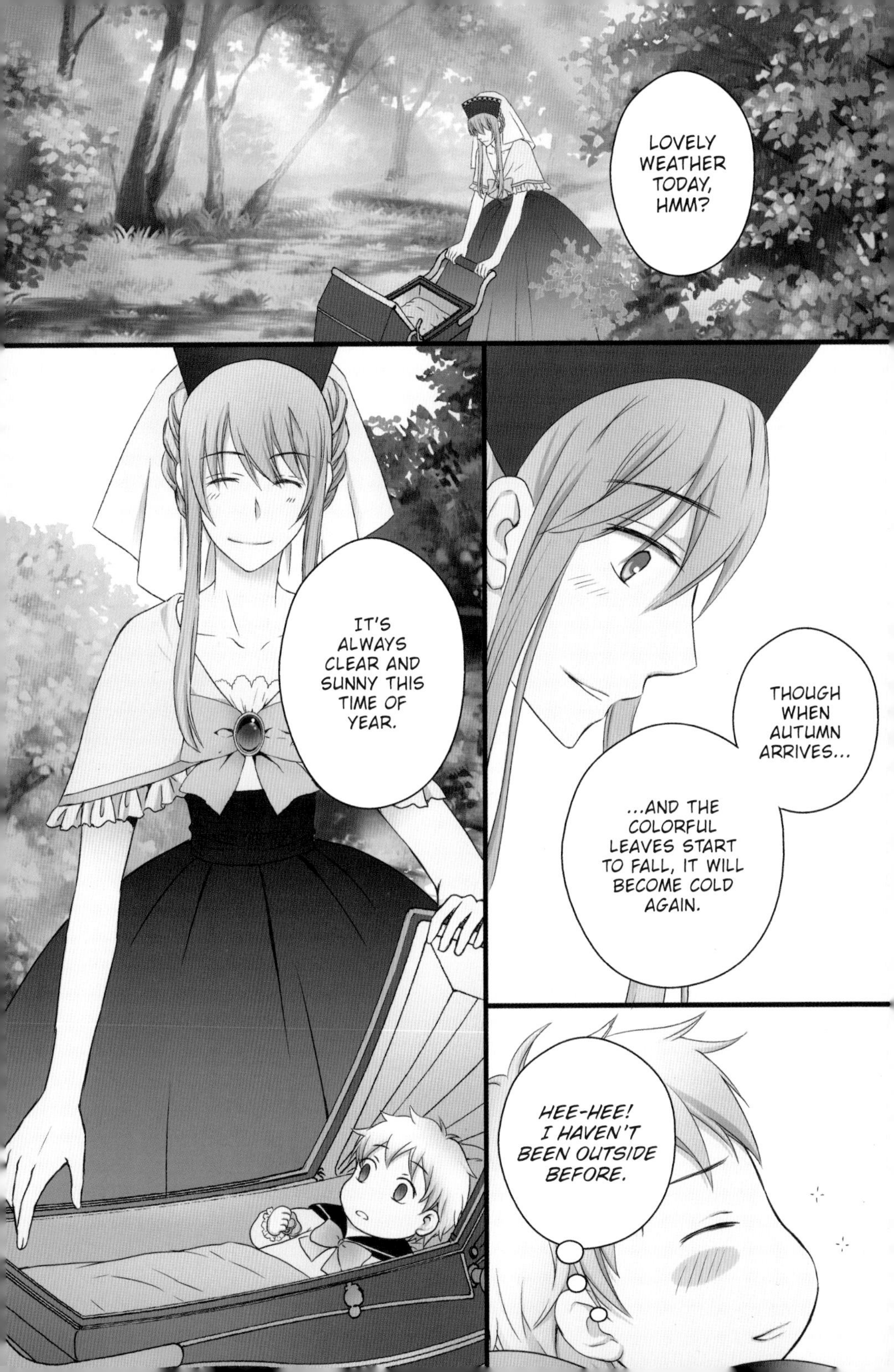
LOVELY WEATHER TODAY, HMM?
IT'S ALWAYS CLEAR AND SUNNY THIS TIME OF YEAR.
THOUGH WHEN AUTUMN ARRIVES...
...AND THE COLORFUL LEAVES START TO FALL, IT WILL BECOME COLD AGAIN.
HEE-HEE! I HAVEN'T BEEN OUTSIDE BEFORE.

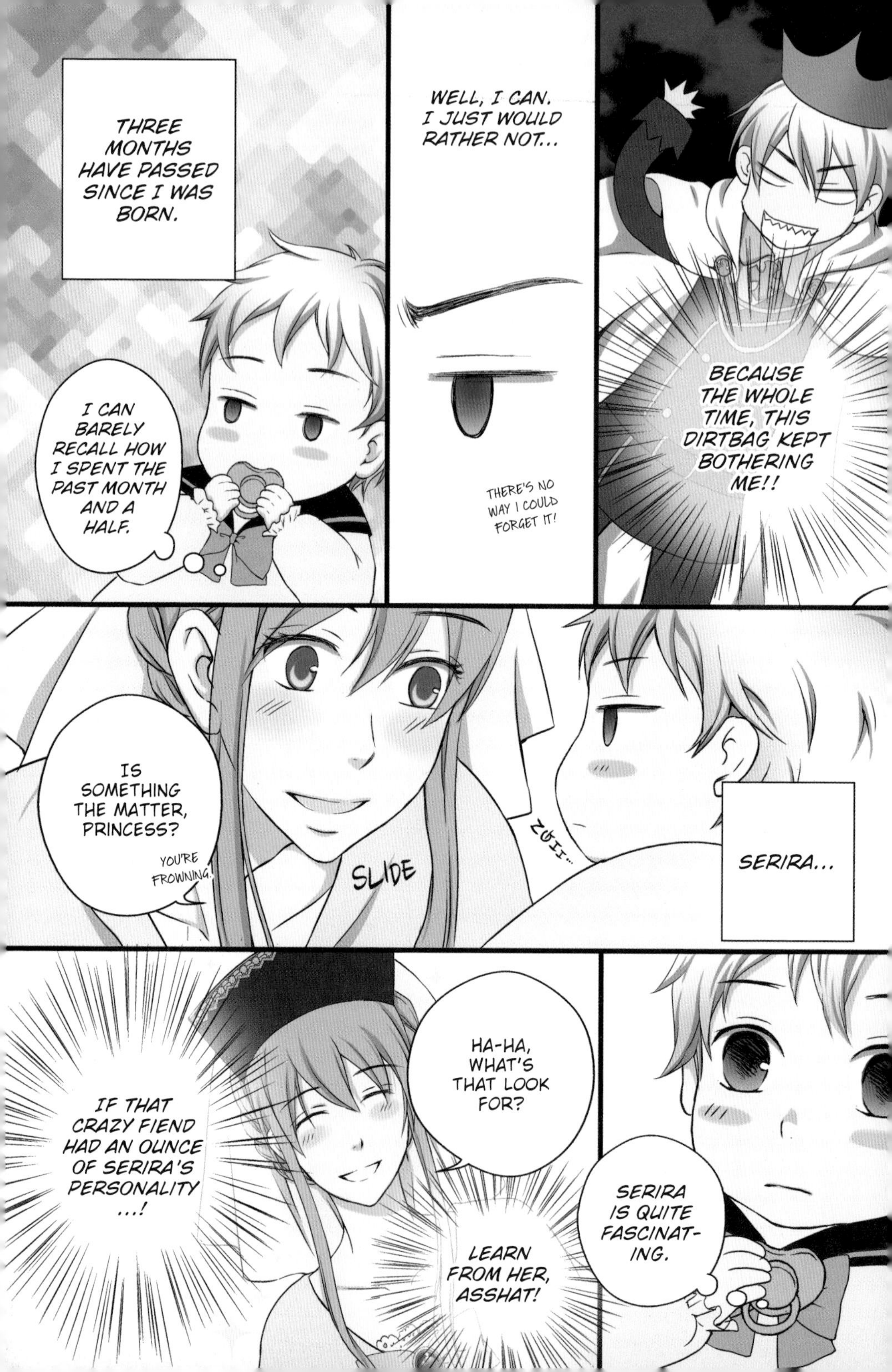
THREE MONTHS HAVE PASSED SINCE I WAS BORN.
I CAN BARELY RECALL HOW I SPENT THE PAST MONTH AND A HALF.
WELL, I CAN. I JUST WOULD RATHER NOT...
THERE'S NO WAY I COULD FORGET IT!
BECAUSE THE WHOLE TIME, THIS DIRTBAG KEPT BOTHERING ME!!
IS SOMETHING THE MATTER, PRINCESS?
YOU'RE FROWNING.
SLIDE
ZOII...
SERIRA...
IF THAT CRAZY FIEND HAD AN OUNCE OF SERIRA'S PERSONALITY ...!
HA-HA, WHAT'S THAT LOOK FOR?
LEARN FROM HER, ASSHAT!
SERIRA IS QUITE FASCINAT-ING.

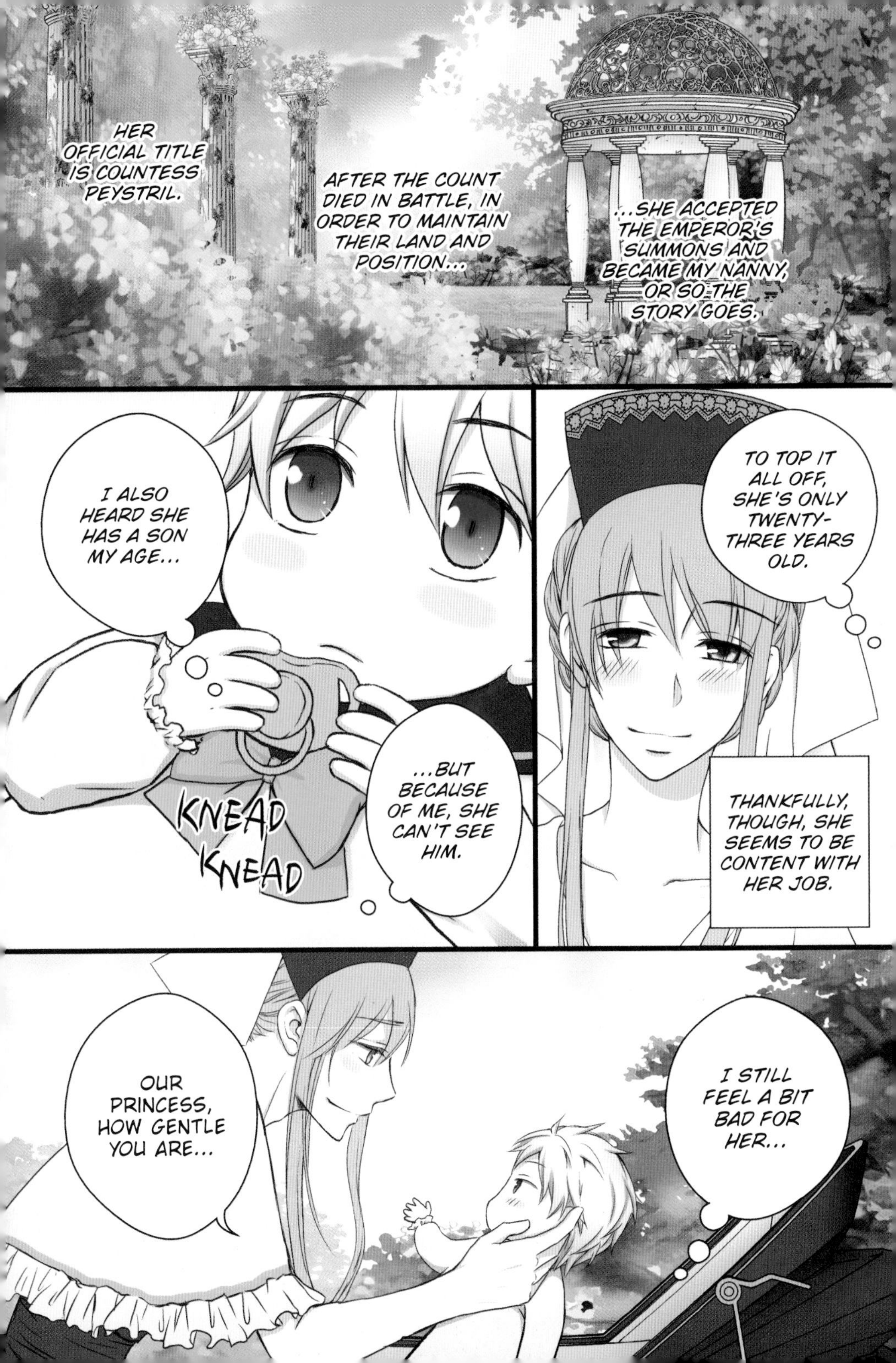
HER OFFICIAL TITLE IS COUNTESS PEYSTRIL.
AFTER THE COUNT DIED IN BATTLE, IN ORDER TO MAINTAIN THEIR LAND AND POSITION...
...SHE ACCEPTED THE EMPEROR'S SUMMONS AND BECAME MY NANNY, OR SO THE STORY GOES.
I ALSO HEARD SHE HAS A SON MY AGE...
KNEAD KNEAD
...BUT BECAUSE OF ME, SHE CAN'T SEE HIM.
TO TOP IT ALL OFF, SHE'S ONLY TWENTY-THREE YEARS OLD.
THANKFULLY, THOUGH, SHE SEEMS TO BE CONTENT WITH HER JOB.
OUR PRINCESS, HOW GENTLE YOU ARE...
I STILL FEEL A BIT BAD FOR HER...

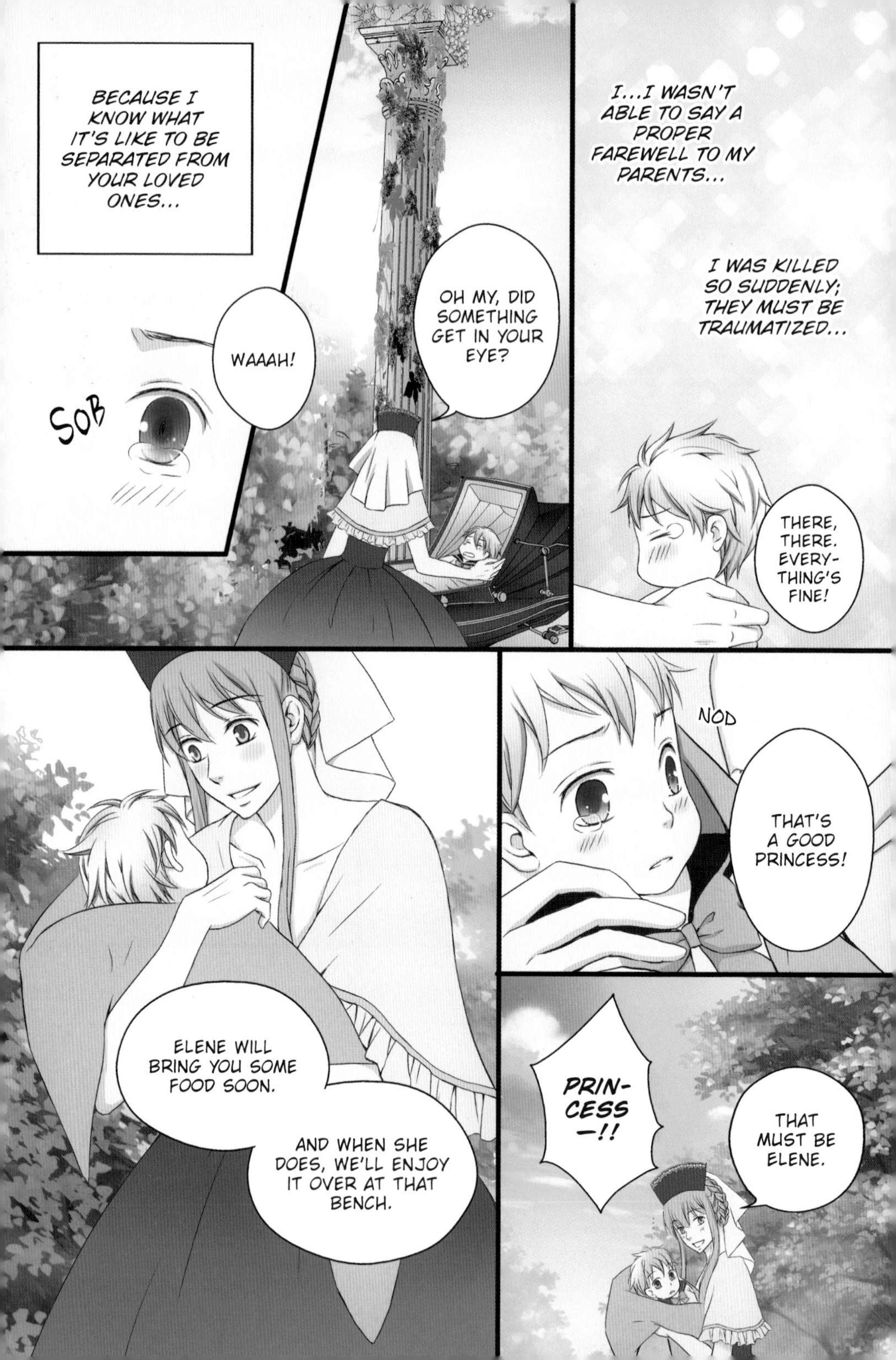
BECAUSE I KNOW WHAT IT'S LIKE TO BE SEPARATED FROM YOUR LOVED ONES...
SOB
WAAAH!
OH MY, DID SOMETHING GET IN YOUR EYE?
I...I WASN'T ABLE TO SAY A PROPER FAREWELL TO MY PARENTS...
I WAS KILLED SO SUDDENLY; THEY MUST BE TRAUMATIZED...
THERE, THERE. EVERYTHING'S FINE!
ELENE WILL BRING YOU SOME FOOD SOON.
AND WHEN SHE DOES, WE'LL ENJOY IT OVER AT THAT BENCH.
NOD
THAT'S A GOOD PRINCESS!
PRINCESS—!!
THAT MUST BE ELENE.

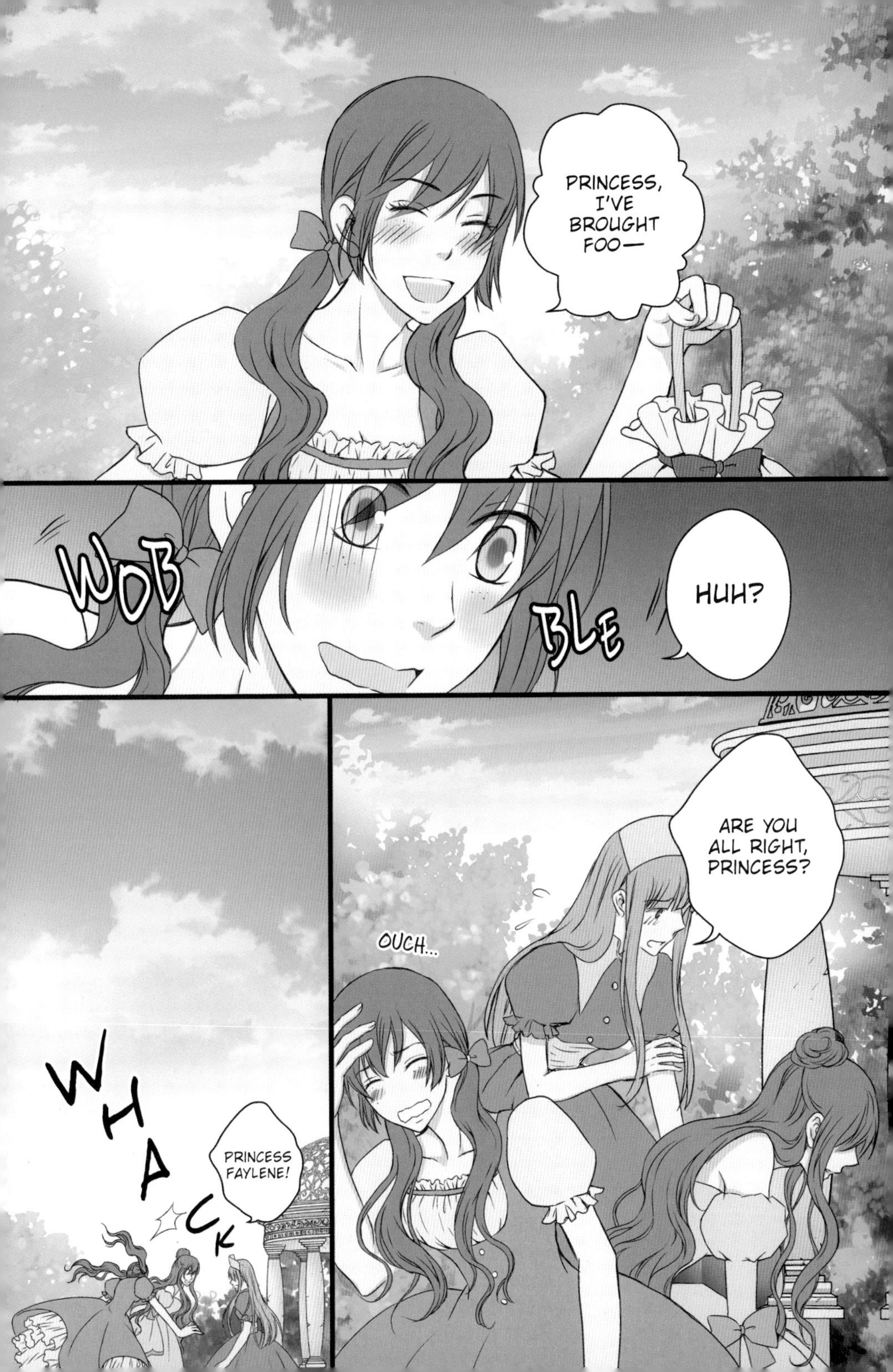
PRINCESS, I'VE BROUGHT FOO—
WOBBLE
HUH?
WHACK
PRINCESS FAYLENE!
ARE YOU ALL RIGHT, PRINCESS?
OUCH...

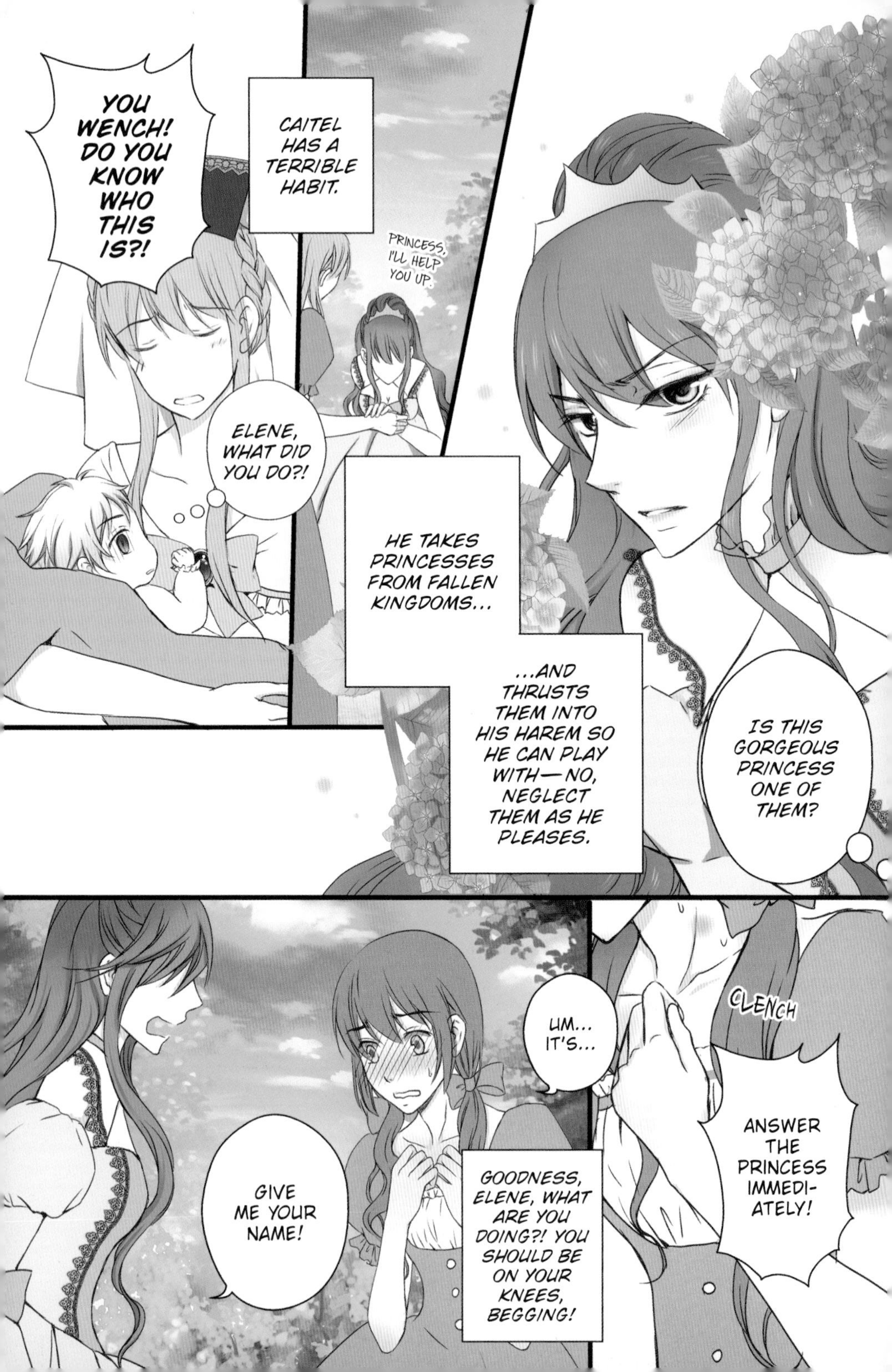
YOU WENCH! DO YOU KNOW WHO THIS IS?!
ELENE, WHAT DID YOU DO?!
CAITEL HAS A TERRIBLE HABIT.
PRINCESS, I'LL HELP YOU UP.
HE TAKES PRINCESSES FROM FALLEN KINGDOMS...
...AND THRUSTS THEM INTO HIS HAREM SO HE CAN PLAY WITH—NO, NEGLECT THEM AS HE PLEASES.
IS THIS GORGEOUS PRINCESS ONE OF THEM?
GIVE ME YOUR NAME!
UM... IT'S...
GOODNESS, ELENE, WHAT ARE YOU DOING?! YOU SHOULD BE ON YOUR KNEES, BEGGING!
CLENCH
ANSWER THE PRINCESS IMMEDI-ATELY!

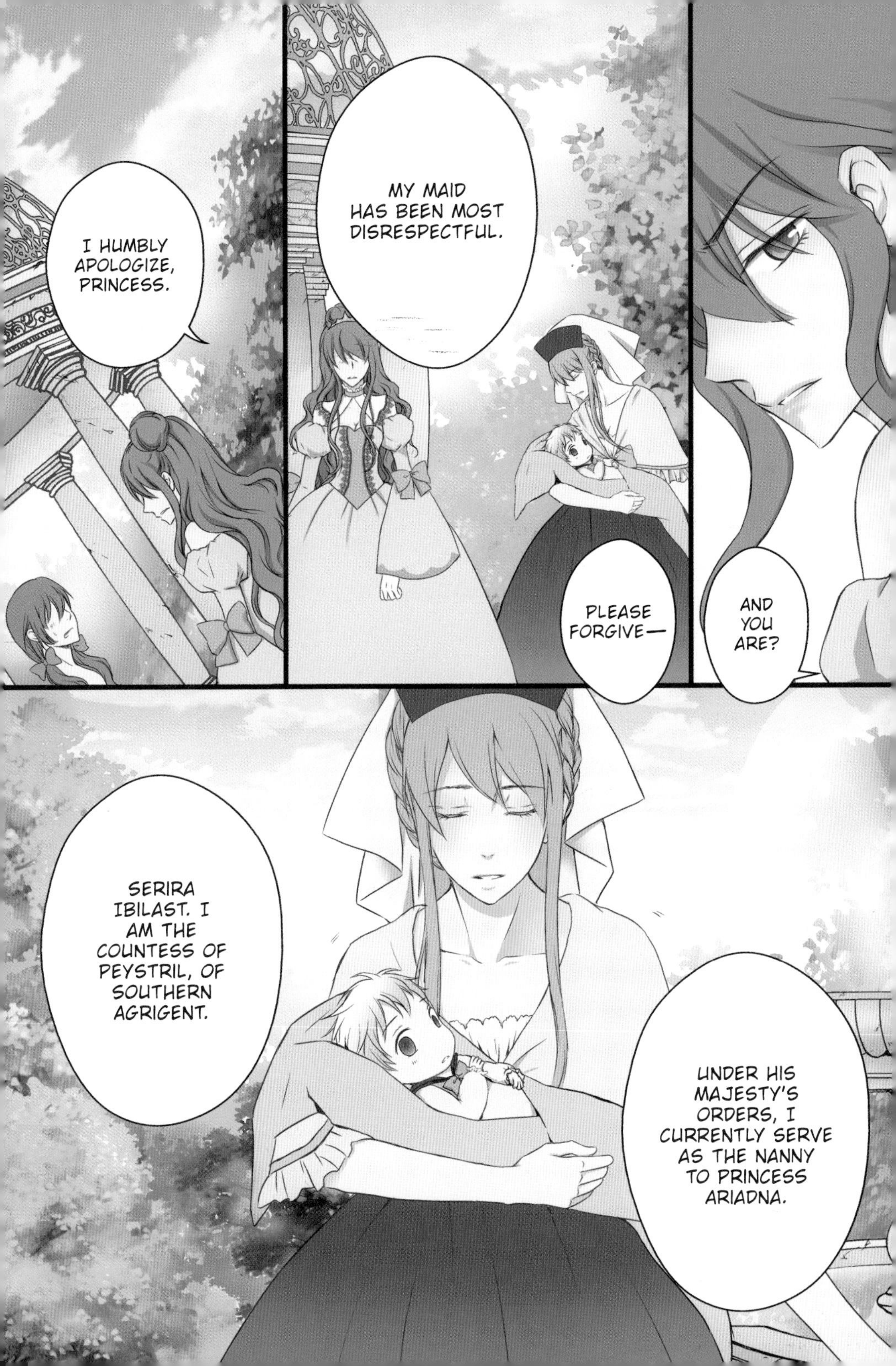
I HUMBLY APOLOGIZE, PRINCESS.
MY MAID HAS BEEN MOST DISRESPECTFUL.
PLEASE FORGIVE—
AND YOU ARE?
SERIRA IBILAST. I AM THE COUNTESS OF PEYSTRIL, OF SOUTHERN AGRIGENT.
UNDER HIS MAJESTY'S ORDERS, I CURRENTLY SERVE AS THE NANNY TO PRINCESS ARIADNA.

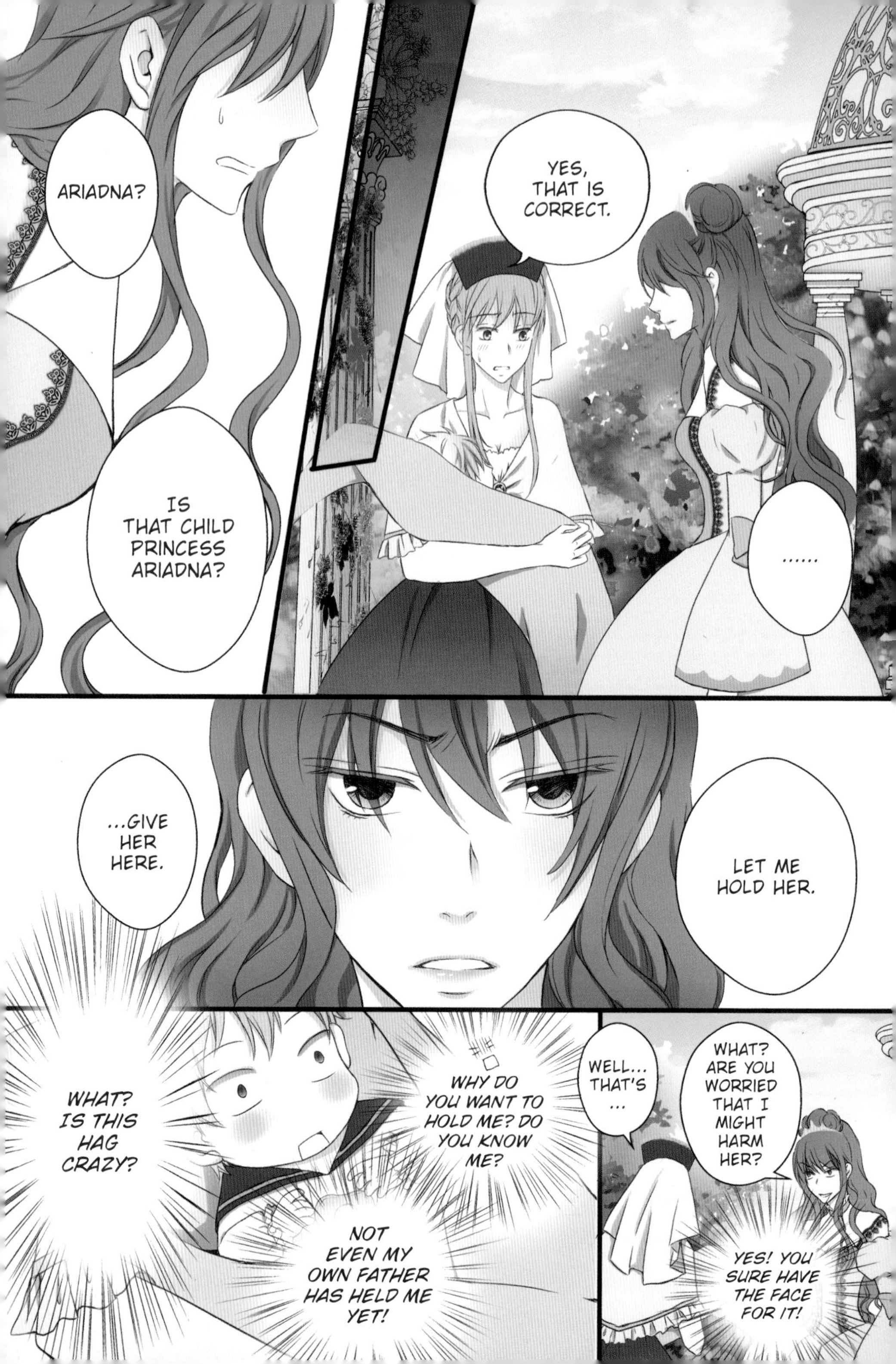

ARIADNA?
IS THAT CHILD PRINCESS ARIADNA?
YES, THAT IS CORRECT.
......
...GIVE HER HERE.
LET ME HOLD HER.
WHAT? IS THIS HAG CRAZY?
WHY DO YOU WANT TO HOLD ME? DO YOU KNOW ME?
NOT EVEN MY OWN FATHER HAS HELD ME YET!
WELL... THAT'S ...
WHAT? ARE YOU WORRIED THAT I MIGHT HARM HER?
YES! YOU SURE HAVE THE FACE FOR IT!

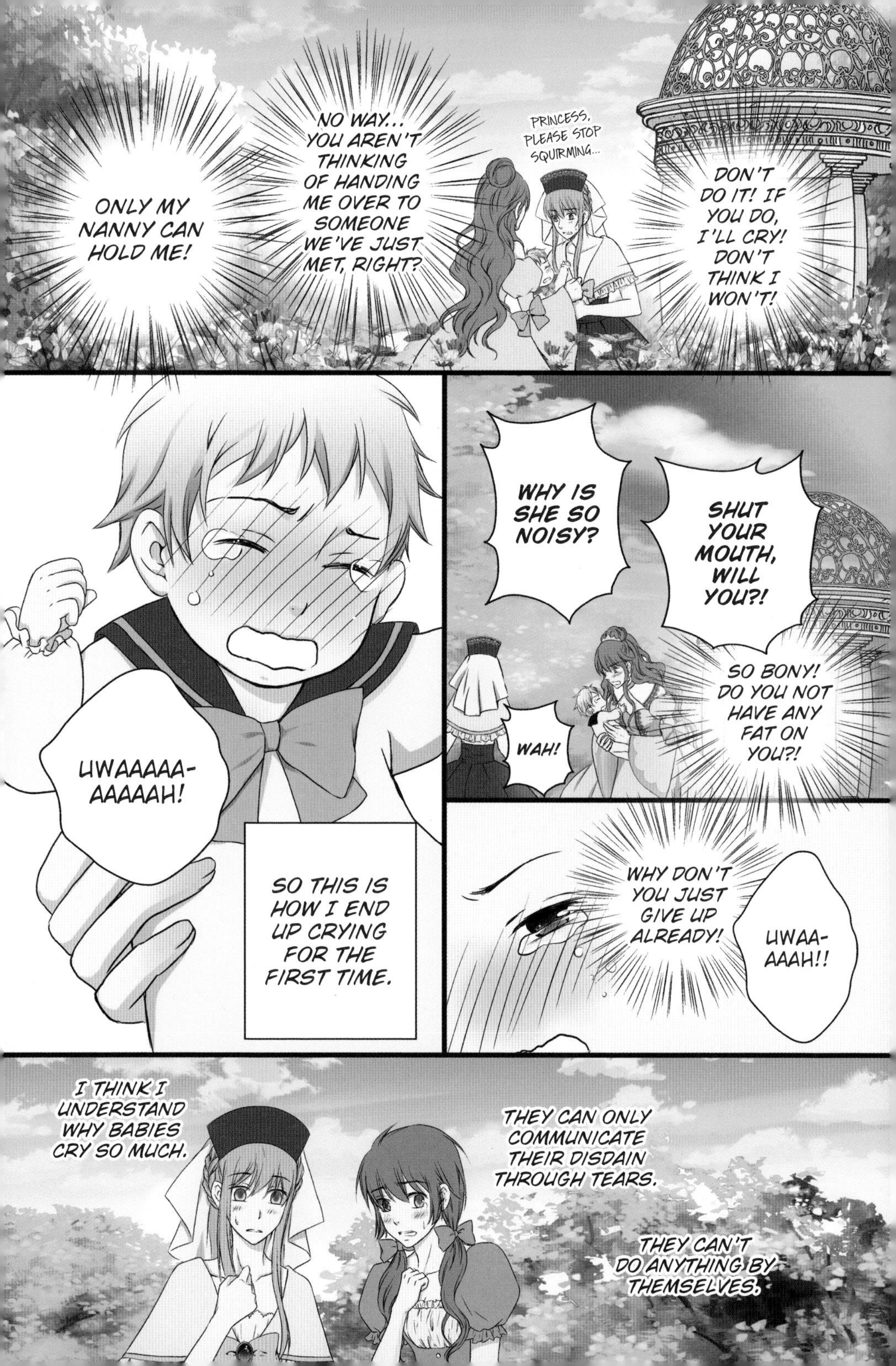
ONLY MY NANNY CAN HOLD ME!
NO WAY... YOU AREN'T THINKING OF HANDING ME OVER TO SOMEONE WE'VE JUST MET, RIGHT?
PRINCESS, PLEASE STOP SQUIRMING...
DON'T DO IT! IF YOU DO, I'LL CRY! DON'T THINK I WON'T!
UWAAAAA-AAAAAH!
SO THIS IS HOW I END UP CRYING FOR THE FIRST TIME.
WHY IS SHE SO NOISY?
SHUT YOUR MOUTH, WILL YOU?!
WAH!
SO BONY! DO YOU NOT HAVE ANY FAT ON YOU?!
WHY DON'T YOU JUST GIVE UP ALREADY!
UWAA-AAAH!!
I THINK I UNDERSTAND WHY BABIES CRY SO MUCH.
THEY CAN ONLY COMMUNICATE THEIR DISDAIN THROUGH TEARS.
THEY CAN'T DO ANYTHING BY THEMSELVES.

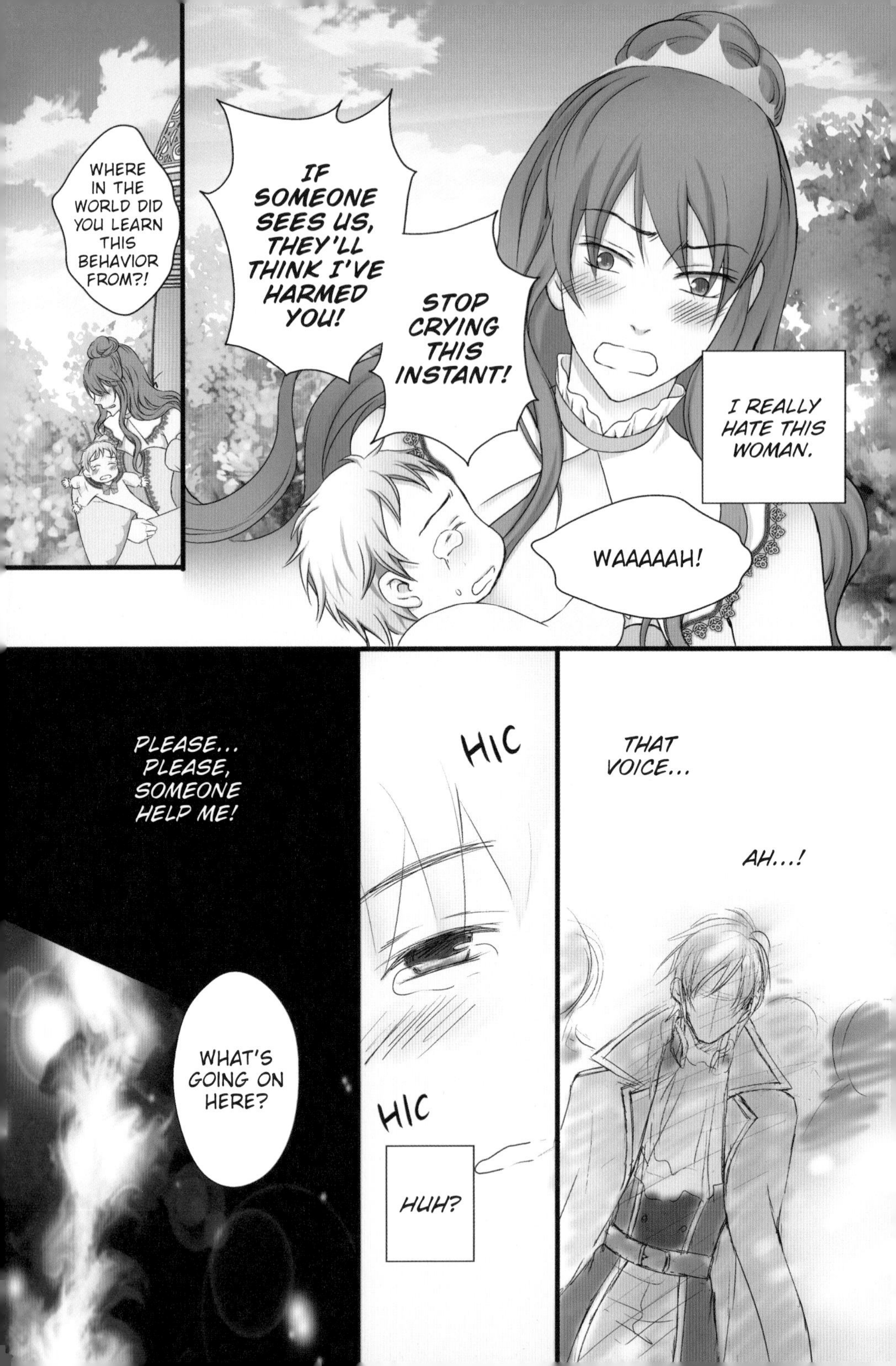
WHERE IN THE WORLD DID YOU LEARN THIS BEHAVIOR FROM?!
IF SOMEONE SEES US, THEY'LL THINK I'VE HARMED YOU!
STOP CRYING THIS INSTANT!
I REALLY HATE THIS WOMAN.
WAAAAAH!
PLEASE... PLEASE, SOMEONE HELP ME!
WHAT'S GOING ON HERE?
HIC
HIC
HUH?
THAT VOICE...
AH...!

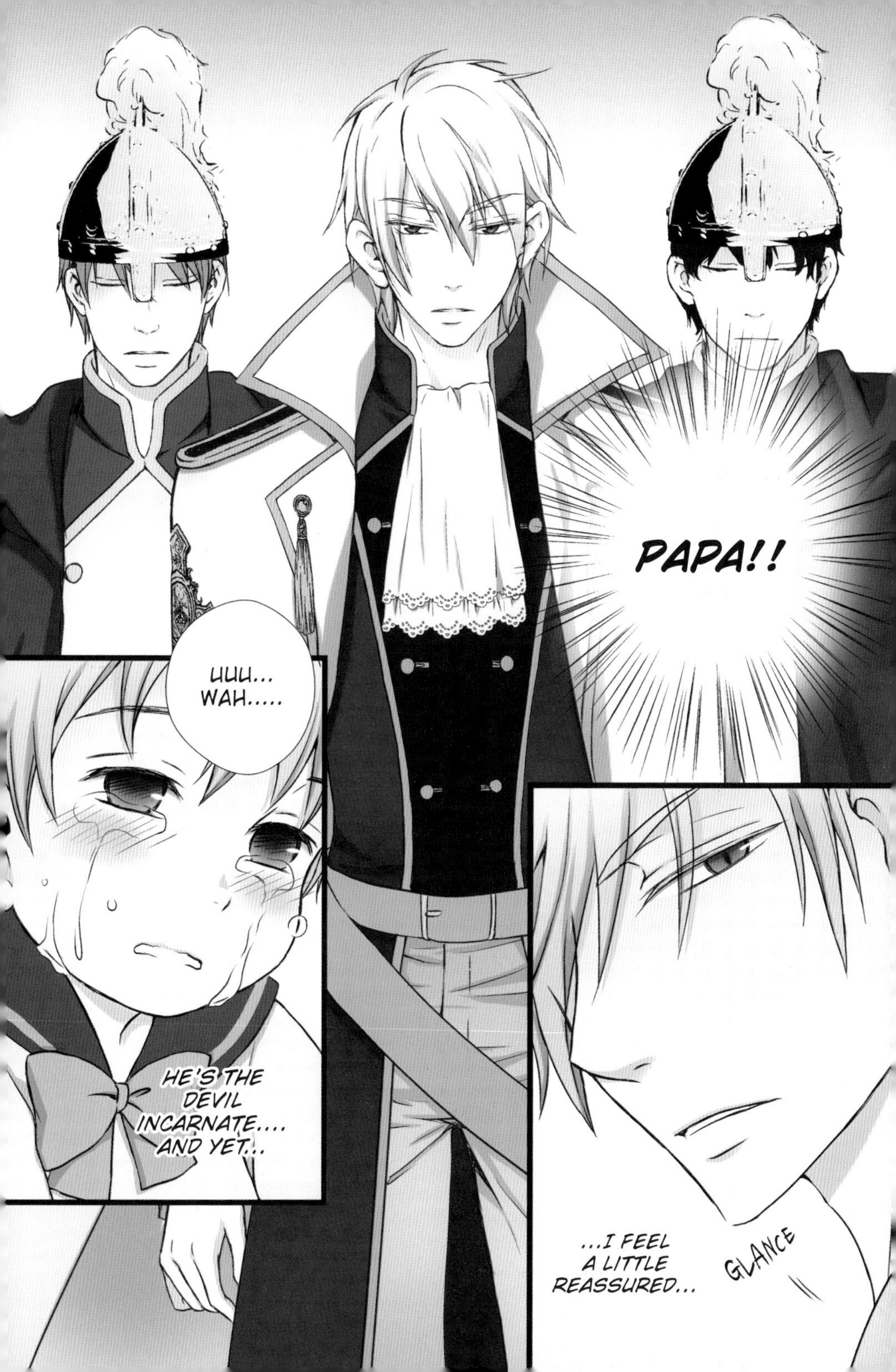
PAPA!!
UUU... WAH.....
HE'S THE DEVIL INCARNATE.... AND YET...
...I FEEL A LITTLE REASSURED...
GLANCE

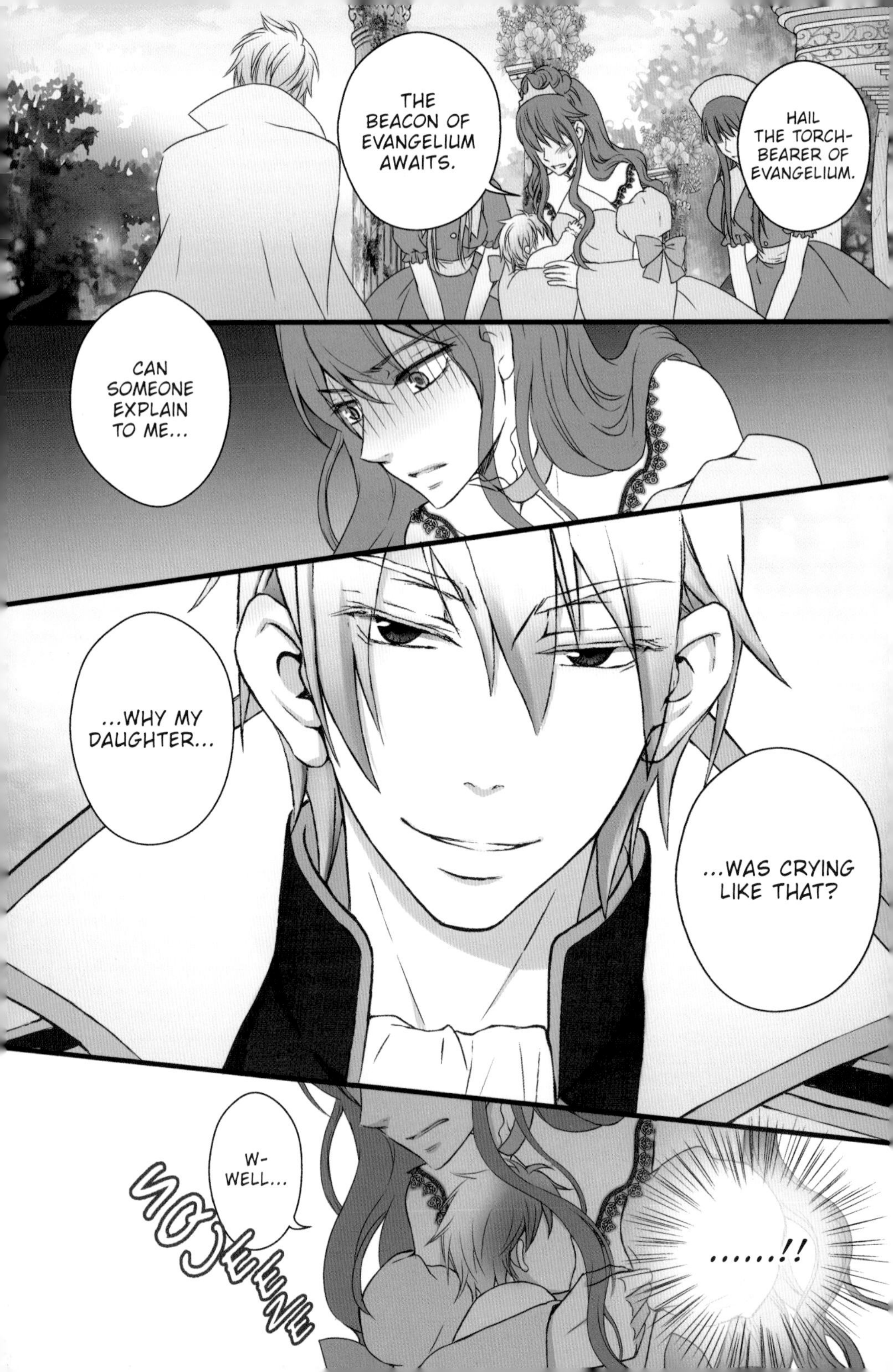
THE BEACON OF EVANGELIUM AWAITS.
HAIL THE TORCH-BEARER OF EVANGELIUM.
CAN SOMEONE EXPLAIN TO ME...
...WHY MY DAUGHTER...
...WAS CRYING LIKE THAT?
W-WELL...
......!!

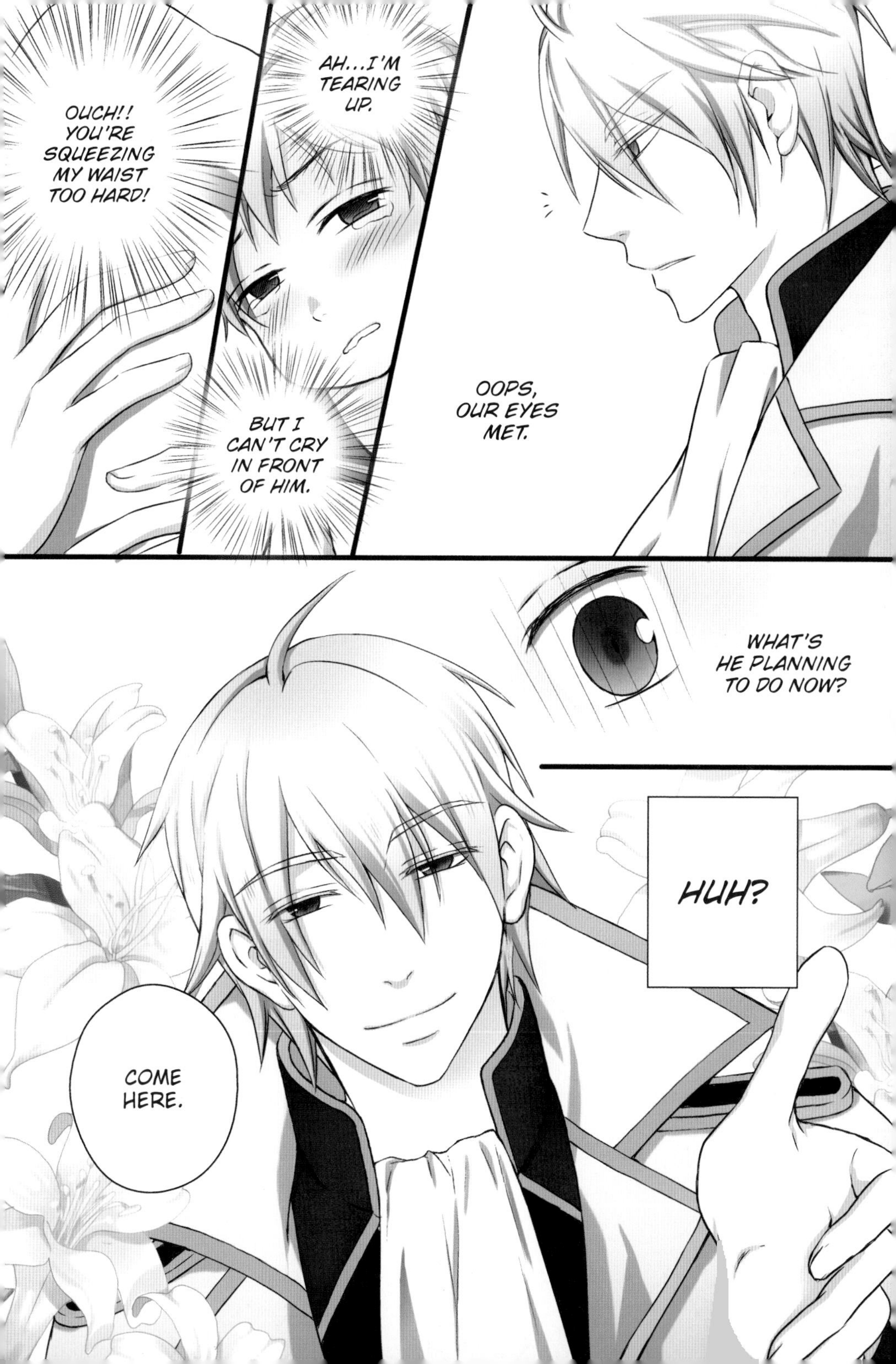
OUCH!! YOU'RE SQUEEZING MY WAIST TOO HARD!
AH...I'M TEARING UP.
BUT I CAN'T CRY IN FRONT OF HIM.
OOPS, OUR EYES MET.
WHAT'S HE PLANNING TO DO NOW?
COME HERE.
HUH?

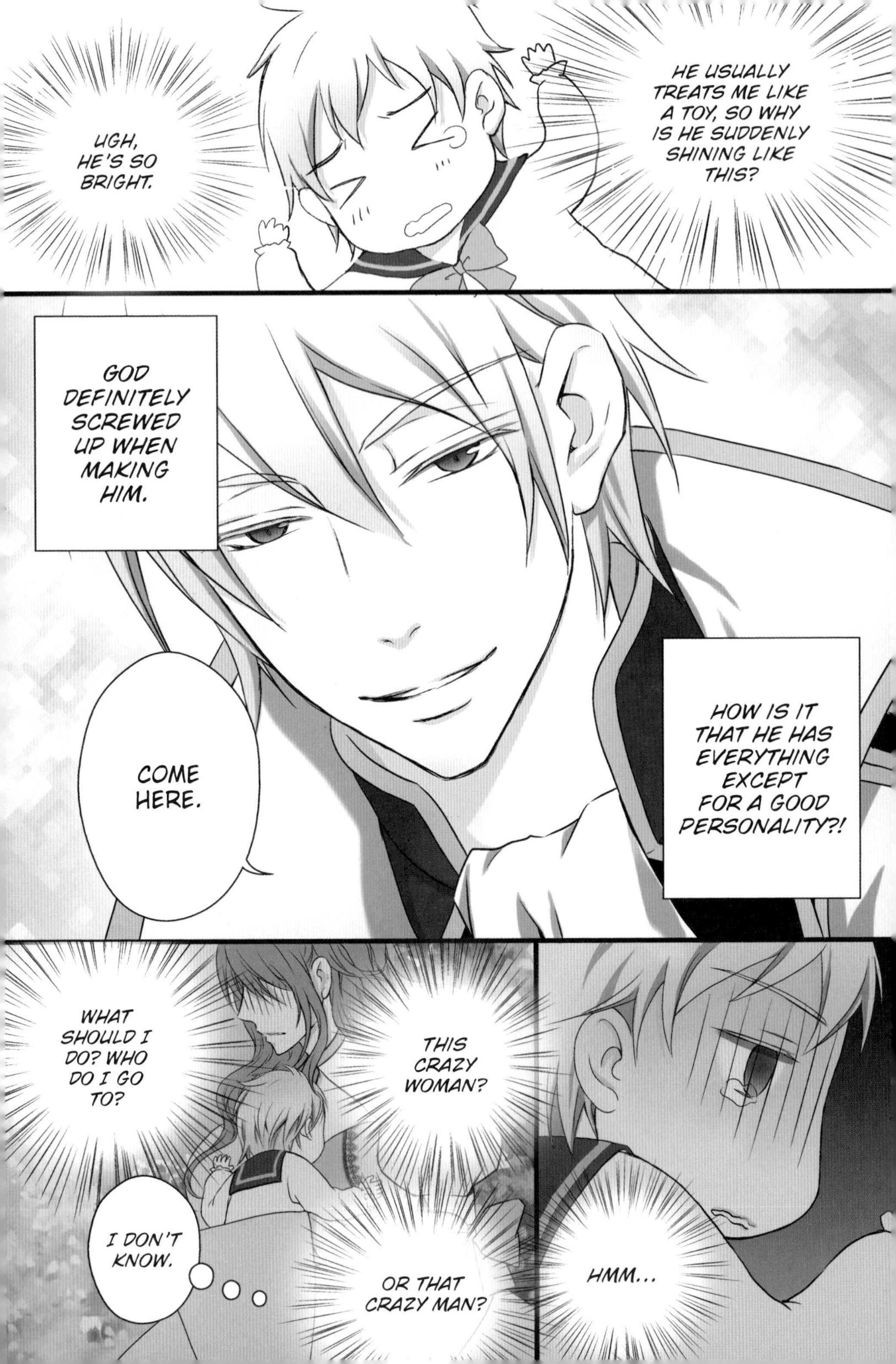
UGH, HE'S SO BRIGHT.
HE USUALLY TREATS ME LIKE A TOY, SO WHY IS HE SUDDENLY SHINING LIKE THIS?
GOD DEFINITELY SCREWED UP WHEN MAKING HIM.
COME HERE.
HOW IS IT THAT HE HAS EVERYTHING EXCEPT FOR A GOOD PERSONALITY?!
WHAT SHOULD I DO? WHO DO I GO TO?
THIS CRAZY WOMAN?
I DON'T KNOW.
OR THAT CRAZY MAN?
HMM...

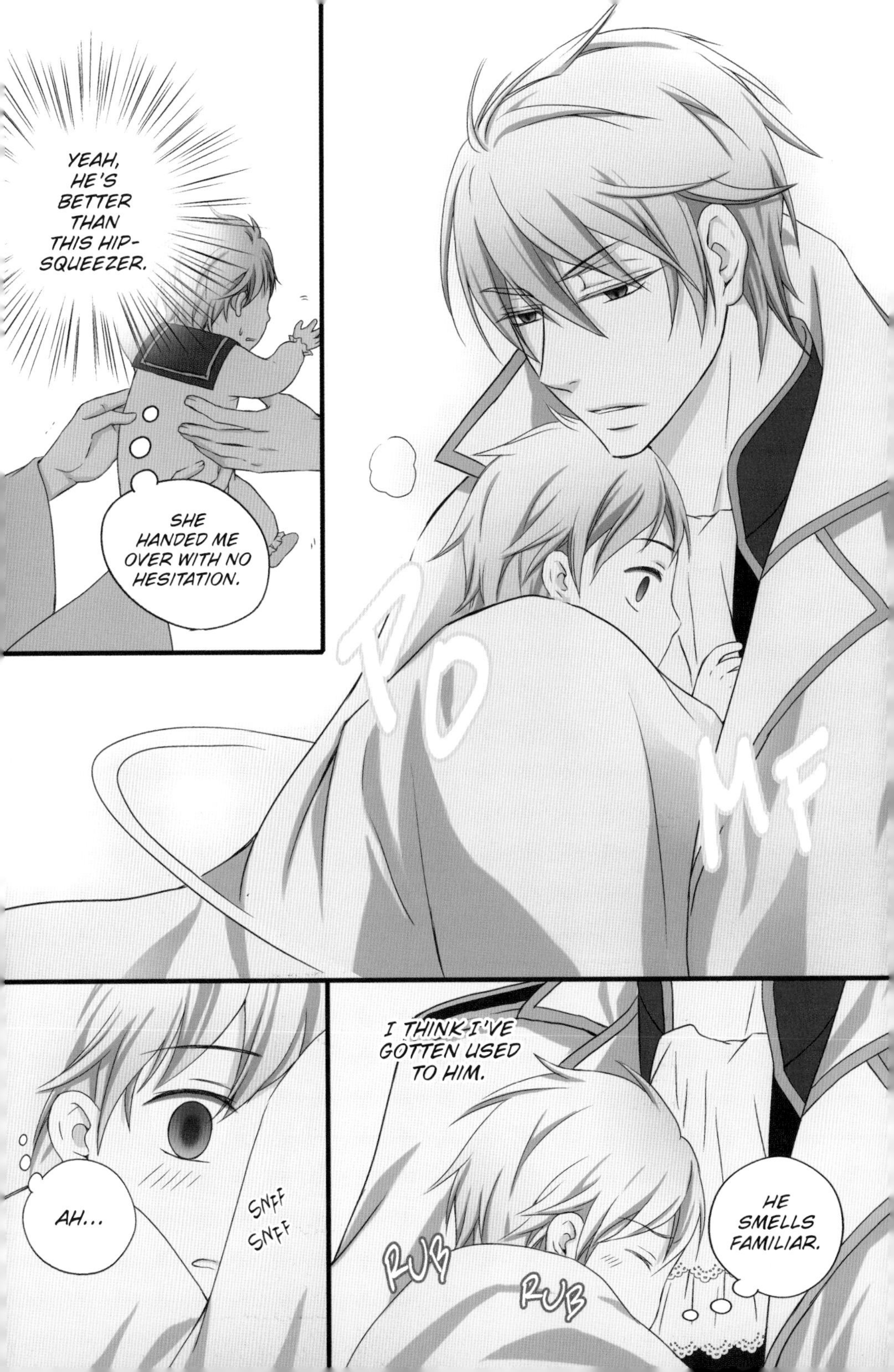
YEAH, HE'S BETTER THAN THIS HIP-SQUEEZER.
SHE HANDED ME OVER WITH NO HESITATION.
POMF
AH...
SNFF SNFF
I THINK I'VE GOTTEN USED TO HIM.
RUB RUB
HE SMELLS FAMILIAR.

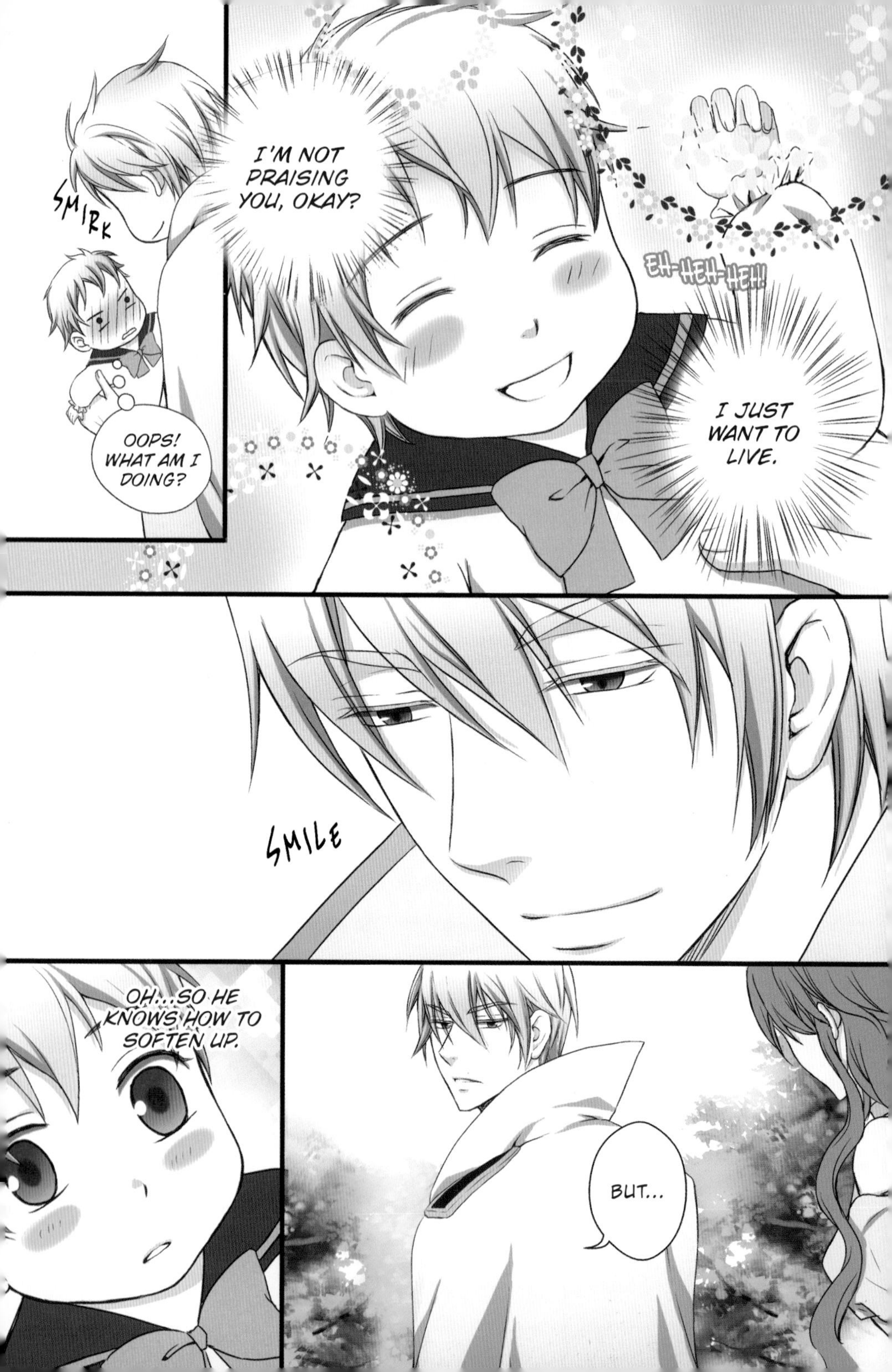
SMIRK
OOPS! WHAT AM I DOING?
I'M NOT PRAISING YOU, OKAY?
EH-HEH-HEH!!
I JUST WANT TO LIVE.
SMILE
OH...SO HE KNOWS HOW TO SOFTEN UP.
BUT...

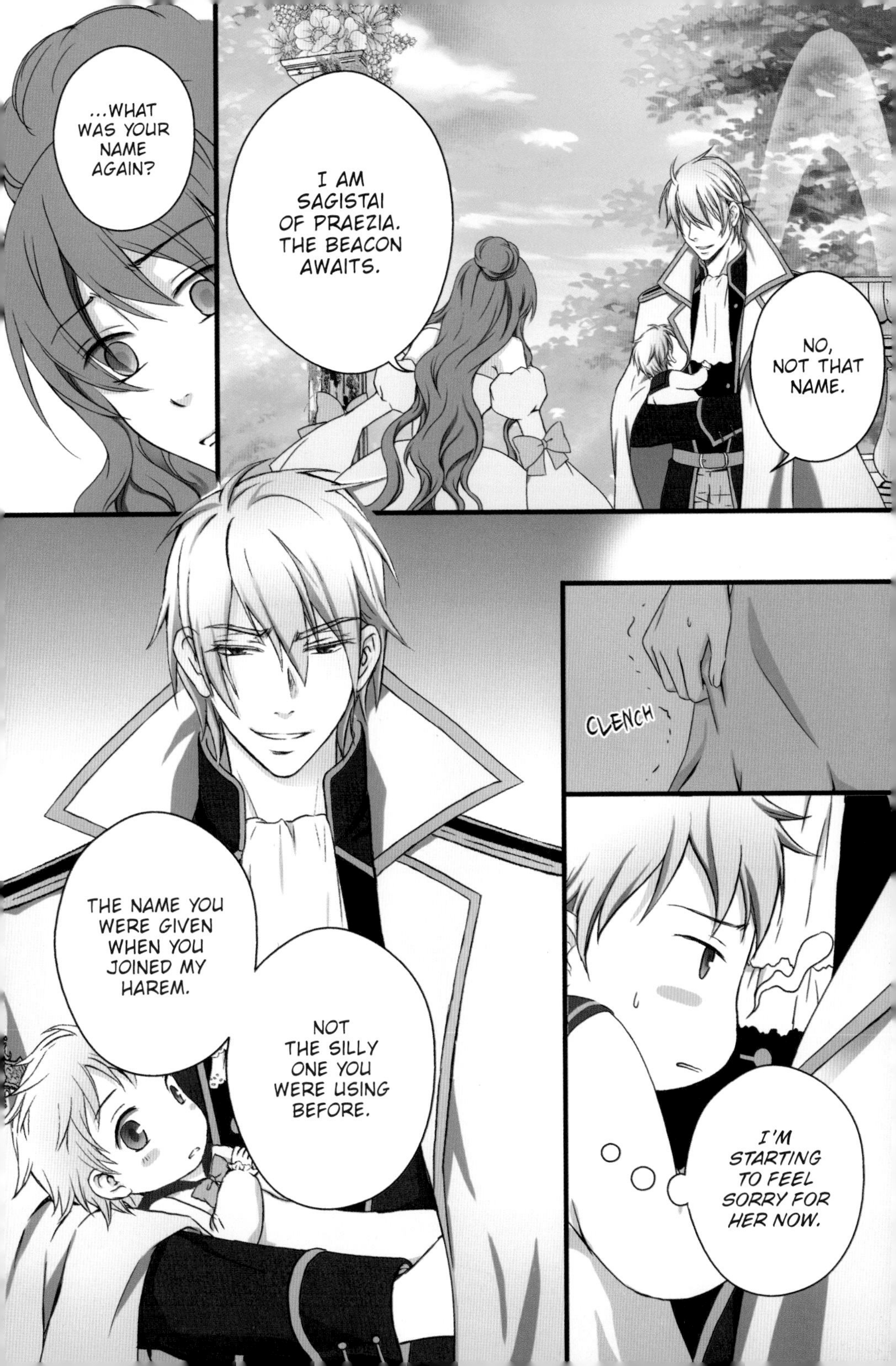
...WHAT WAS YOUR NAME AGAIN?
I AM SAGISTAI OF PRAEZIA. THE BEACON AWAITS.
NO, NOT THAT NAME.
THE NAME YOU WERE GIVEN WHEN YOU JOINED MY HAREM.
NOT THE SILLY ONE YOU WERE USING BEFORE.
CLENCH
I'M STARTING TO FEEL SORRY FOR HER NOW.

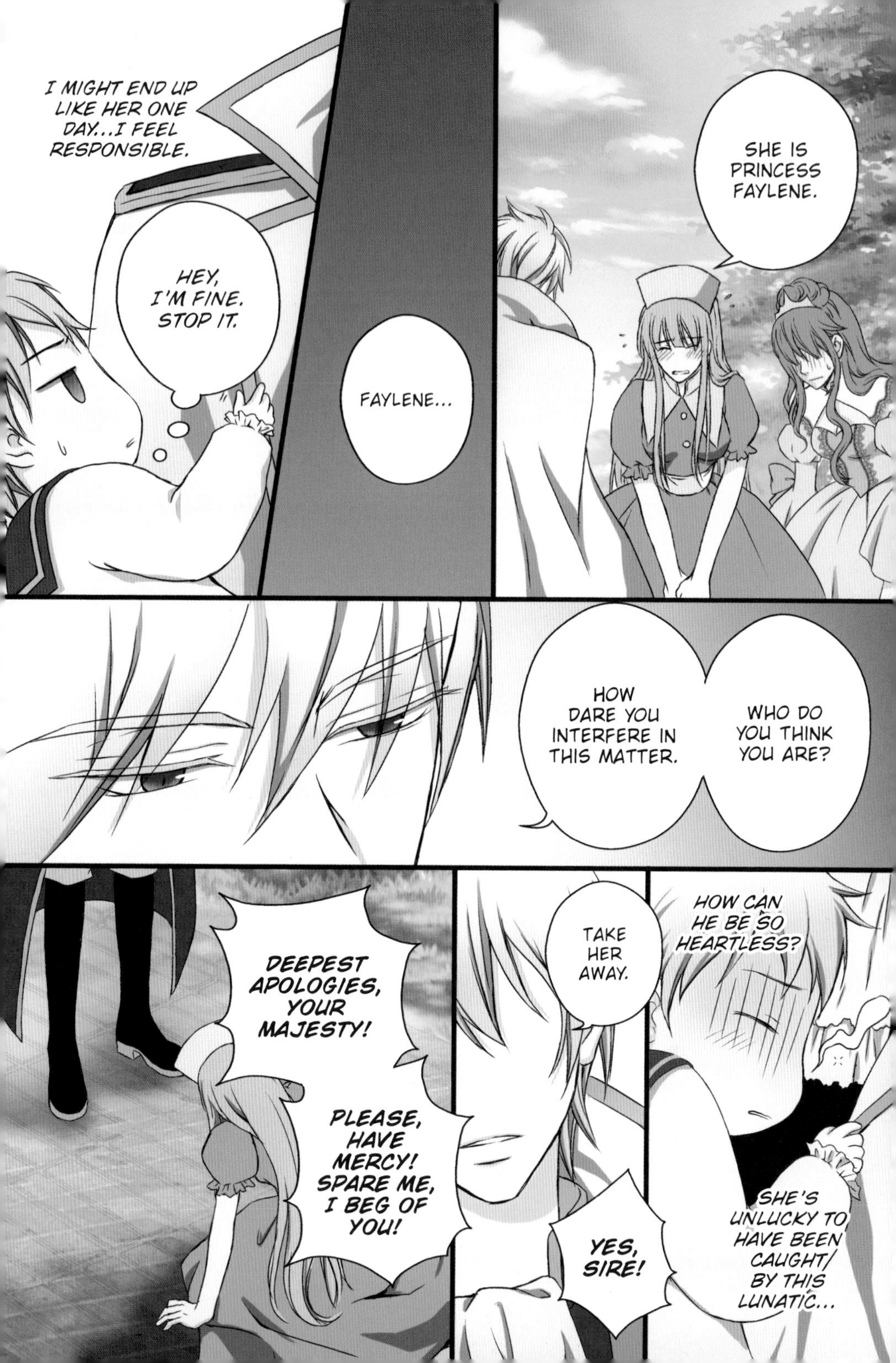
I MIGHT END UP LIKE HER ONE DAY...I FEEL RESPONSIBLE.
HEY, I'M FINE. STOP IT.
FAYLENE...
SHE IS PRINCESS FAYLENE.
HOW DARE YOU INTERFERE IN THIS MATTER.
WHO DO YOU THINK YOU ARE?
DEEPEST APOLOGIES, YOUR MAJESTY!
PLEASE, HAVE MERCY! SPARE ME, I BEG OF YOU!
TAKE HER AWAY.
YES, SIRE!
HOW CAN HE BE SO HEARTLESS?
SHE'S UNLUCKY TO HAVE BEEN CAUGHT BY THIS LUNATIC...

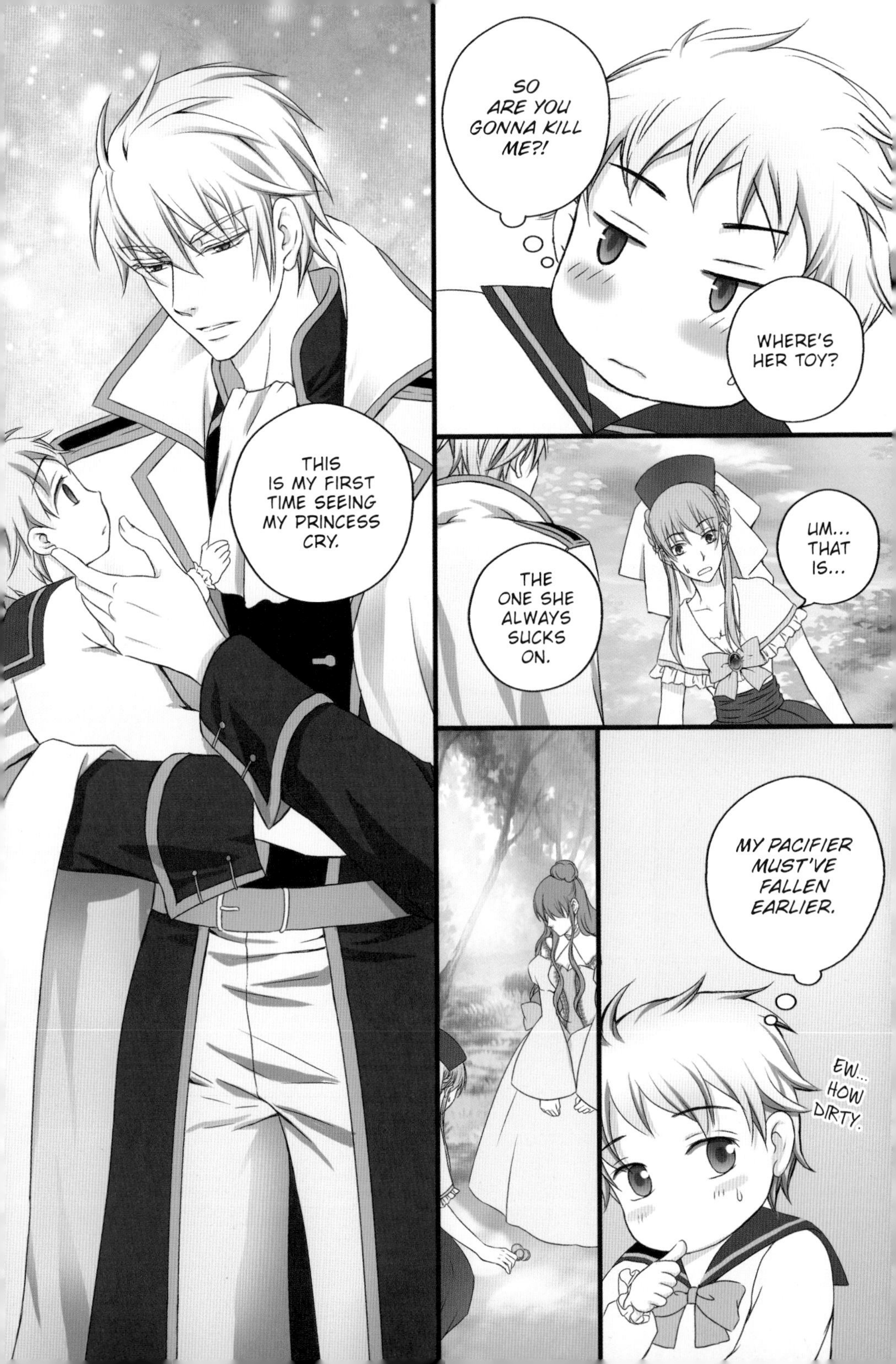
THIS IS MY FIRST TIME SEEING MY PRINCESS CRY.
SO ARE YOU GONNA KILL ME?!
WHERE'S HER TOY?
THE ONE SHE ALWAYS SUCKS ON.
UM... THAT IS...
MY PACIFIER MUST'VE FALLEN EARLIER.
EW... HOW DIRTY.

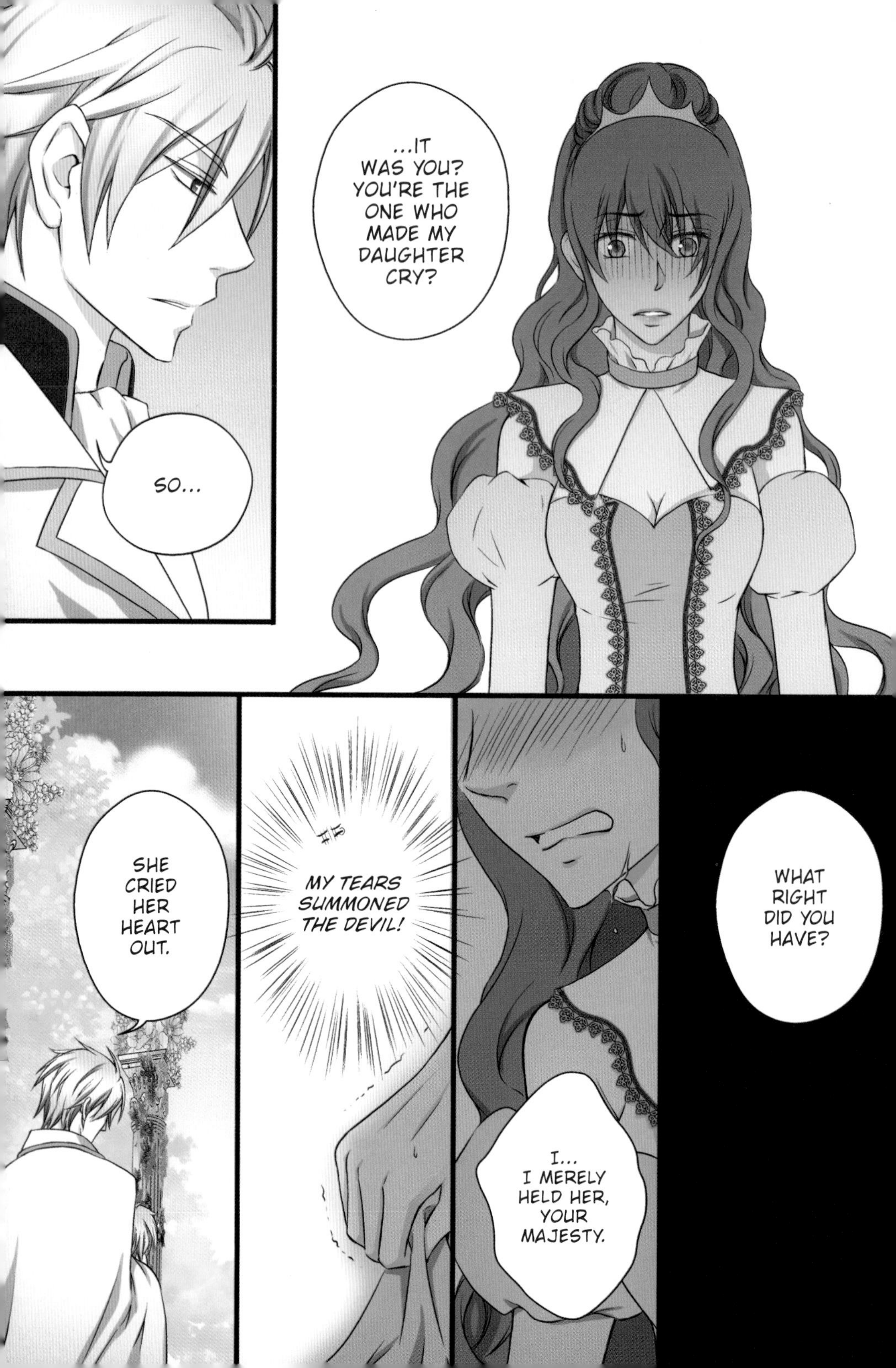
SO...
...IT WAS YOU? YOU'RE THE ONE WHO MADE MY DAUGHTER CRY?
SHE CRIED HER HEART OUT.
MY TEARS SUMMONED THE DEVIL!
WHAT RIGHT DID YOU HAVE?
I... I MERELY HELD HER, YOUR MAJESTY.

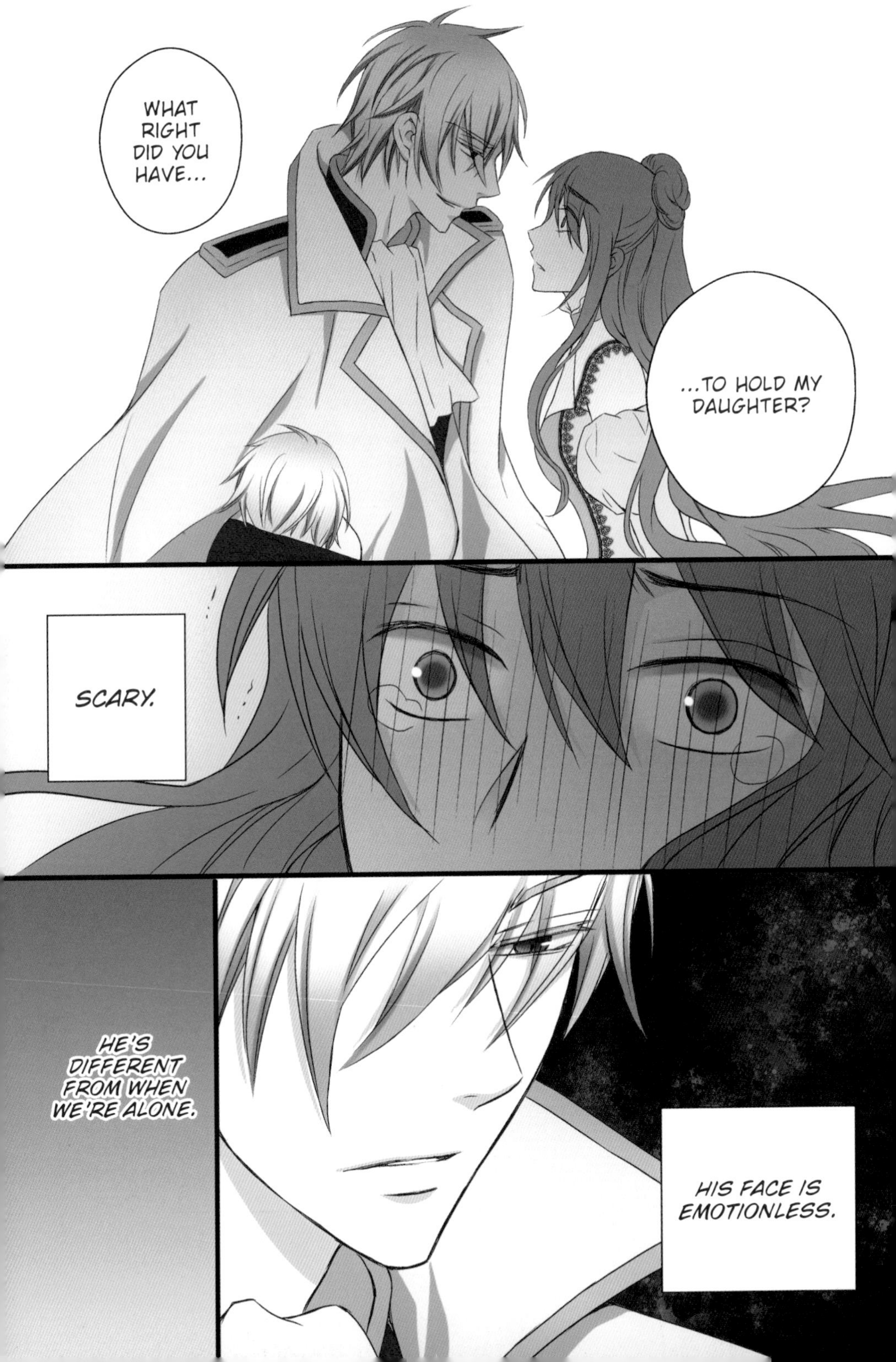
WHAT RIGHT DID YOU HAVE...
...TO HOLD MY DAUGHTER?
SCARY.
HE'S DIFFERENT FROM WHEN WE'RE ALONE.
HIS FACE IS EMOTIONLESS.

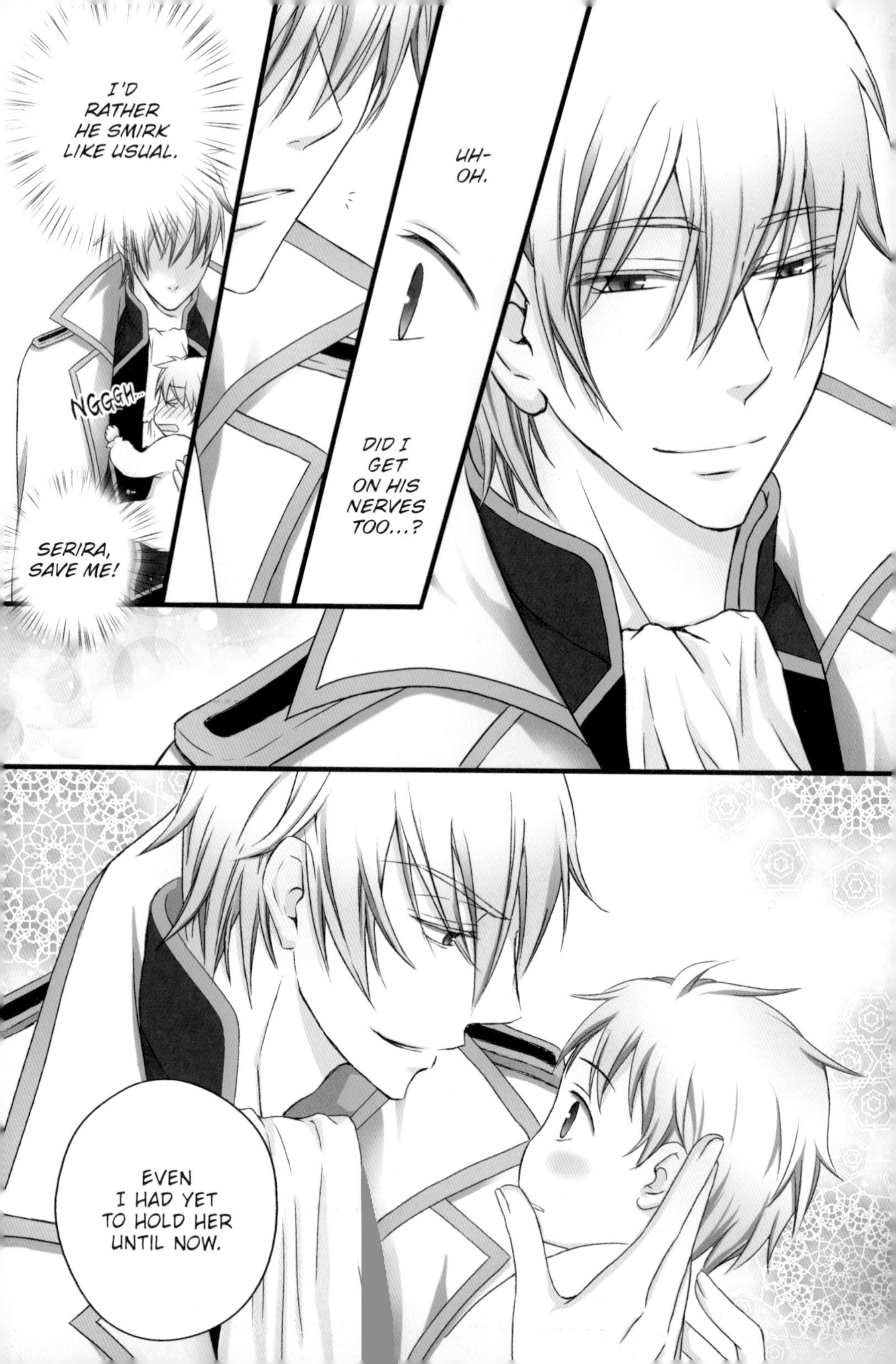
I'D RATHER HE SMIRK LIKE USUAL.
NGGGH...
SERIRA, SAVE ME!
UH-OH.
DID I GET ON HIS NERVES TOO...?
EVEN I HAD YET TO HOLD HER UNTIL NOW.

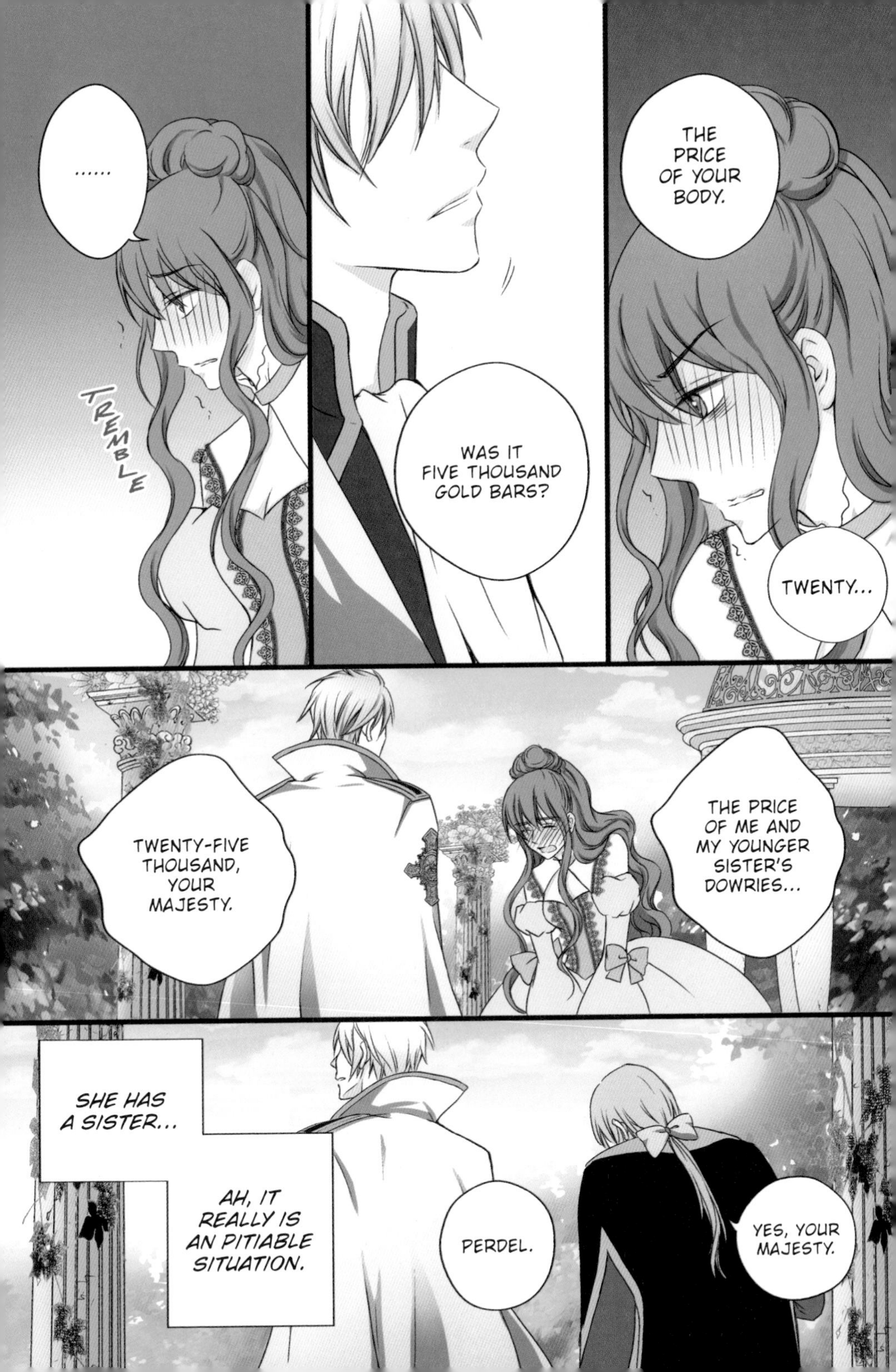
......
TREMBLE
WAS IT FIVE THOUSAND GOLD BARS?
THE PRICE OF YOUR BODY.
TWENTY...
TWENTY-FIVE THOUSAND, YOUR MAJESTY.
THE PRICE OF ME AND MY YOUNGER SISTER'S DOWRIES...
SHE HAS A SISTER...
AH, IT REALLY IS AN PITIABLE SITUATION.
PERDEL.
YES, YOUR MAJESTY.

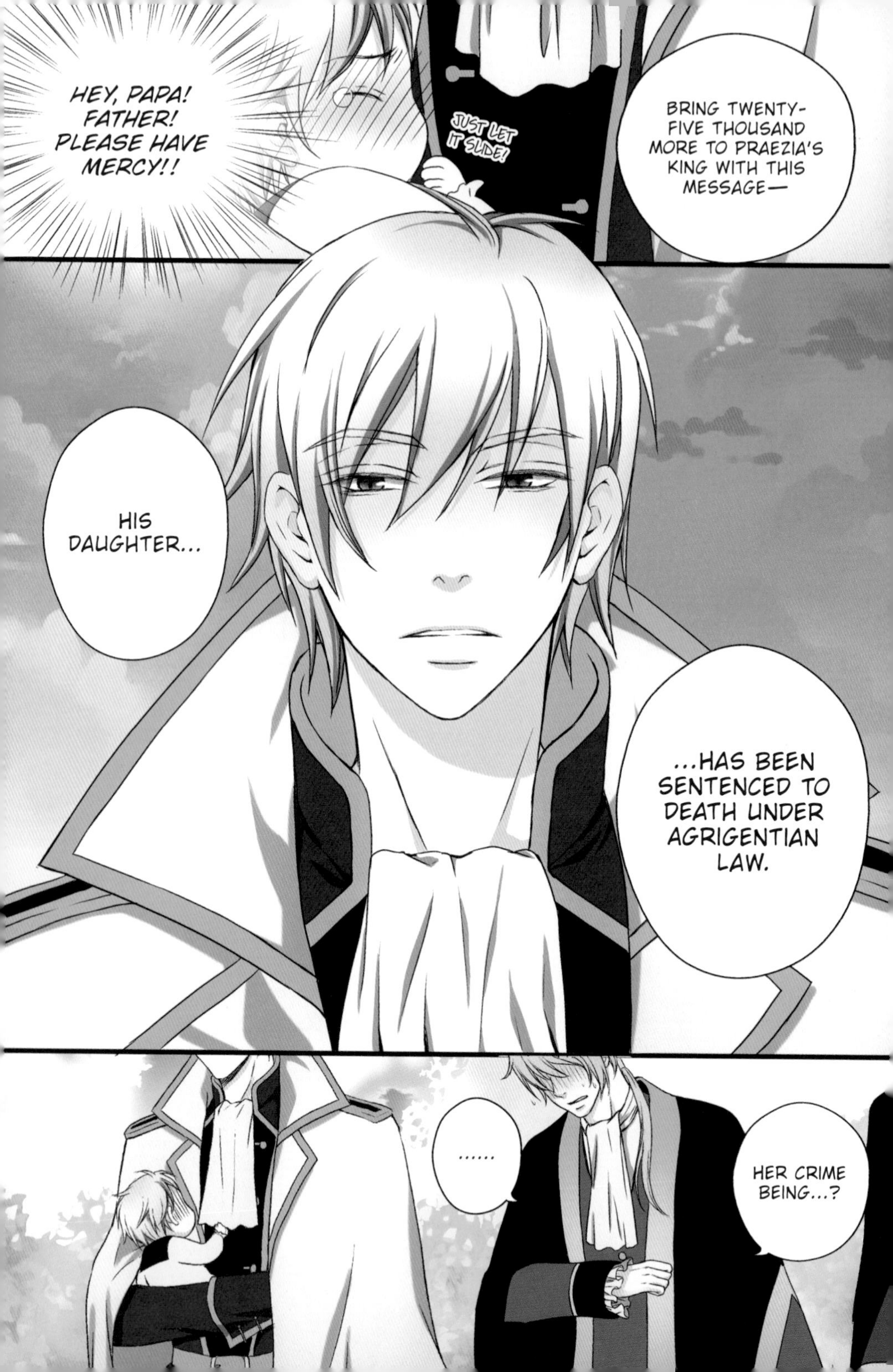
HEY, PAPA! FATHER! PLEASE HAVE MERCY!!
JUST LET IT SLIDE!
BRING TWENTY-FIVE THOUSAND MORE TO PRAEZIA'S KING WITH THIS MESSAGE—
HIS DAUGHTER...
...HAS BEEN SENTENCED TO DEATH UNDER AGRIGENTIAN LAW.
......
HER CRIME BEING...?

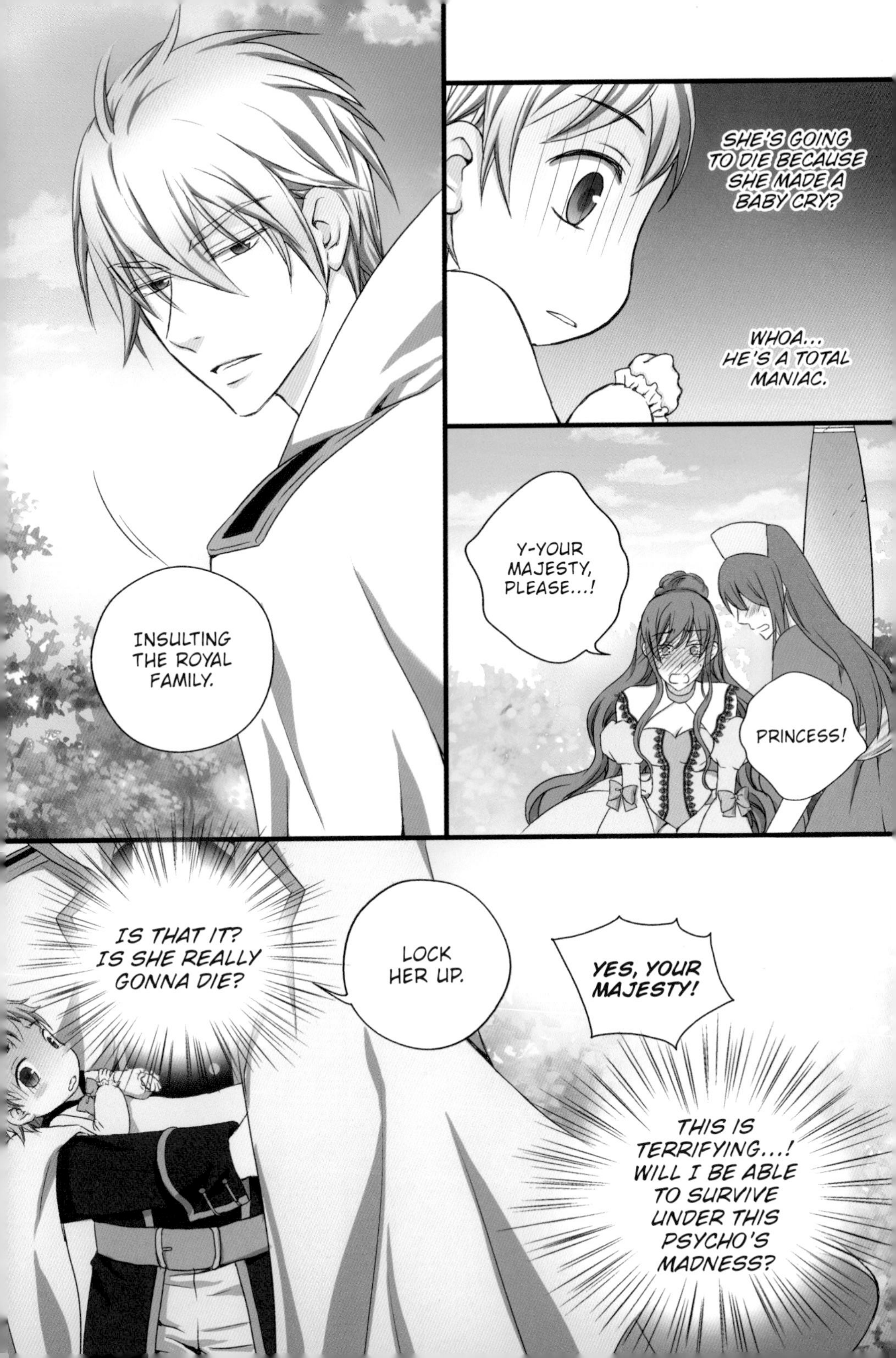
INSULTING THE ROYAL FAMILY.
SHE'S GOING TO DIE BECAUSE SHE MADE A BABY CRY?
WHOA... HE'S A TOTAL MANIAC.
Y-YOUR MAJESTY, PLEASE...!
PRINCESS!
IS THAT IT? IS SHE REALLY GONNA DIE?
LOCK HER UP.
YES, YOUR MAJESTY!
THIS IS TERRIFYING...! WILL I BE ABLE TO SURVIVE UNDER THIS PSYCHO'S MADNESS?

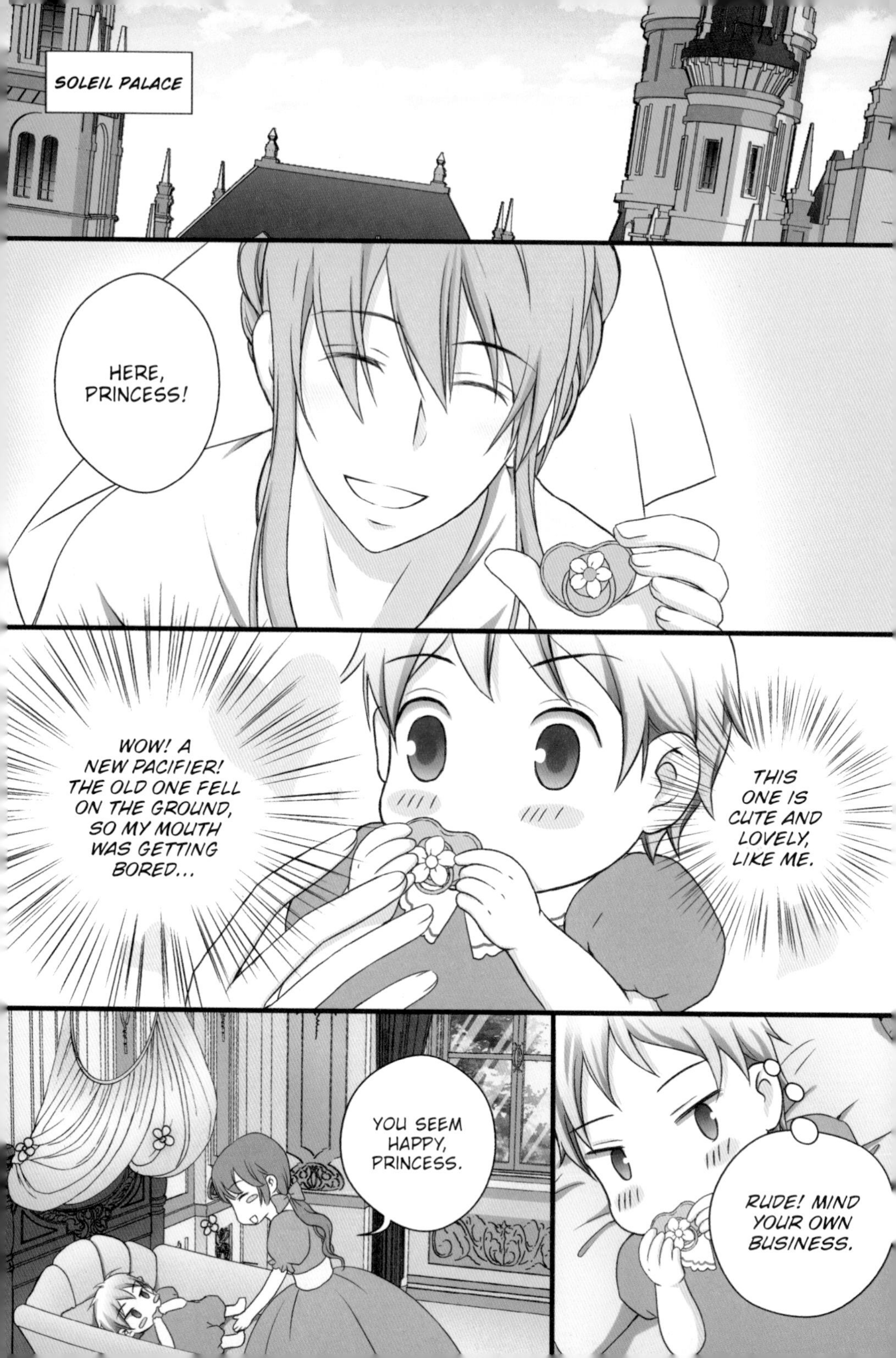
SOLEIL PALACE
HERE, PRINCESS!
WOW! A NEW PACIFIER! THE OLD ONE FELL ON THE GROUND, SO MY MOUTH WAS GETTING BORED...
THIS ONE IS CUTE AND LOVELY, LIKE ME.
YOU SEEM HAPPY, PRINCESS.
RUDE! MIND YOUR OWN BUSINESS.

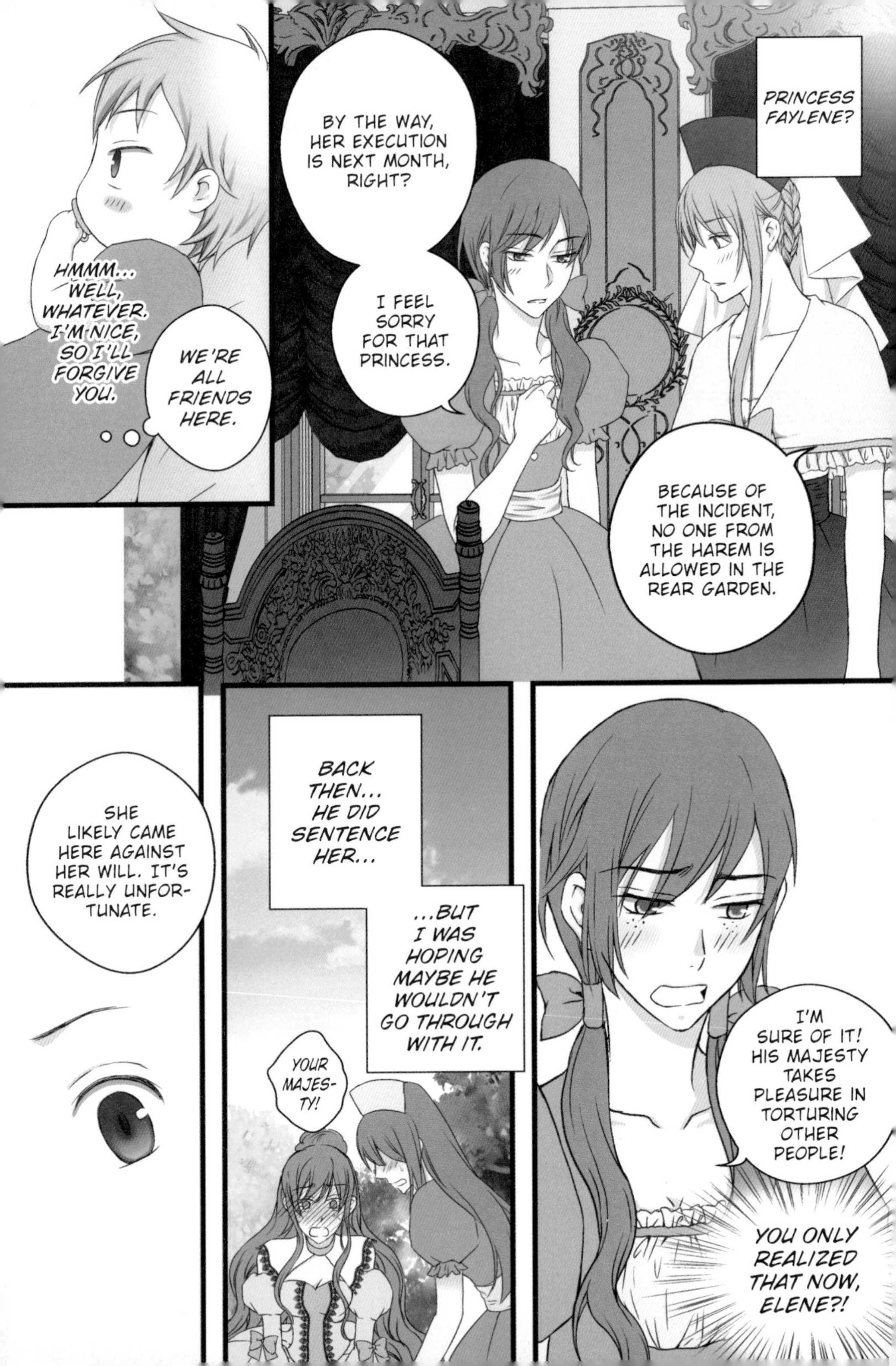
HMMM... WELL, WHATEVER. I'M NICE, SO I'LL FORGIVE YOU.
WE'RE ALL FRIENDS HERE.
BY THE WAY, HER EXECUTION IS NEXT MONTH, RIGHT?
PRINCESS FAYLENE?
I FEEL SORRY FOR THAT PRINCESS.
BECAUSE OF THE INCIDENT, NO ONE FROM THE HAREM IS ALLOWED IN THE REAR GARDEN.
SHE LIKELY CAME HERE AGAINST HER WILL. IT'S REALLY UNFOR-TUNATE.
BACK THEN... HE DID SENTENCE HER...
...BUT I WAS HOPING MAYBE HE WOULDN'T GO THROUGH WITH IT.
YOUR MAJES-TY!
I'M SURE OF IT! HIS MAJESTY TAKES PLEASURE IN TORTURING OTHER PEOPLE!
YOU ONLY REALIZED THAT NOW, ELENE?!

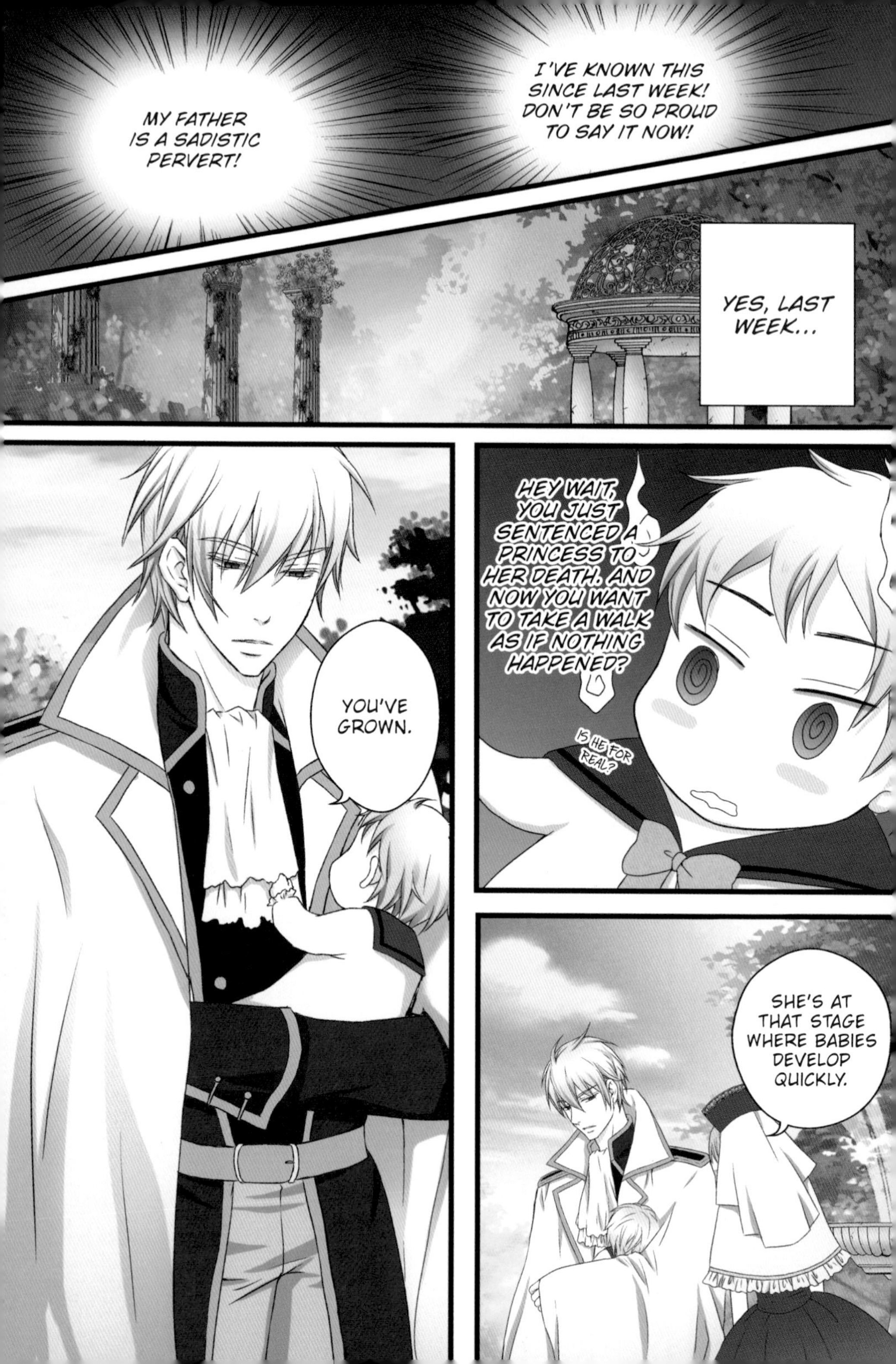
MY FATHER IS A SADISTIC PERVERT!
I'VE KNOWN THIS SINCE LAST WEEK! DON'T BE SO PROUD TO SAY IT NOW!
YES, LAST WEEK...
YOU'VE GROWN.
HEY WAIT, YOU JUST SENTENCED A PRINCESS TO HER DEATH. AND NOW YOU WANT TO TAKE A WALK AS IF NOTHING HAPPENED?
IS HE FOR REAL?
SHE'S AT THAT STAGE WHERE BABIES DEVELOP QUICKLY.

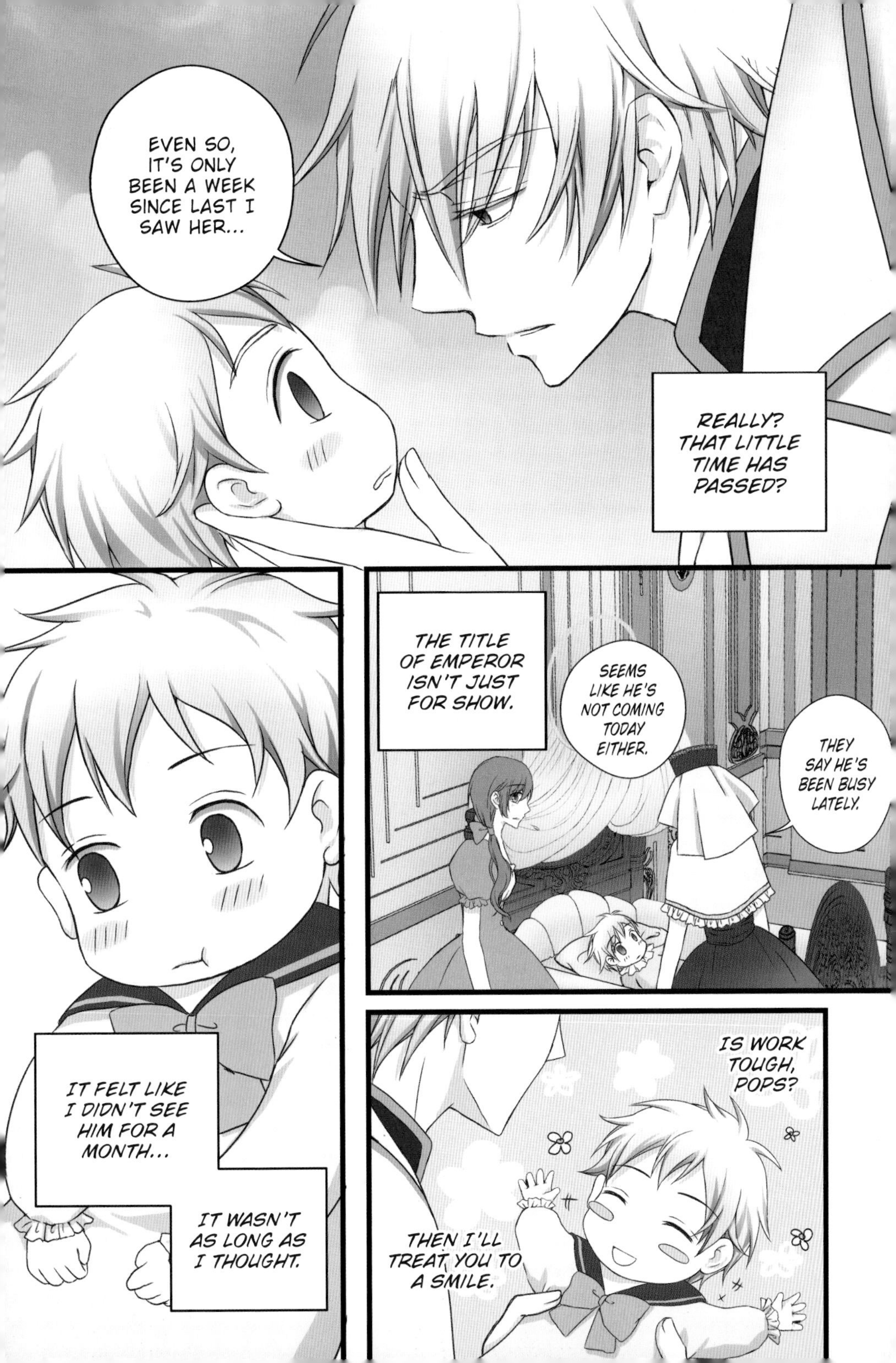
EVEN SO, IT'S ONLY BEEN A WEEK SINCE LAST I SAW HER...
REALLY? THAT LITTLE TIME HAS PASSED?
THE TITLE OF EMPEROR ISN'T JUST FOR SHOW.
SEEMS LIKE HE'S NOT COMING TODAY EITHER.
THEY SAY HE'S BEEN BUSY LATELY.
IT FELT LIKE I DIDN'T SEE HIM FOR A MONTH...
IT WASN'T AS LONG AS I THOUGHT.
IS WORK TOUGH, POPS?
THEN I'LL TREAT YOU TO A SMILE.

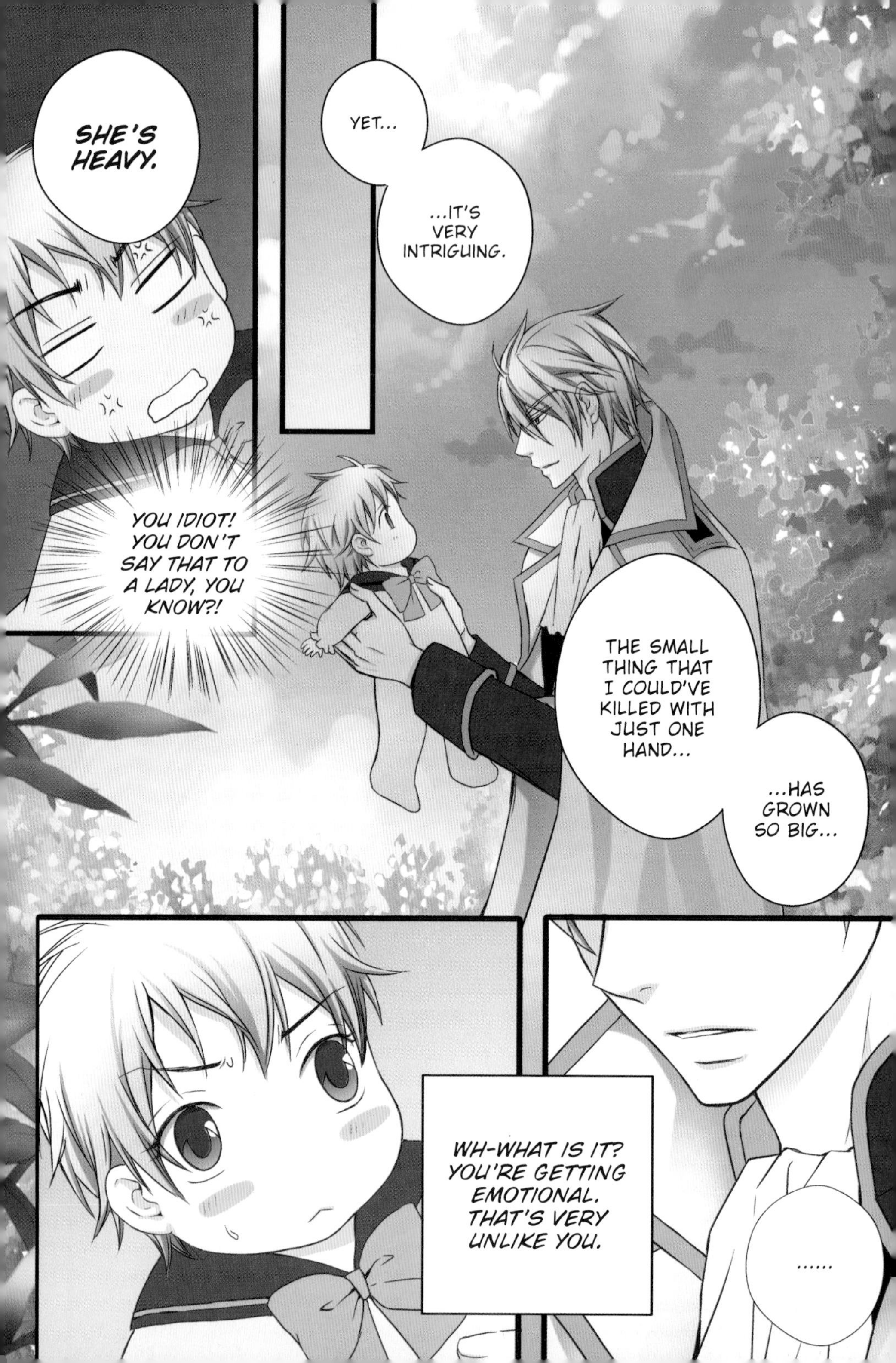

SHE'S HEAVY.
YOU IDIOT! YOU DON'T SAY THAT TO A LADY, YOU KNOW?!
YET...
...IT'S VERY INTRIGUING.
THE SMALL THING THAT I COULD'VE KILLED WITH JUST ONE HAND...
...HAS GROWN SO BIG...
WH-WHAT IS IT? YOU'RE GETTING EMOTIONAL. THAT'S VERY UNLIKE YOU.
......

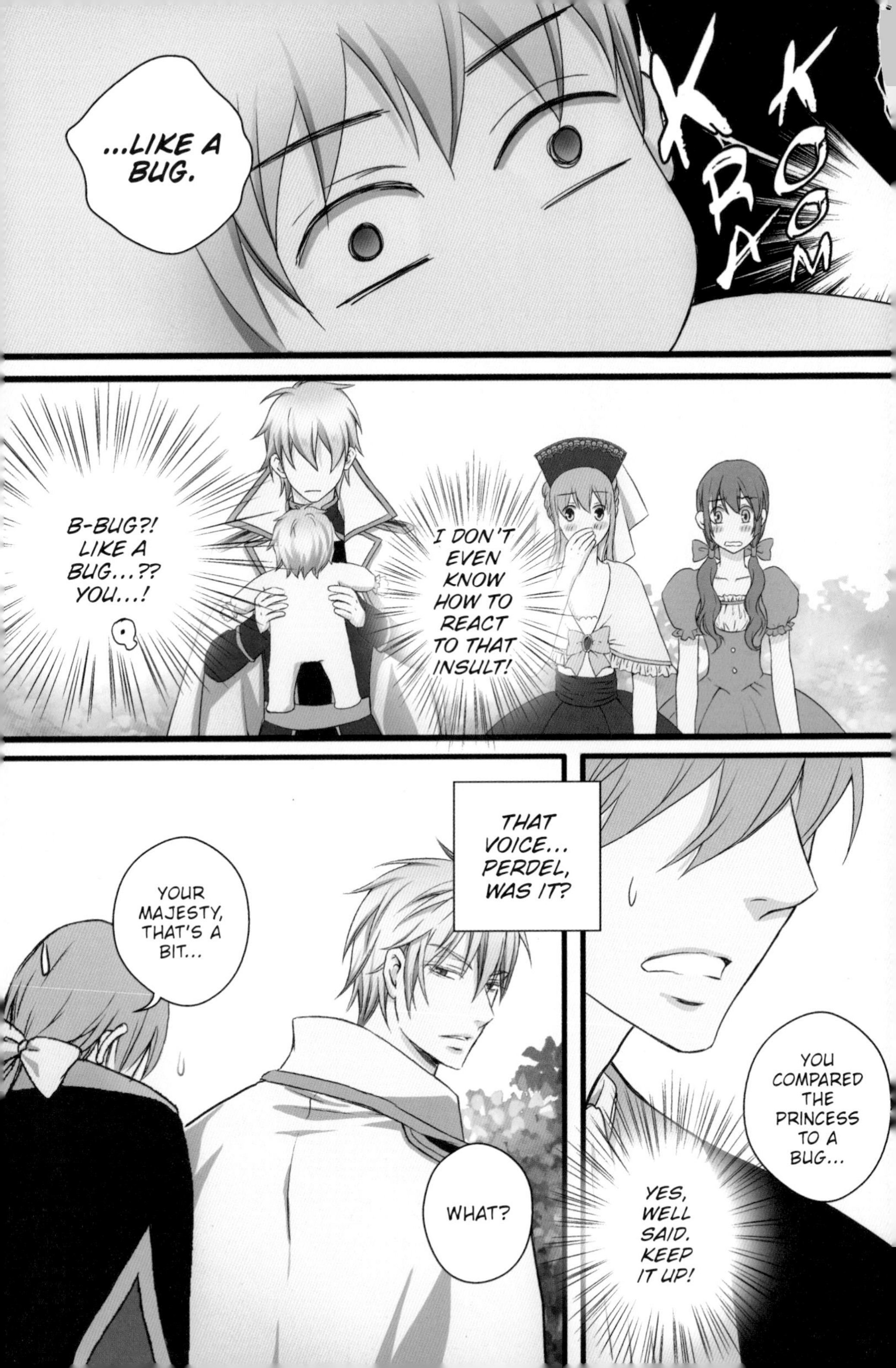
...LIKE A BUG.
KRAKOOM
B-BUG?! LIKE A BUG...?? YOU...!
I DON'T EVEN KNOW HOW TO REACT TO THAT INSULT!
YOUR MAJESTY, THAT'S A BIT...
THAT VOICE... PERDEL, WAS IT?
WHAT?
YOU COMPARED THE PRINCESS TO A BUG...
YES, WELL SAID. KEEP IT UP!

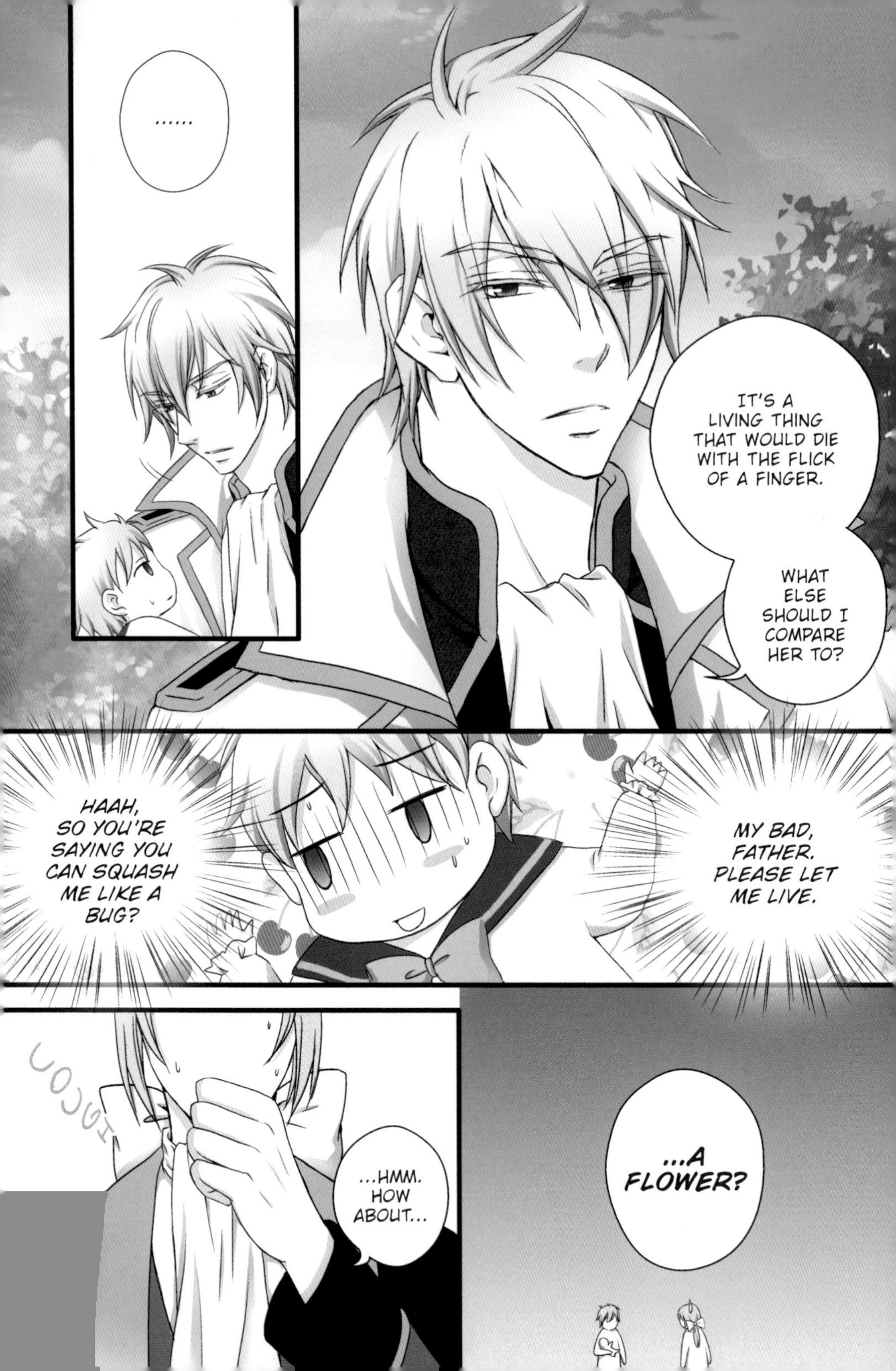
......
IT'S A LIVING THING THAT WOULD DIE WITH THE FLICK OF A FINGER.
WHAT ELSE SHOULD I COMPARE HER TO?
HAAH, SO YOU'RE SAYING YOU CAN SQUASH ME LIKE A BUG?
MY BAD, FATHER. PLEASE LET ME LIVE.
...HMM. HOW ABOUT...
...A FLOWER?

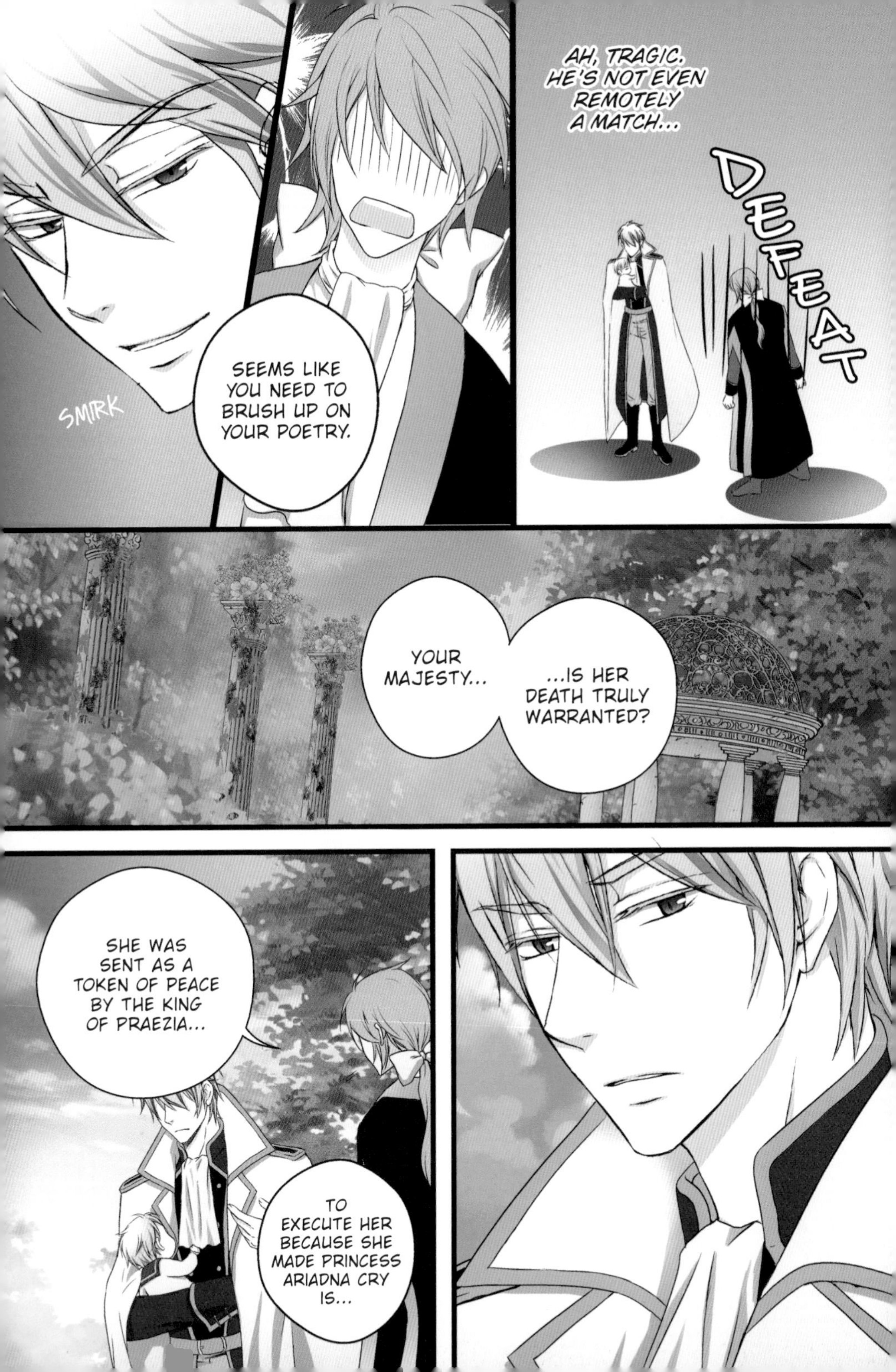
SMIRK
SEEMS LIKE YOU NEED TO BRUSH UP ON YOUR POETRY.
AH, TRAGIC. HE'S NOT EVEN REMOTELY A MATCH...
DEFEAT
YOUR MAJESTY...
...IS HER DEATH TRULY WARRANTED?
SHE WAS SENT AS A TOKEN OF PEACE BY THE KING OF PRAEZIA...
TO EXECUTE HER BECAUSE SHE MADE PRINCESS ARIADNA CRY IS...

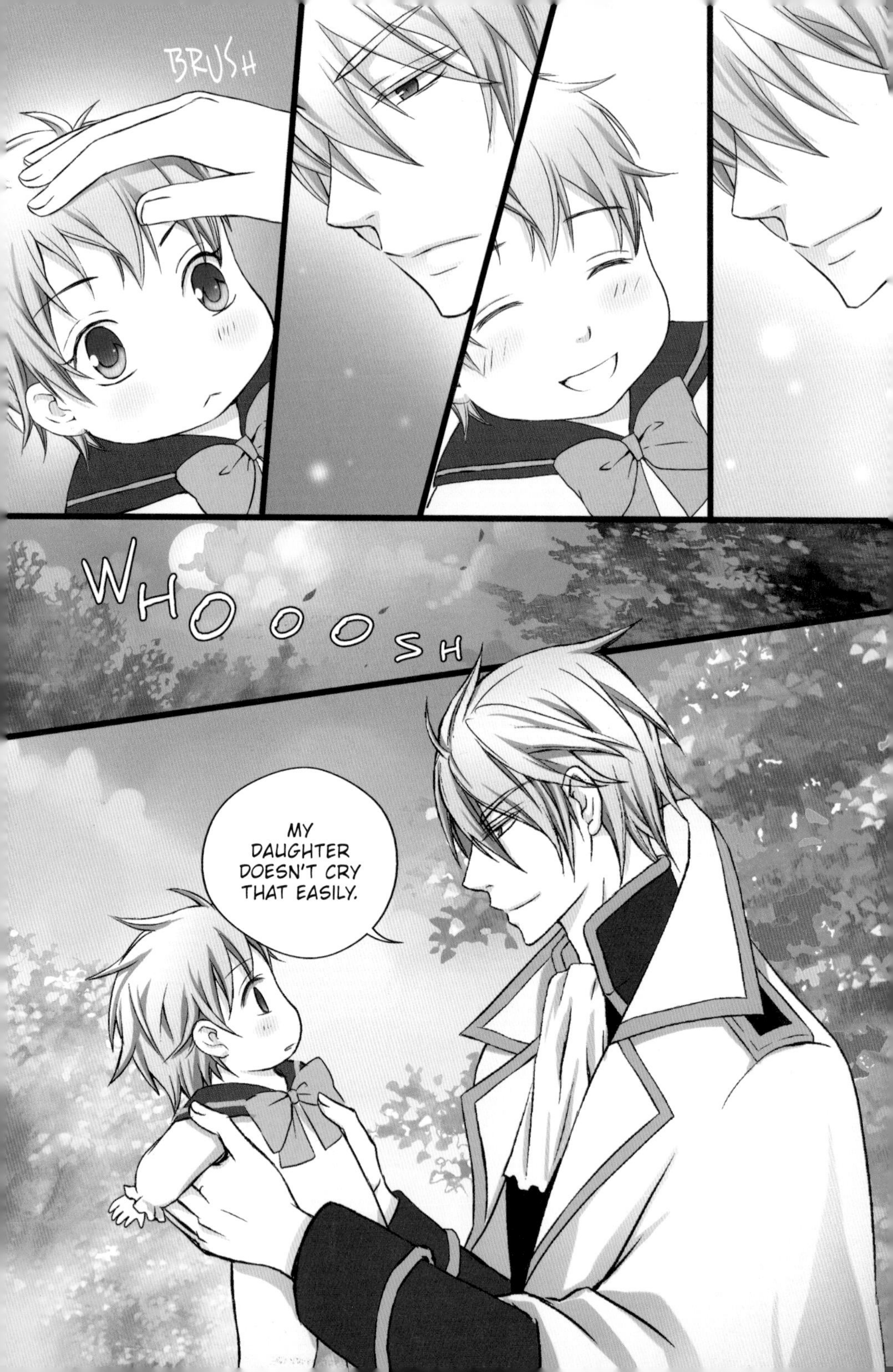
BRUSH
WHOOOSH
MY DAUGHTER DOESN'T CRY THAT EASILY.

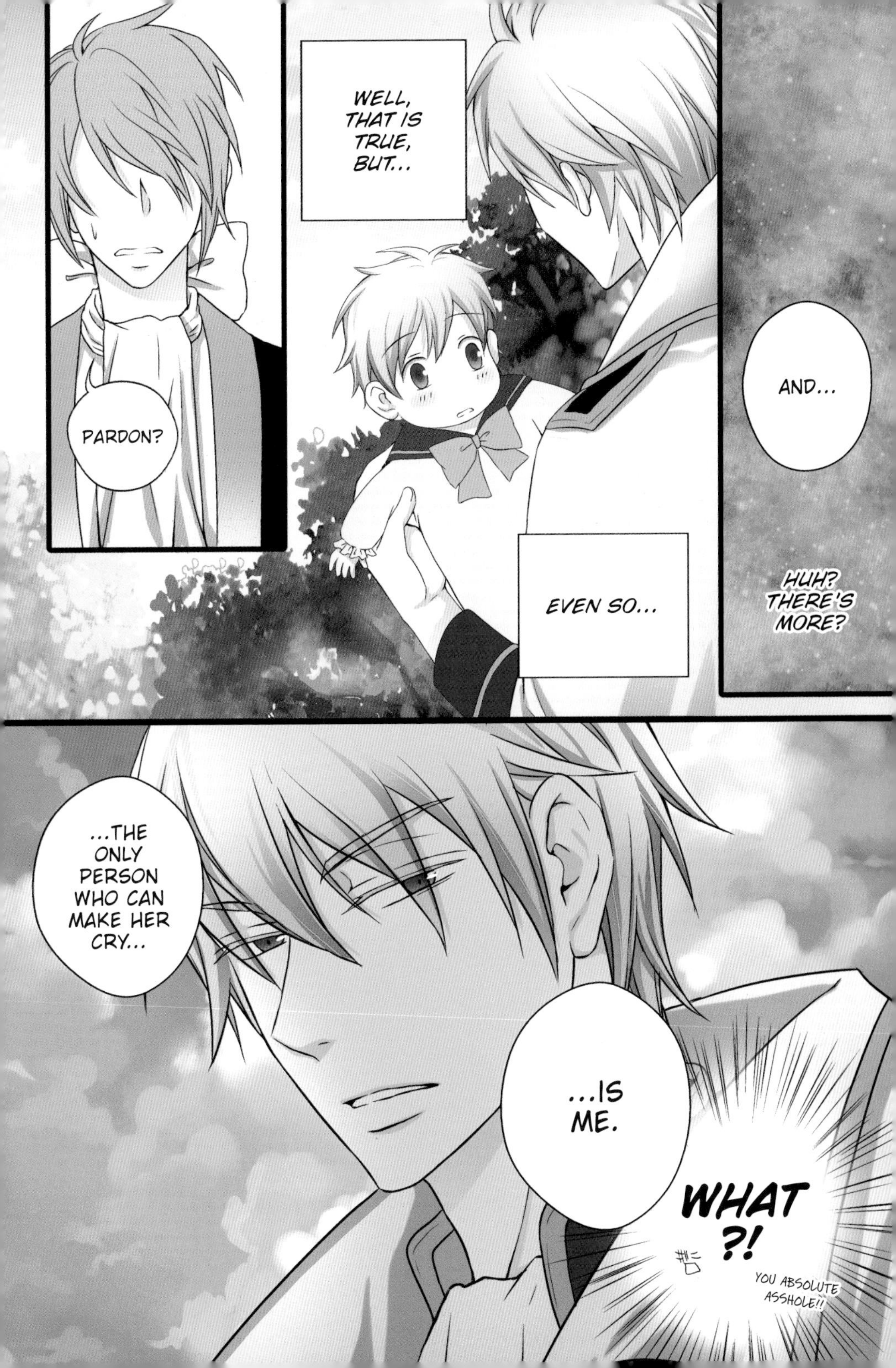
PARDON?
WELL, THAT IS TRUE, BUT...
EVEN SO...
AND...
HUH? THERE'S MORE?
...THE ONLY PERSON WHO CAN MAKE HER CRY...
...IS ME.
WHAT?!
YOU ABSOLUTE ASSHOLE!!

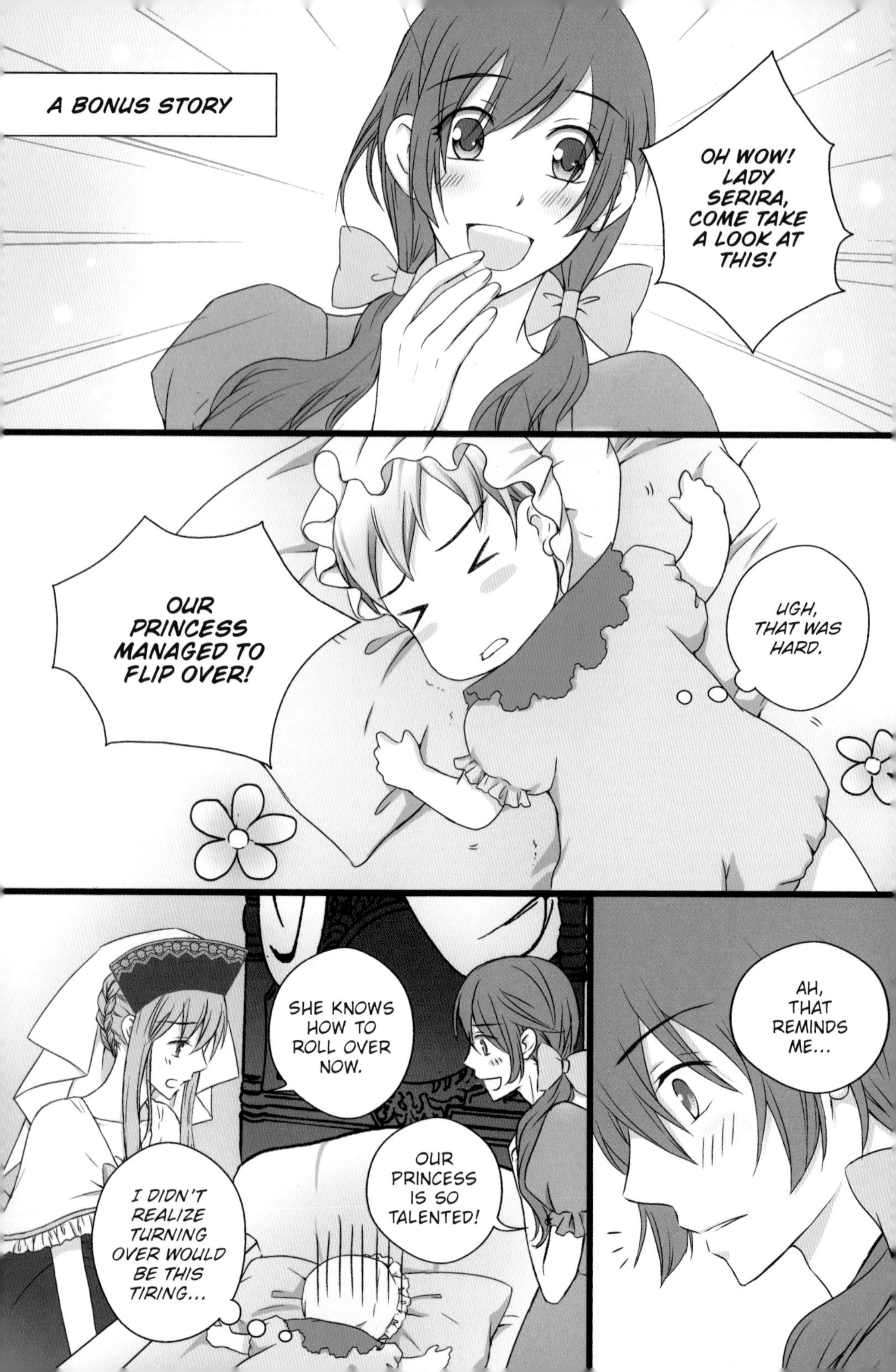
A BONUS STORY
OH WOW! LADY SERIRA, COME TAKE A LOOK AT THIS!
OUR PRINCESS MANAGED TO FLIP OVER!
UGH, THAT WAS HARD.
SHE KNOWS HOW TO ROLL OVER NOW.
OUR PRINCESS IS SO TALENTED!
I DIDN'T REALIZE TURNING OVER WOULD BE THIS TIRING...
AH, THAT REMINDS ME...

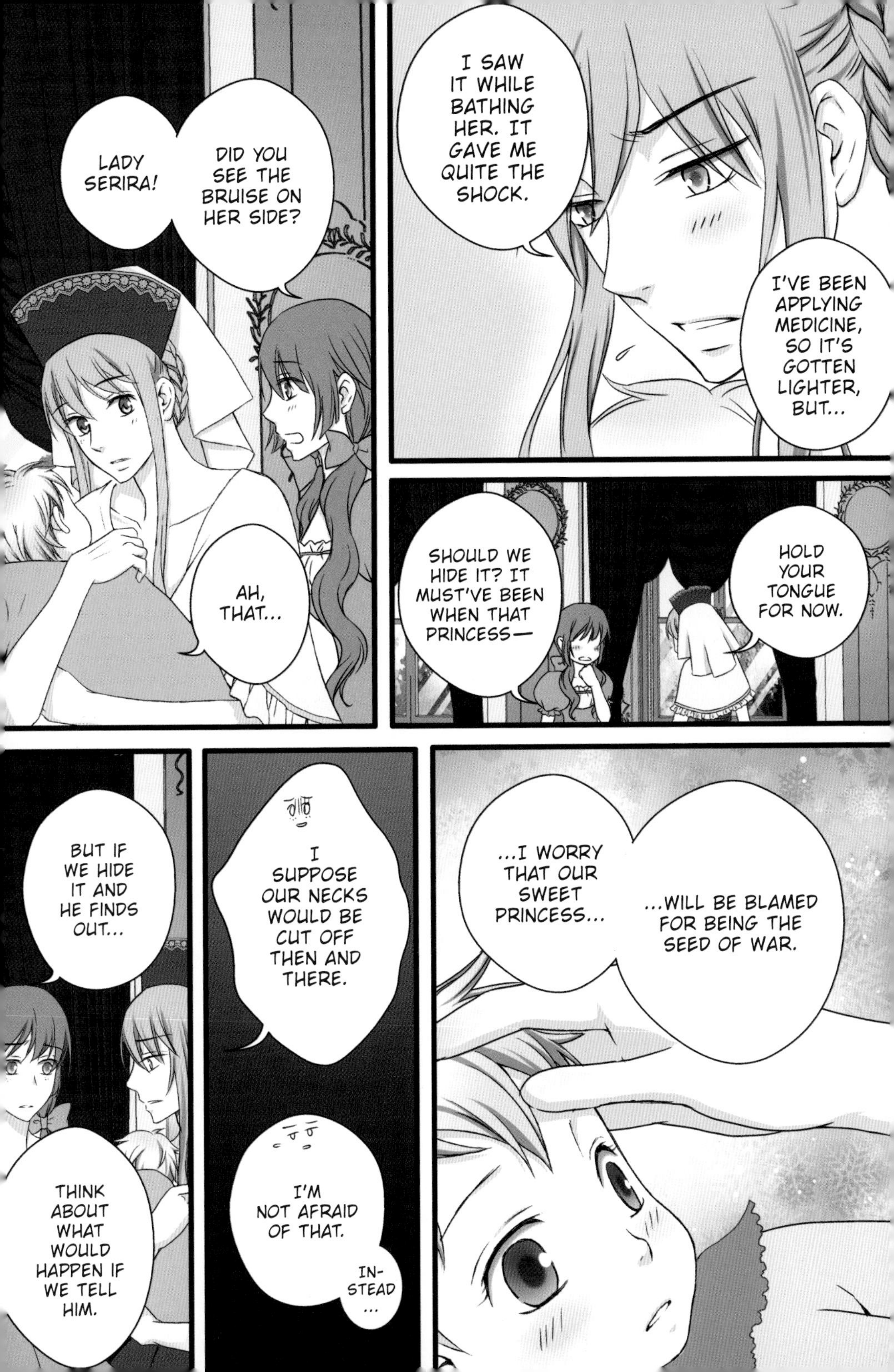
LADY SERIRA!
DID YOU SEE THE BRUISE ON HER SIDE?
AH, THAT...
I SAW IT WHILE BATHING HER. IT GAVE ME QUITE THE SHOCK.
I'VE BEEN APPLYING MEDICINE, SO IT'S GOTTEN LIGHTER, BUT...
SHOULD WE HIDE IT? IT MUST'VE BEEN WHEN THAT PRINCESS—
HOLD YOUR TONGUE FOR NOW.
BUT IF WE HIDE IT AND HE FINDS OUT...
THINK ABOUT WHAT WOULD HAPPEN IF WE TELL HIM.
I SUPPOSE OUR NECKS WOULD BE CUT OFF THEN AND THERE.
I'M NOT AFRAID OF THAT.
IN-STEAD...
...I WORRY THAT OUR SWEET PRINCESS...
...WILL BE BLAMED FOR BEING THE SEED OF WAR.

You're My Papa! (1)

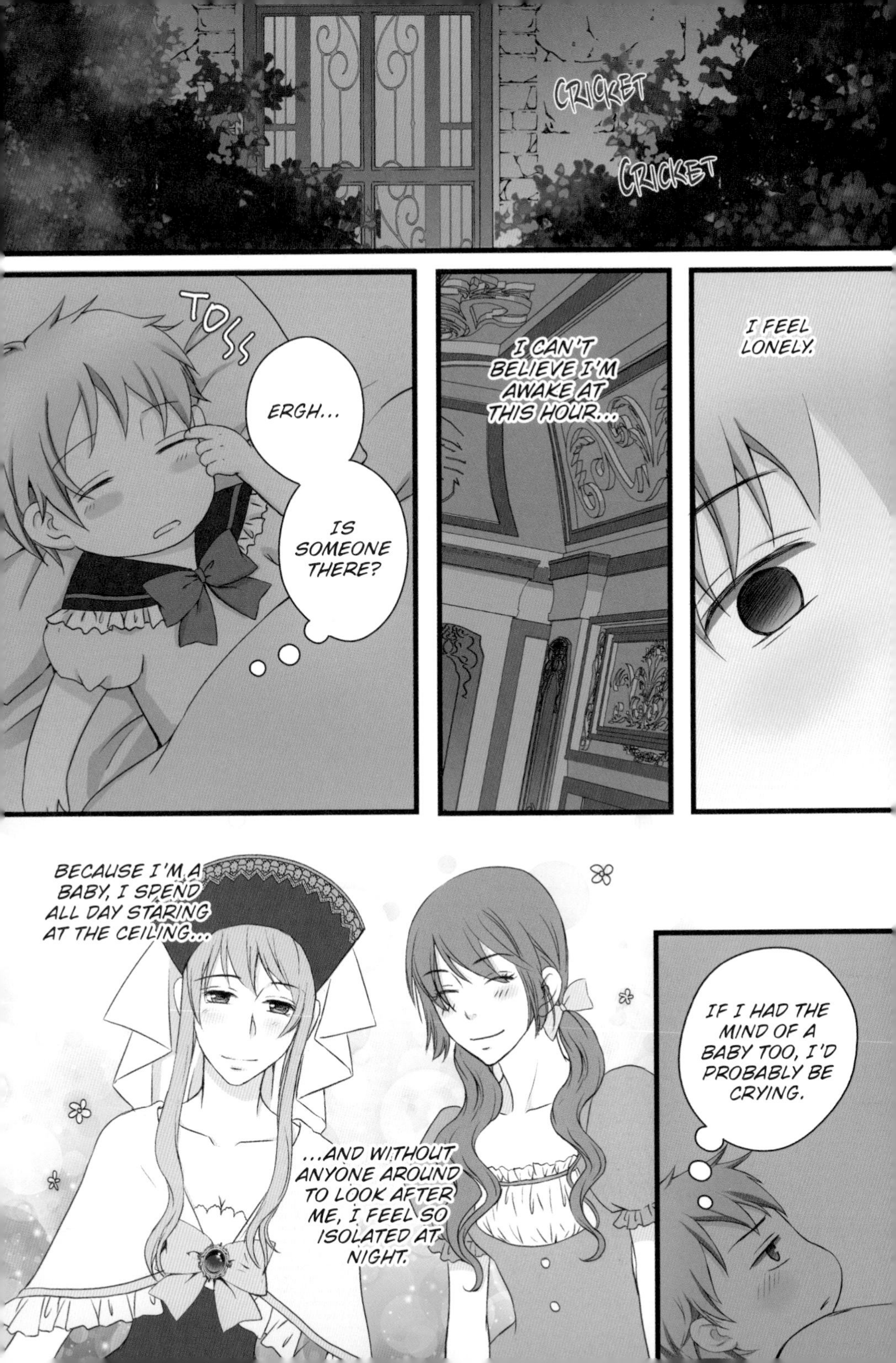
CRICKET
CRICKET
TOSS
ERGH...
IS SOMEONE THERE?
I CAN'T BELIEVE I'M AWAKE AT THIS HOUR...
I FEEL LONELY.
BECAUSE I'M A BABY, I SPEND ALL DAY STARING AT THE CEILING...
...AND WITHOUT ANYONE AROUND TO LOOK AFTER ME, I FEEL SO ISOLATED AT NIGHT.
IF I HAD THE MIND OF A BABY TOO, I'D PROBABLY BE CRYING.

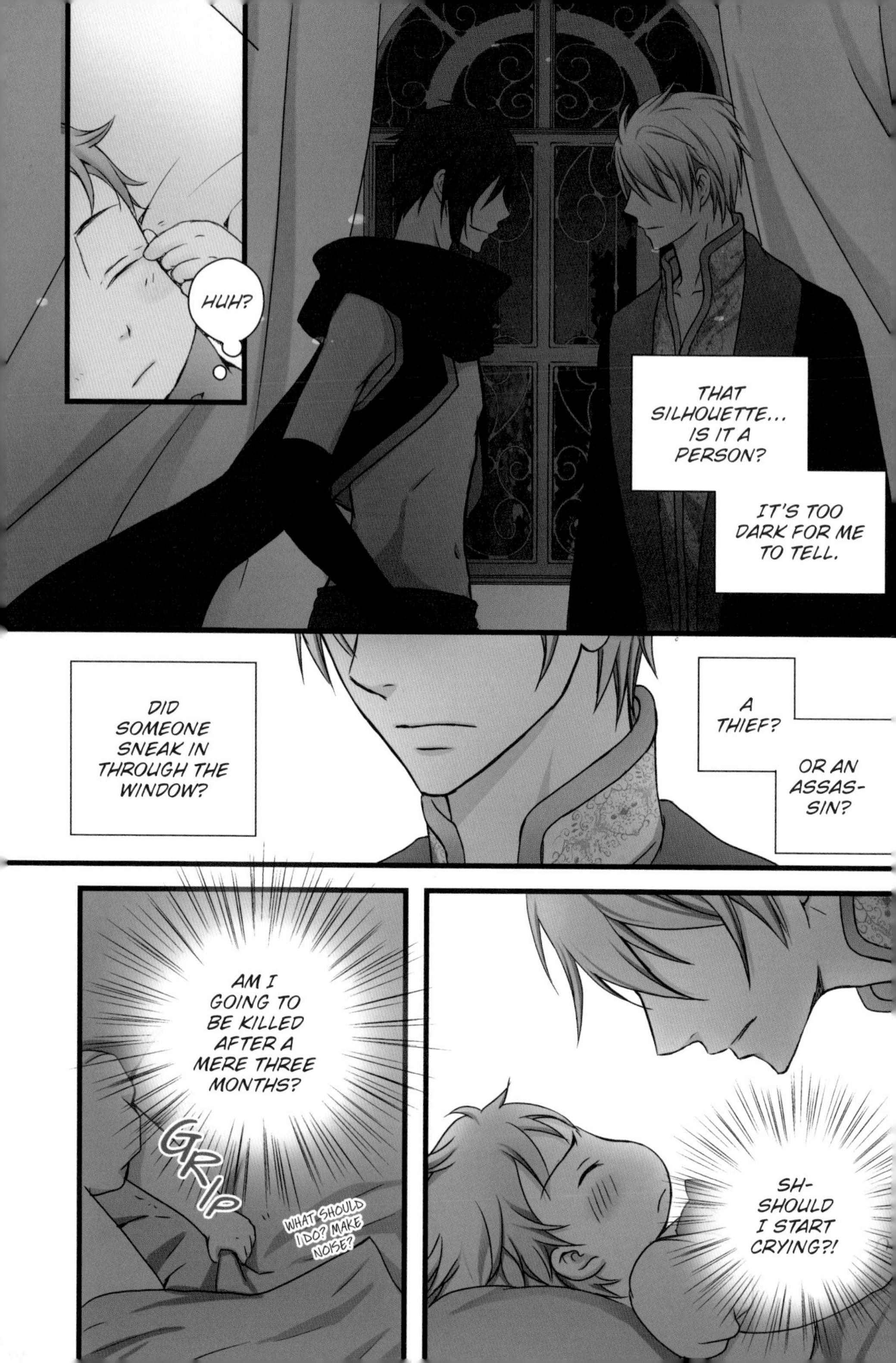
HUH?
THAT SILHOUETTE... IS IT A PERSON?
IT'S TOO DARK FOR ME TO TELL.
DID SOMEONE SNEAK IN THROUGH THE WINDOW?
A THIEF?
OR AN ASSAS-SIN?
AM I GOING TO BE KILLED AFTER A MERE THREE MONTHS?
GRIP
WHAT SHOULD I DO? MAKE NOISE?
SH-SHOULD I START CRYING?!

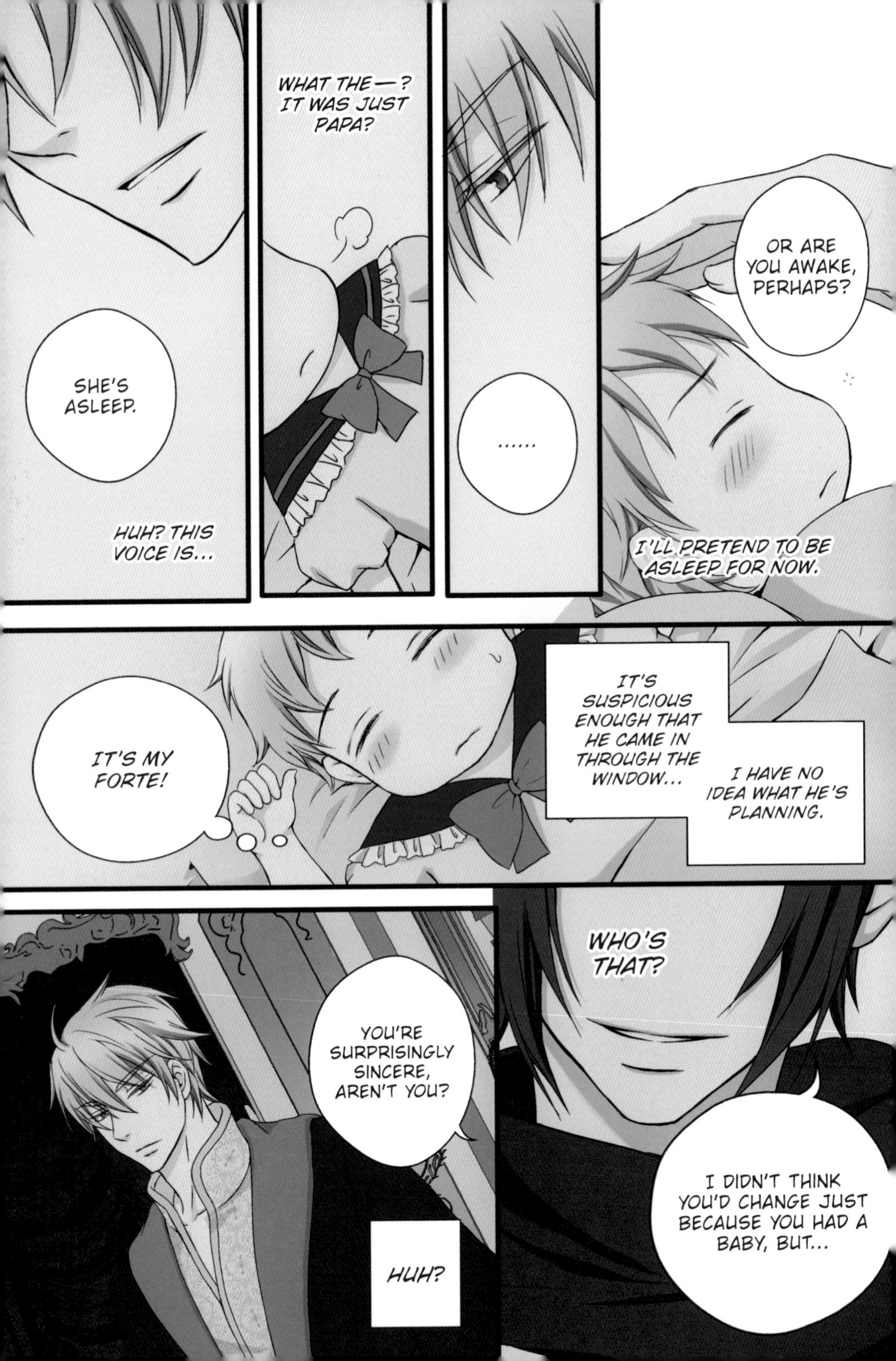
SHE'S ASLEEP.
HUH? THIS VOICE IS...
WHAT THE—? IT WAS JUST PAPA?
......
OR ARE YOU AWAKE, PERHAPS?
I'LL PRETEND TO BE ASLEEP FOR NOW.
IT'S MY FORTE!
IT'S SUSPICIOUS ENOUGH THAT HE CAME IN THROUGH THE WINDOW...
I HAVE NO IDEA WHAT HE'S PLANNING.
YOU'RE SURPRISINGLY SINCERE, AREN'T YOU?
HUH?
WHO'S THAT?
I DIDN'T THINK YOU'D CHANGE JUST BECAUSE YOU HAD A BABY, BUT...

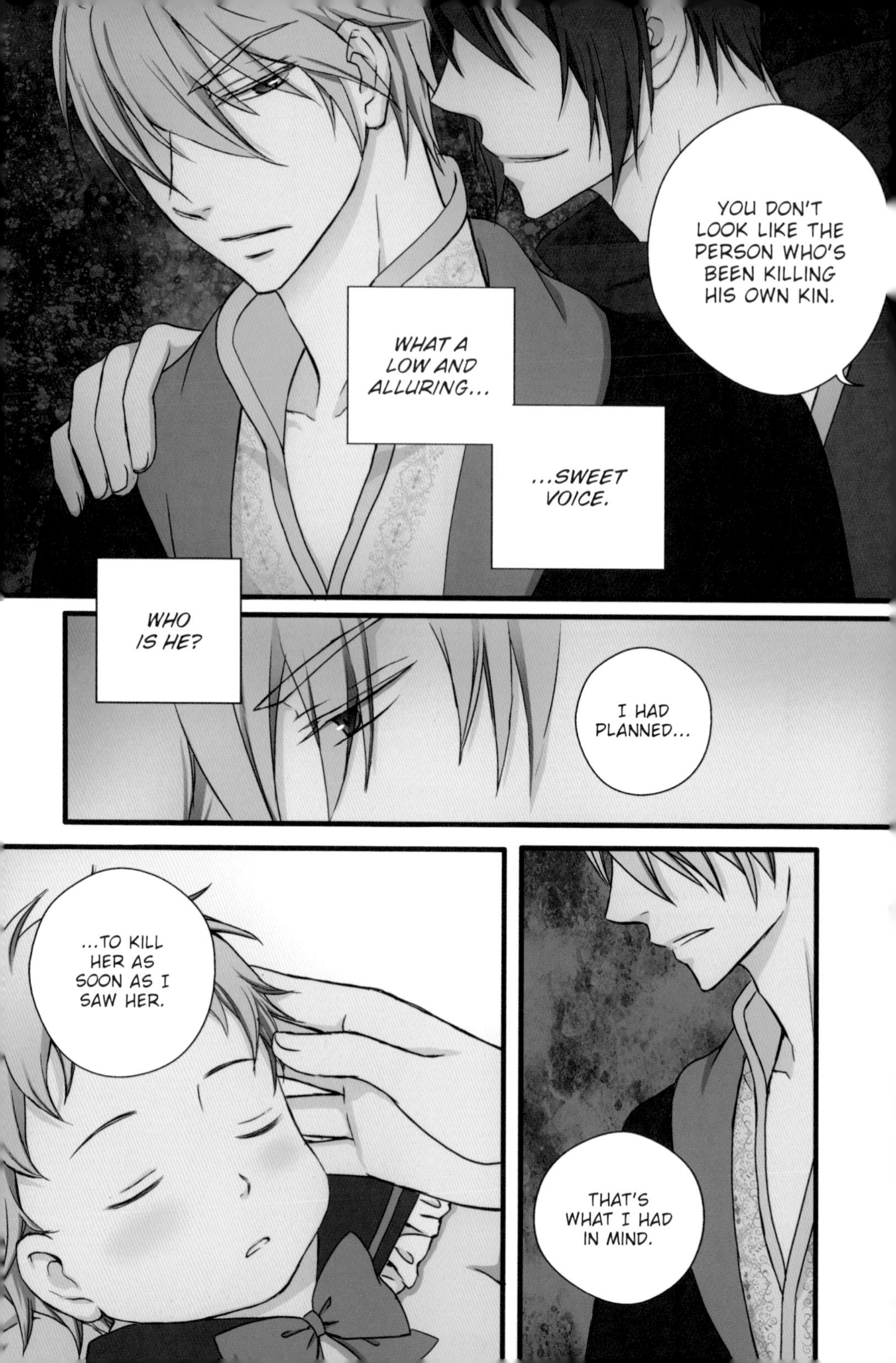
YOU DON'T LOOK LIKE THE PERSON WHO'S BEEN KILLING HIS OWN KIN.
WHAT A LOW AND ALLURING...
...SWEET VOICE.
WHO IS HE?
I HAD PLANNED...
...TO KILL HER AS SOON AS I SAW HER.
THAT'S WHAT I HAD IN MIND.

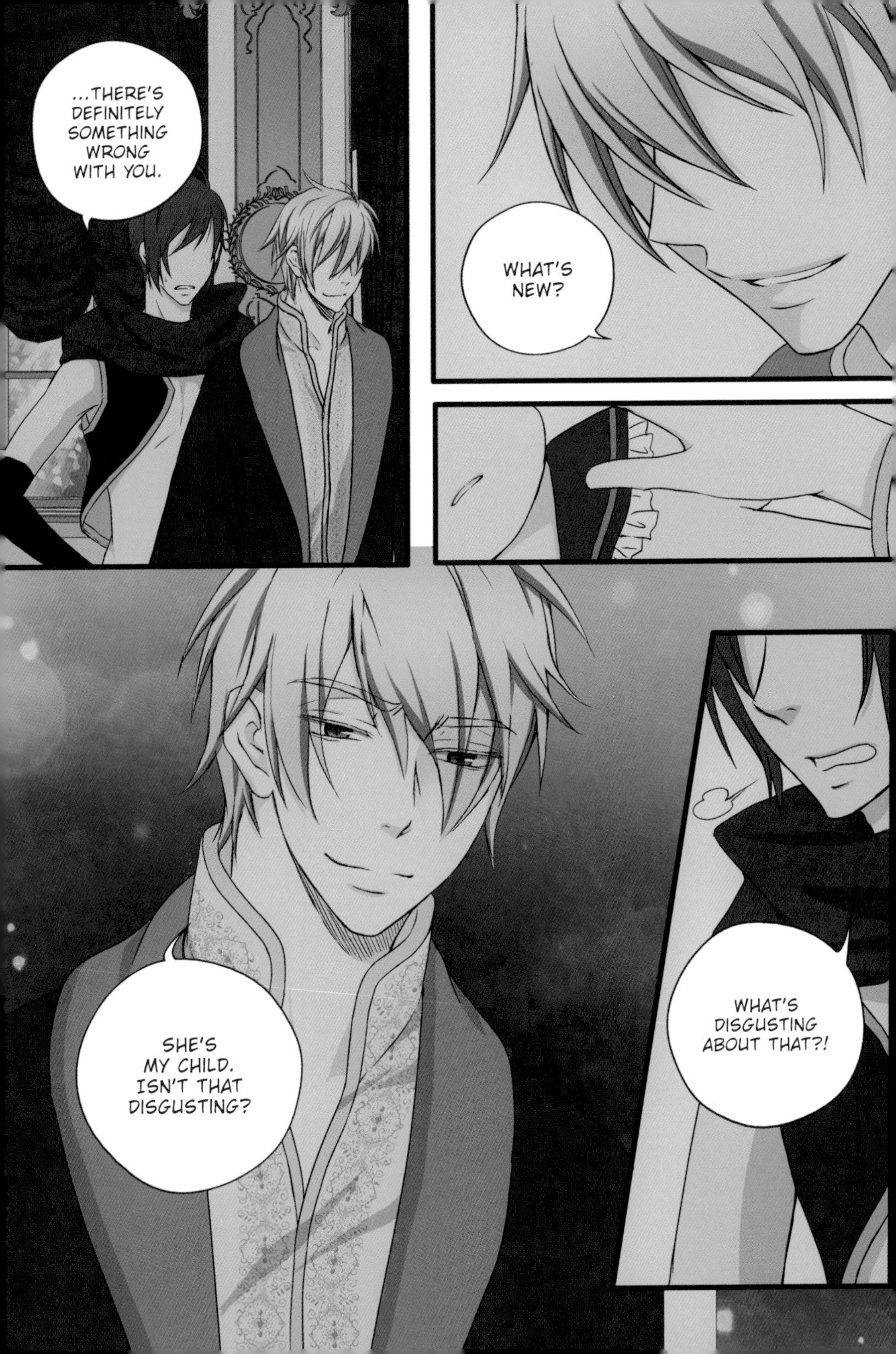
...THERE'S DEFINITELY SOMETHING WRONG WITH YOU.
WHAT'S NEW?
SHE'S MY CHILD. ISN'T THAT DISGUSTING?
WHAT'S DISGUSTING ABOUT THAT?!

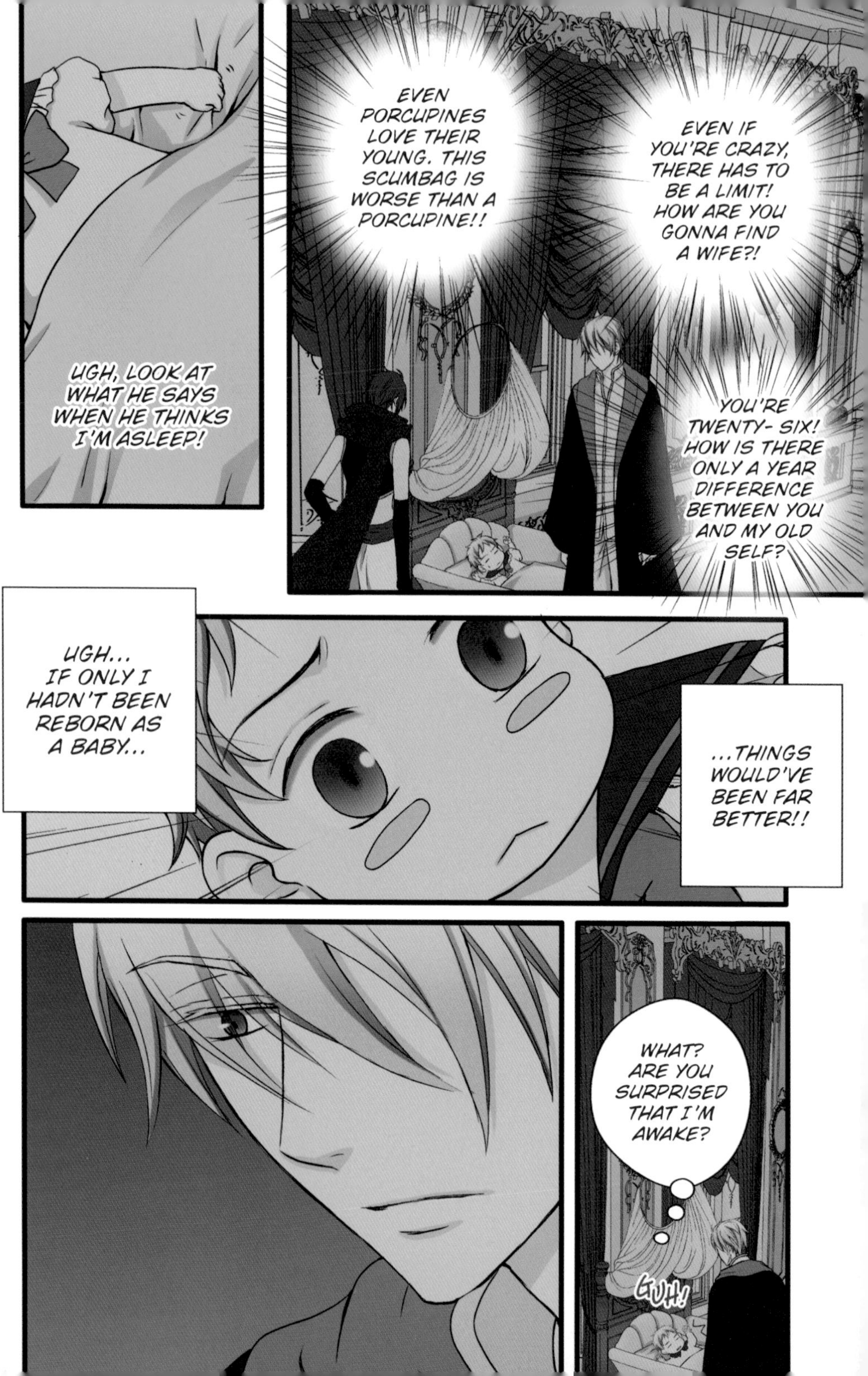
UGH, LOOK AT WHAT HE SAYS WHEN HE THINKS I'M ASLEEP!
EVEN PORCUPINES LOVE THEIR YOUNG. THIS SCUMBAG IS WORSE THAN A PORCUPINE!!
EVEN IF YOU'RE CRAZY, THERE HAS TO BE A LIMIT! HOW ARE YOU GONNA FIND A WIFE?!
YOU'RE TWENTY- SIX! HOW IS THERE ONLY A YEAR DIFFERENCE BETWEEN YOU AND MY OLD SELF?
UGH... IF ONLY I HADN'T BEEN REBORN AS A BABY...
...THINGS WOULD'VE BEEN FAR BETTER!!
WHAT? ARE YOU SURPRISED THAT I'M AWAKE?
GUH!

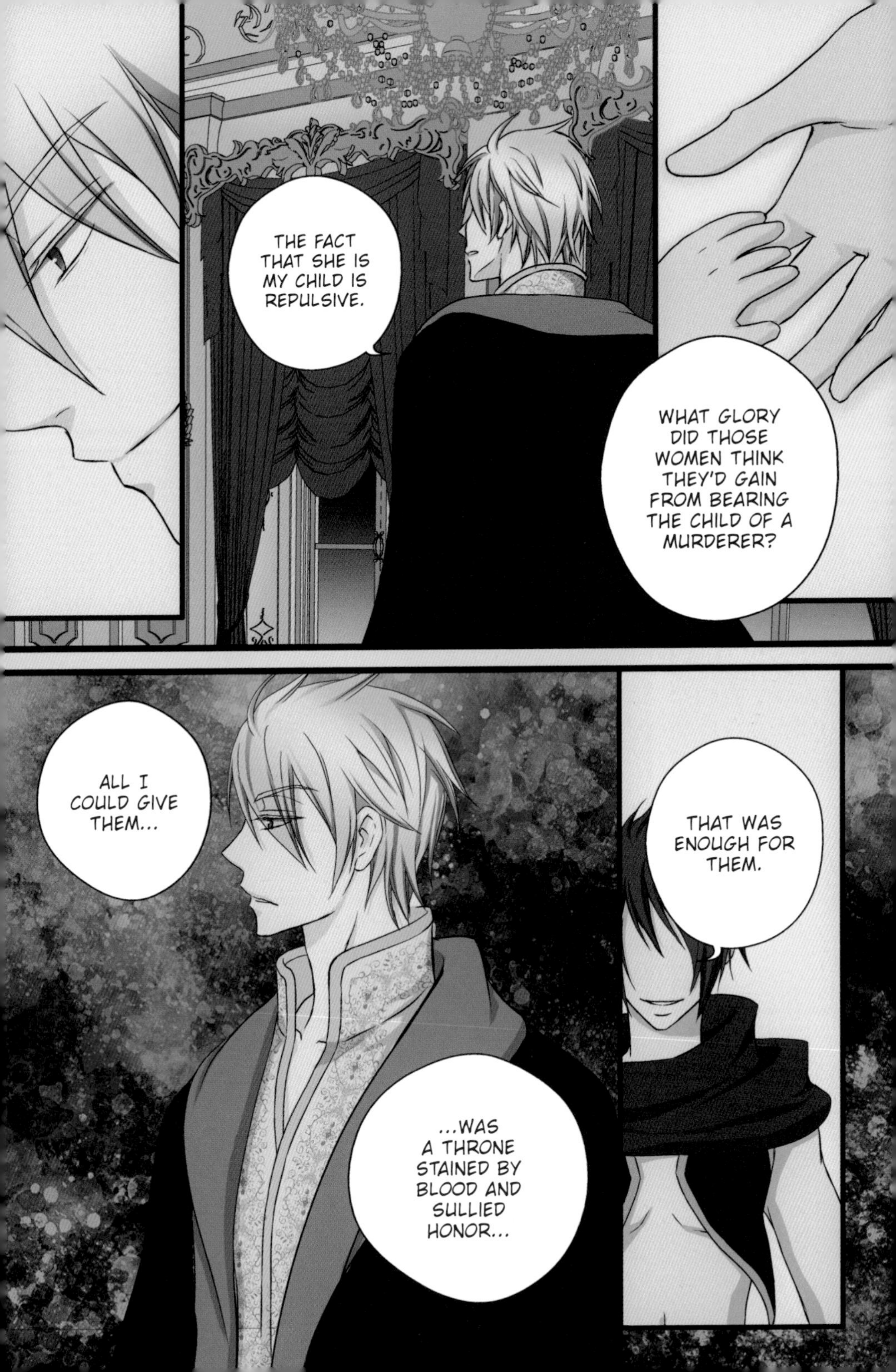
THE FACT THAT SHE IS MY CHILD IS REPULSIVE.
WHAT GLORY DID THOSE WOMEN THINK THEY'D GAIN FROM BEARING THE CHILD OF A MURDERER?
ALL I COULD GIVE THEM...
...WAS A THRONE STAINED BY BLOOD AND SULLIED HONOR...
THAT WAS ENOUGH FOR THEM.

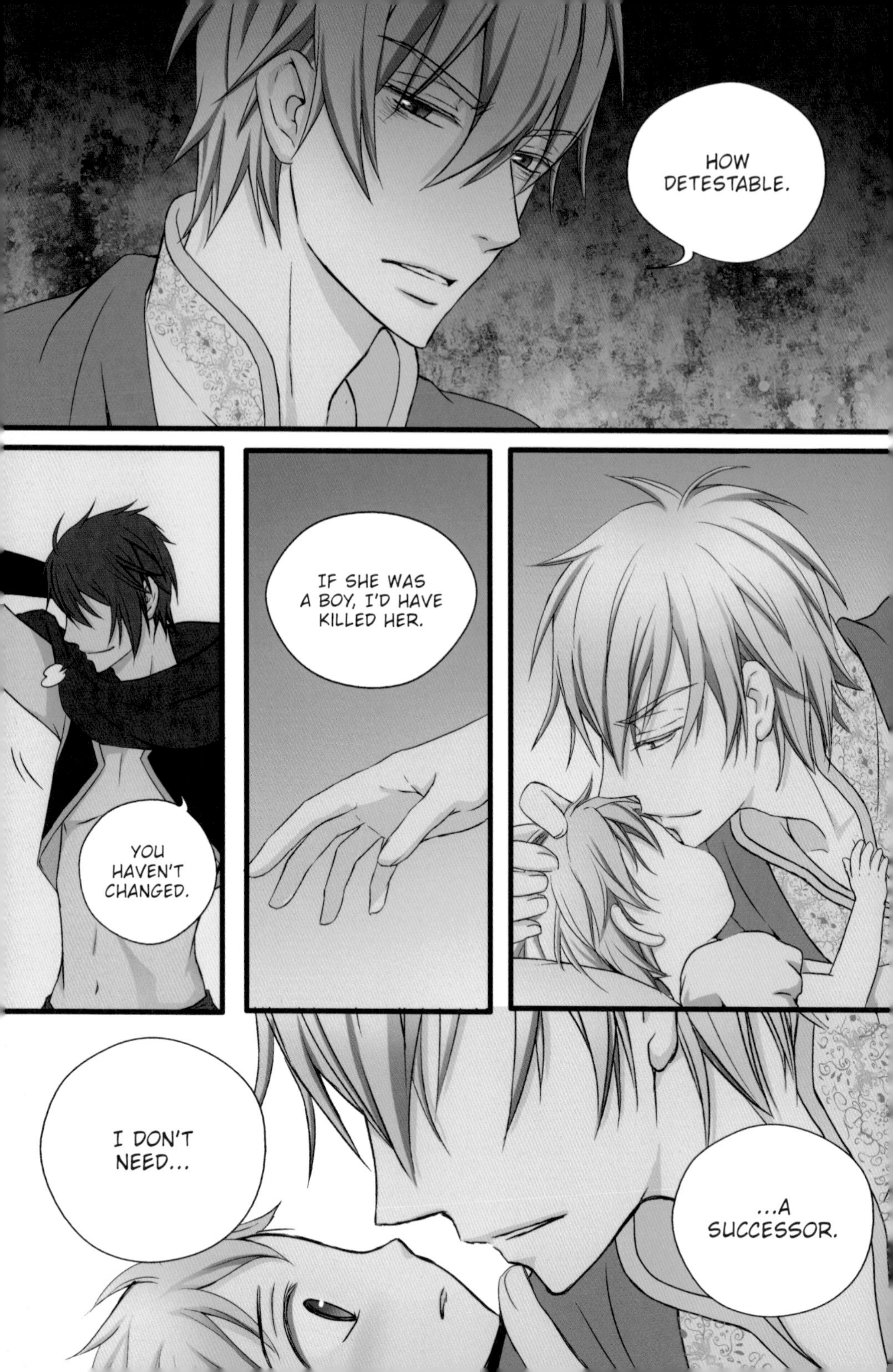
HOW DETESTABLE.
YOU HAVEN'T CHANGED.
IF SHE WAS A BOY, I'D HAVE KILLED HER.
I DON'T NEED...
...A SUCCESSOR.

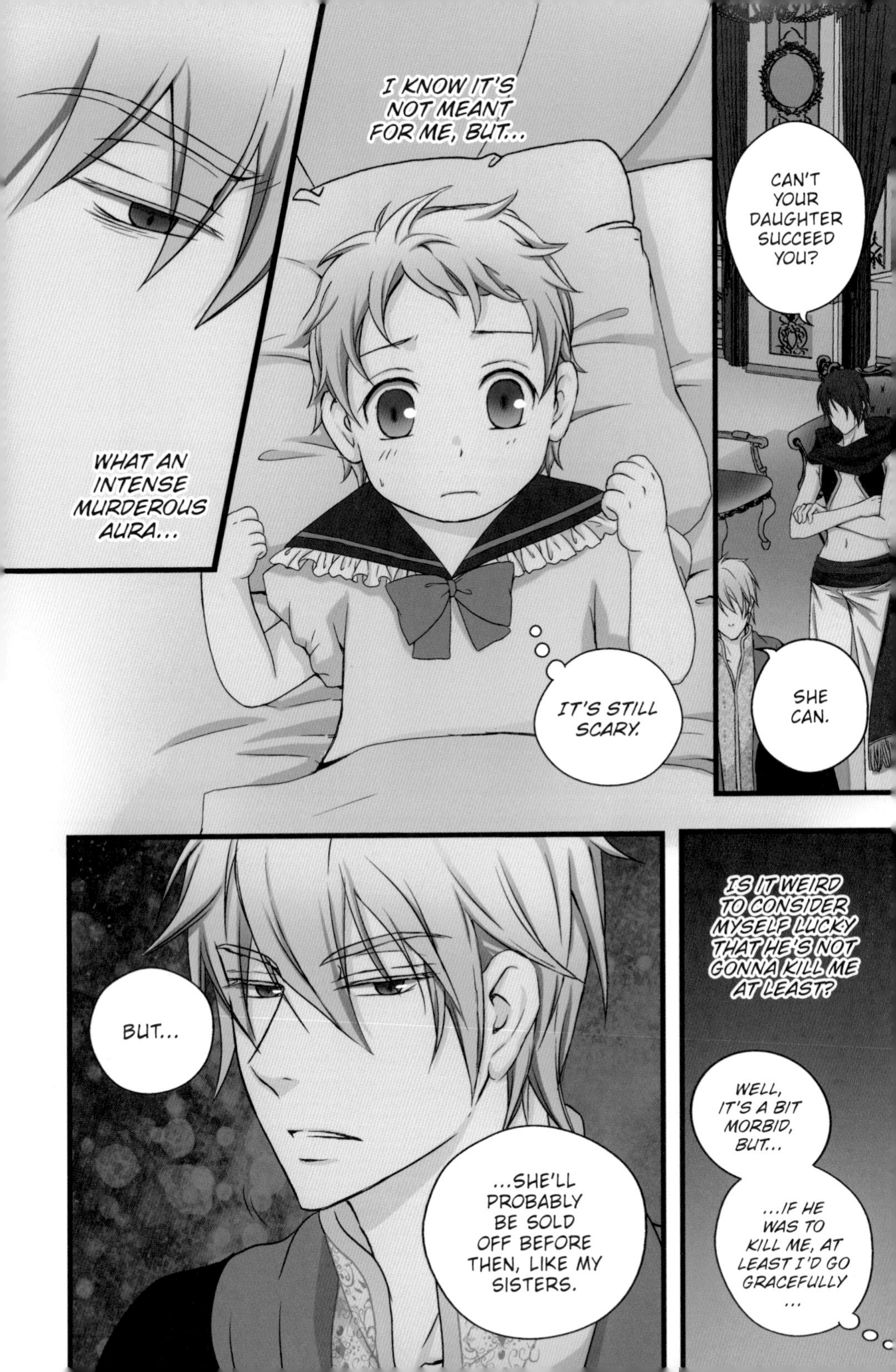
WHAT AN INTENSE MURDEROUS AURA...
I KNOW IT'S NOT MEANT FOR ME, BUT...
IT'S STILL SCARY.
CAN'T YOUR DAUGHTER SUCCEED YOU?
SHE CAN.
BUT...
...SHE'LL PROBABLY BE SOLD OFF BEFORE THEN, LIKE MY SISTERS.
IS IT WEIRD TO CONSIDER MYSELF LUCKY THAT HE'S NOT GONNA KILL ME AT LEAST?
WELL, IT'S A BIT MORBID, BUT...
...IF HE WAS TO KILL ME, AT LEAST I'D GO GRACEFULLY...

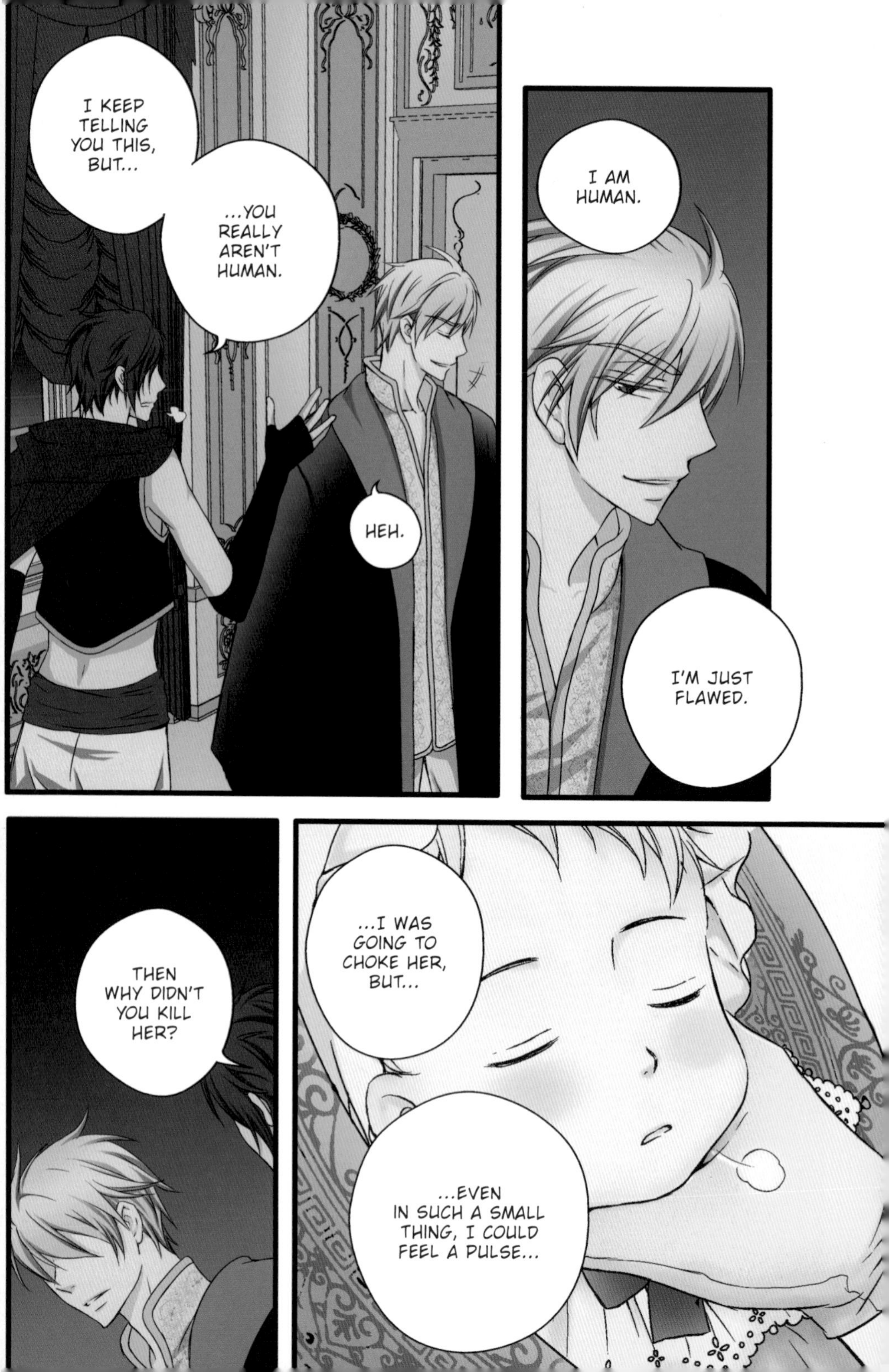
I KEEP TELLING YOU THIS, BUT...
...YOU REALLY AREN'T HUMAN.
HEH.
I AM HUMAN.
I'M JUST FLAWED.
THEN WHY DIDN'T YOU KILL HER?
...I WAS GOING TO CHOKE HER, BUT...
...EVEN IN SUCH A SMALL THING, I COULD FEEL A PULSE...

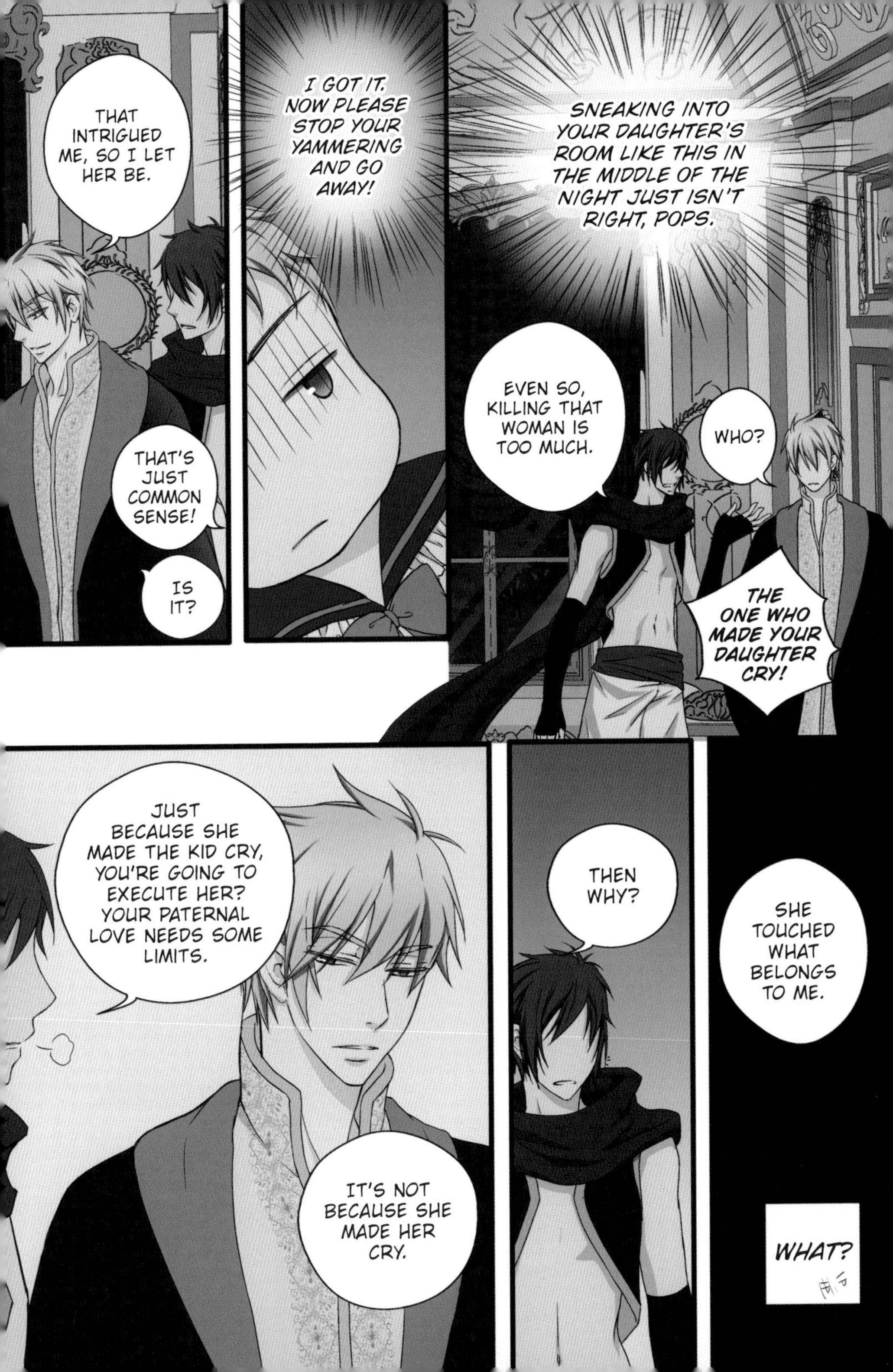
THAT INTRIGUED ME, SO I LET HER BE.
THAT'S JUST COMMON SENSE!
IS IT?
I GOT IT. NOW PLEASE STOP YOUR YAMMERING AND GO AWAY!
SNEAKING INTO YOUR DAUGHTER'S ROOM LIKE THIS IN THE MIDDLE OF THE NIGHT JUST ISN'T RIGHT, POPS.
EVEN SO, KILLING THAT WOMAN IS TOO MUCH.
WHO?
THE ONE WHO MADE YOUR DAUGHTER CRY!
JUST BECAUSE SHE MADE THE KID CRY, YOU'RE GOING TO EXECUTE HER? YOUR PATERNAL LOVE NEEDS SOME LIMITS.
IT'S NOT BECAUSE SHE MADE HER CRY.
THEN WHY?
SHE TOUCHED WHAT BELONGS TO ME.
WHAT?

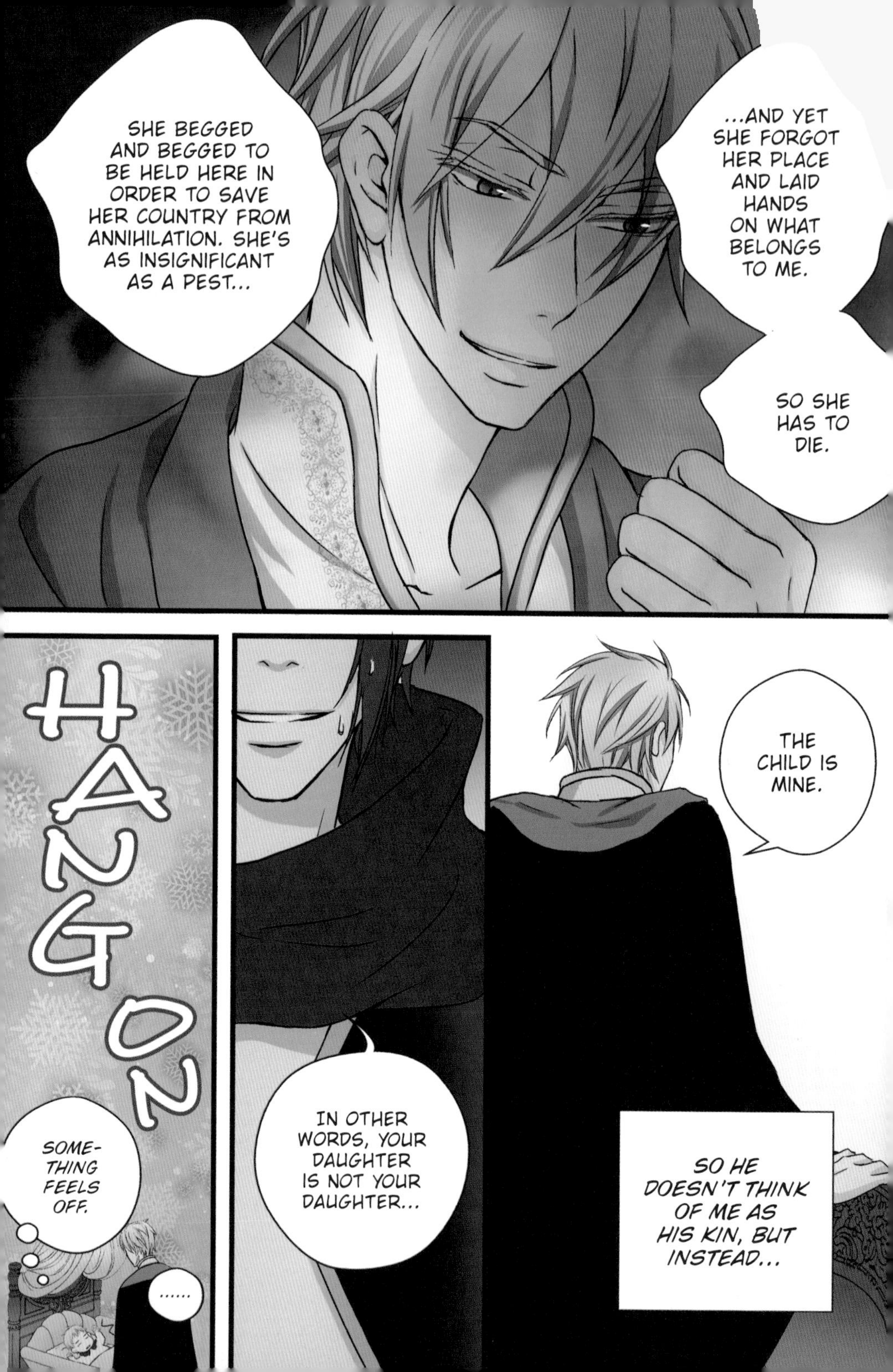

SHE BEGGED AND BEGGED TO BE HELD HERE IN ORDER TO SAVE HER COUNTRY FROM ANNIHILATION. SHE'S AS INSIGNIFICANT AS A PEST...
...AND YET SHE FORGOT HER PLACE AND LAID HANDS ON WHAT BELONGS TO ME.
SO SHE HAS TO DIE.
HANG ON
SOME-THING FEELS OFF.
......
THE CHILD IS MINE.
IN OTHER WORDS, YOUR DAUGHTER IS NOT YOUR DAUGHTER...
SO HE DOESN'T THINK OF ME AS HIS KIN, BUT INSTEAD...

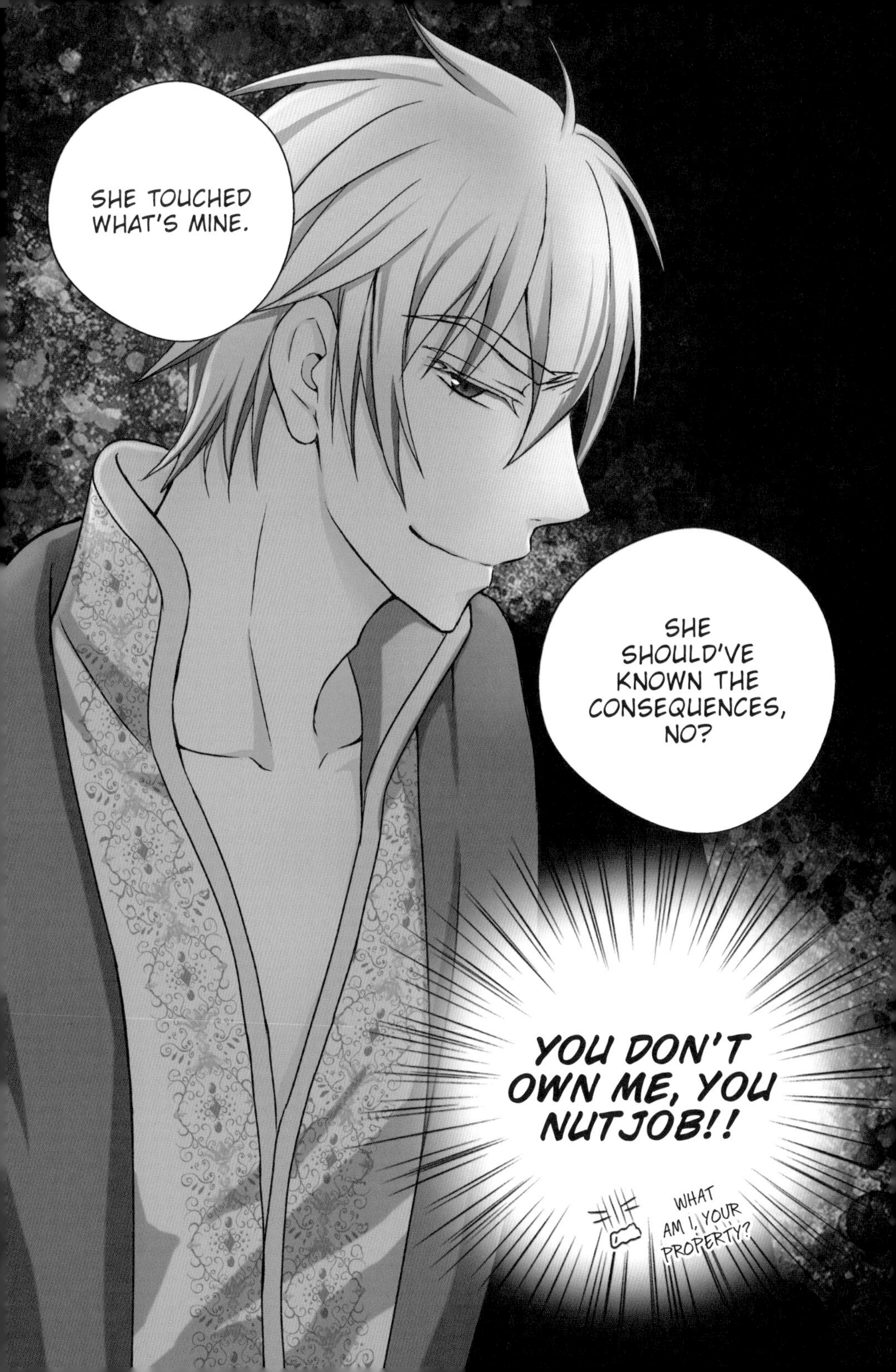
SHE TOUCHED WHAT'S MINE.
SHE SHOULD'VE KNOWN THE CONSEQUENCES, NO?
YOU DON'T OWN ME, YOU NUTJOB!!
WHAT AM I, YOUR PROPERTY?

DAUGHTER
OF THE
EMPEROR

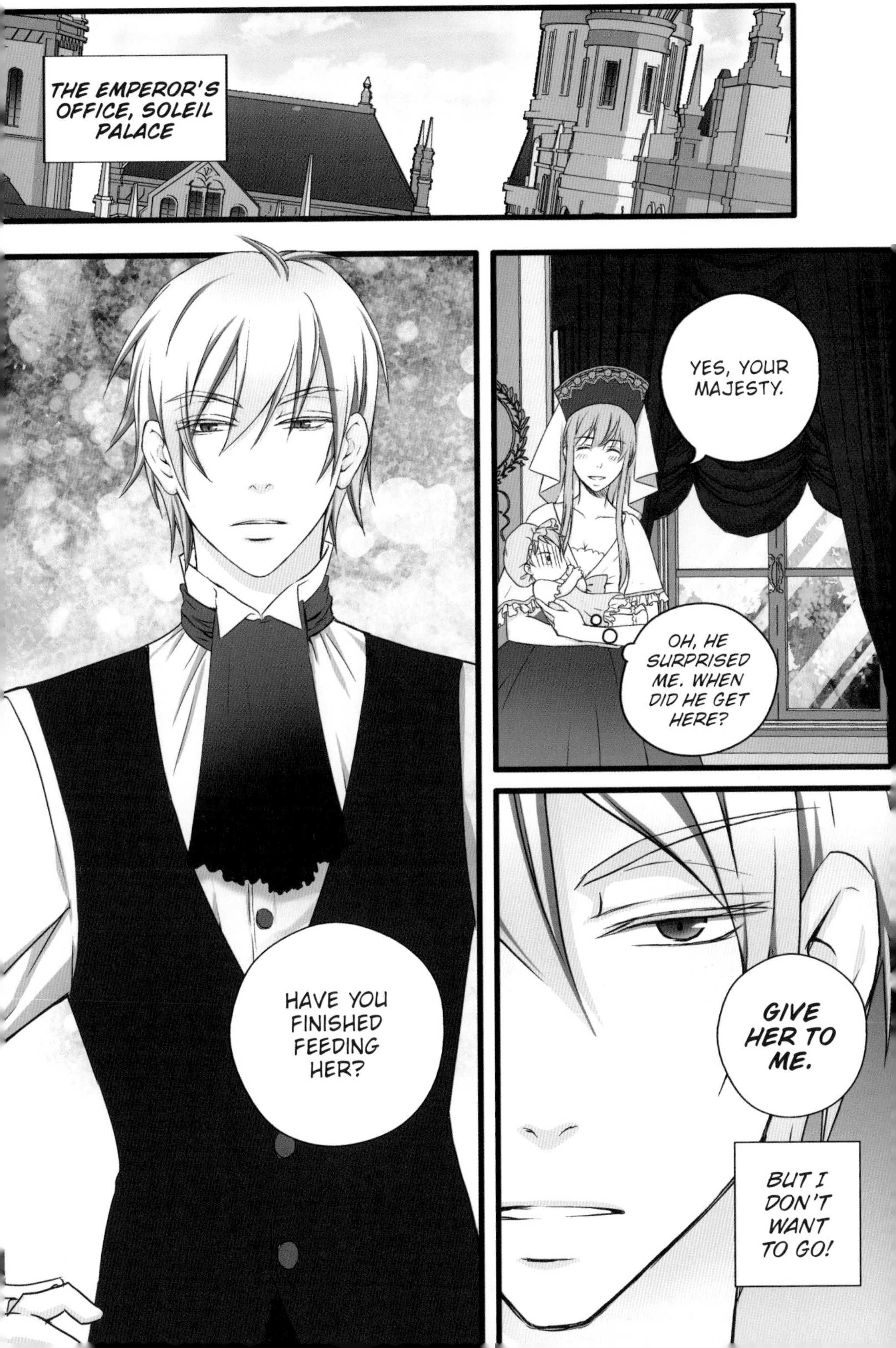
THE EMPEROR'S OFFICE, SOLEIL PALACE
HAVE YOU FINISHED FEEDING HER?
YES, YOUR MAJESTY.
OH, HE SURPRISED ME. WHEN DID HE GET HERE?
GIVE HER TO ME.
BUT I DON'T WANT TO GO!

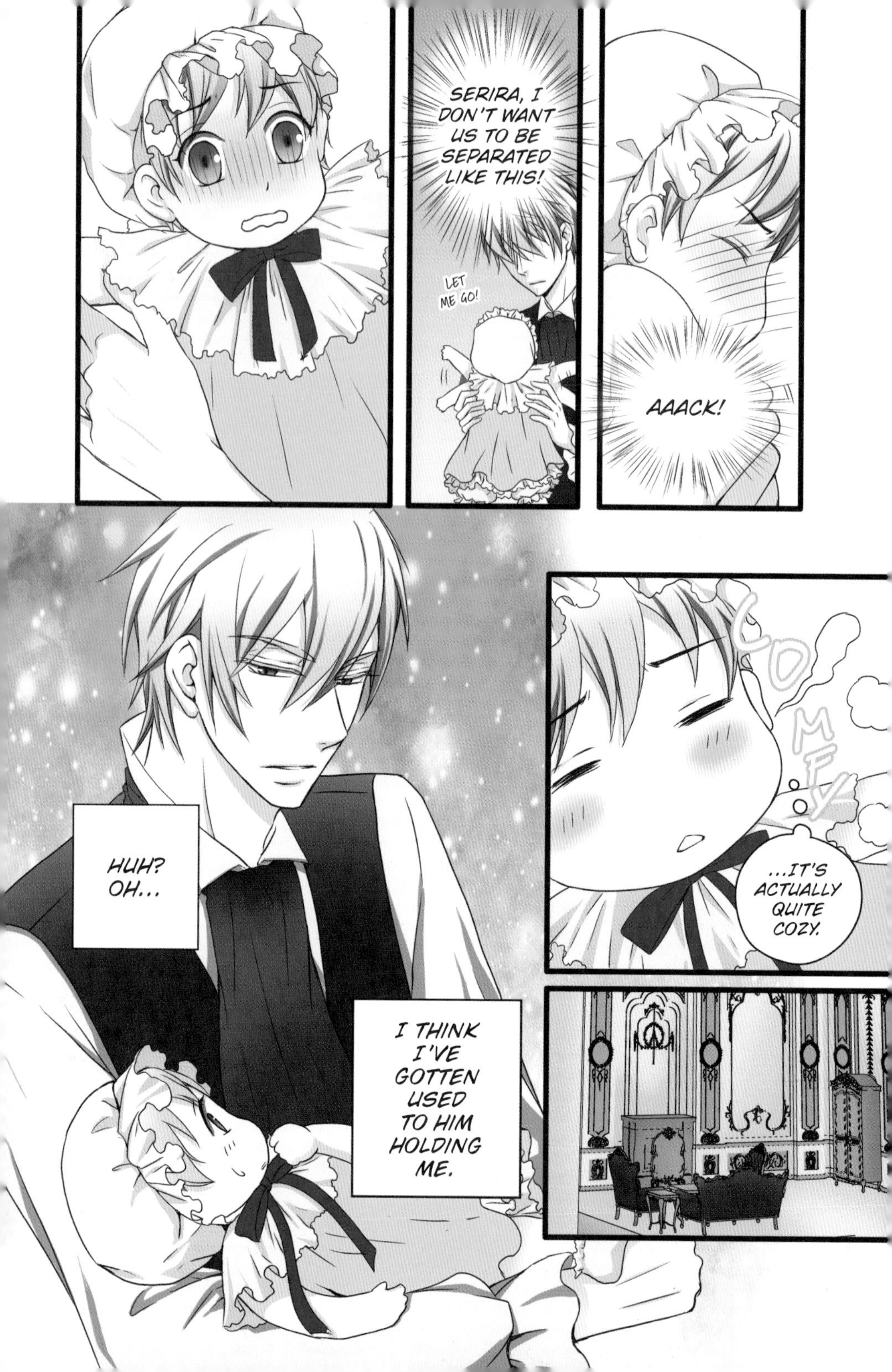
SERIRA, I DON'T WANT US TO BE SEPARATED LIKE THIS!
LET ME GO!
AAACK!
HUH? OH...
I THINK I'VE GOTTEN USED TO HIM HOLDING ME.
COMFY
...IT'S ACTUALLY QUITE COZY.

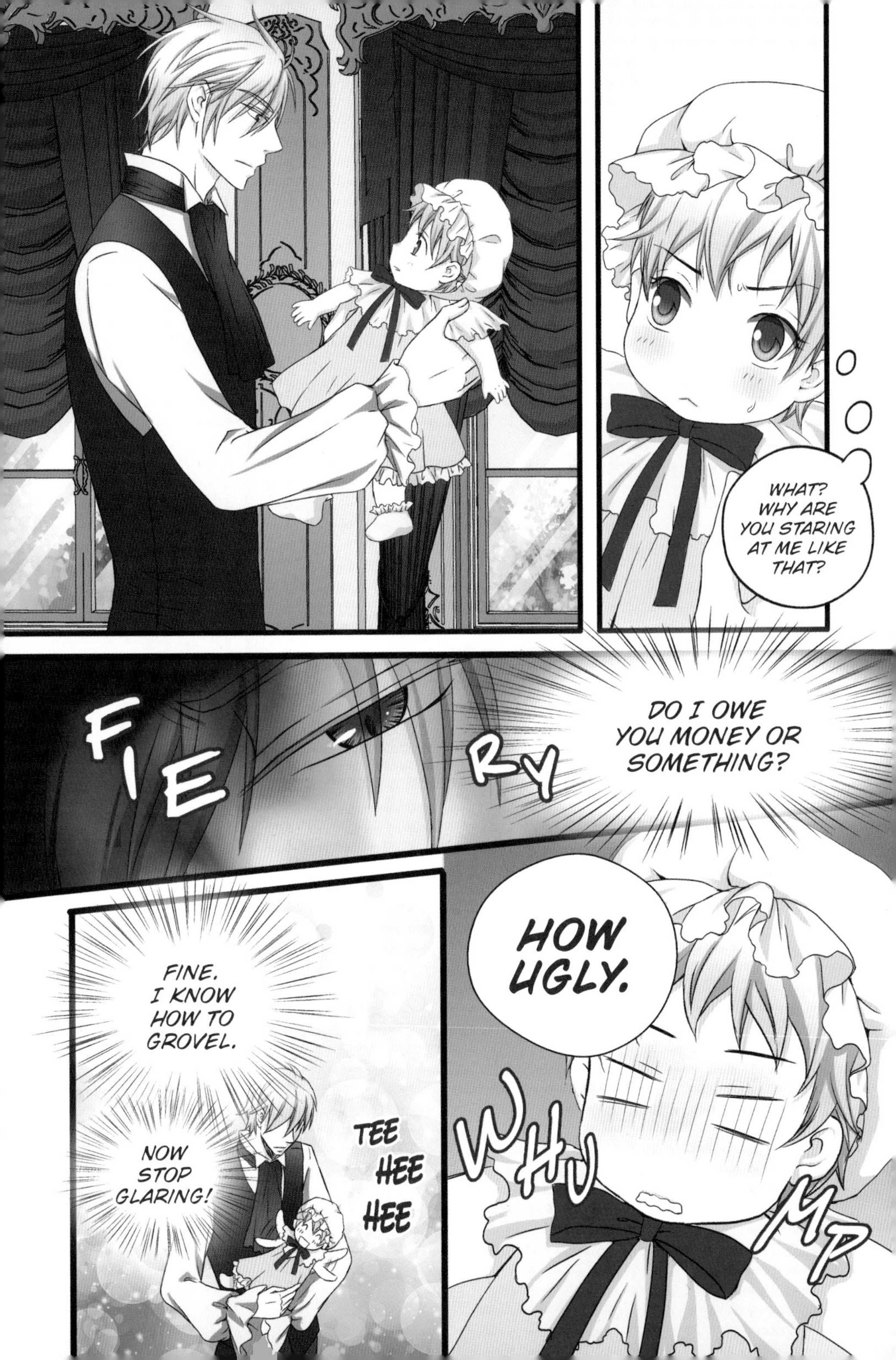
WHAT? WHY ARE YOU STARING AT ME LIKE THAT?
FIERY
DO I OWE YOU MONEY OR SOMETHING?
FINE. I KNOW HOW TO GROVEL.
NOW STOP GLARING!
TEE HEE HEE
HOW UGLY.
WHUMP

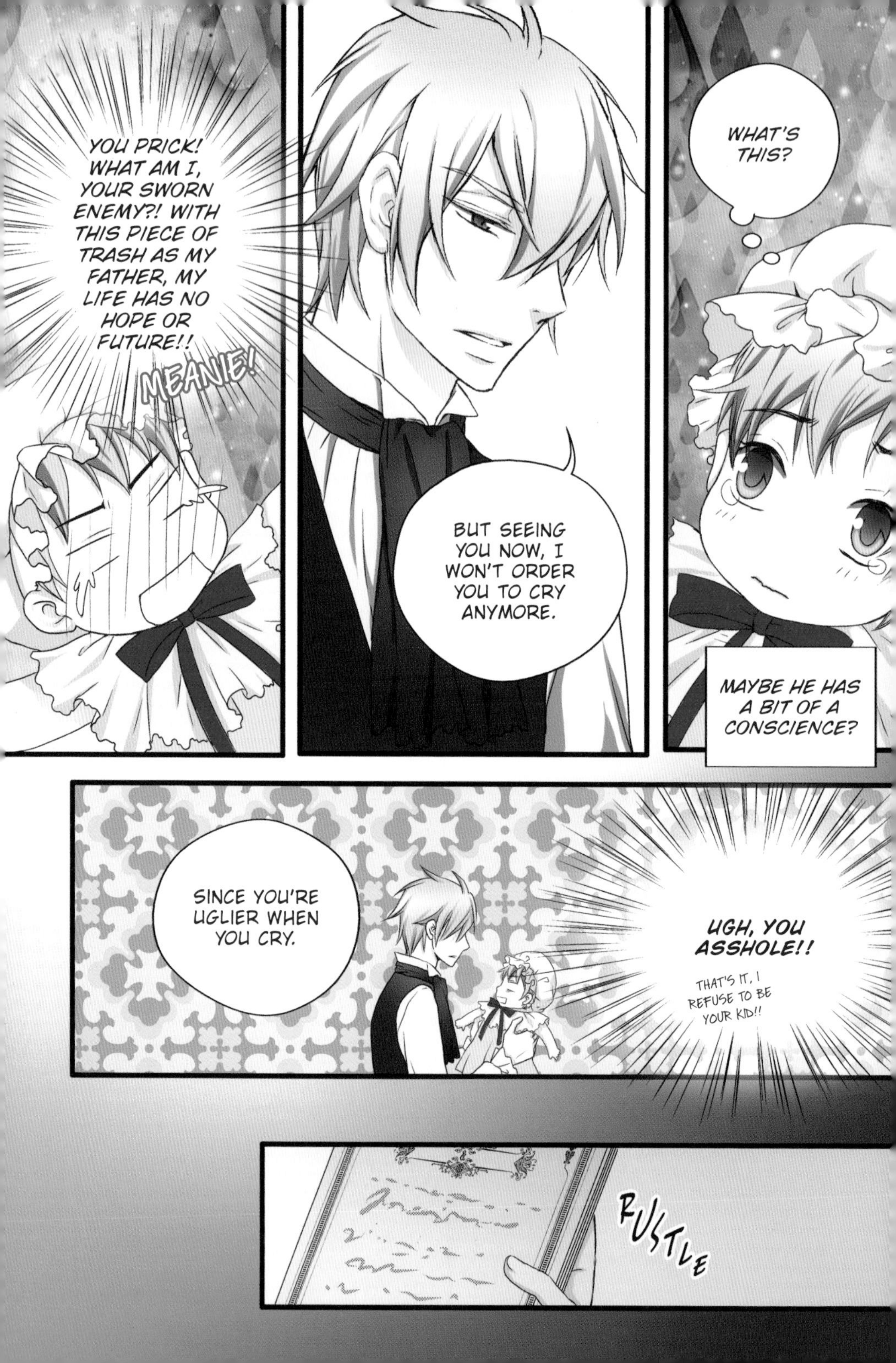
YOU PRICK! WHAT AM I, YOUR SWORN ENEMY?! WITH THIS PIECE OF TRASH AS MY FATHER, MY LIFE HAS NO HOPE OR FUTURE!!
MEANIE!
BUT SEEING YOU NOW, I WON'T ORDER YOU TO CRY ANYMORE.
WHAT'S THIS?
MAYBE HE HAS A BIT OF A CONSCIENCE?
SINCE YOU'RE UGLIER WHEN YOU CRY.
UGH, YOU ASSHOLE!!
THAT'S IT, I REFUSE TO BE YOUR KID!!
RUSTLE

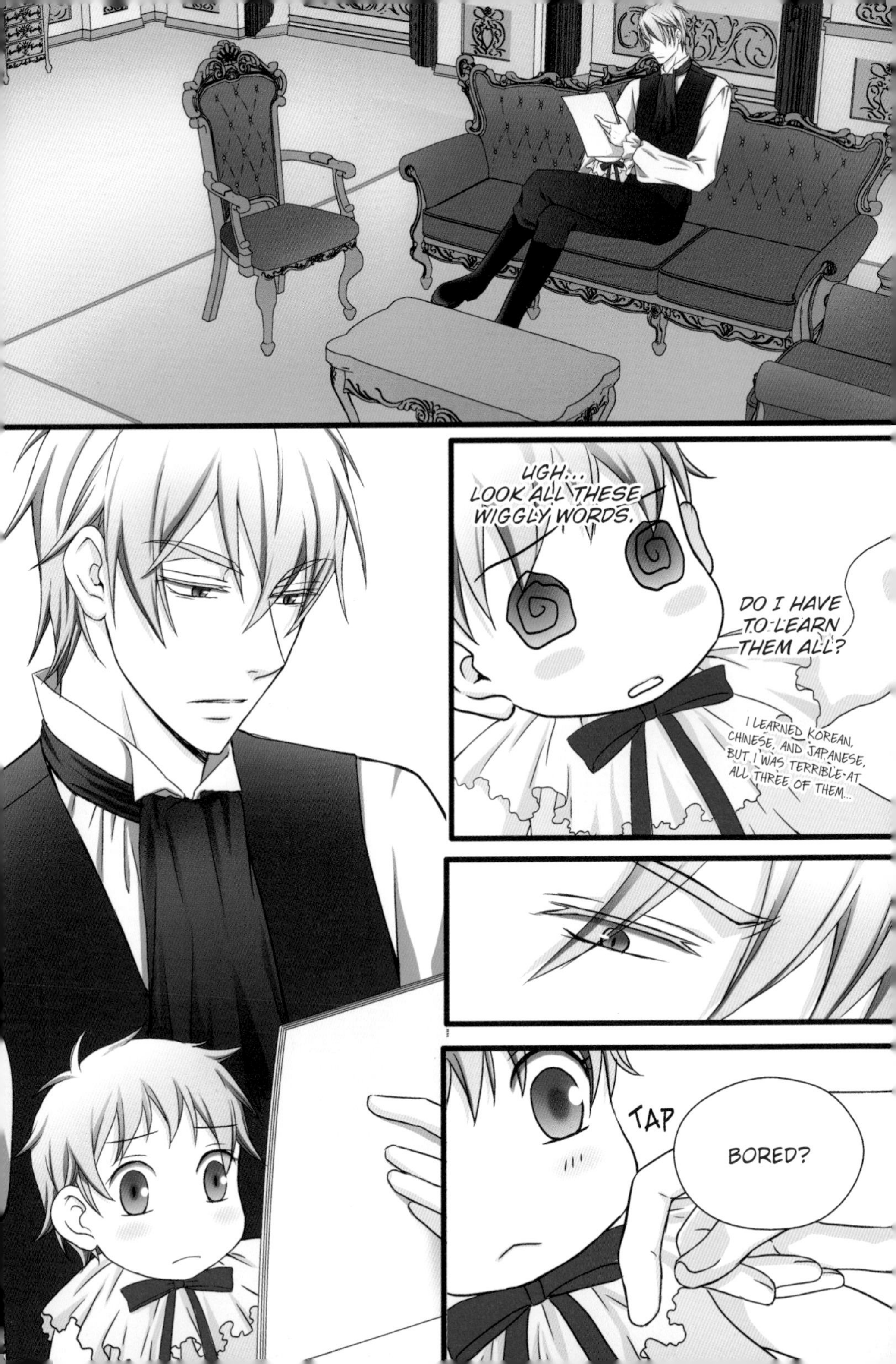
UGH... LOOK ALL THESE WIGGLY WORDS.
DO I HAVE TO LEARN THEM ALL?
I LEARNED KOREAN, CHINESE, AND JAPANESE, BUT I WAS TERRIBLE AT ALL THREE OF THEM...
TAP
BORED?

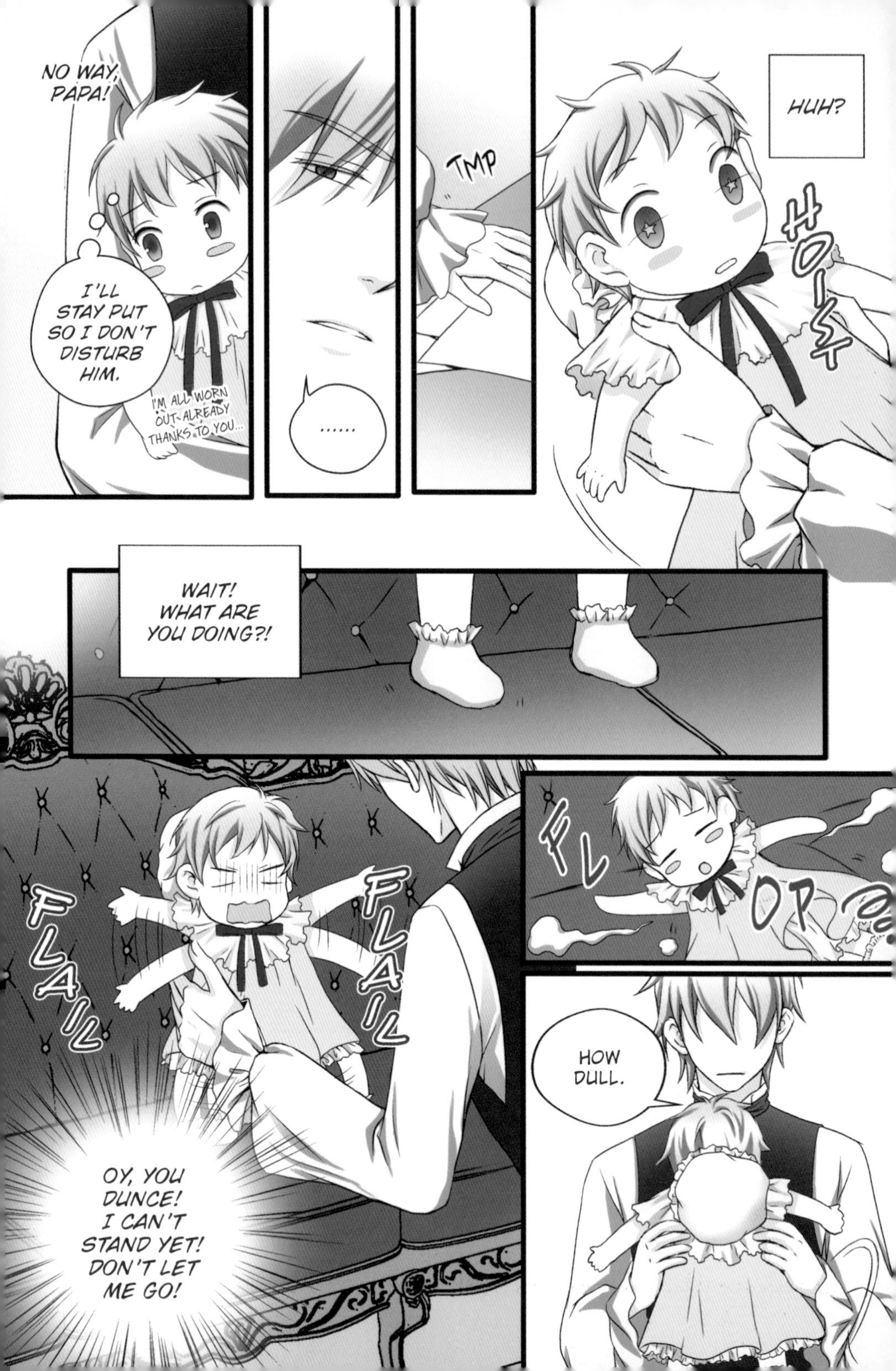
NO WAY, PAPA!
I'LL STAY PUT SO I DON'T DISTURB HIM.
I'M ALL WORN OUT ALREADY THANKS TO YOU...
......
TMP
HUH?
HOIST
WAIT! WHAT ARE YOU DOING?!
FLAIL
FLAIL
OY, YOU DUNCE! I CAN'T STAND YET! DON'T LET ME GO!
FLOP
HOW DULL.

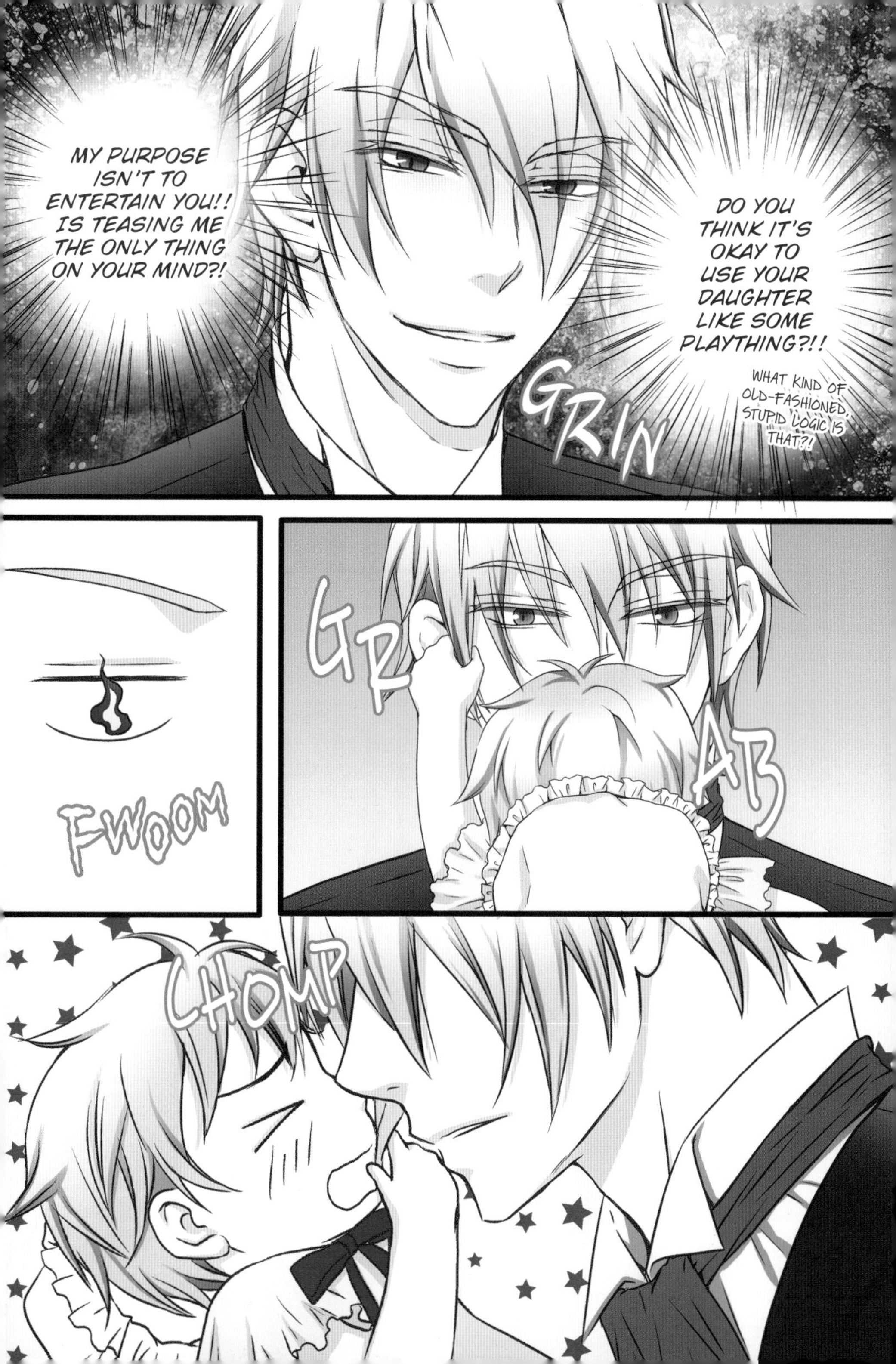
MY PURPOSE ISN'T TO ENTERTAIN YOU!! IS TEASING ME THE ONLY THING ON YOUR MIND?!
DO YOU THINK IT'S OKAY TO USE YOUR DAUGHTER LIKE SOME PLAYTHING?!!
GRIN
WHAT KIND OF OLD-FASHIONED, STUPID LOGIC IS THAT?!
FWOOM
GRAB
CHOMP

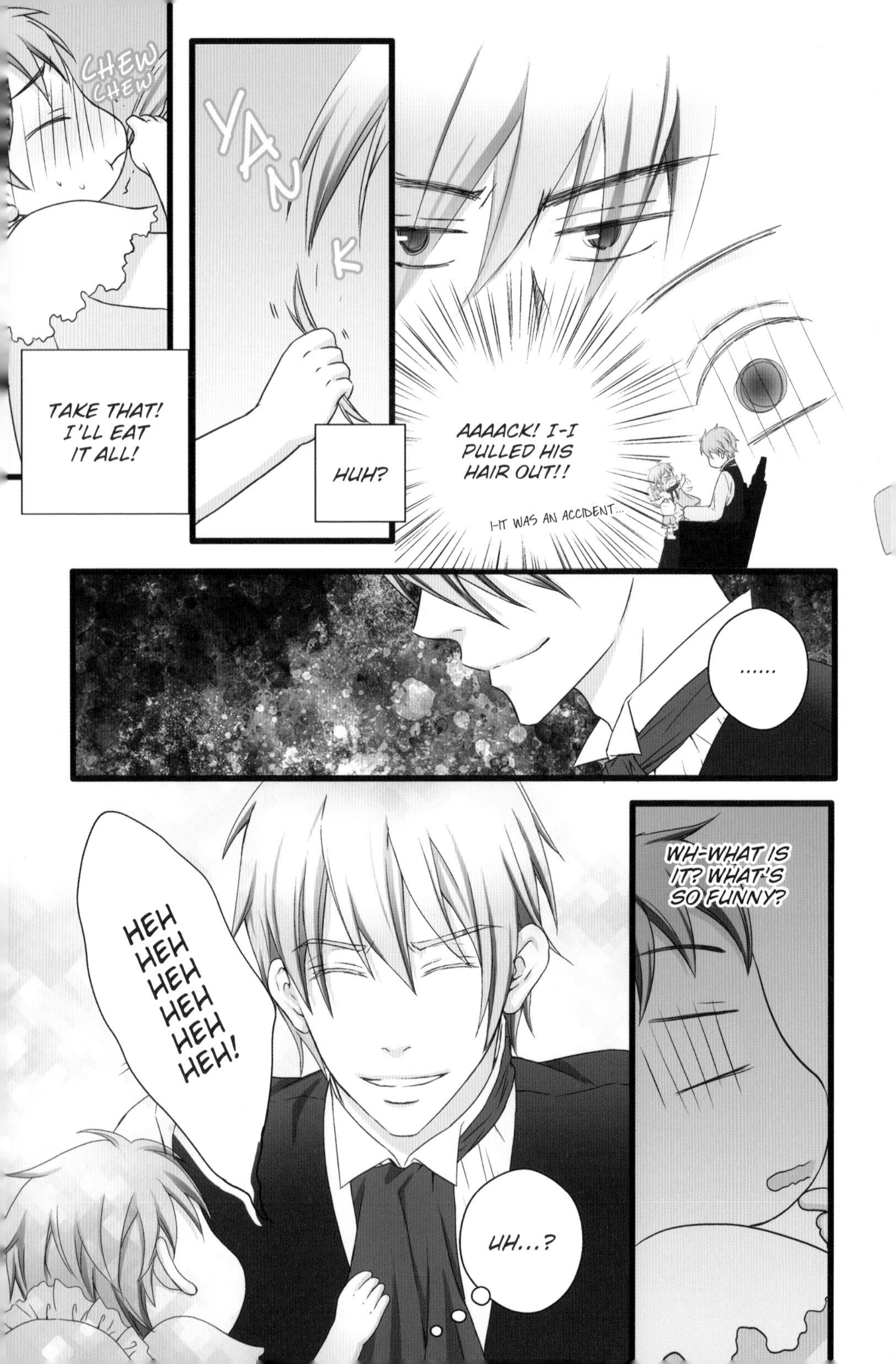

CHEW CHEW
TAKE THAT! I'LL EAT IT ALL!
YANK
HUH?
AAAACK! I-I PULLED HIS HAIR OUT!!
I-IT WAS AN ACCIDENT...
......
HEH HEH HEH HEH HEH HEH!
UH...?
WH-WHAT IS IT? WHAT'S SO FUNNY?

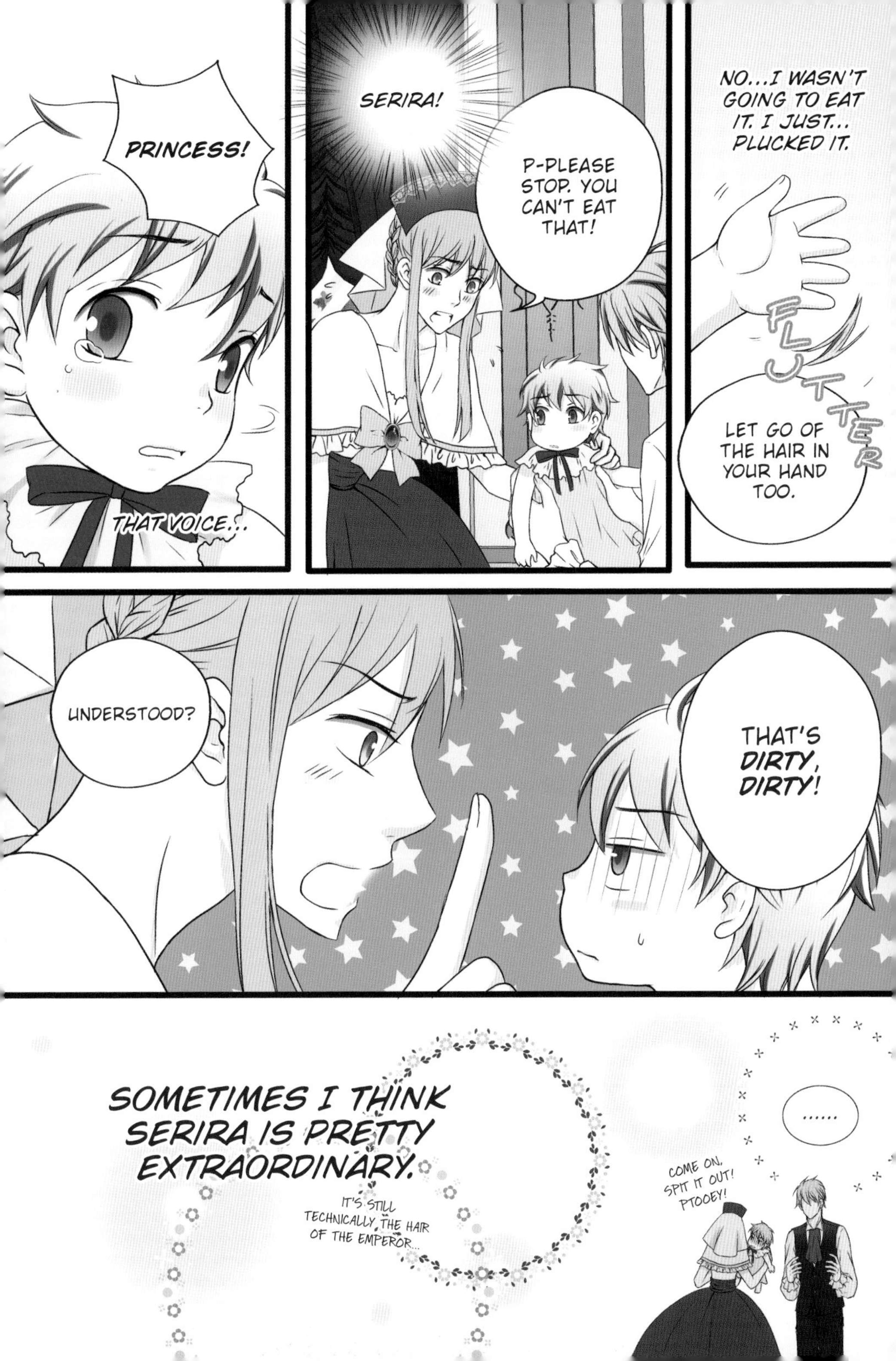
PRINCESS!
THAT VOICE...
SERIRA!
P-PLEASE STOP. YOU CAN'T EAT THAT!
NO...I WASN'T GOING TO EAT IT. I JUST... PLUCKED IT.
FLUTTER
LET GO OF THE HAIR IN YOUR HAND TOO.
UNDERSTOOD?
THAT'S DIRTY, DIRTY!
SOMETIMES I THINK SERIRA IS PRETTY EXTRAORDINARY.
IT'S STILL TECHNICALLY THE HAIR OF THE EMPEROR...
......
COME ON, SPIT IT OUT! PTOOEY!

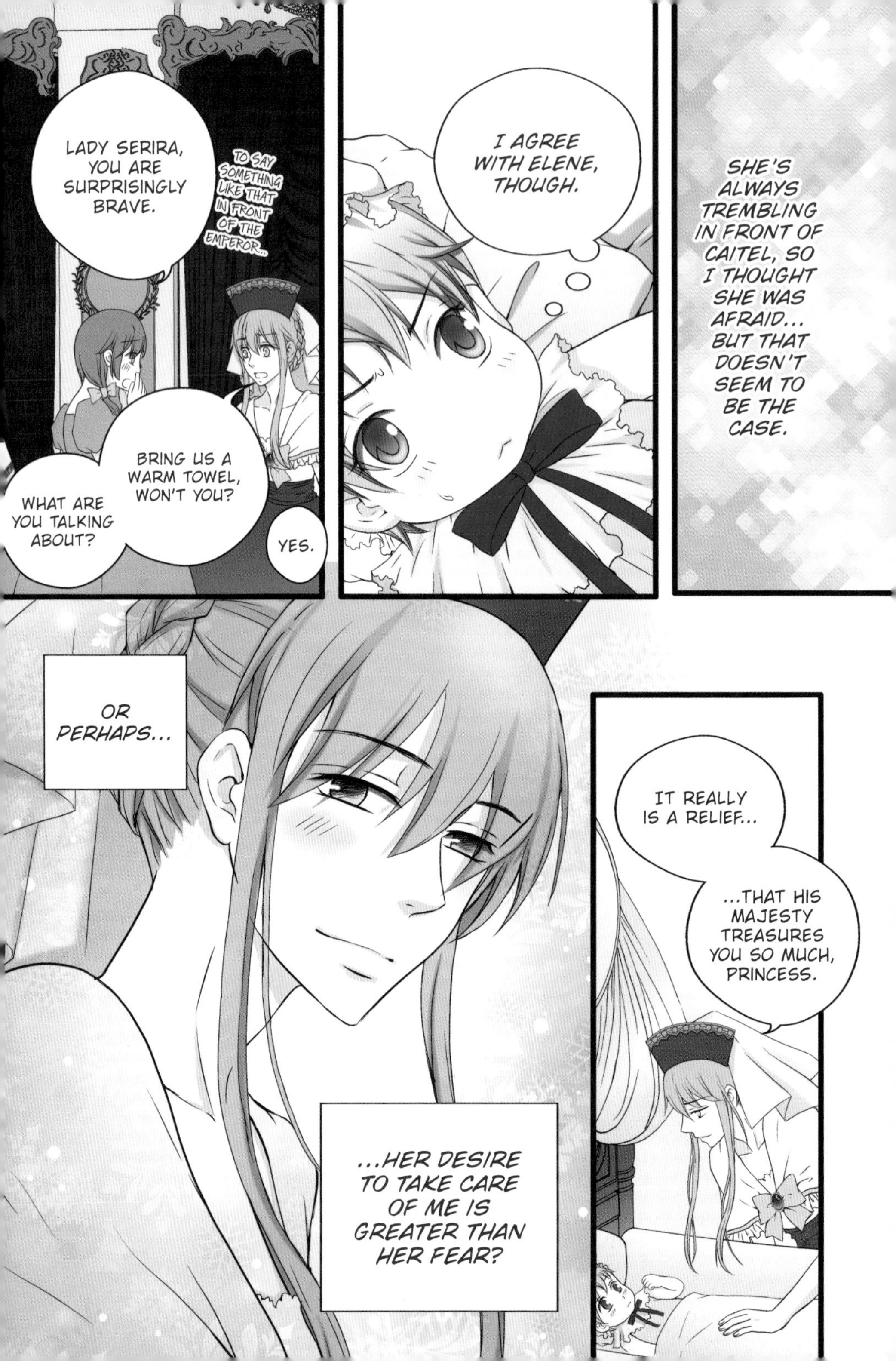
LADY SERIRA, YOU ARE SURPRISINGLY BRAVE.
TO SAY SOMETHING LIKE THAT IN FRONT OF THE EMPEROR...
BRING US A WARM TOWEL, WON'T YOU?
WHAT ARE YOU TALKING ABOUT?
YES.
I AGREE WITH ELENE, THOUGH.
SHE'S ALWAYS TREMBLING IN FRONT OF CAITEL, SO I THOUGHT SHE WAS AFRAID... BUT THAT DOESN'T SEEM TO BE THE CASE.
OR PERHAPS...
IT REALLY IS A RELIEF...
...THAT HIS MAJESTY TREASURES YOU SO MUCH, PRINCESS.
...HER DESIRE TO TAKE CARE OF ME IS GREATER THAN HER FEAR?

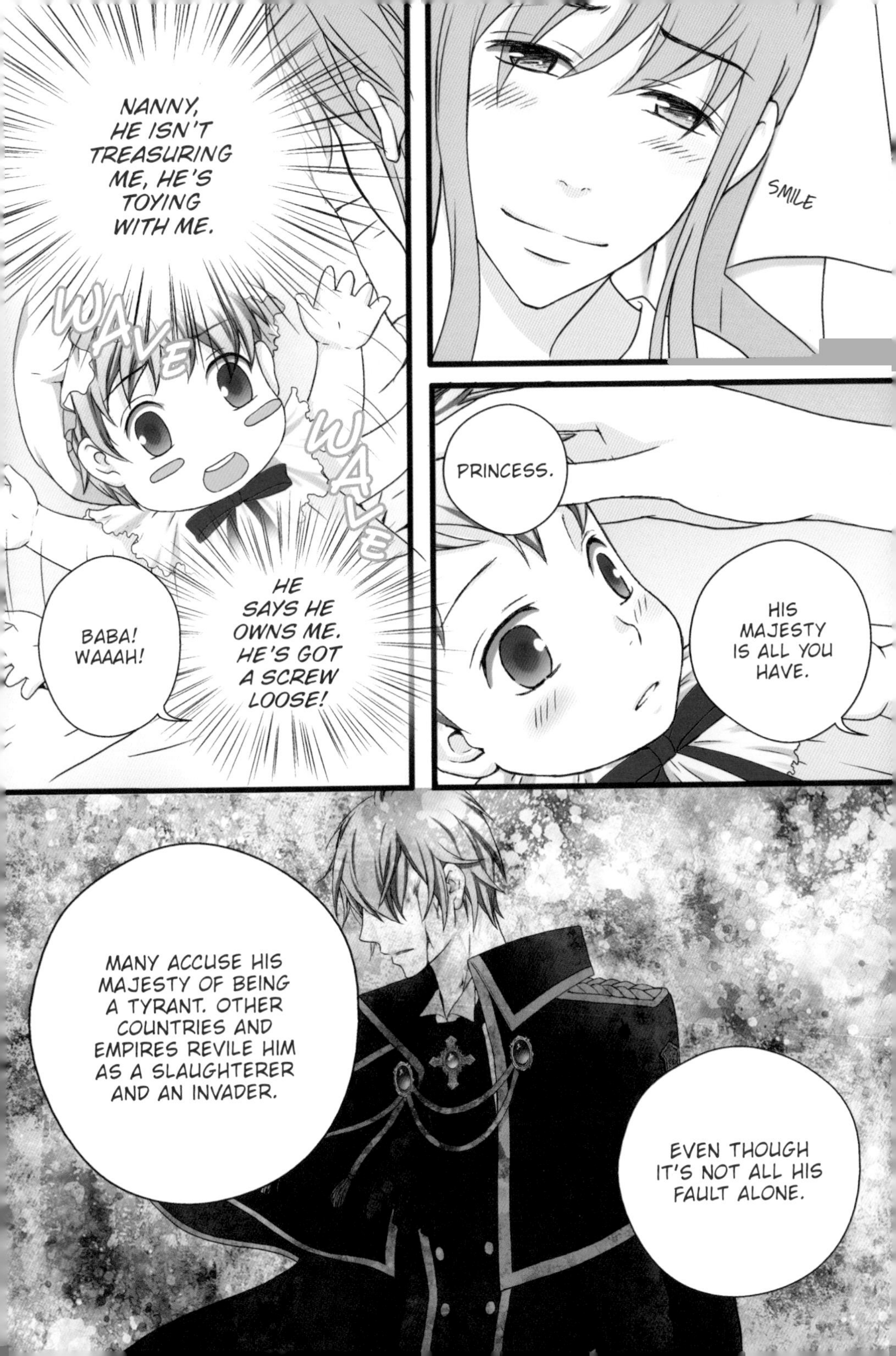
NANNY, HE ISN'T TREASURING ME, HE'S TOYING WITH ME.
WAVE
WAVE
BABA! WAAAH!
HE SAYS HE OWNS ME. HE'S GOT A SCREW LOOSE!
SMILE
PRINCESS.
HIS MAJESTY IS ALL YOU HAVE.
MANY ACCUSE HIS MAJESTY OF BEING A TYRANT. OTHER COUNTRIES AND EMPIRES REVILE HIM AS A SLAUGHTERER AND AN INVADER.
EVEN THOUGH IT'S NOT ALL HIS FAULT ALONE.

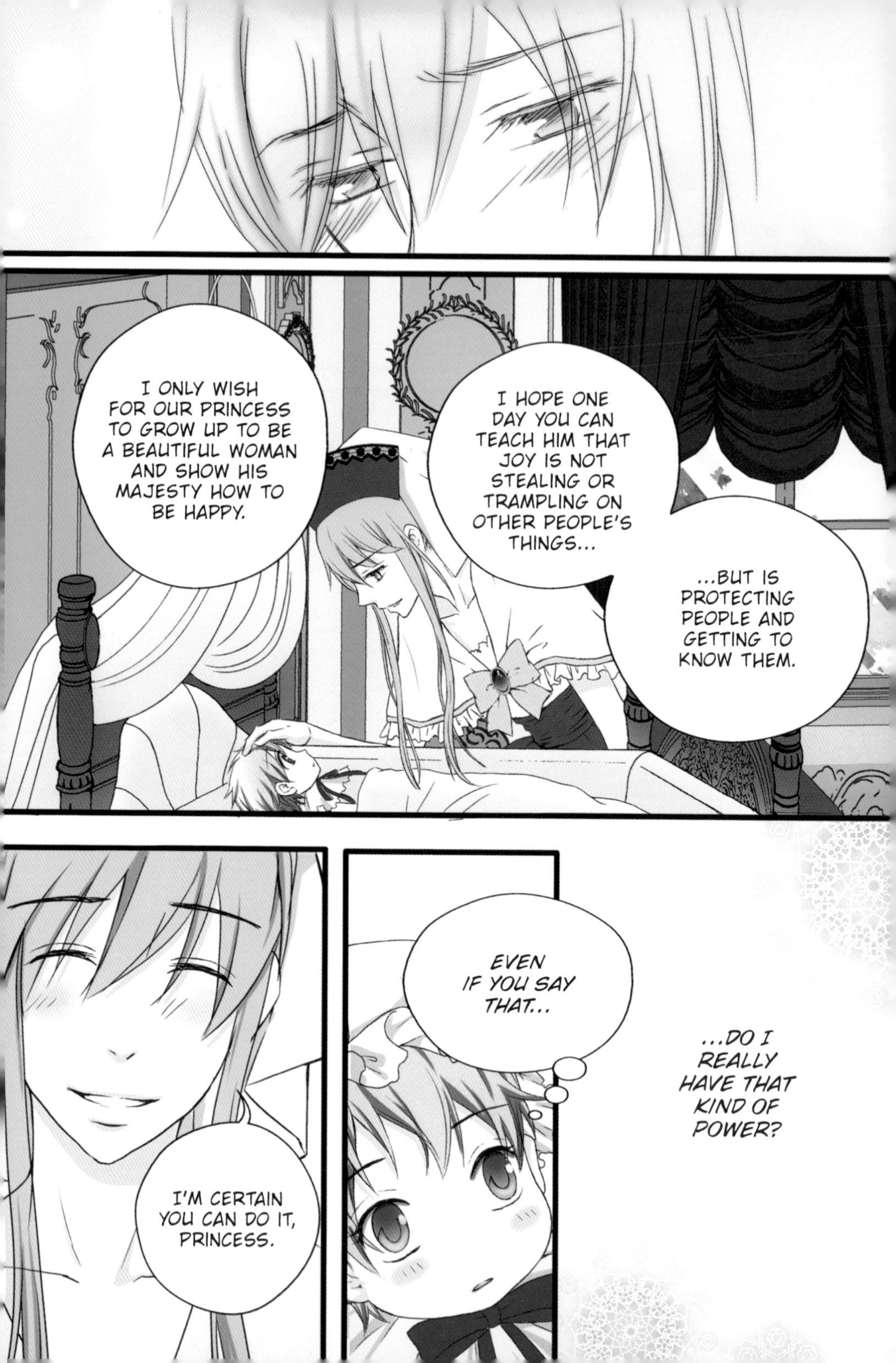
I ONLY WISH FOR OUR PRINCESS TO GROW UP TO BE A BEAUTIFUL WOMAN AND SHOW HIS MAJESTY HOW TO BE HAPPY.
I HOPE ONE DAY YOU CAN TEACH HIM THAT JOY IS NOT STEALING OR TRAMPLING ON OTHER PEOPLE'S THINGS...
...BUT IS PROTECTING PEOPLE AND GETTING TO KNOW THEM.
I'M CERTAIN YOU CAN DO IT, PRINCESS.
EVEN IF YOU SAY THAT...
...DO I REALLY HAVE THAT KIND OF POWER?

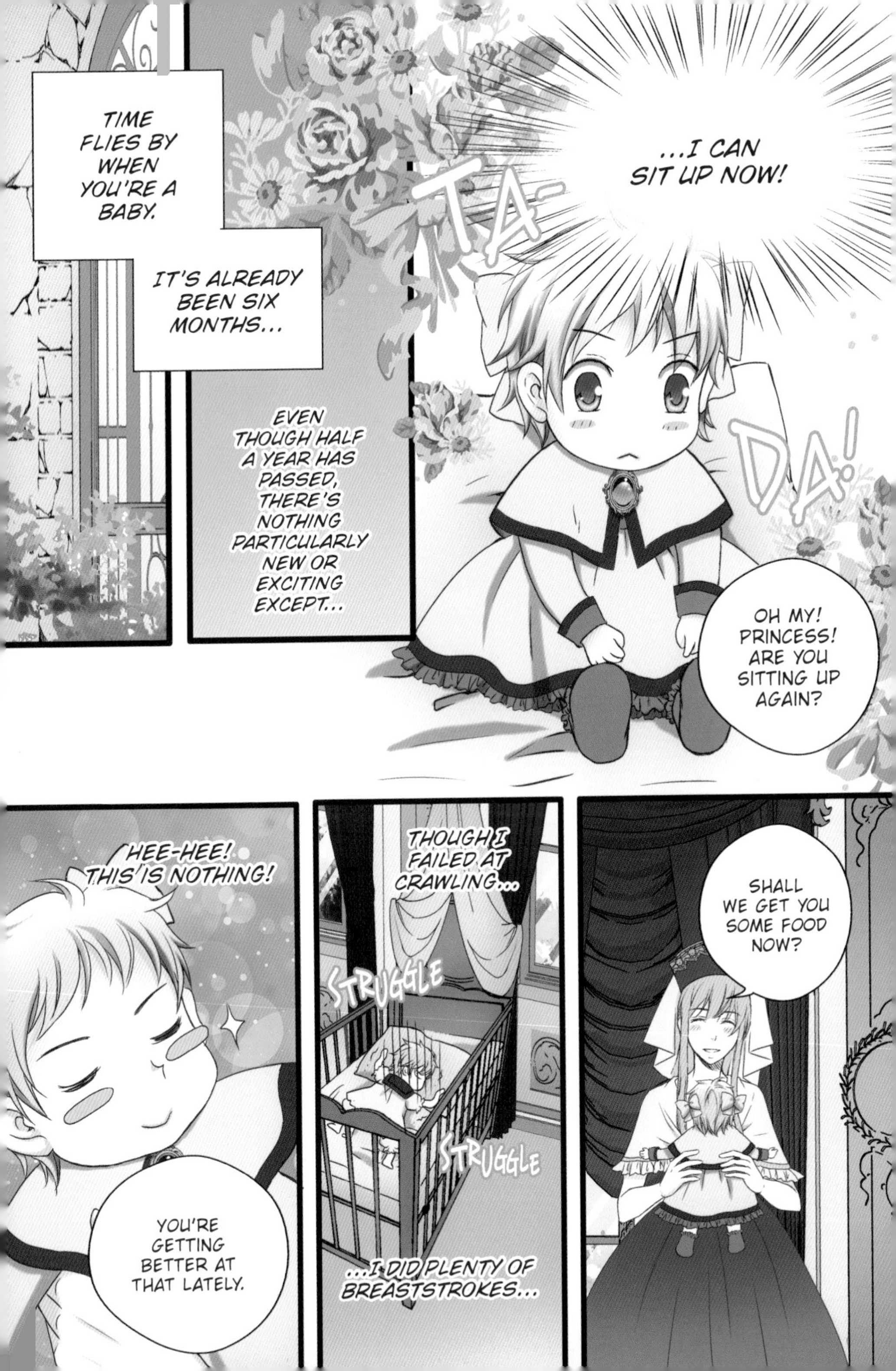

TIME FLIES BY WHEN YOU'RE A BABY.
IT'S ALREADY BEEN SIX MONTHS...
EVEN THOUGH HALF A YEAR HAS PASSED, THERE'S NOTHING PARTICULARLY NEW OR EXCITING EXCEPT...
TA-
...I CAN SIT UP NOW!
DA!
OH MY! PRINCESS! ARE YOU SITTING UP AGAIN?
HEE-HEE! THIS IS NOTHING!
YOU'RE GETTING BETTER AT THAT LATELY.
THOUGH I FAILED AT CRAWLING...
STRUGGLE
STRUGGLE
...I DID PLENTY OF BREASTSTROKES...
SHALL WE GET YOU SOME FOOD NOW?

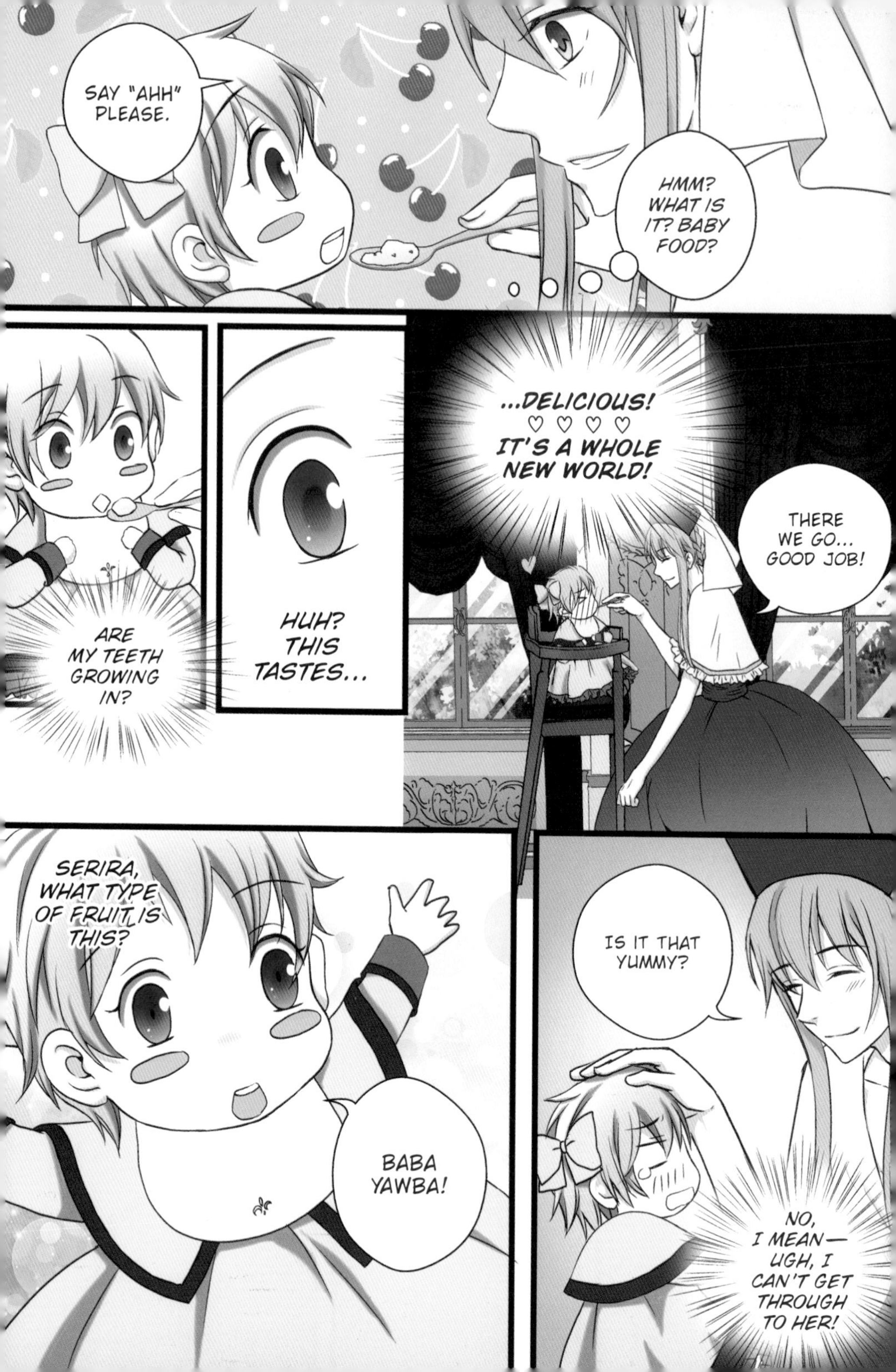
SAY "AHH" PLEASE.
HMM? WHAT IS IT? BABY FOOD?
ARE MY TEETH GROWING IN?
HUH? THIS TASTES...
...DELICIOUS! ♡ ♡ ♡ ♡ IT'S A WHOLE NEW WORLD!
THERE WE GO... GOOD JOB!
SERIRA, WHAT TYPE OF FRUIT IS THIS?
BABA YAWBA!
IS IT THAT YUMMY?
NO, I MEAN— UGH, I CAN'T GET THROUGH TO HER!

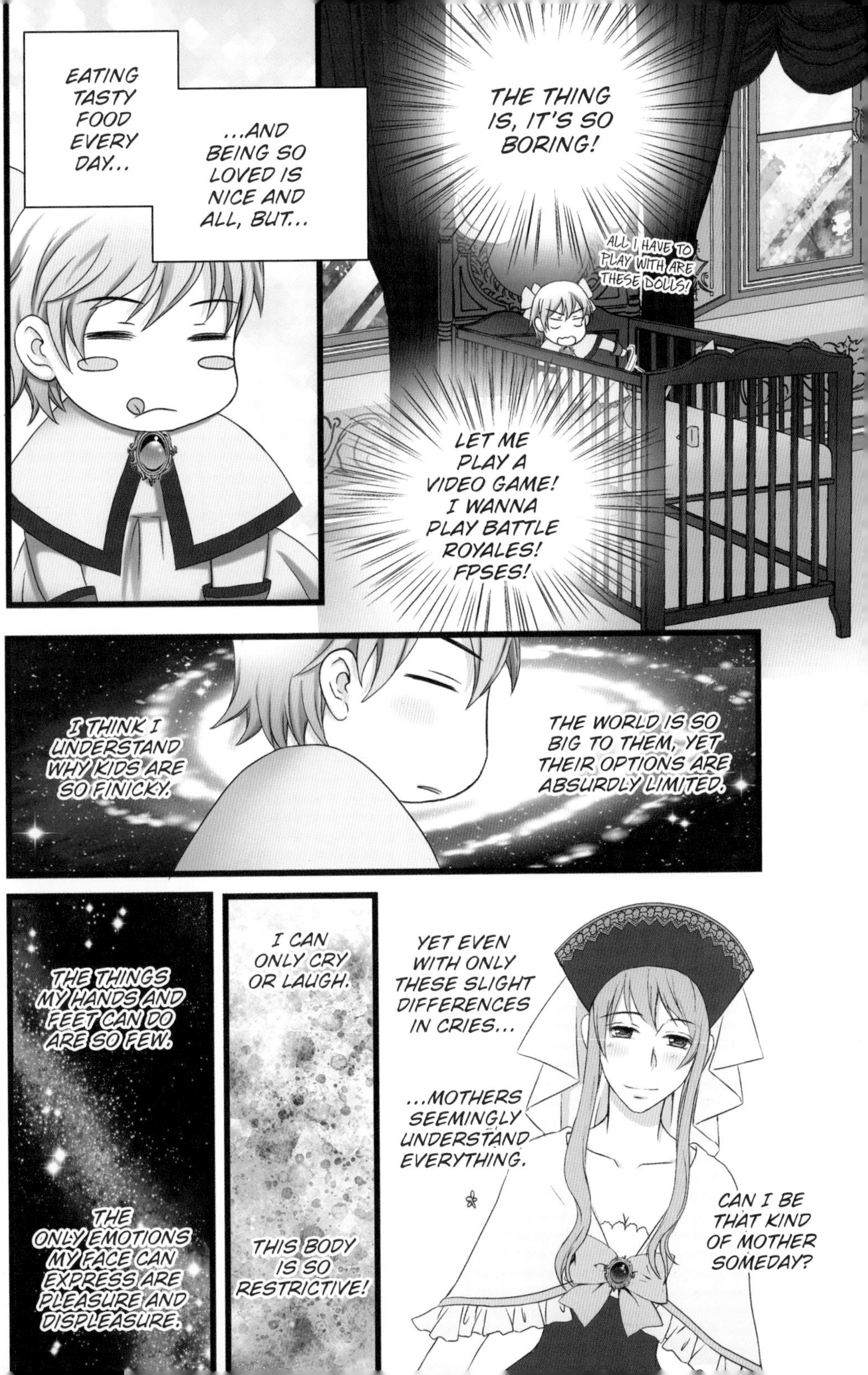
EATING TASTY FOOD EVERY DAY...
...AND BEING SO LOVED IS NICE AND ALL, BUT...
THE THING IS, IT'S SO BORING!
ALL I HAVE TO PLAY WITH ARE THESE DOLLS!
LET ME PLAY A VIDEO GAME! I WANNA PLAY BATTLE ROYALES! FPSES!
I THINK I UNDERSTAND WHY KIDS ARE SO FINICKY.
THE WORLD IS SO BIG TO THEM, YET THEIR OPTIONS ARE ABSURDLY LIMITED.
THE THINGS MY HANDS AND FEET CAN DO ARE SO FEW.
THE ONLY EMOTIONS MY FACE CAN EXPRESS ARE PLEASURE AND DISPLEASURE.
I CAN ONLY CRY OR LAUGH.
THIS BODY IS SO RESTRICTIVE!
YET EVEN WITH ONLY THESE SLIGHT DIFFERENCES IN CRIES...
...MOTHERS SEEMINGLY UNDERSTAND EVERYTHING.
CAN I BE THAT KIND OF MOTHER SOMEDAY?

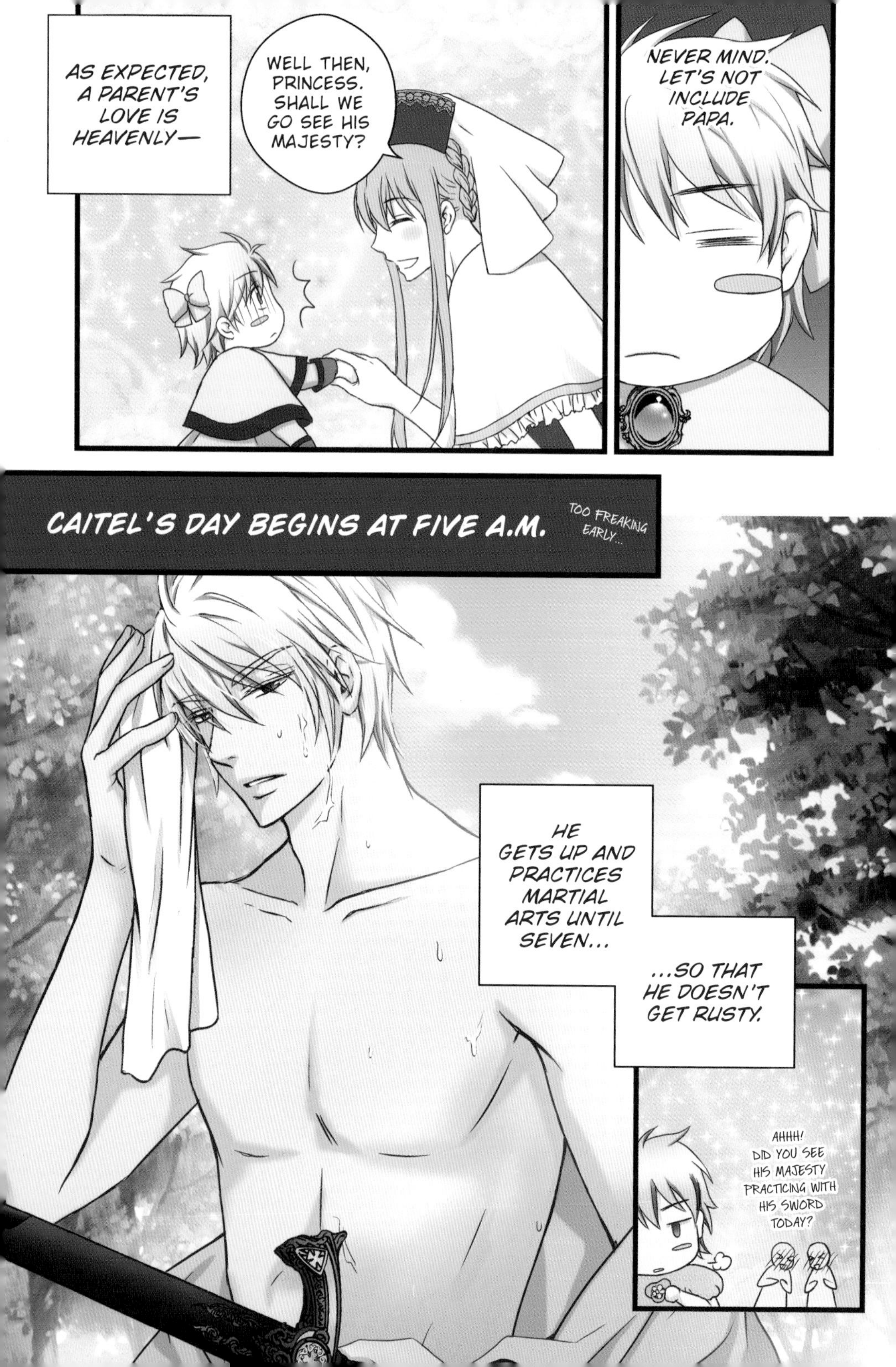
AS EXPECTED, A PARENT'S LOVE IS HEAVENLY—
WELL THEN, PRINCESS. SHALL WE GO SEE HIS MAJESTY?
NEVER MIND. LET'S NOT INCLUDE PAPA.
CAITEL'S DAY BEGINS AT FIVE A.M.
TOO FREAKING EARLY...
HE GETS UP AND PRACTICES MARTIAL ARTS UNTIL SEVEN...
...SO THAT HE DOESN'T GET RUSTY.
AHHH! DID YOU SEE HIS MAJESTY PRACTICING WITH HIS SWORD TODAY?

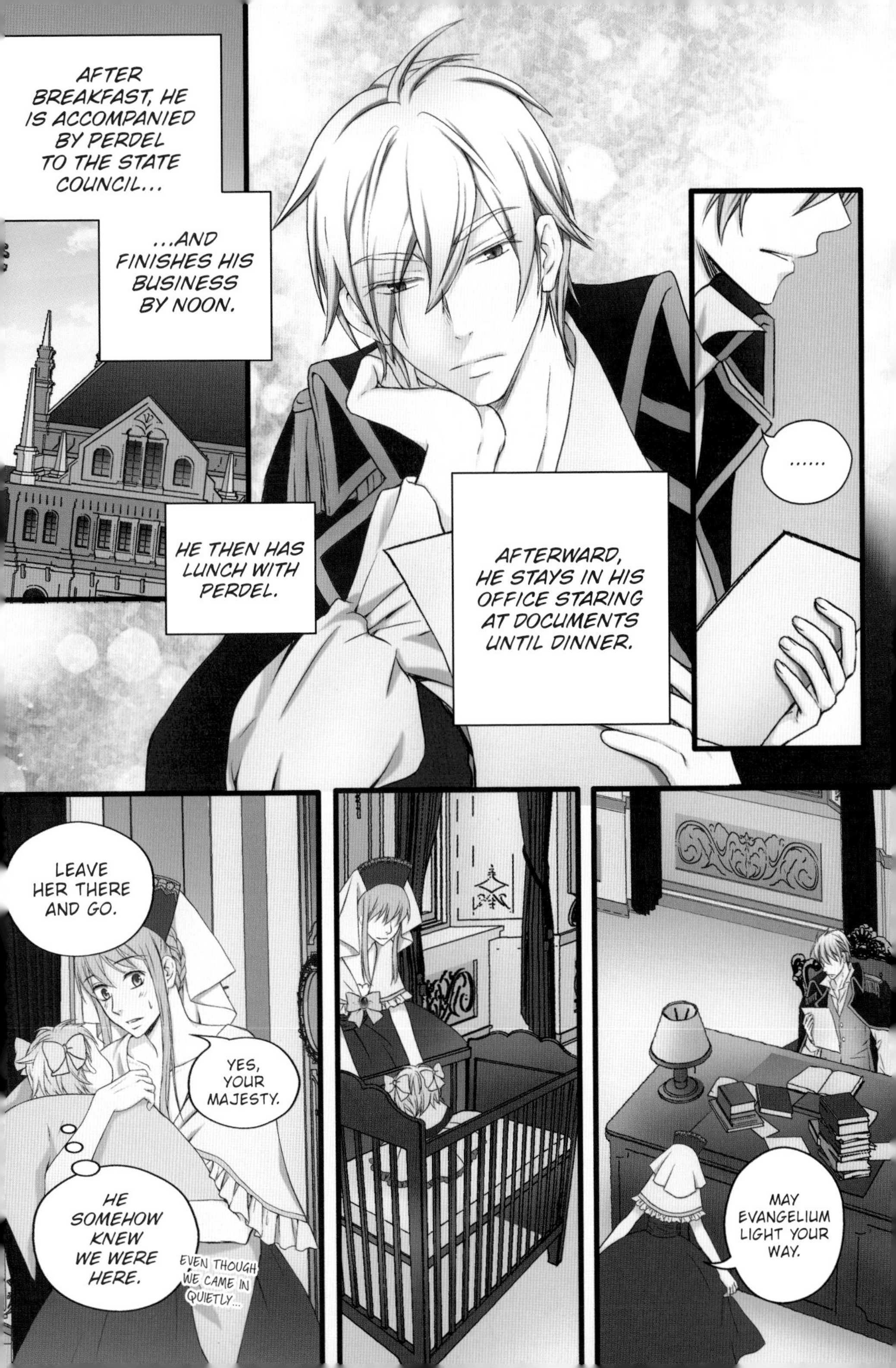
AFTER BREAKFAST, HE IS ACCOMPANIED BY PERDEL TO THE STATE COUNCIL...
...AND FINISHES HIS BUSINESS BY NOON.
HE THEN HAS LUNCH WITH PERDEL.
AFTERWARD, HE STAYS IN HIS OFFICE STARING AT DOCUMENTS UNTIL DINNER.
......
LEAVE HER THERE AND GO.
YES, YOUR MAJESTY.
HE SOMEHOW KNEW WE WERE HERE.
EVEN THOUGH WE CAME IN QUIETLY...
MAY EVANGELIUM LIGHT YOUR WAY.

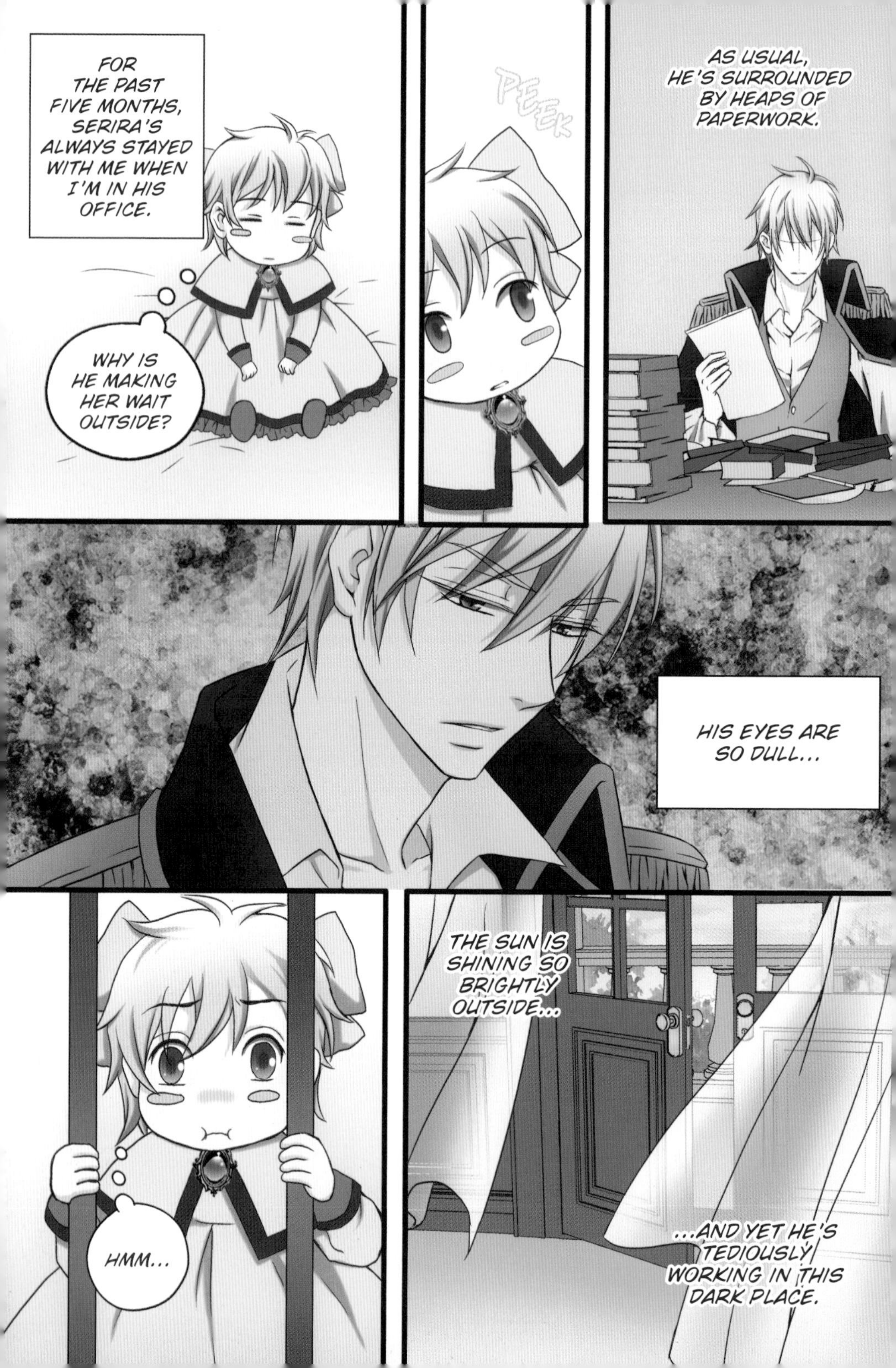
FOR THE PAST FIVE MONTHS, SERIRA'S ALWAYS STAYED WITH ME WHEN I'M IN HIS OFFICE.
WHY IS HE MAKING HER WAIT OUTSIDE?
PEEEK
AS USUAL, HE'S SURROUNDED BY HEAPS OF PAPERWORK.
HIS EYES ARE SO DULL...
HMM...
THE SUN IS SHINING SO BRIGHTLY OUTSIDE...
...AND YET HE'S TEDIOUSLY WORKING IN THIS DARK PLACE.

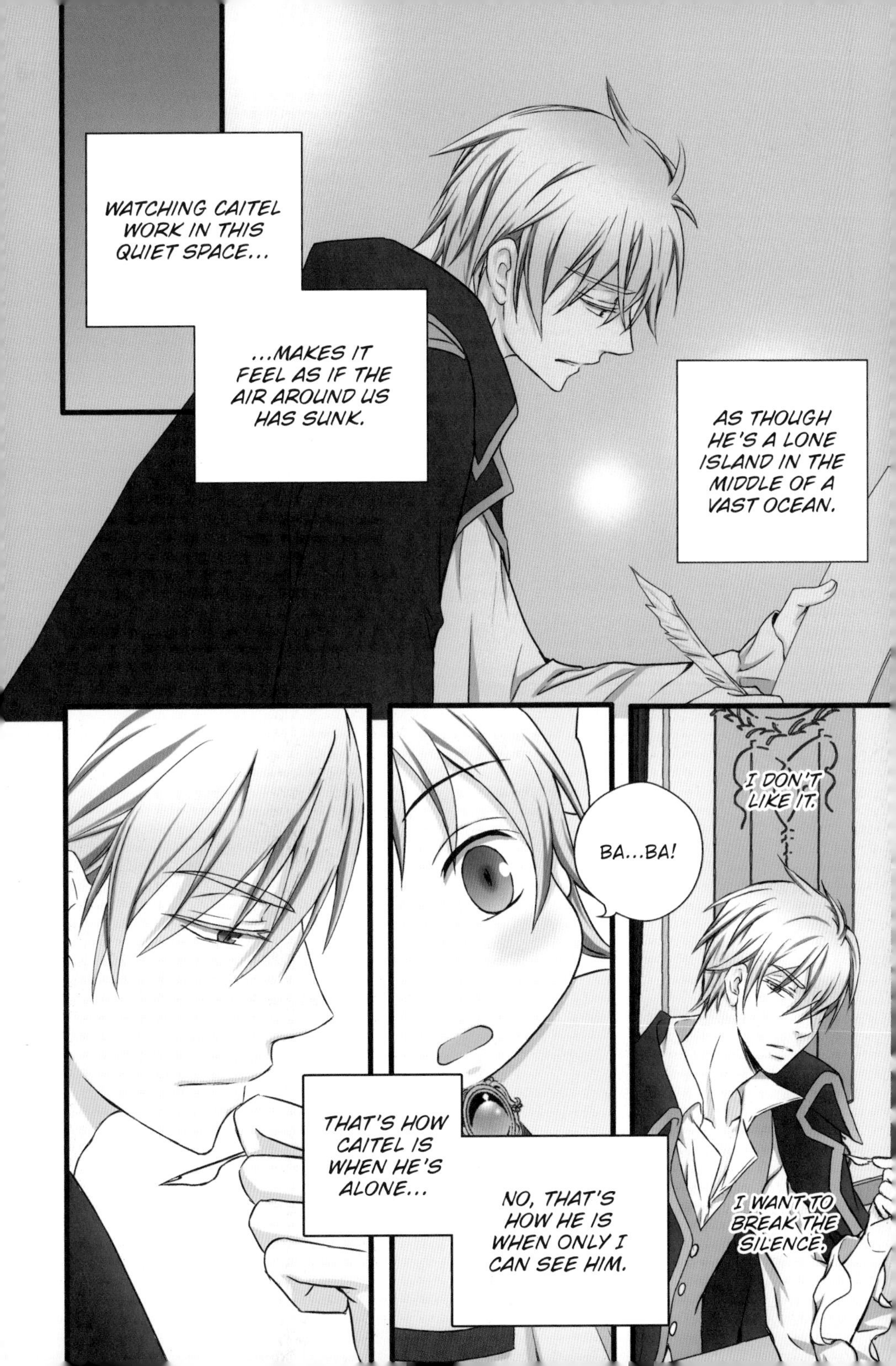
WATCHING CAITEL WORK IN THIS QUIET SPACE...
...MAKES IT FEEL AS IF THE AIR AROUND US HAS SUNK.
AS THOUGH HE'S A LONE ISLAND IN THE MIDDLE OF A VAST OCEAN.
BA...BA!
THAT'S HOW CAITEL IS WHEN HE'S ALONE...
NO, THAT'S HOW HE IS WHEN ONLY I CAN SEE HIM.
I DON'T LIKE IT.
I WANT TO BREAK THE SILENCE.

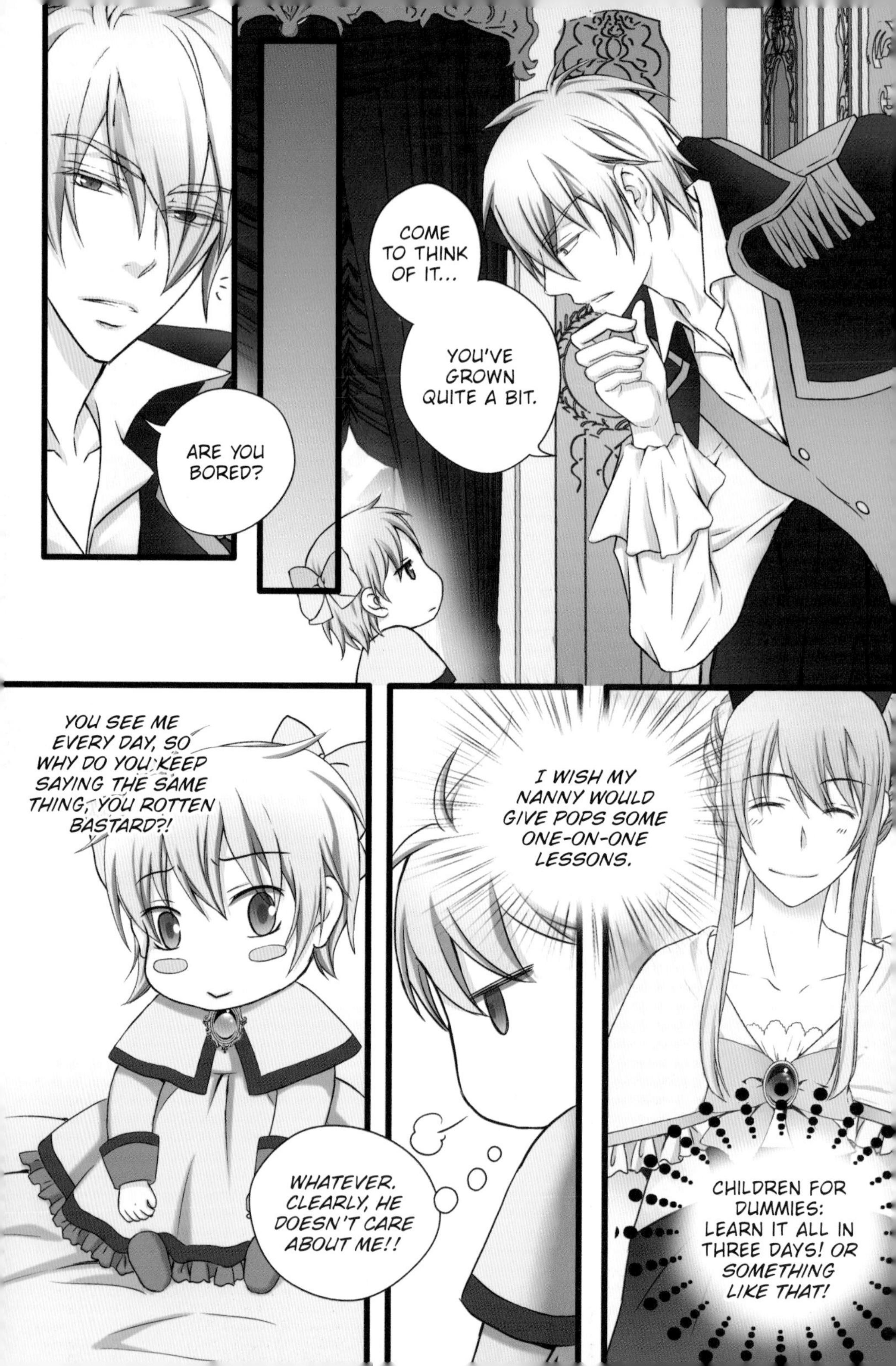
ARE YOU BORED?
COME TO THINK OF IT...
YOU'VE GROWN QUITE A BIT.
YOU SEE ME EVERY DAY, SO WHY DO YOU KEEP SAYING THE SAME THING, YOU ROTTEN BASTARD?!
WHATEVER. CLEARLY, HE DOESN'T CARE ABOUT ME!!
I WISH MY NANNY WOULD GIVE POPS SOME ONE-ON-ONE LESSONS.
CHILDREN FOR DUMMIES: LEARN IT ALL IN THREE DAYS! OR SOMETHING LIKE THAT!

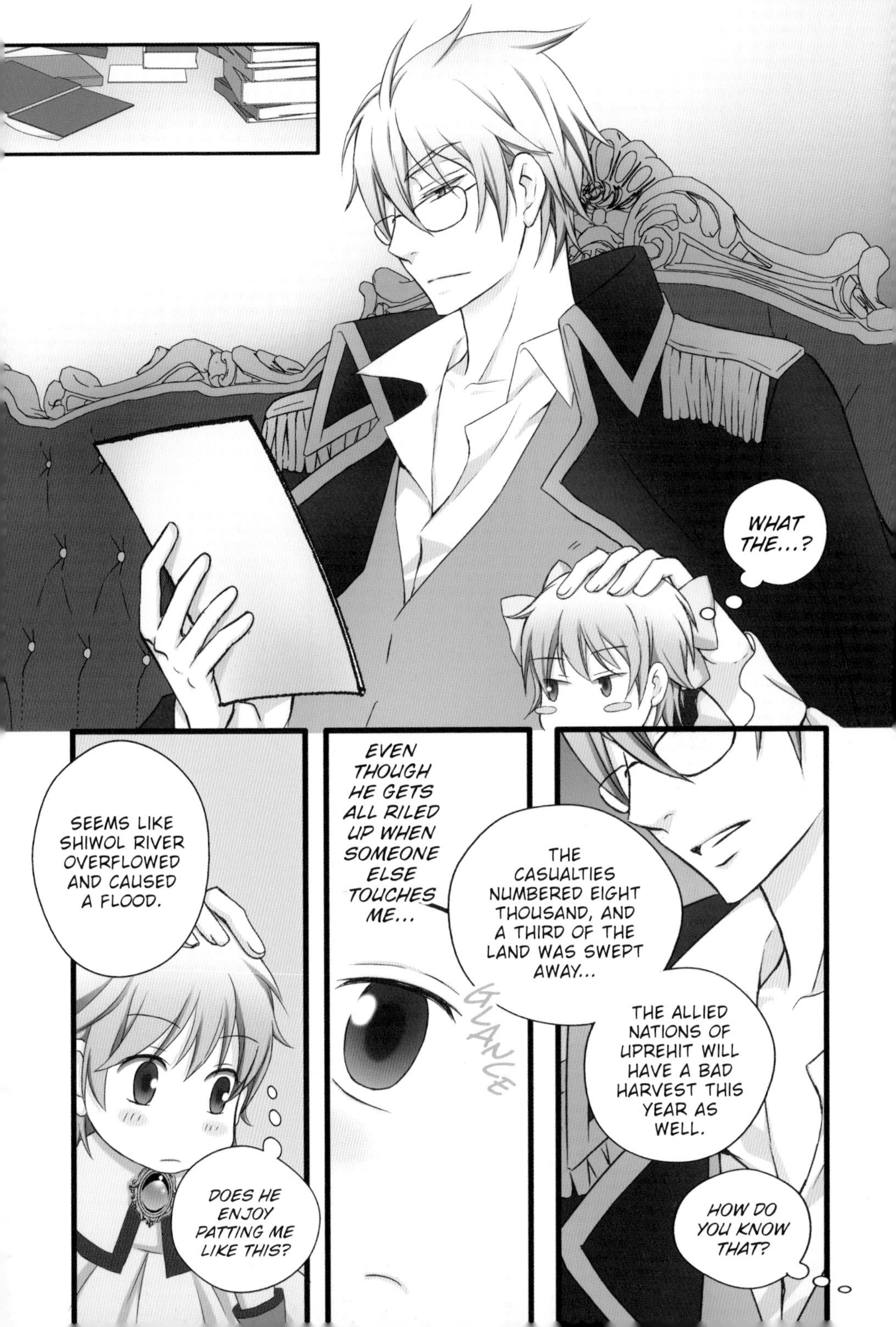
WHAT THE...?
SEEMS LIKE SHIWOL RIVER OVERFLOWED AND CAUSED A FLOOD.
DOES HE ENJOY PATTING ME LIKE THIS?
EVEN THOUGH HE GETS ALL RILED UP WHEN SOMEONE ELSE TOUCHES ME...
GLANCE
THE CASUALTIES NUMBERED EIGHT THOUSAND, AND A THIRD OF THE LAND WAS SWEPT AWAY...
THE ALLIED NATIONS OF UPREHIT WILL HAVE A BAD HARVEST THIS YEAR AS WELL.
HOW DO YOU KNOW THAT?

YOU'RE TALKING TO A KID WHO DOESN'T KNOW WHAT COVENTRY IS.

IF I CAN PROVOKE THEIR NEIGHBORING COUNTRY, COVENTRY, I MIGHT BE ABLE TO CONQUER THEIR TERRITORY QUITE EASILY.

NOT BAD, HUH?

GAZE

...SINCE WE'VE ENDED UP SEEING EACH OTHER SO FREQUENTLY, THERE'S NO POINT IN FAKE SMILING AT CAITEL.

I DID SO IN THE BEGINNING BECAUSE I THOUGHT MY LIFE WAS GOING TO END...

...BUT SURPRISINGLY, HE DOESN'T GO WILD AND THREATEN TO KILL ME ANYMORE.

SO I'VE GOTTEN BRAVER AND USUALLY JUST SIT HERE LOOKING EMOTIONLESS.

SMILING TAKES SO MUCH EFFORT.

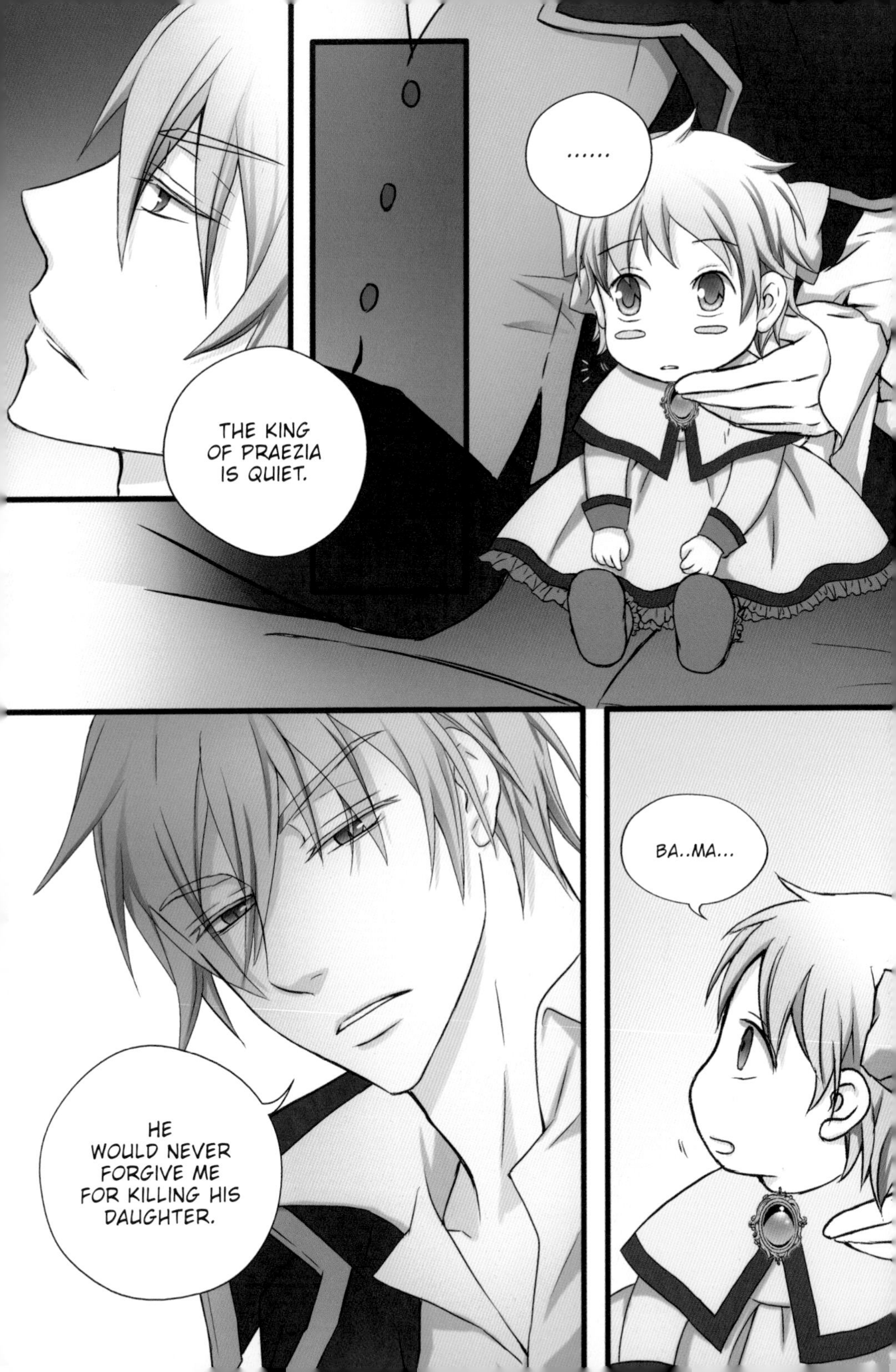
THE KING OF PRAEZIA IS QUIET.
......
HE WOULD NEVER FORGIVE ME FOR KILLING HIS DAUGHTER.
BA..MA...

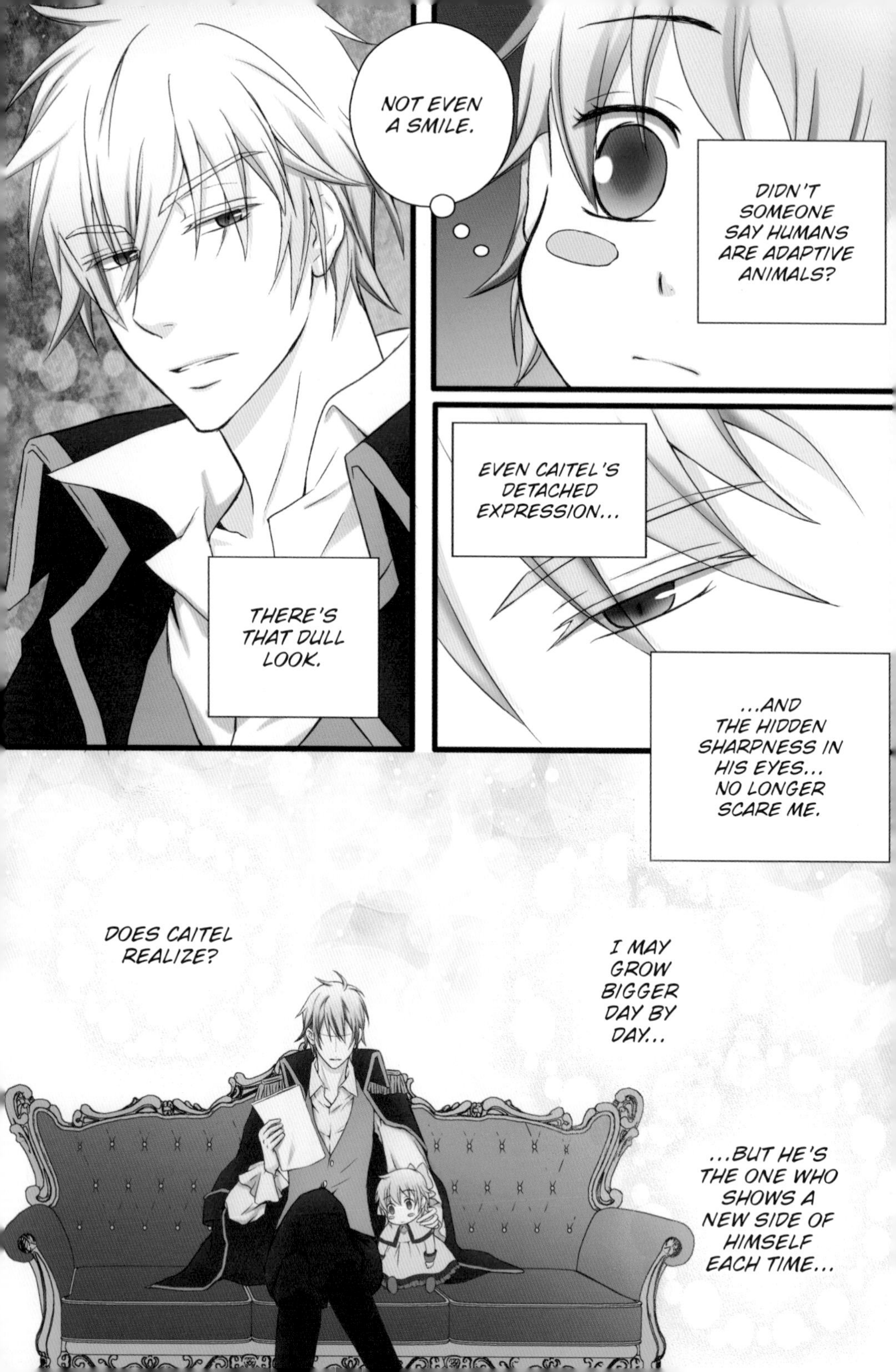
THERE'S THAT DULL LOOK.
NOT EVEN A SMILE.
DIDN'T SOMEONE SAY HUMANS ARE ADAPTIVE ANIMALS?
EVEN CAITEL'S DETACHED EXPRESSION...
...AND THE HIDDEN SHARPNESS IN HIS EYES... NO LONGER SCARE ME.
DOES CAITEL REALIZE?
I MAY GROW BIGGER DAY BY DAY...
...BUT HE'S THE ONE WHO SHOWS A NEW SIDE OF HIMSELF EACH TIME...

You're My Papa! (2)

DAUGHTER
OF THE
EMPEROR

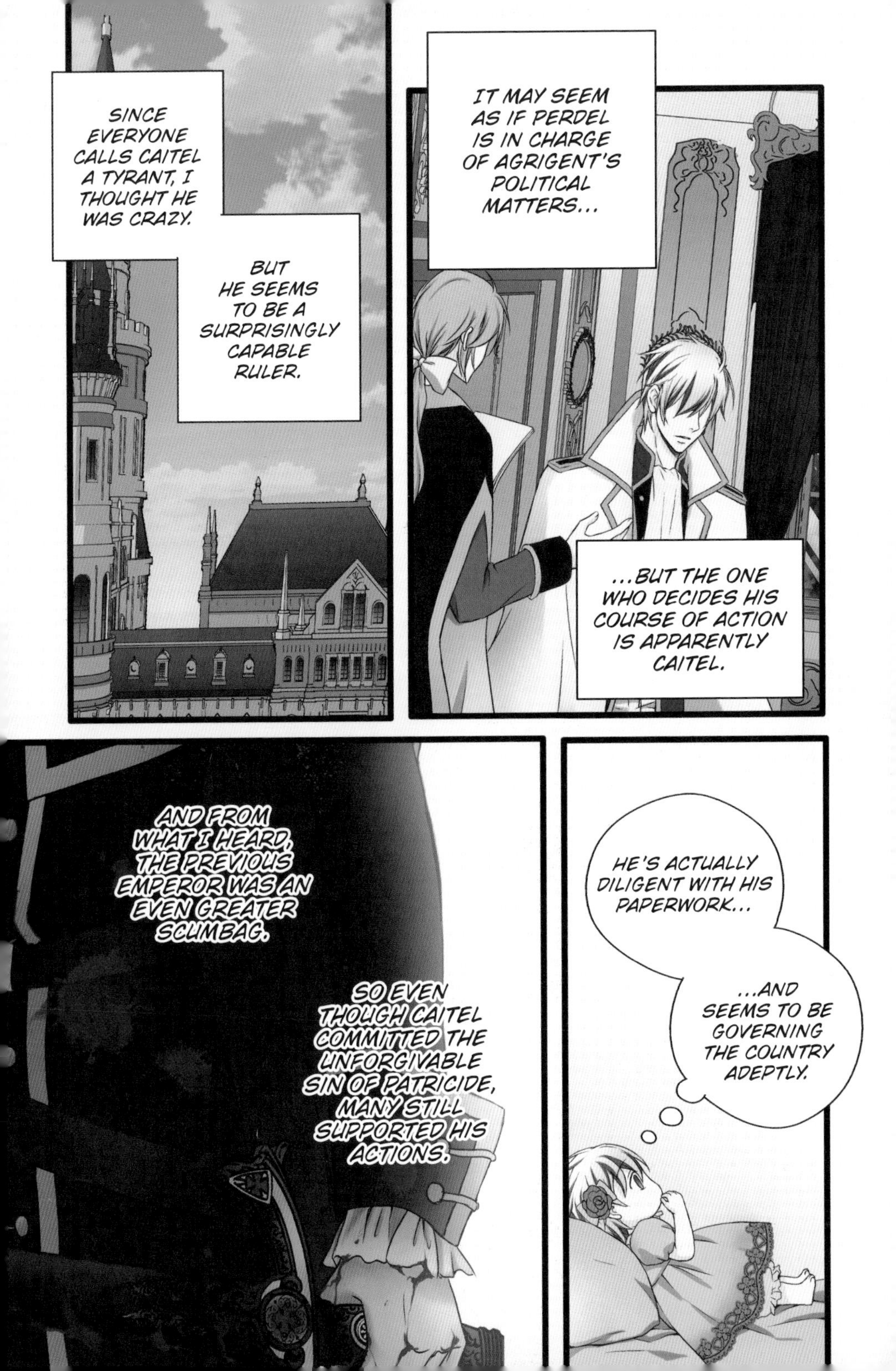
SINCE EVERYONE CALLS CAITEL A TYRANT, I THOUGHT HE WAS CRAZY.
BUT HE SEEMS TO BE A SURPRISINGLY CAPABLE RULER.
IT MAY SEEM AS IF PERDEL IS IN CHARGE OF AGRIGENT'S POLITICAL MATTERS...
...BUT THE ONE WHO DECIDES HIS COURSE OF ACTION IS APPARENTLY CAITEL.
AND FROM WHAT I HEARD, THE PREVIOUS EMPEROR WAS AN EVEN GREATER SCUMBAG.
SO EVEN THOUGH CAITEL COMMITTED THE UNFORGIVABLE SIN OF PATRICIDE, MANY STILL SUPPORTED HIS ACTIONS.
HE'S ACTUALLY DILIGENT WITH HIS PAPERWORK...
...AND SEEMS TO BE GOVERNING THE COUNTRY ADEPTLY.

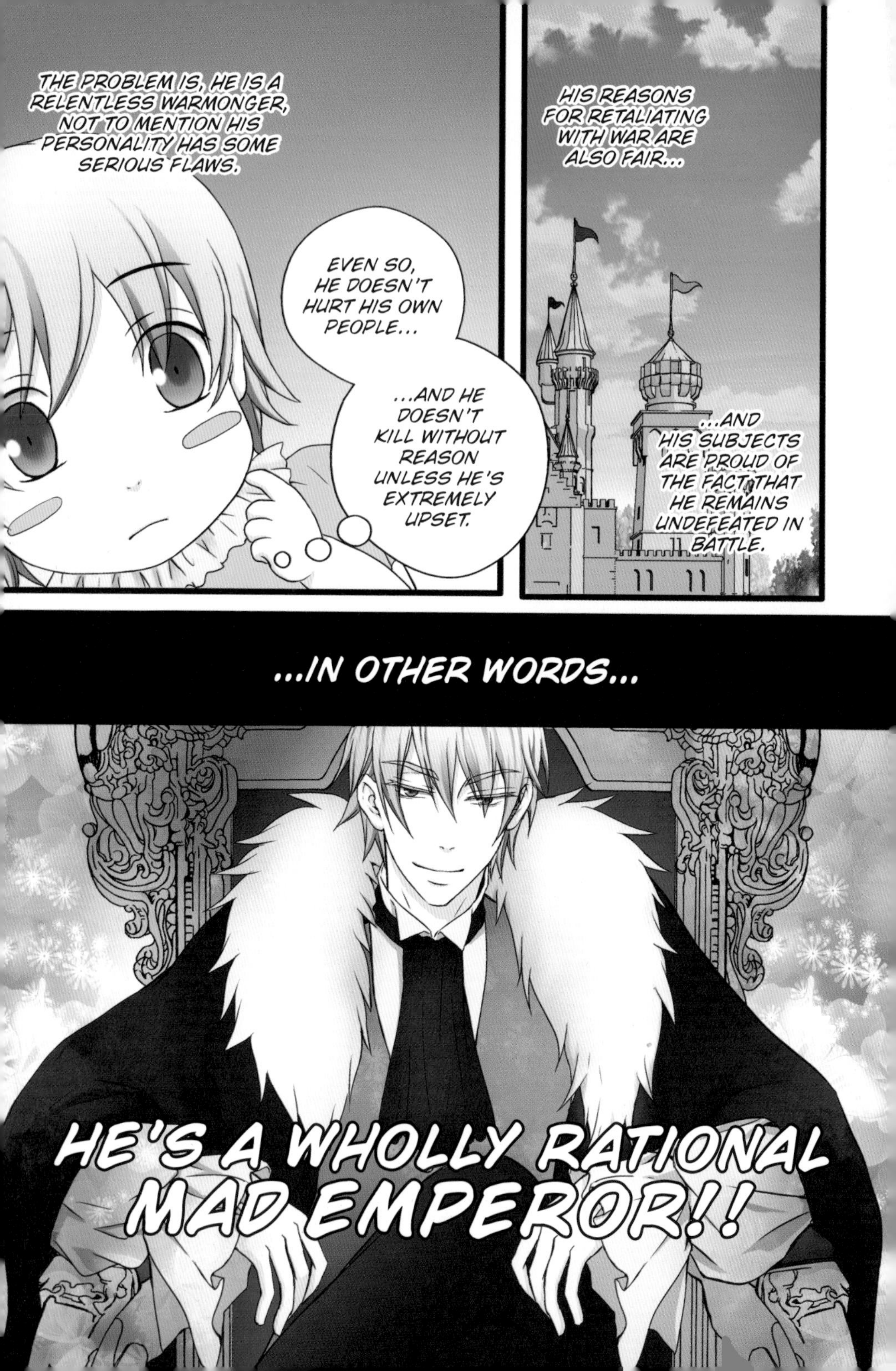
HIS REASONS FOR RETALIATING WITH WAR ARE ALSO FAIR...
...AND HIS SUBJECTS ARE PROUD OF THE FACT THAT HE REMAINS UNDEFEATED IN BATTLE.
THE PROBLEM IS, HE IS A RELENTLESS WARMONGER, NOT TO MENTION HIS PERSONALITY HAS SOME SERIOUS FLAWS.
EVEN SO, HE DOESN'T HURT HIS OWN PEOPLE...
...AND HE DOESN'T KILL WITHOUT REASON UNLESS HE'S EXTREMELY UPSET.
...IN OTHER WORDS...
HE'S A WHOLLY RATIONAL MAD EMPEROR!!

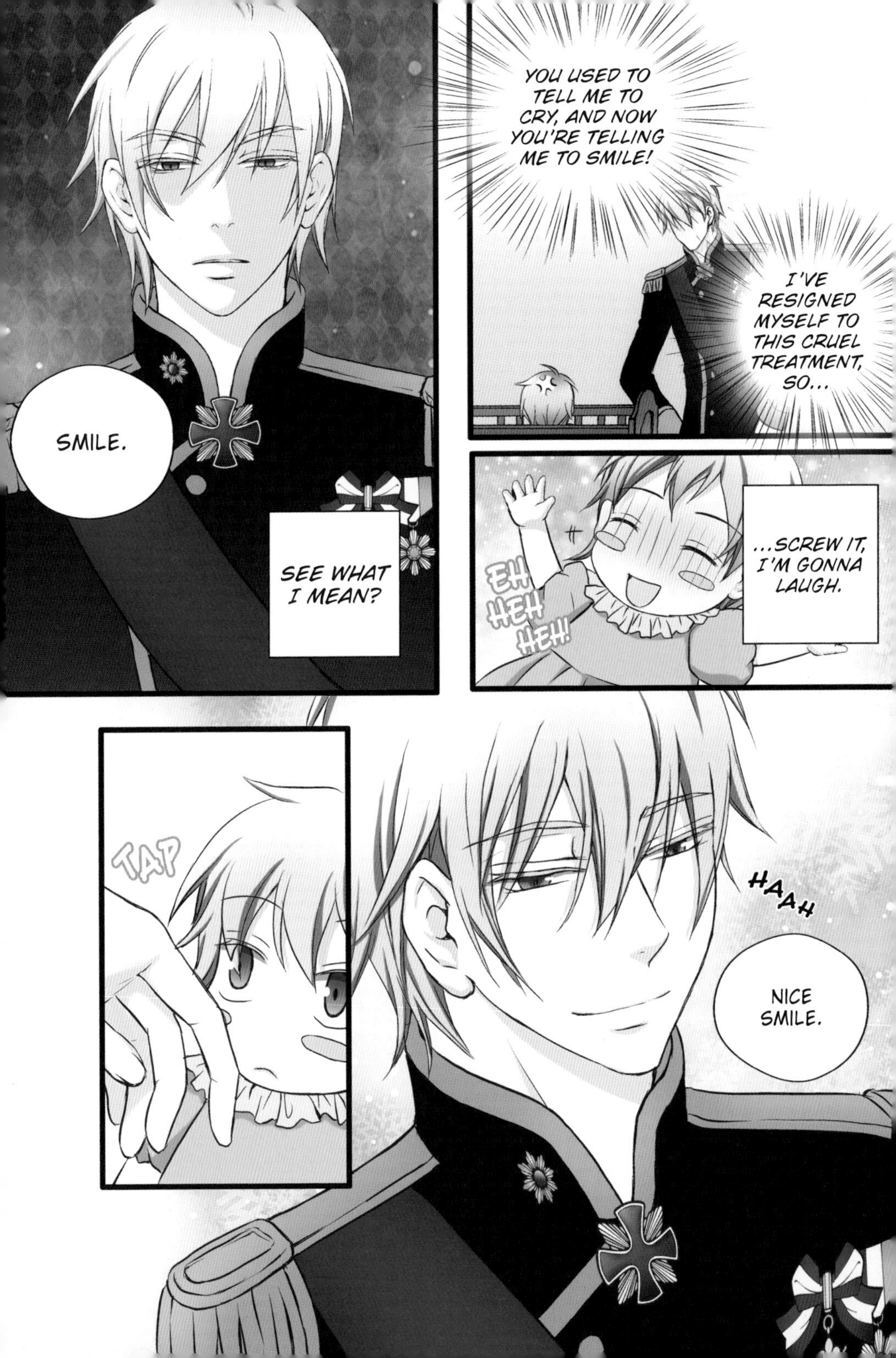
SMILE.
SEE WHAT I MEAN?
YOU USED TO TELL ME TO CRY, AND NOW YOU'RE TELLING ME TO SMILE!
I'VE RESIGNED MYSELF TO THIS CRUEL TREATMENT, SO...
EH HEH HEH!
...SCREW IT, I'M GONNA LAUGH.
TAP
HAAH
NICE SMILE.

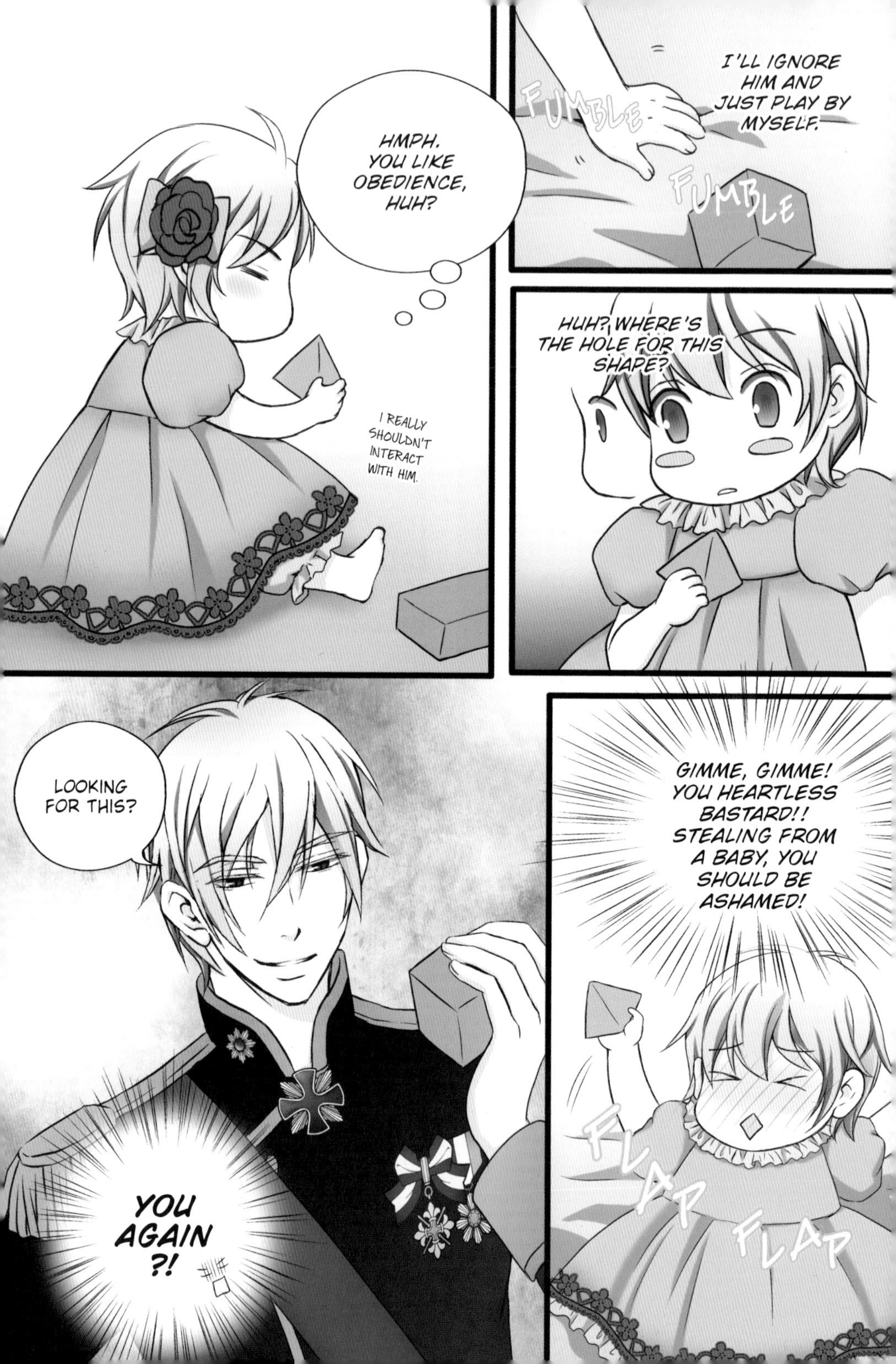
HMPH. YOU LIKE OBEDIENCE, HUH?
I REALLY SHOULDN'T INTERACT WITH HIM.
I'LL IGNORE HIM AND JUST PLAY BY MYSELF.
FUMBLE
FUMBLE
HUH? WHERE'S THE HOLE FOR THIS SHAPE?
LOOKING FOR THIS?
YOU AGAIN ?!
GIMME, GIMME! YOU HEARTLESS BASTARD!! STEALING FROM A BABY, YOU SHOULD BE ASHAMED!
FLAP
FLAP

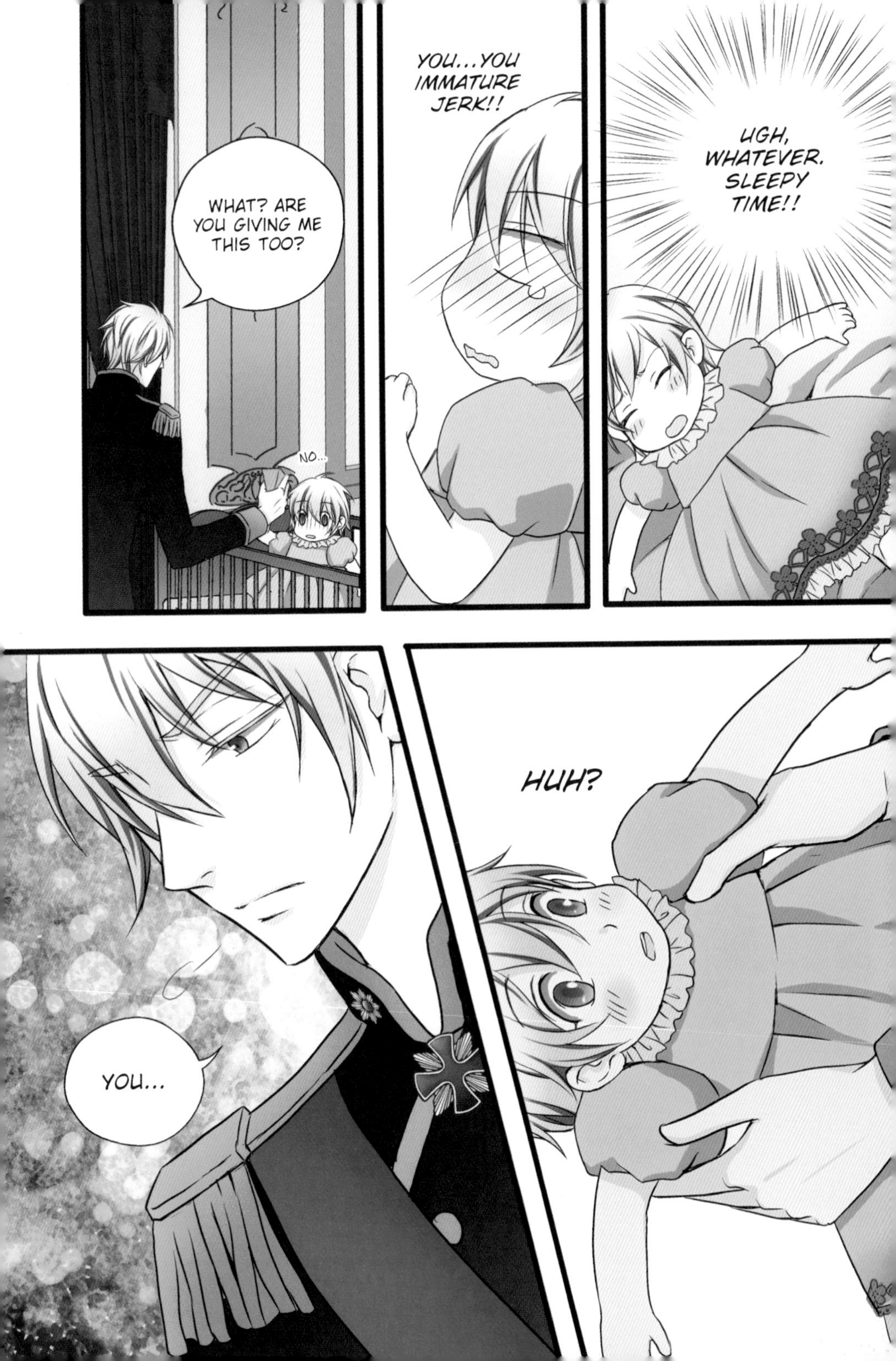
WHAT? ARE YOU GIVING ME THIS TOO?
NO...
YOU...YOU IMMATURE JERK!!
UGH, WHATEVER. SLEEPY TIME!!
YOU...
HUH?

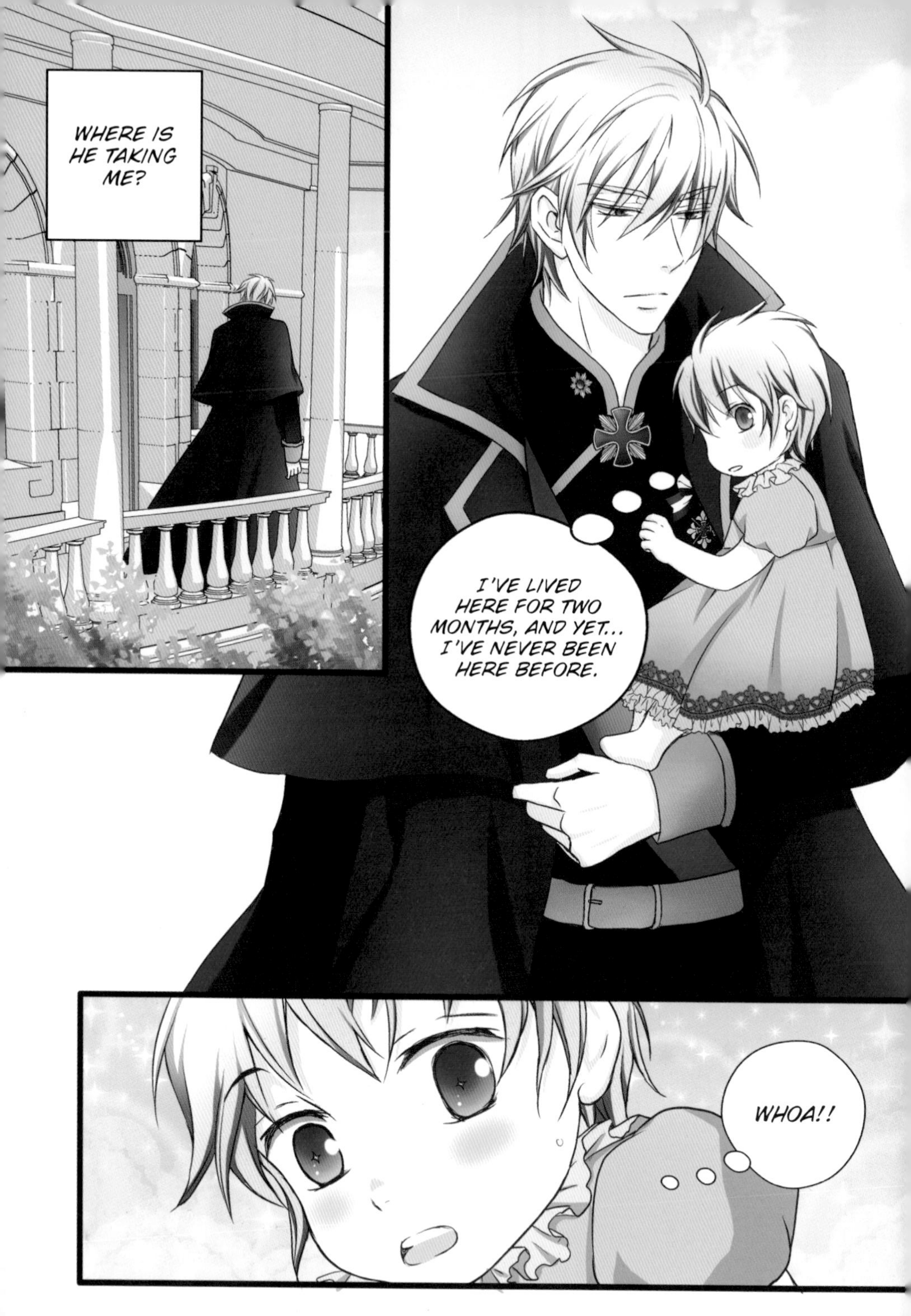
WHERE IS HE TAKING ME?
I'VE LIVED HERE FOR TWO MONTHS, AND YET... I'VE NEVER BEEN HERE BEFORE.
WHOA!!

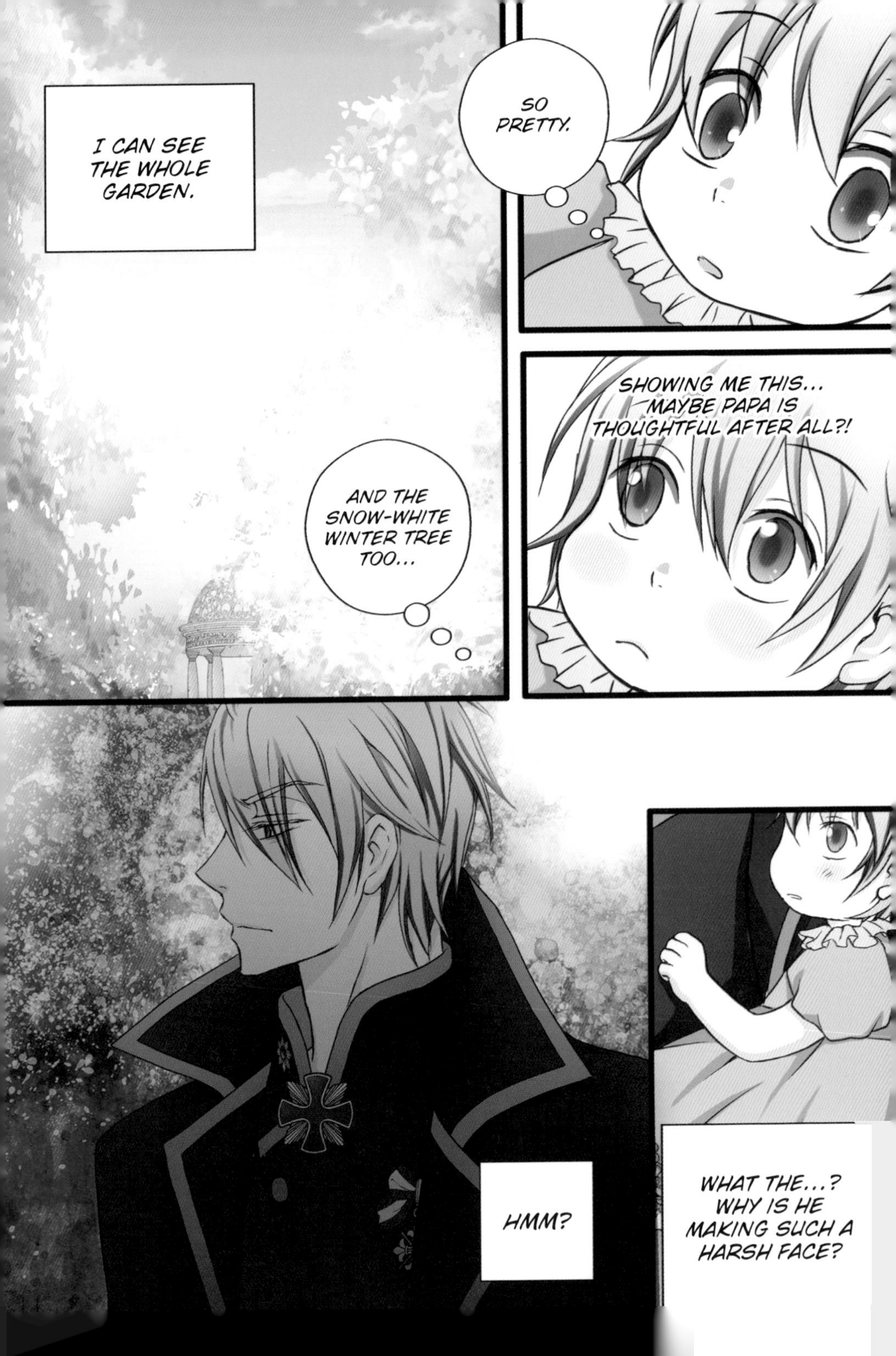
I CAN SEE THE WHOLE GARDEN.
AND THE SNOW-WHITE WINTER TREE TOO...
SO PRETTY.
SHOWING ME THIS... MAYBE PAPA IS THOUGHTFUL AFTER ALL?!
HMM?
WHAT THE...? WHY IS HE MAKING SUCH A HARSH FACE?

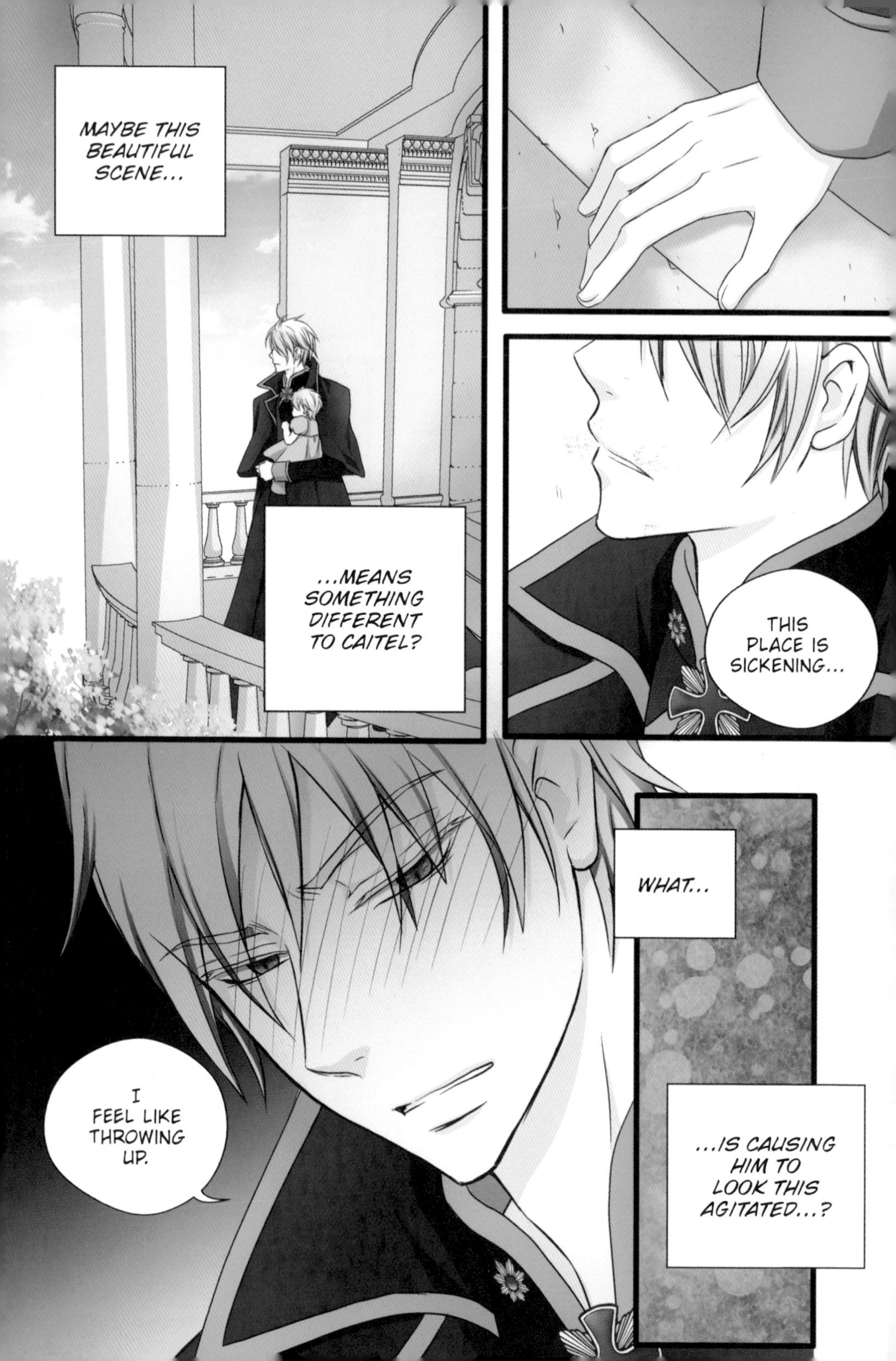
MAYBE THIS BEAUTIFUL SCENE...
...MEANS SOMETHING DIFFERENT TO CAITEL?
THIS PLACE IS SICKENING...
WHAT...
I FEEL LIKE THROWING UP.
...IS CAUSING HIM TO LOOK THIS AGITATED...?

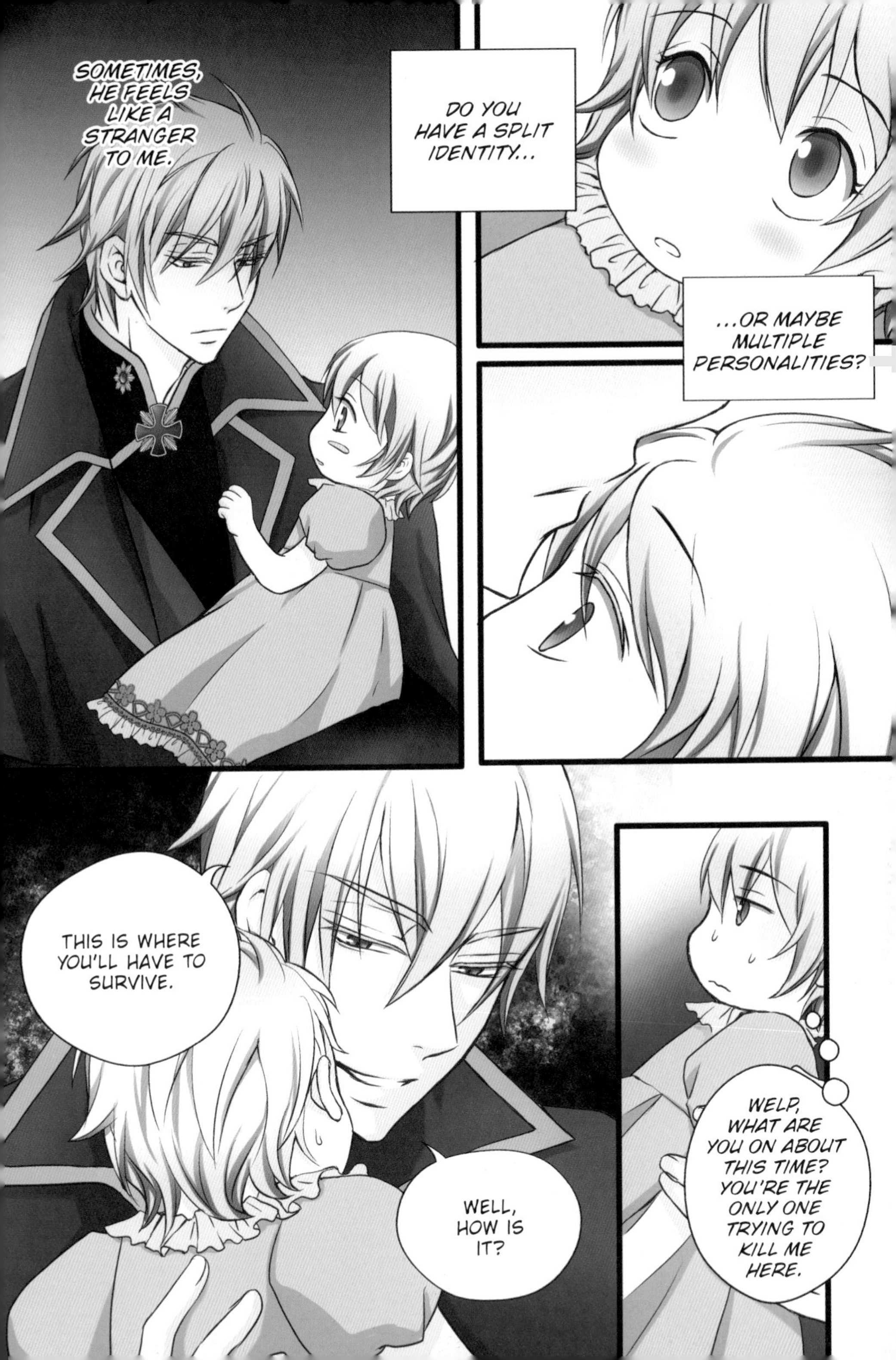
SOMETIMES, HE FEELS LIKE A STRANGER TO ME.
DO YOU HAVE A SPLIT IDENTITY...
...OR MAYBE MULTIPLE PERSONALITIES?
THIS IS WHERE YOU'LL HAVE TO SURVIVE.
WELL, HOW IS IT?
WELP, WHAT ARE YOU ON ABOUT THIS TIME? YOU'RE THE ONLY ONE TRYING TO KILL ME HERE.

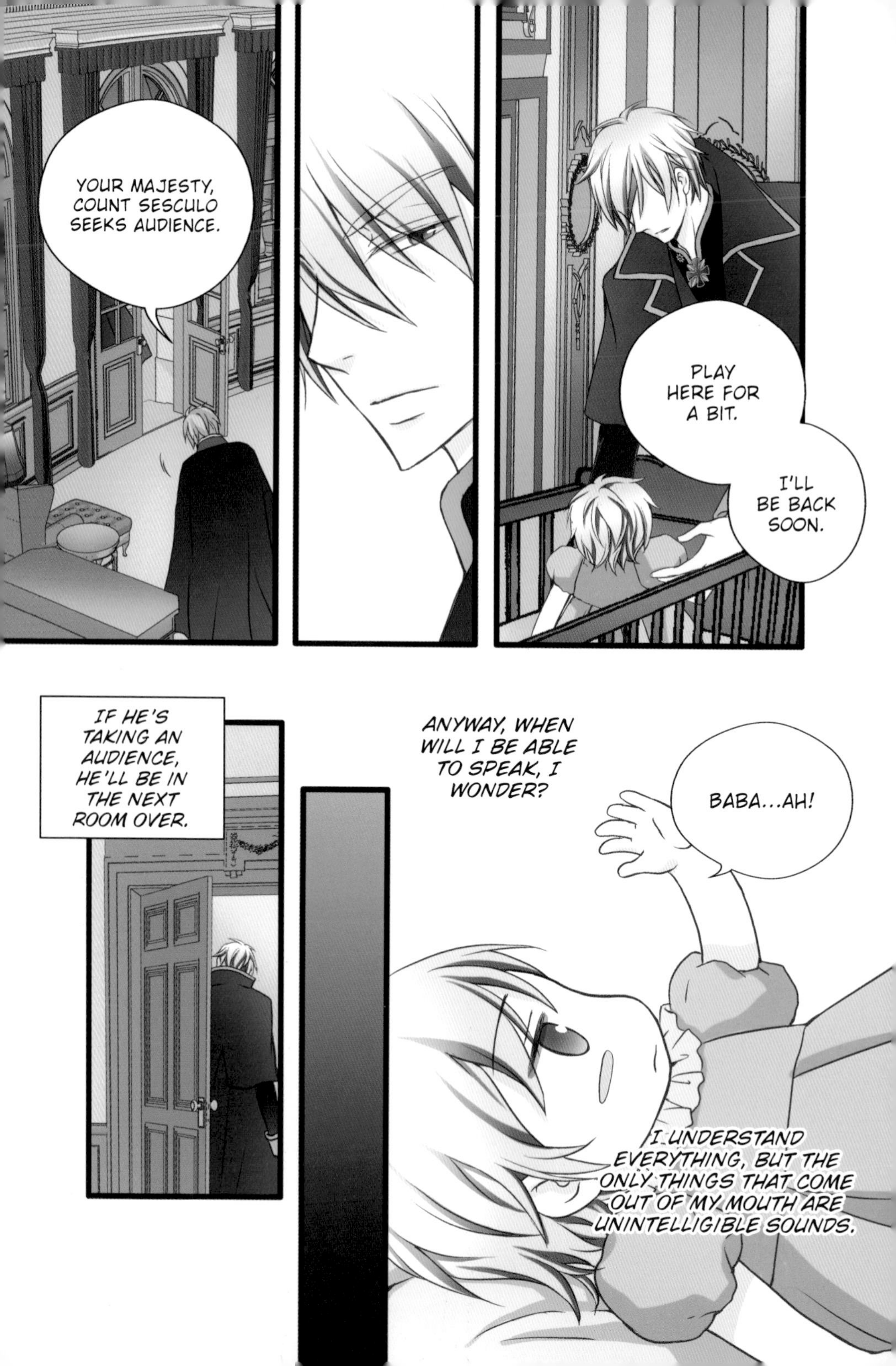
YOUR MAJESTY, COUNT SESCULO SEEKS AUDIENCE.
PLAY HERE FOR A BIT.
I'LL BE BACK SOON.
IF HE'S TAKING AN AUDIENCE, HE'LL BE IN THE NEXT ROOM OVER.
ANYWAY, WHEN WILL I BE ABLE TO SPEAK, I WONDER?
BABA...AH!
I UNDERSTAND EVERYTHING, BUT THE ONLY THINGS THAT COME OUT OF MY MOUTH ARE UNINTELLIGIBLE SOUNDS.

THOUGH ACCORDING TO MY NANNY, I'LL IMPROVE IF I PRACTICE, RIGHT? SERIRA WOULDN'T LIE.

HUH?

CREEEEAK

I'LL KEEP PRACTICING SO THAT I CAN CALL MY LUNATIC FATHER A CRAZED BASTARD.

RUSTLE

TA-DAA!

A MAID MUST BE HERE TO CLEAN.

ANYWAY, TIME TO FOCUS ON MY TOES!

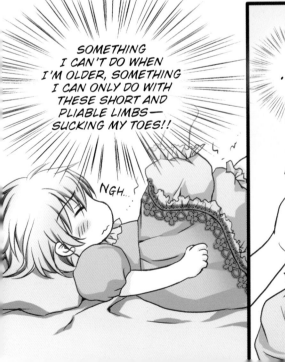

SOMETHING I CAN'T DO WHEN I'M OLDER, SOMETHING I CAN ONLY DO WITH THESE SHORT AND PLIABLE LIMBS— SUCKING MY TOES!!

NGH...

...?!

OH? I DID IT! WOW, I REALLY DID IT!

THIS IS THE FLEXIBILITY OF A BABY!! MY THIGH DOESN'T EVEN FEEL STRAINED!

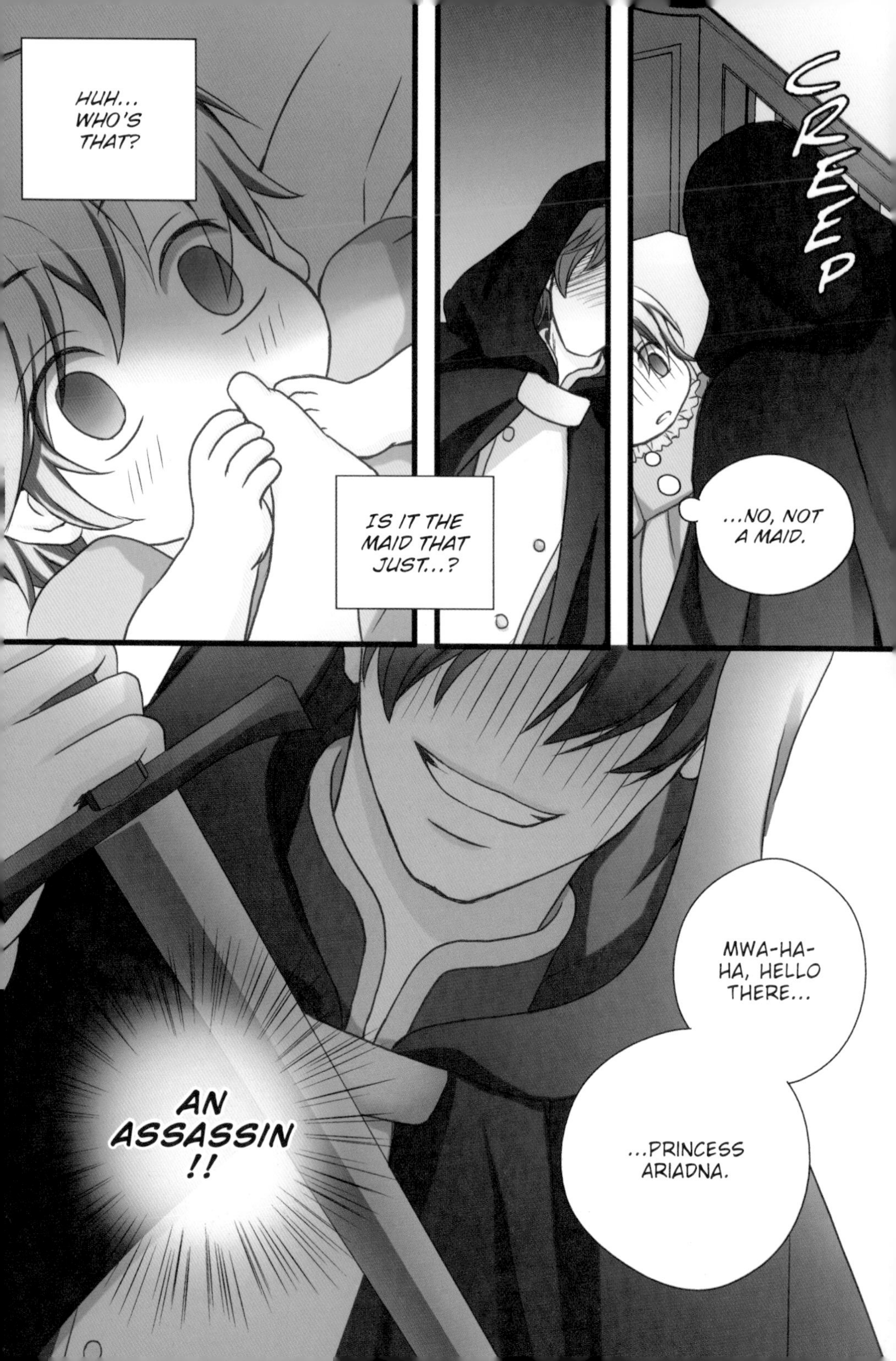
HUH... WHO'S THAT?
IS IT THE MAID THAT JUST...?
CREEP
...NO, NOT A MAID.
MWA-HA-HA, HELLO THERE...
...PRINCESS ARIADNA.
AN ASSASSIN!!

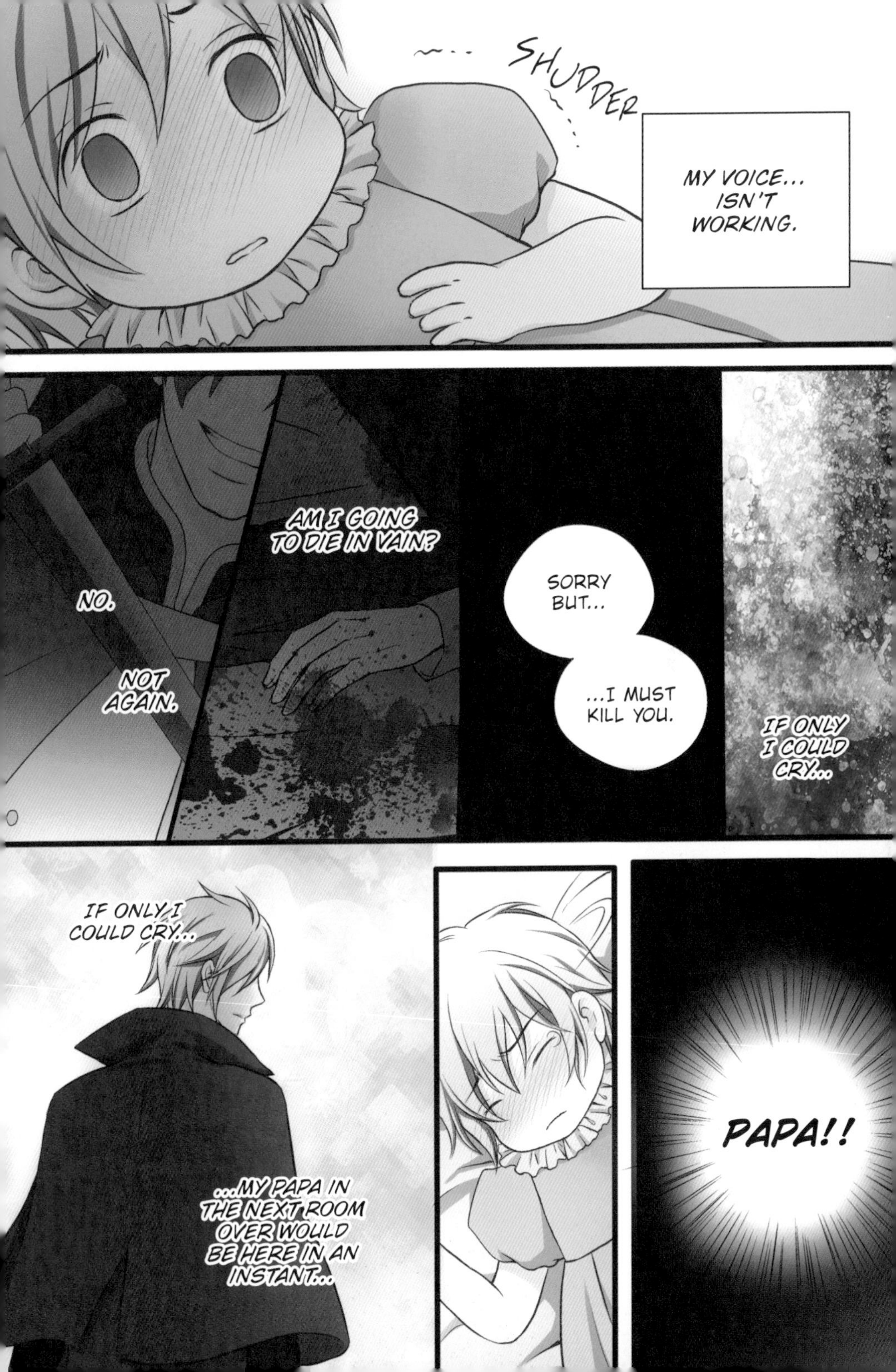
~...
SHUDDER
MY VOICE... ISN'T WORKING.
AM I GOING TO DIE IN VAIN?
NO.
NOT AGAIN.
SORRY BUT...
...I MUST KILL YOU.
IF ONLY I COULD CRY...
IF ONLY I COULD CRY...
...MY PAPA IN THE NEXT ROOM OVER WOULD BE HERE IN AN INSTANT...
PAPA!!

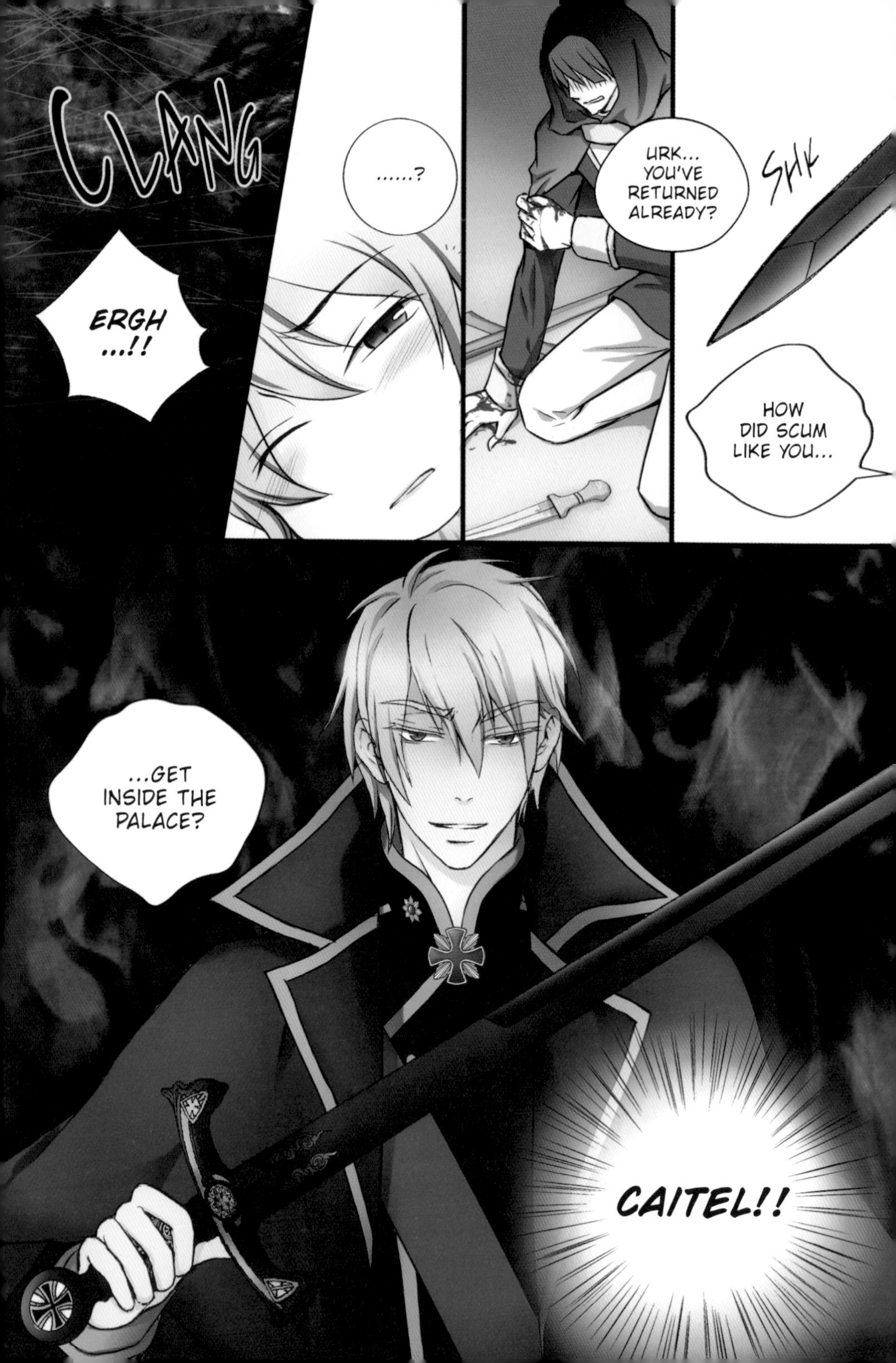

CLANG
ERGH ...!!
......?
URK... YOU'VE RETURNED ALREADY?
SHK
HOW DID SCUM LIKE YOU...
...GET INSIDE THE PALACE?
CAITEL!!

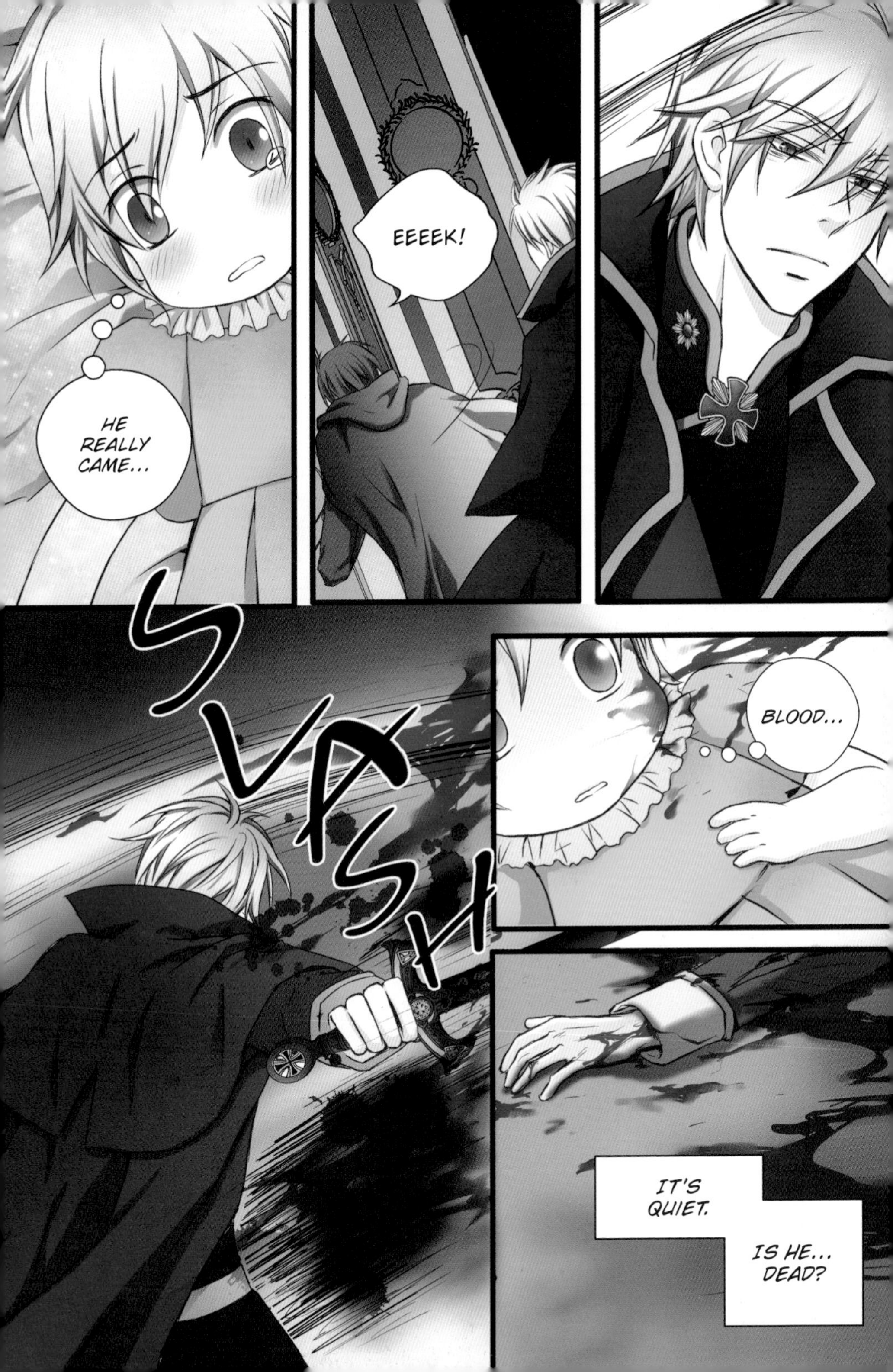
HE REALLY CAME...
EEEEK!
SLASH
BLOOD...
IT'S QUIET.
IS HE... DEAD?

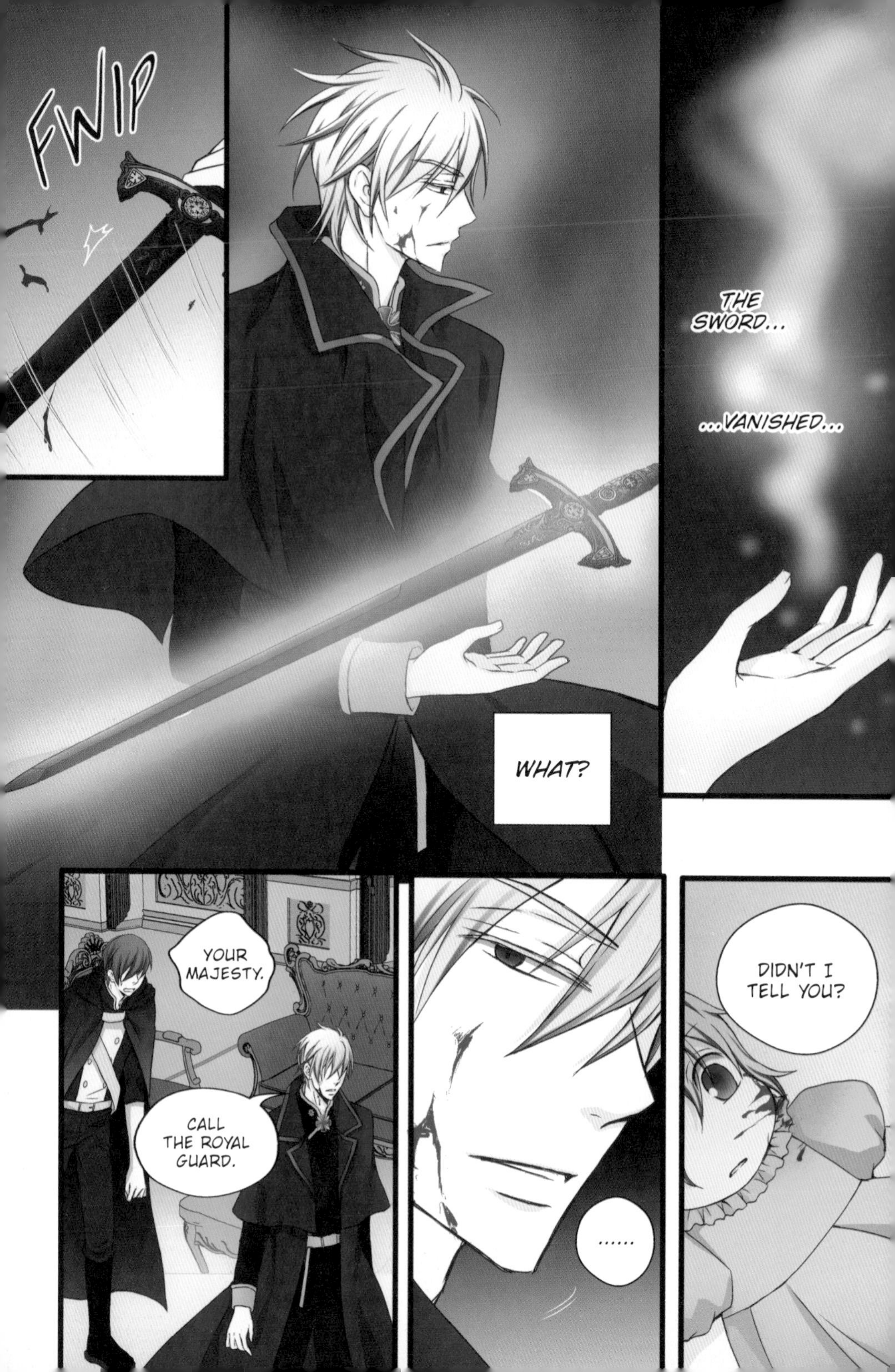
FWIP
THE SWORD...
...VANISHED...
WHAT?
YOUR MAJESTY.
CALL THE ROYAL GUARD.
......
DIDN'T I TELL YOU?

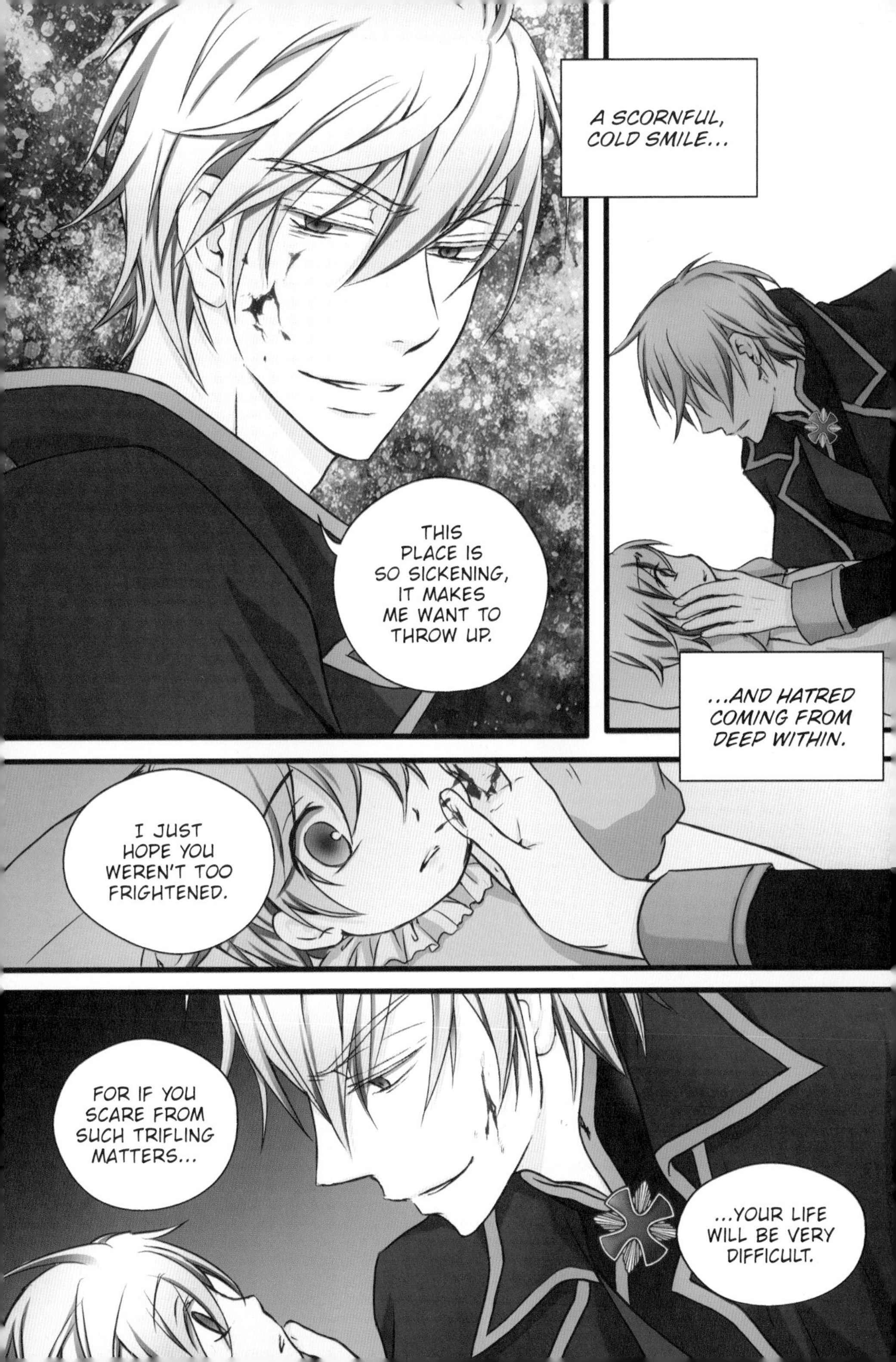
THIS PLACE IS SO SICKENING, IT MAKES ME WANT TO THROW UP.
A SCORNFUL, COLD SMILE...
...AND HATRED COMING FROM DEEP WITHIN.
I JUST HOPE YOU WEREN'T TOO FRIGHTENED.
FOR IF YOU SCARE FROM SUCH TRIFLING MATTERS...
...YOUR LIFE WILL BE VERY DIFFICULT.

OH NO... SHE FEELS SO COLD.

WHY IS SERIRA SO SHAKEN UP?

I'M THE ONE WHO'S TRAUMATIZED...

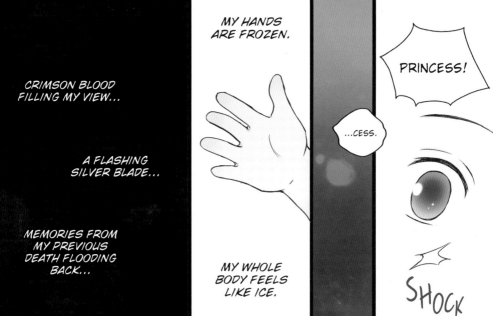

CRIMSON BLOOD FILLING MY VIEW...

A FLASHING SILVER BLADE...

MEMORIES FROM MY PREVIOUS DEATH FLOODING BACK...

MY HANDS ARE FROZEN.

MY WHOLE BODY FEELS LIKE ICE.

PRINCESS!

...CESS.

SHOCK

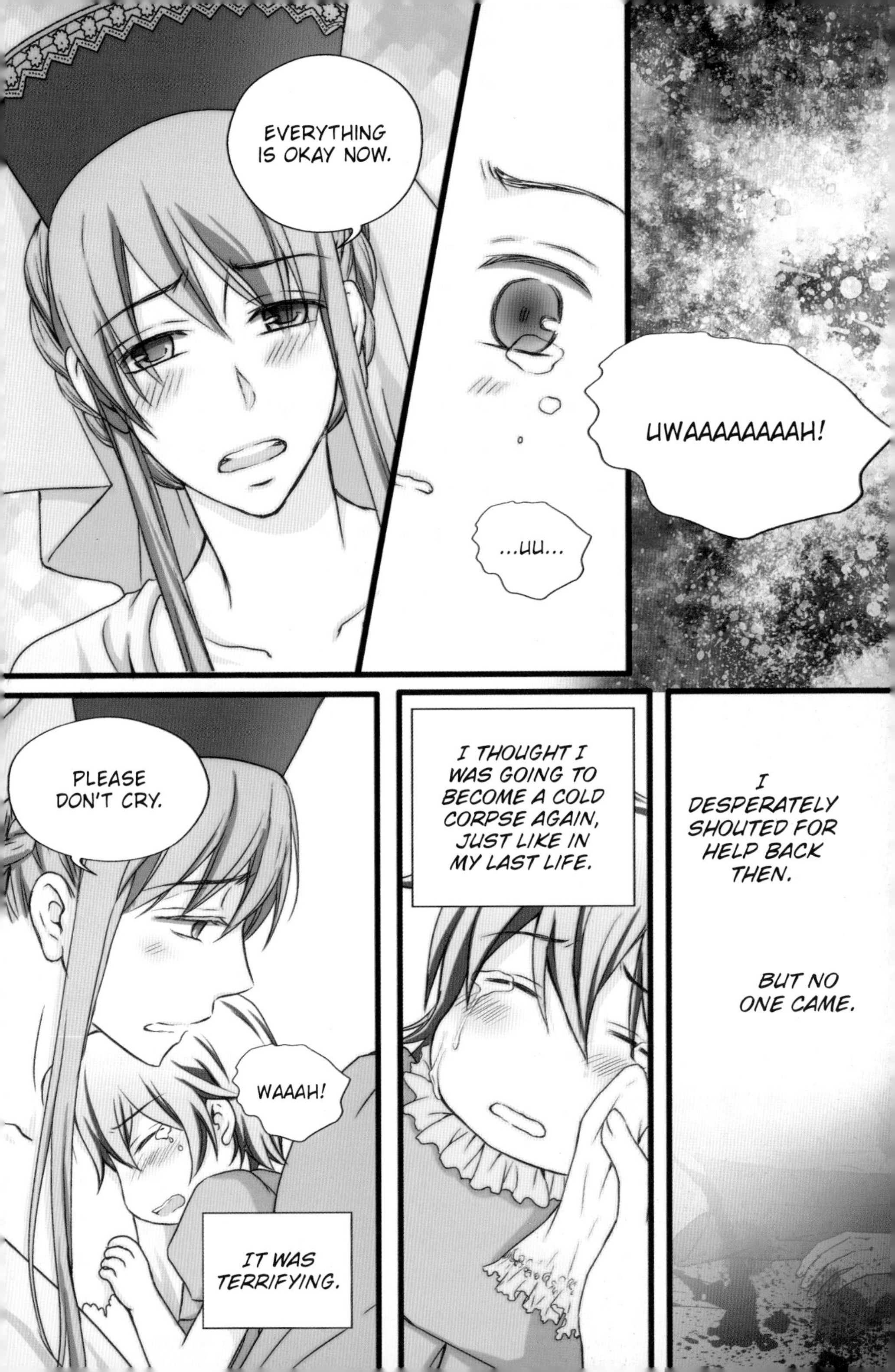
EVERYTHING IS OKAY NOW.
...UU...
UWAAAAAAAAH!
PLEASE DON'T CRY.
WAAAH!
IT WAS TERRIFYING.
I THOUGHT I WAS GOING TO BECOME A COLD CORPSE AGAIN, JUST LIKE IN MY LAST LIFE.
I DESPERATELY SHOUTED FOR HELP BACK THEN.
BUT NO ONE CAME.

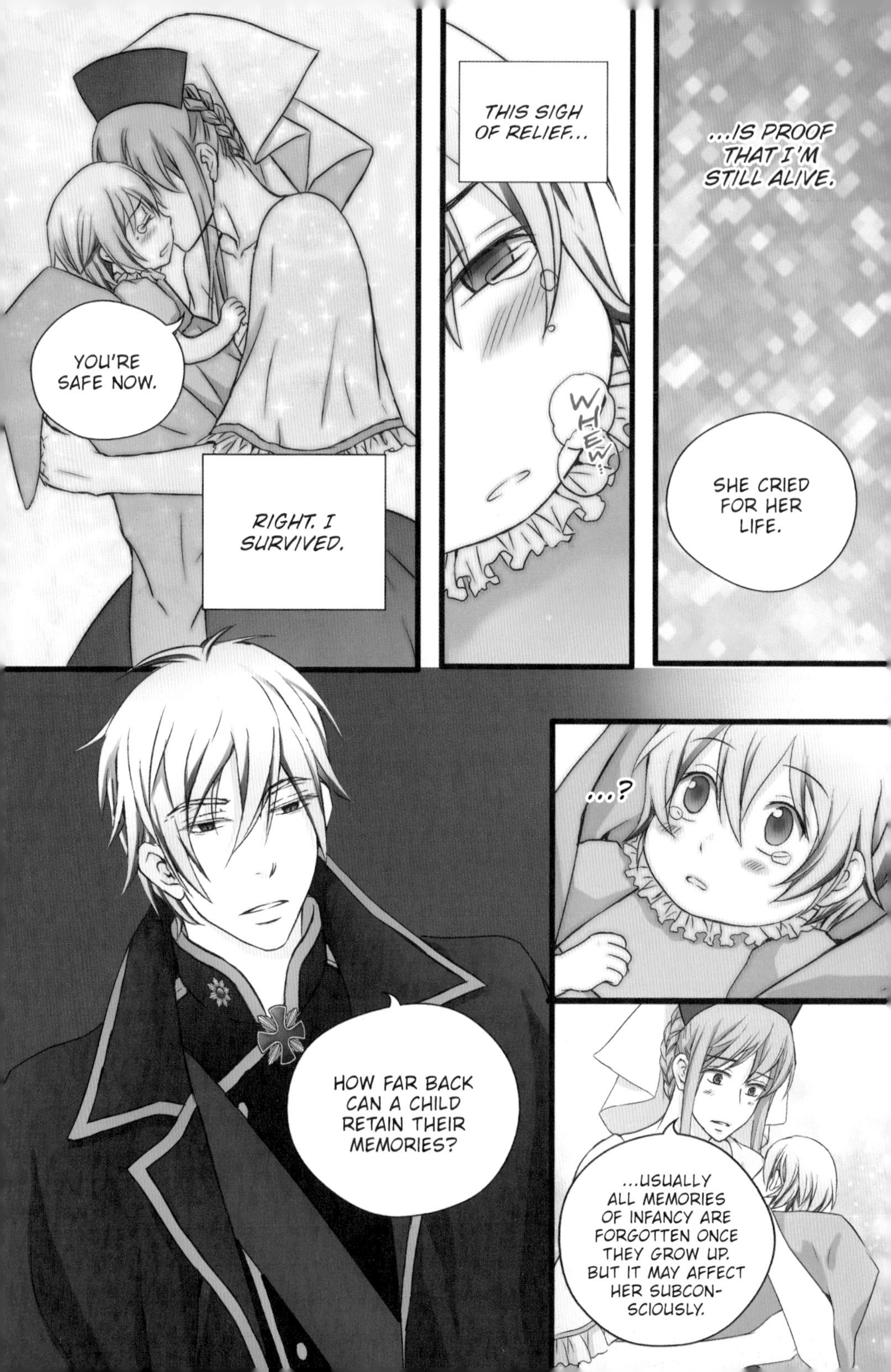
YOU'RE SAFE NOW.
RIGHT. I SURVIVED.
THIS SIGH OF RELIEF...
WHEW...
...IS PROOF THAT I'M STILL ALIVE.
SHE CRIED FOR HER LIFE.
HOW FAR BACK CAN A CHILD RETAIN THEIR MEMORIES?
...?
...USUALLY ALL MEMORIES OF INFANCY ARE FORGOTTEN ONCE THEY GROW UP. BUT IT MAY AFFECT HER SUBCON-SCIOUSLY.

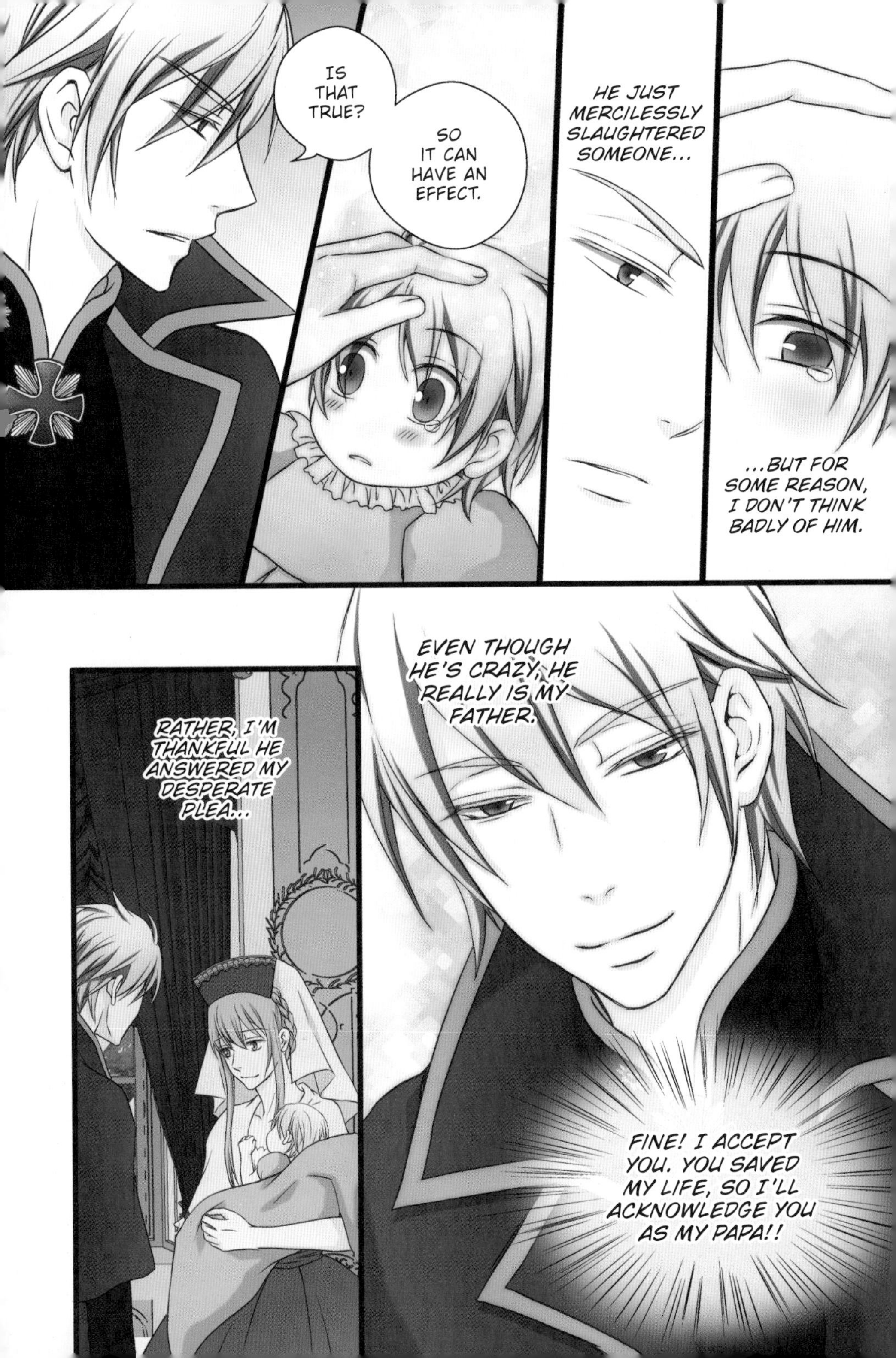
IS THAT TRUE?
SO IT CAN HAVE AN EFFECT.
HE JUST MERCILESSLY SLAUGHTERED SOMEONE...
...BUT FOR SOME REASON, I DON'T THINK BADLY OF HIM.
RATHER, I'M THANKFUL HE ANSWERED MY DESPERATE PLEA...
EVEN THOUGH HE'S CRAZY, HE REALLY IS MY FATHER.
FINE! I ACCEPT YOU. YOU SAVED MY LIFE, SO I'LL ACKNOWLEDGE YOU AS MY PAPA!!

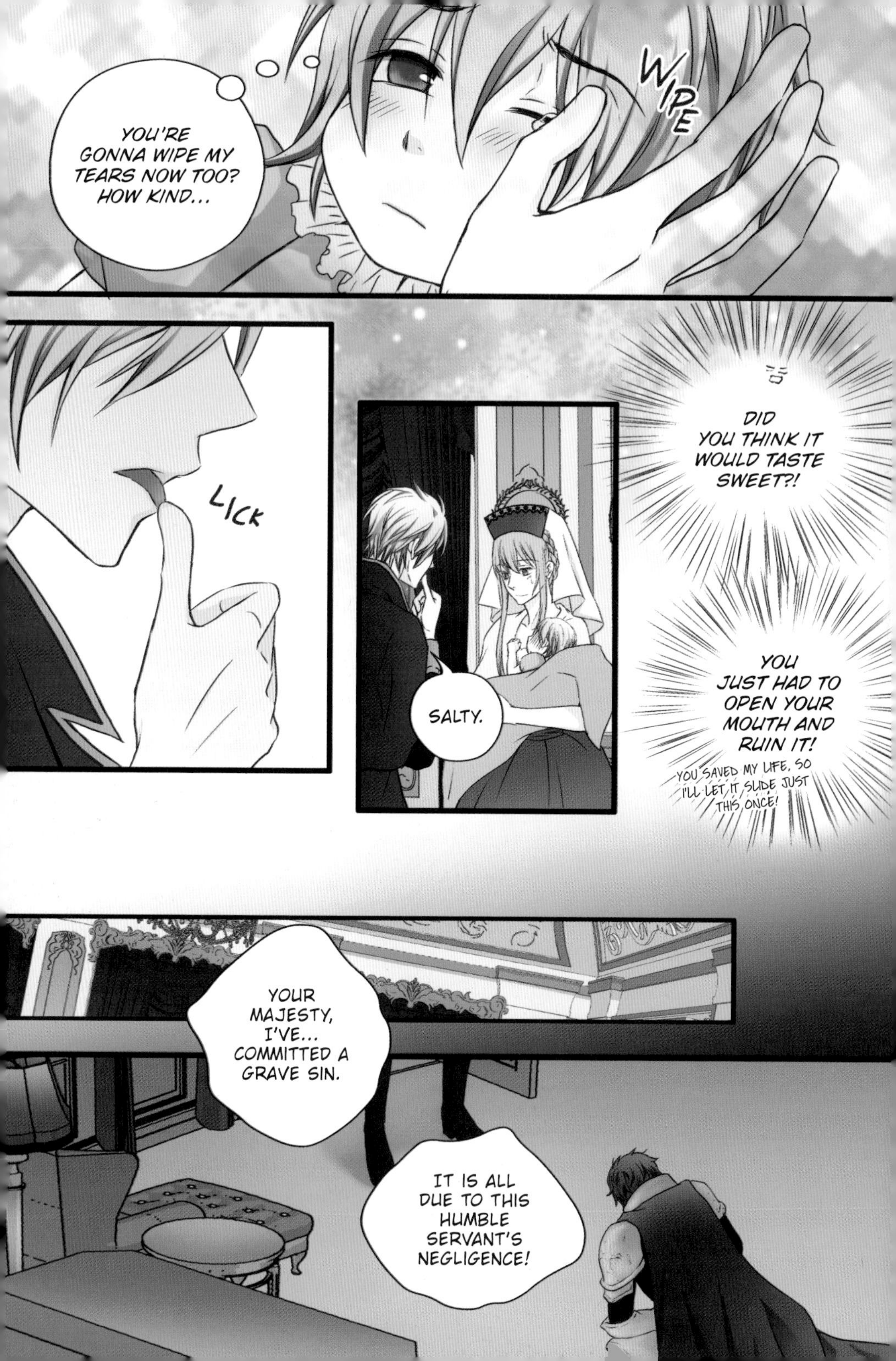
YOU'RE GONNA WIPE MY TEARS NOW TOO? HOW KIND...
WIPE
LICK
SALTY.
DID YOU THINK IT WOULD TASTE SWEET?!
YOU JUST HAD TO OPEN YOUR MOUTH AND RUIN IT!
YOU SAVED MY LIFE, SO I'LL LET IT SLIDE JUST THIS ONCE!
YOUR MAJESTY, I'VE... COMMITTED A GRAVE SIN.
IT IS ALL DUE TO THIS HUMBLE SERVANT'S NEGLIGENCE!

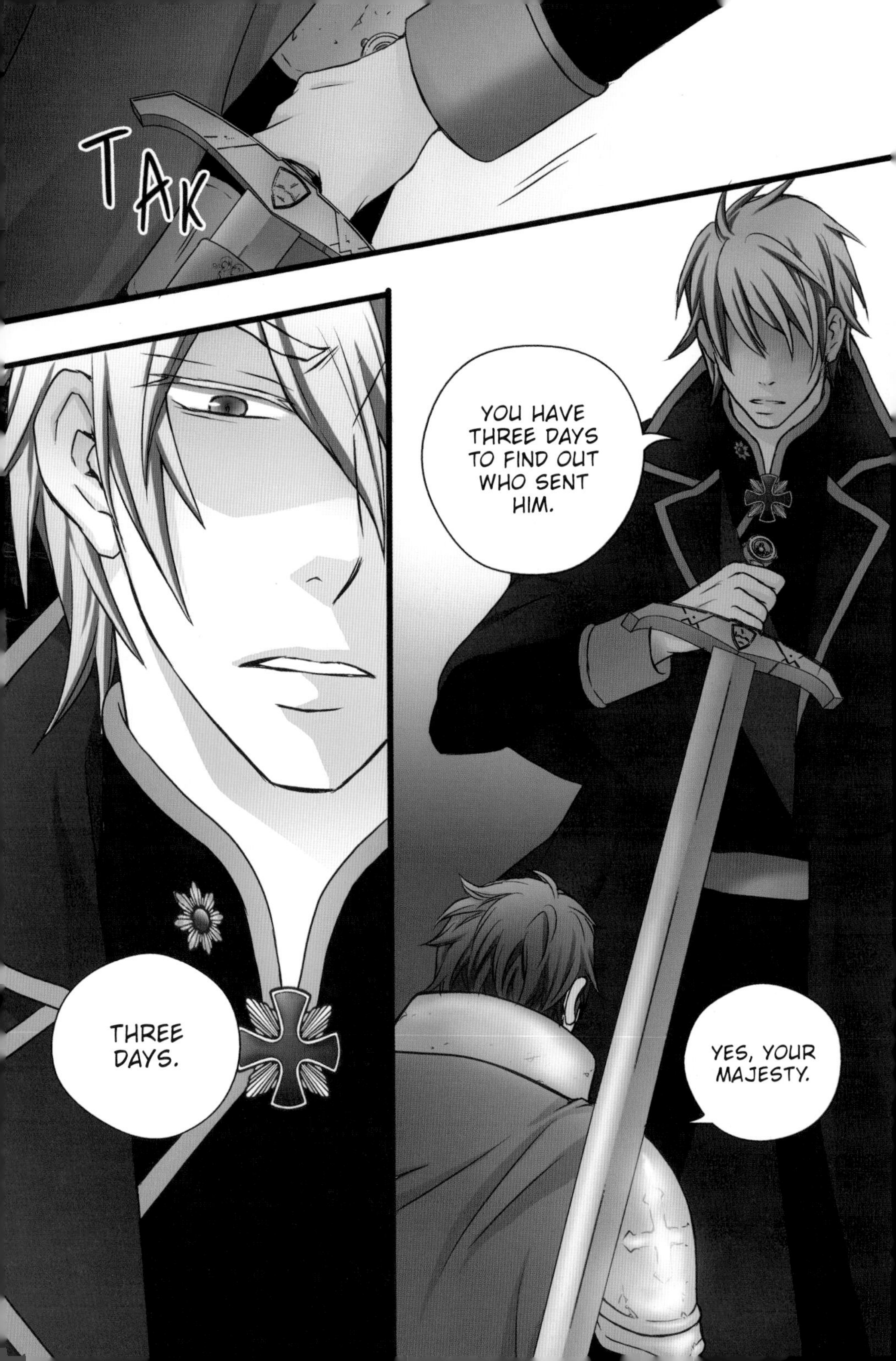
TAK
THREE DAYS.
YOU HAVE THREE DAYS TO FIND OUT WHO SENT HIM.
YES, YOUR MAJESTY.

IF YOU FAIL, CONSIDER YOUR LIFE FORFEIT.
SHF
SKAARE
WHY ARE YOU SUDDENLY ACTING LIKE WE'RE CLOSE?
WE'RE NOT QUITE THERE YET, PAPA.
HUH? WHY'S HE SMILING?

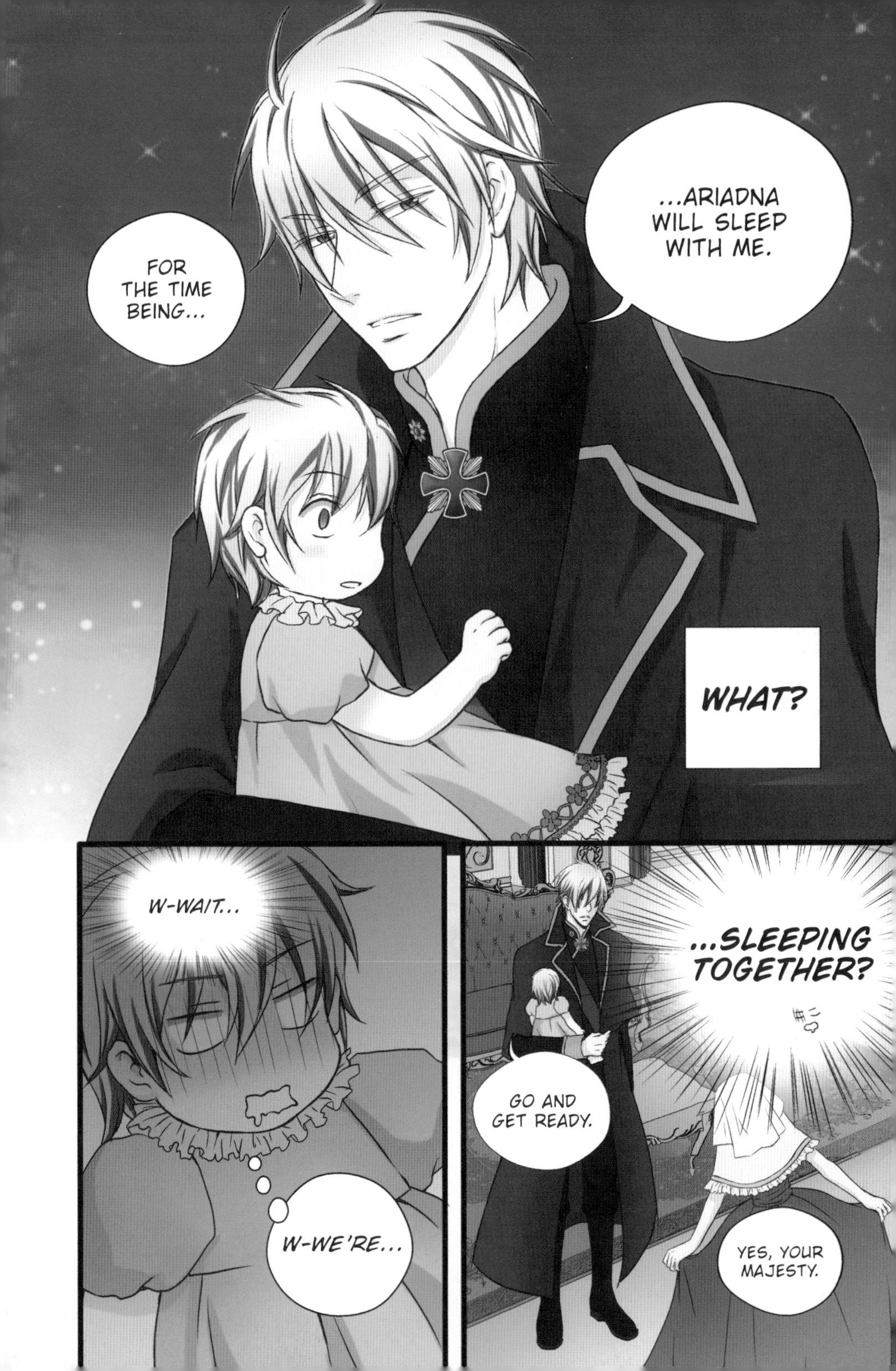
FOR THE TIME BEING...
...ARIADNA WILL SLEEP WITH ME.
WHAT?
W-WAIT...
W-WE'RE...
...SLEEPING TOGETHER?
GO AND GET READY.
YES, YOUR MAJESTY.

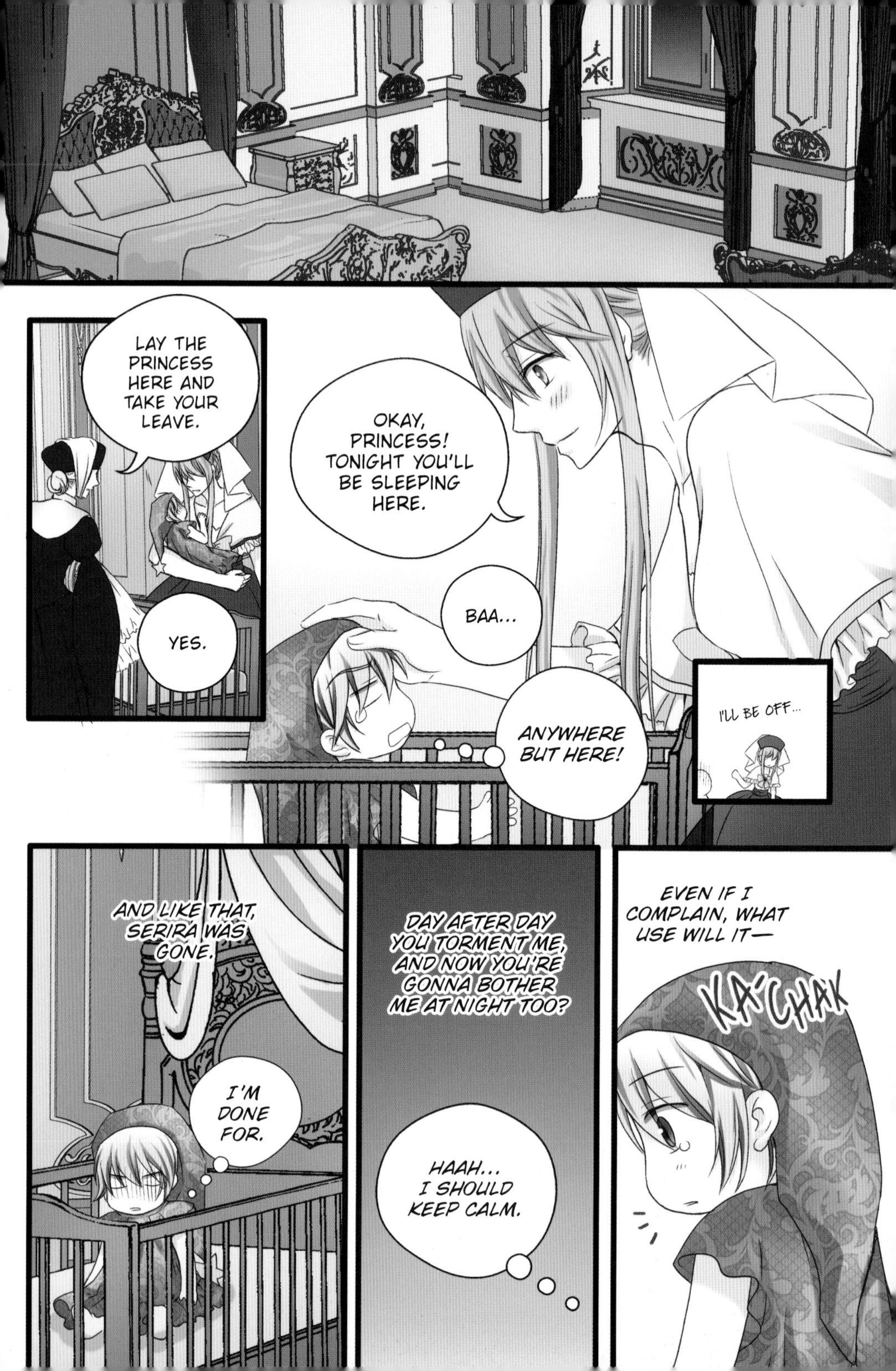
LAY THE PRINCESS HERE AND TAKE YOUR LEAVE.
YES.
OKAY, PRINCESS! TONIGHT YOU'LL BE SLEEPING HERE.
BAA...
ANYWHERE BUT HERE!
I'LL BE OFF...
AND LIKE THAT, SERIRA WAS GONE.
I'M DONE FOR.
DAY AFTER DAY YOU TORMENT ME, AND NOW YOU'RE GONNA BOTHER ME AT NIGHT TOO?
HAAH... I SHOULD KEEP CALM.
EVEN IF I COMPLAIN, WHAT USE WILL IT—
KA'CHAK

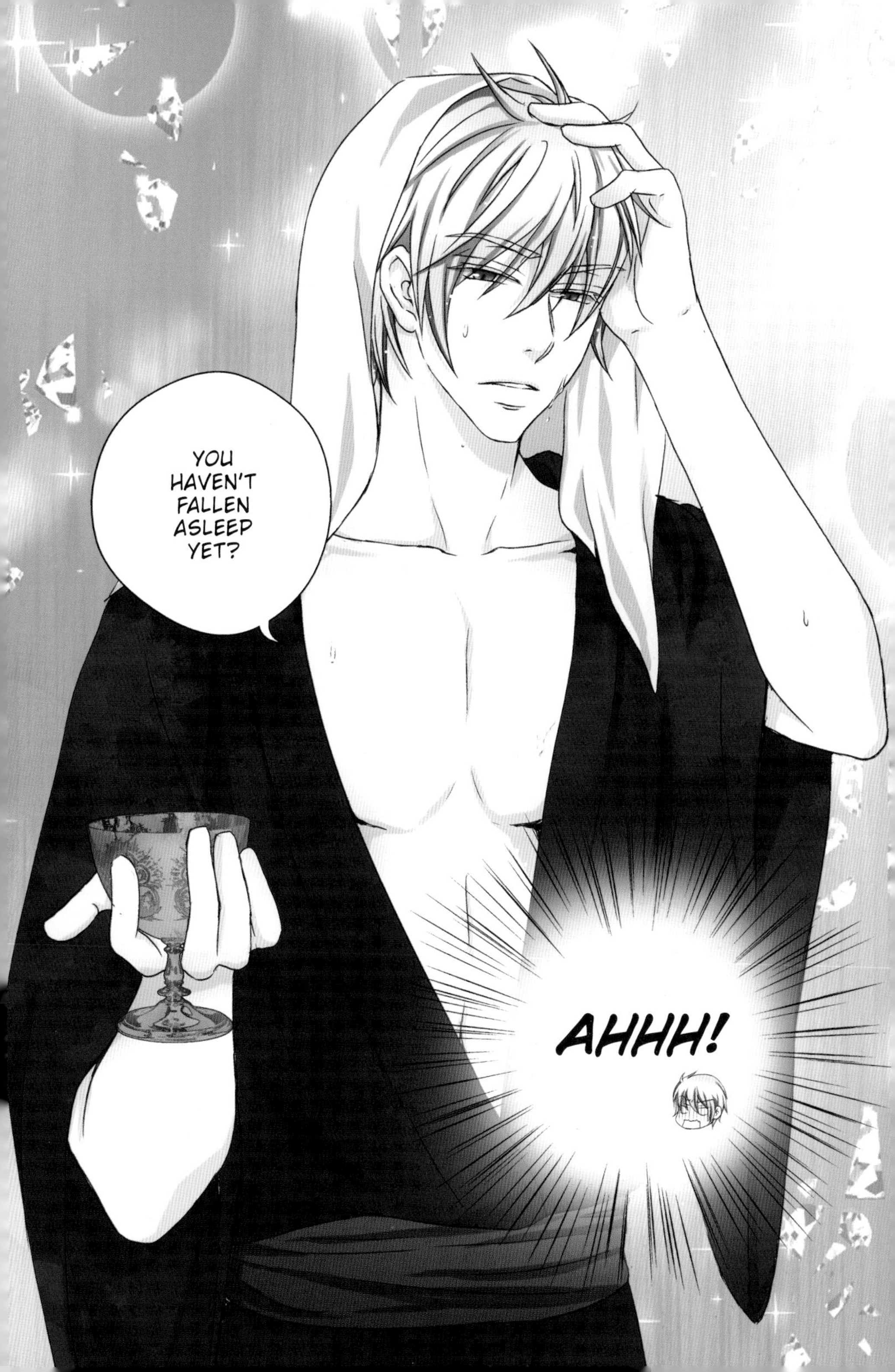
YOU HAVEN'T FALLEN ASLEEP YET?
AHHH!

WHY IS HE SHOWING SO MUCH SKIN?

I MAY BE YOUR DAUGHTER, BUT HAVE SOME DECENCY!

TAP

WHAT'S THE MATTER?

HIS FLUSHED SKIN STRAIGHT OUT OF THE SHOWER...

...HIS DRIPPING WET HAIR...

...AND THE REFRESHING SCENT FILLING THE AIR...

IS SOMETHING WRONG?

MOM! THIS IS DEFINITELY WRONG!

I'VE ALWAYS DREAMED OF THIS TYPE OF SCENARIO, BUT...

A TOAST TO YOUR BEAUTIFUL EYES!!

...NOT LIKE THIS! NO WAY!

THIS MAN IS MY PAPA!!

DAMN IT! WHY?! A HOTTIE IS RIGHT IN FRONT OF MY EYES, BUT I CAN'T FLIRT WITH HIM!!

YES, THERE'S SOMETHING WRONG WITH MY HEART!!

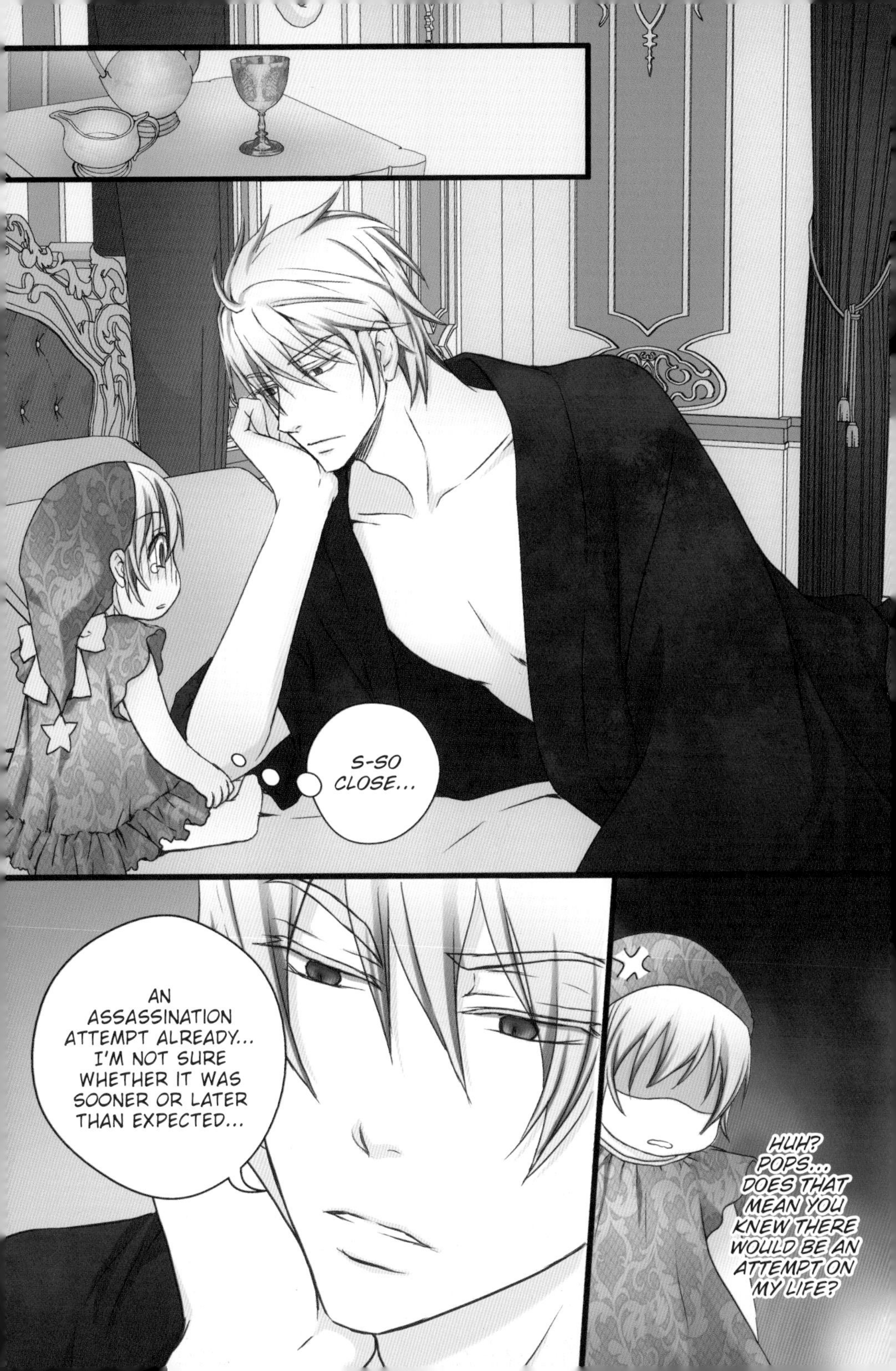
S-SO CLOSE...
AN ASSASSINATION ATTEMPT ALREADY... I'M NOT SURE WHETHER IT WAS SOONER OR LATER THAN EXPECTED...
HUH? POPS... DOES THAT MEAN YOU KNEW THERE WOULD BE AN ATTEMPT ON MY LIFE?

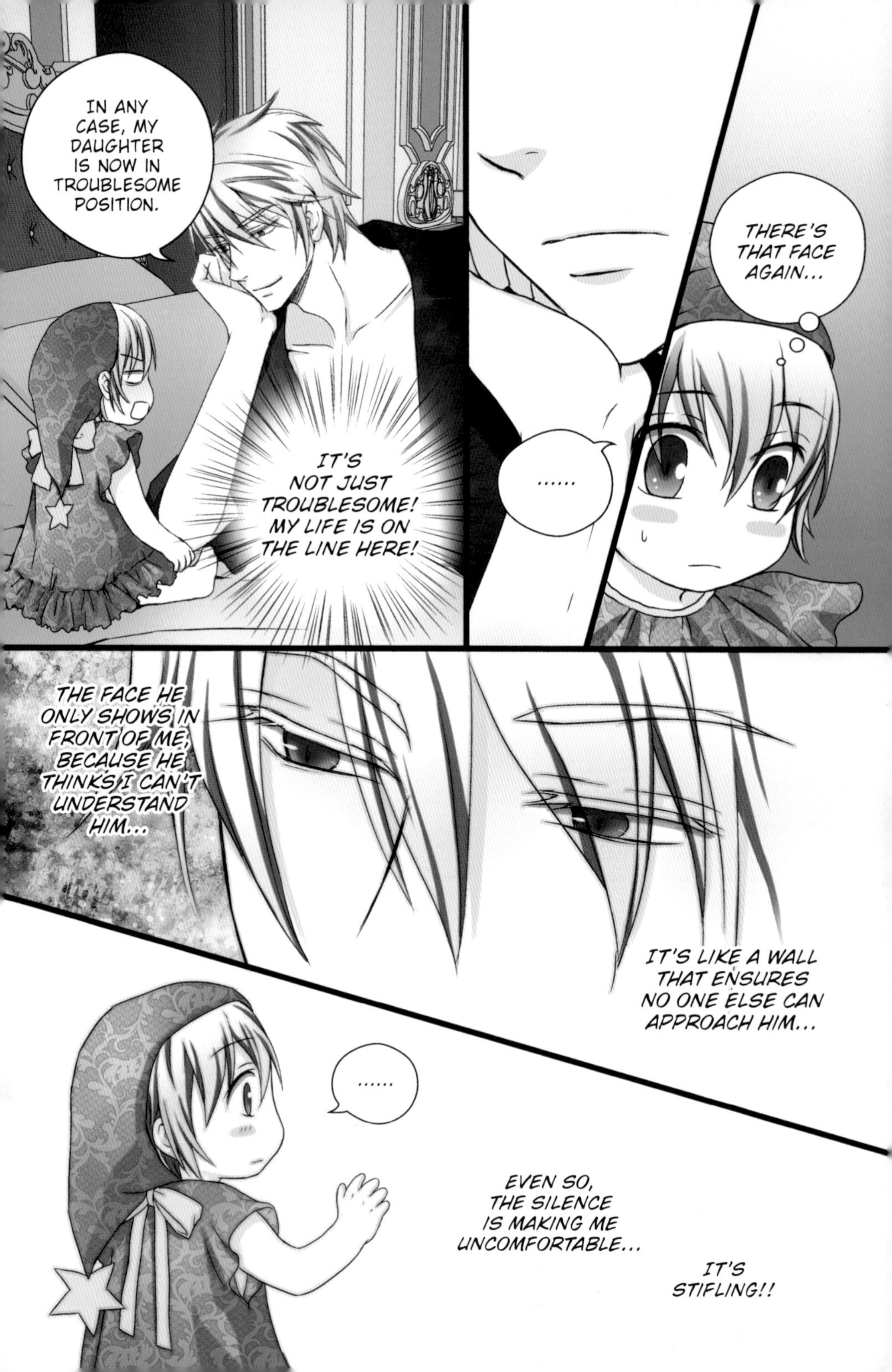
IN ANY CASE, MY DAUGHTER IS NOW IN TROUBLESOME POSITION.
IT'S NOT JUST TROUBLESOME! MY LIFE IS ON THE LINE HERE!
......
THERE'S THAT FACE AGAIN...
THE FACE HE ONLY SHOWS IN FRONT OF ME, BECAUSE HE THINKS I CAN'T UNDERSTAND HIM...
IT'S LIKE A WALL THAT ENSURES NO ONE ELSE CAN APPROACH HIM...
......
EVEN SO, THE SILENCE IS MAKING ME UNCOMFORTABLE...
IT'S STIFLING!!

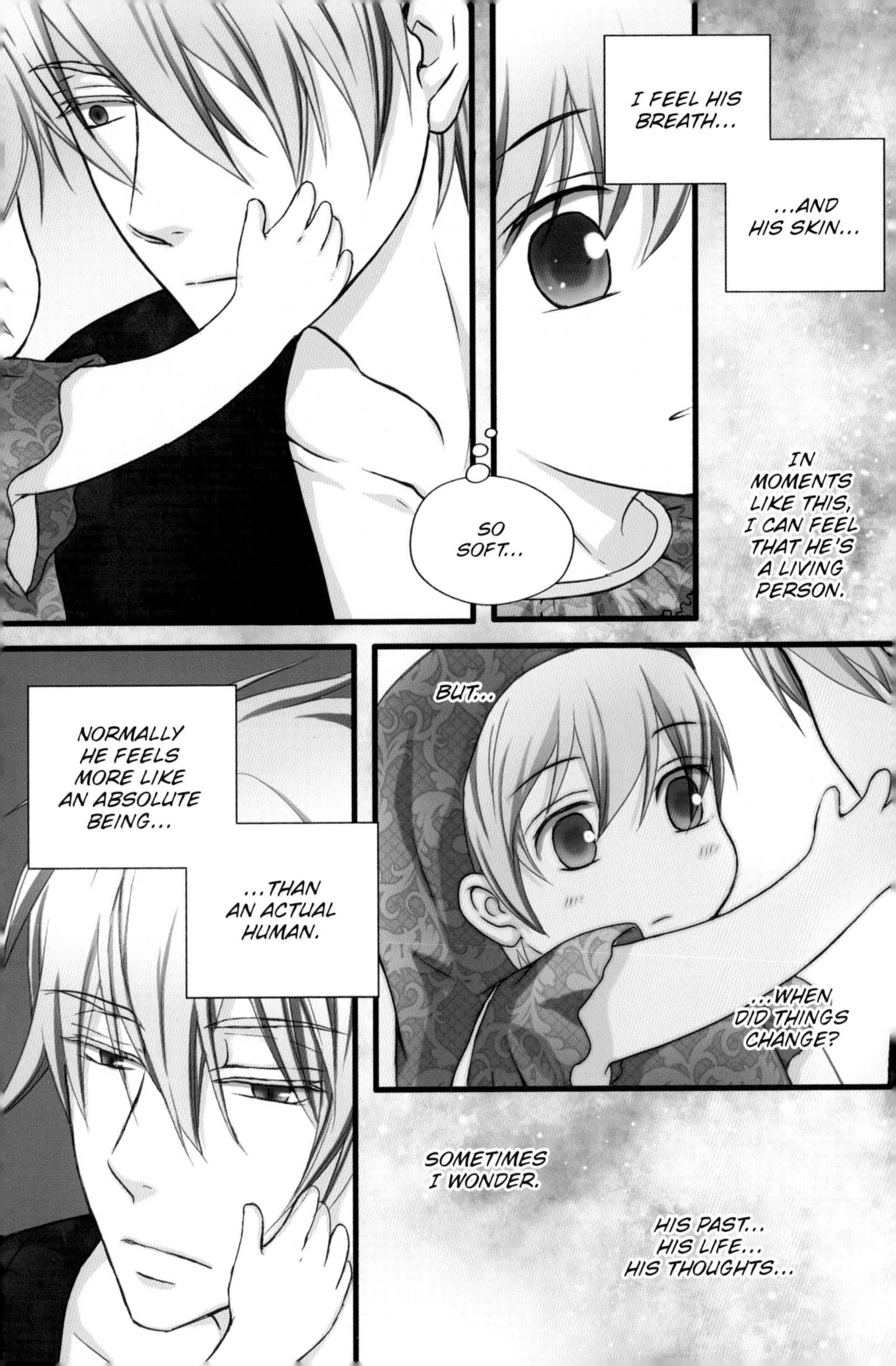

I FEEL HIS BREATH...
...AND HIS SKIN...
SO SOFT...
IN MOMENTS LIKE THIS, I CAN FEEL THAT HE'S A LIVING PERSON.
NORMALLY HE FEELS MORE LIKE AN ABSOLUTE BEING...
...THAN AN ACTUAL HUMAN.
BUT...
...WHEN DID THINGS CHANGE?
SOMETIMES I WONDER.
HIS PAST... HIS LIFE... HIS THOUGHTS...

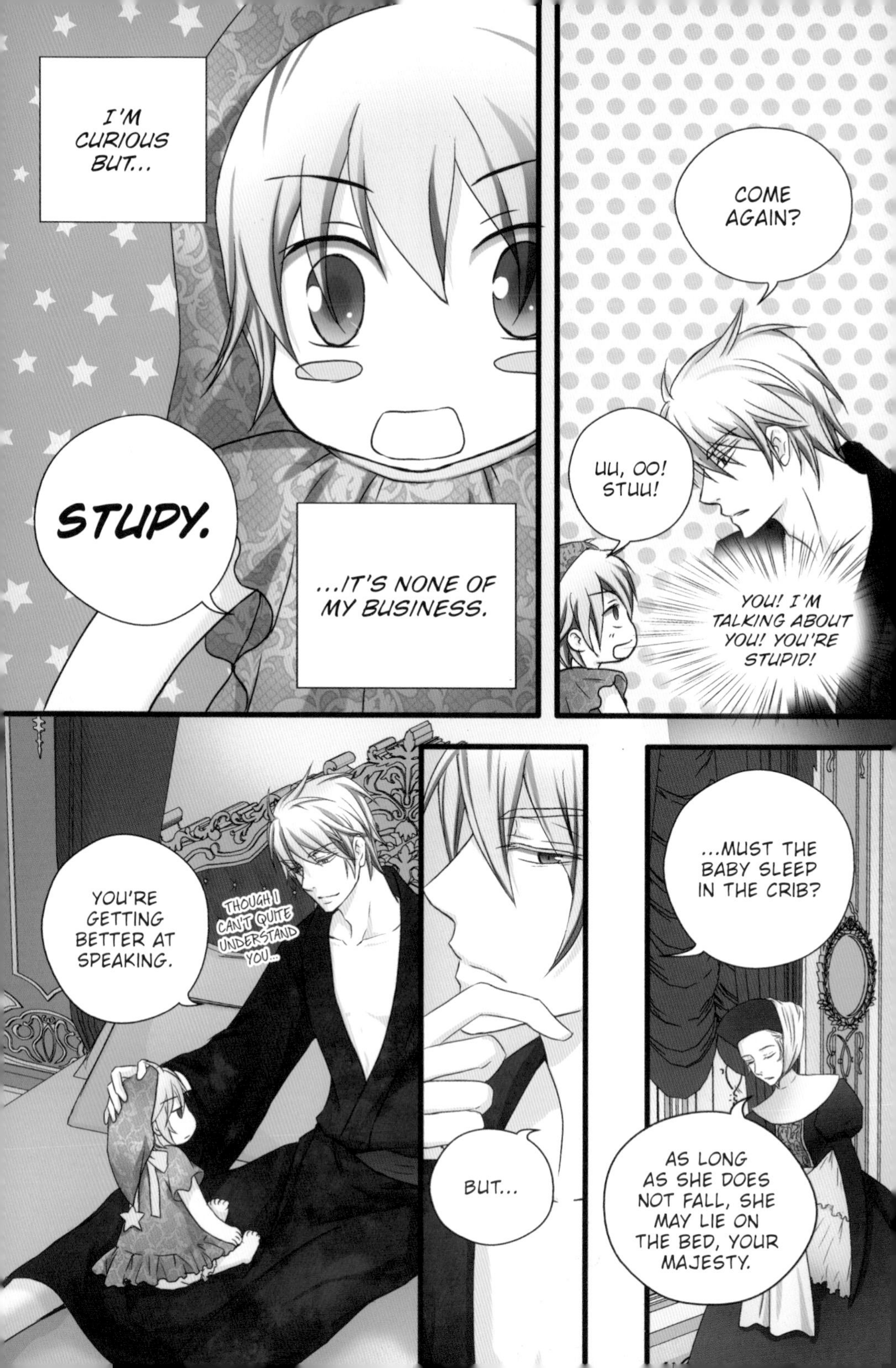
I'M CURIOUS BUT...
STUPY.
...IT'S NONE OF MY BUSINESS.
COME AGAIN?
UU, OO! STUU!
YOU! I'M TALKING ABOUT YOU! YOU'RE STUPID!
YOU'RE GETTING BETTER AT SPEAKING.
THOUGH I CAN'T QUITE UNDERSTAND YOU...
BUT...
...MUST THE BABY SLEEP IN THE CRIB?
AS LONG AS SHE DOES NOT FALL, SHE MAY LIE ON THE BED, YOUR MAJESTY.

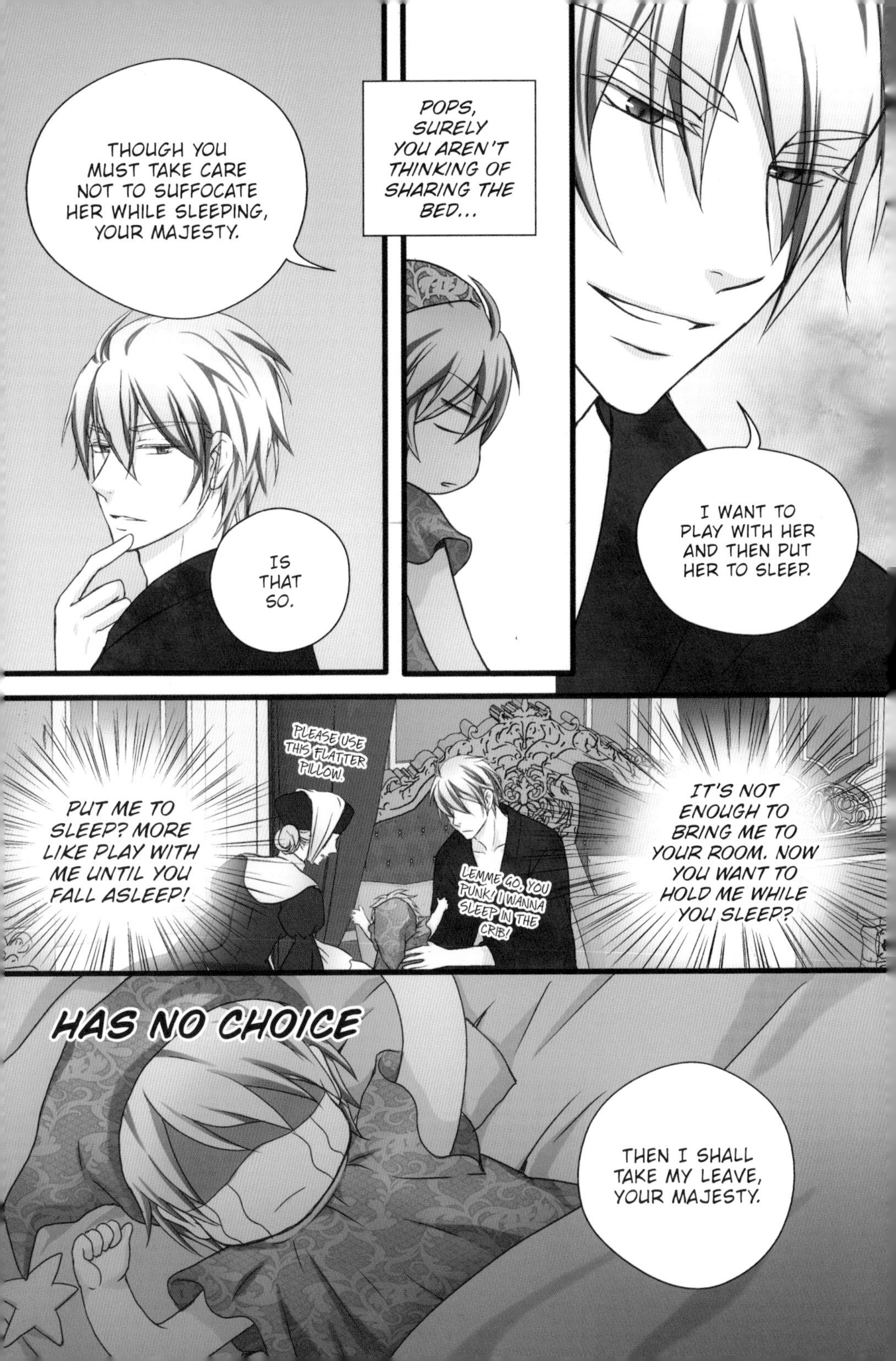
THOUGH YOU MUST TAKE CARE NOT TO SUFFOCATE HER WHILE SLEEPING, YOUR MAJESTY.
IS THAT SO.
POPS, SURELY YOU AREN'T THINKING OF SHARING THE BED...
I WANT TO PLAY WITH HER AND THEN PUT HER TO SLEEP.
PUT ME TO SLEEP? MORE LIKE PLAY WITH ME UNTIL YOU FALL ASLEEP!
PLEASE USE THIS FLATTER PILLOW.
LEMME GO, YOU PUNK! I WANNA SLEEP IN THE CRIB!
IT'S NOT ENOUGH TO BRING ME TO YOUR ROOM. NOW YOU WANT TO HOLD ME WHILE YOU SLEEP?
HAS NO CHOICE
THEN I SHALL TAKE MY LEAVE, YOUR MAJESTY.

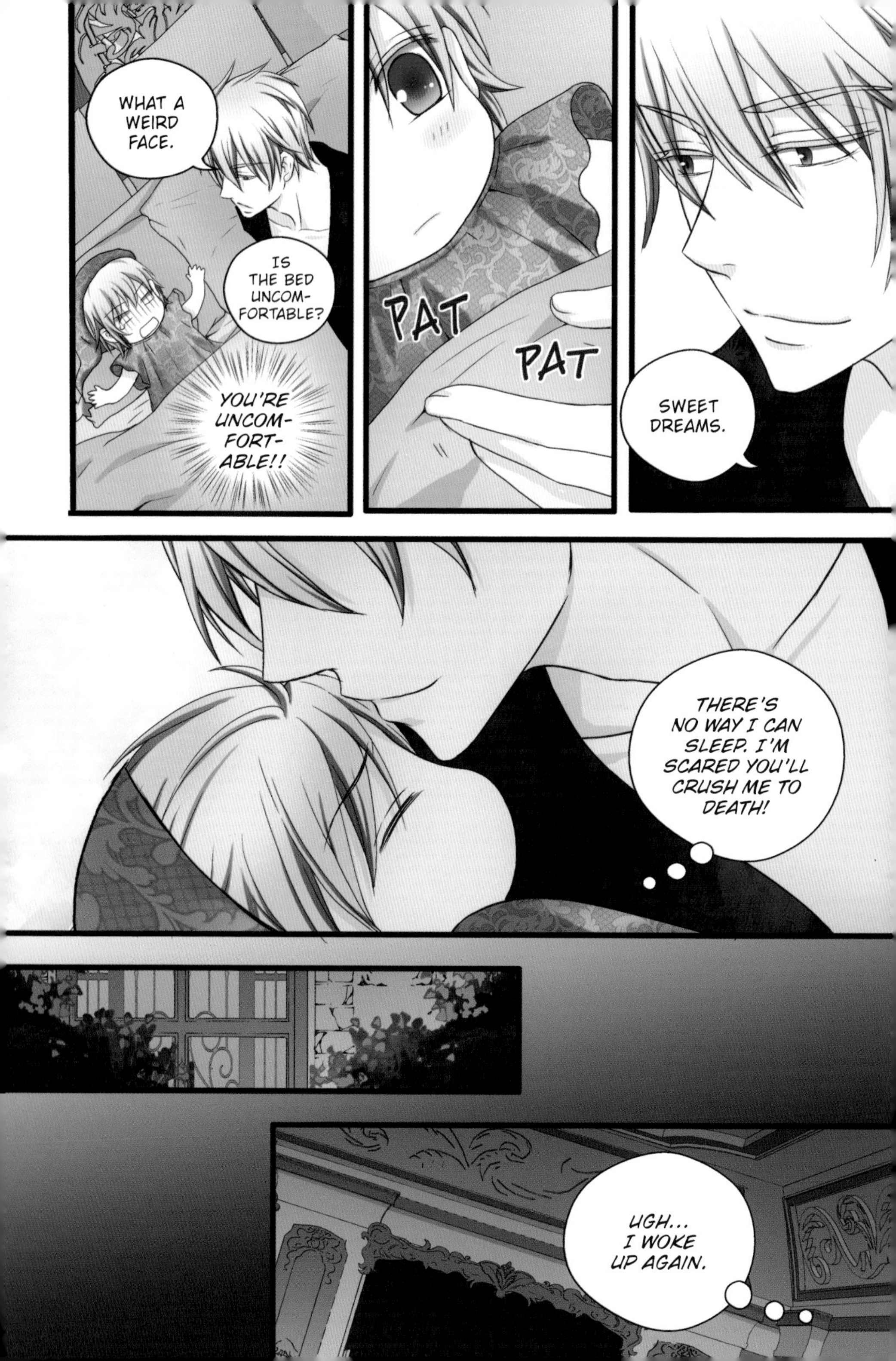
WHAT A WEIRD FACE.
IS THE BED UNCOM-FORTABLE?
YOU'RE UNCOM-FORT-ABLE!!
PAT
PAT
SWEET DREAMS.
THERE'S NO WAY I CAN SLEEP. I'M SCARED YOU'LL CRUSH ME TO DEATH!
UGH... I WOKE UP AGAIN.

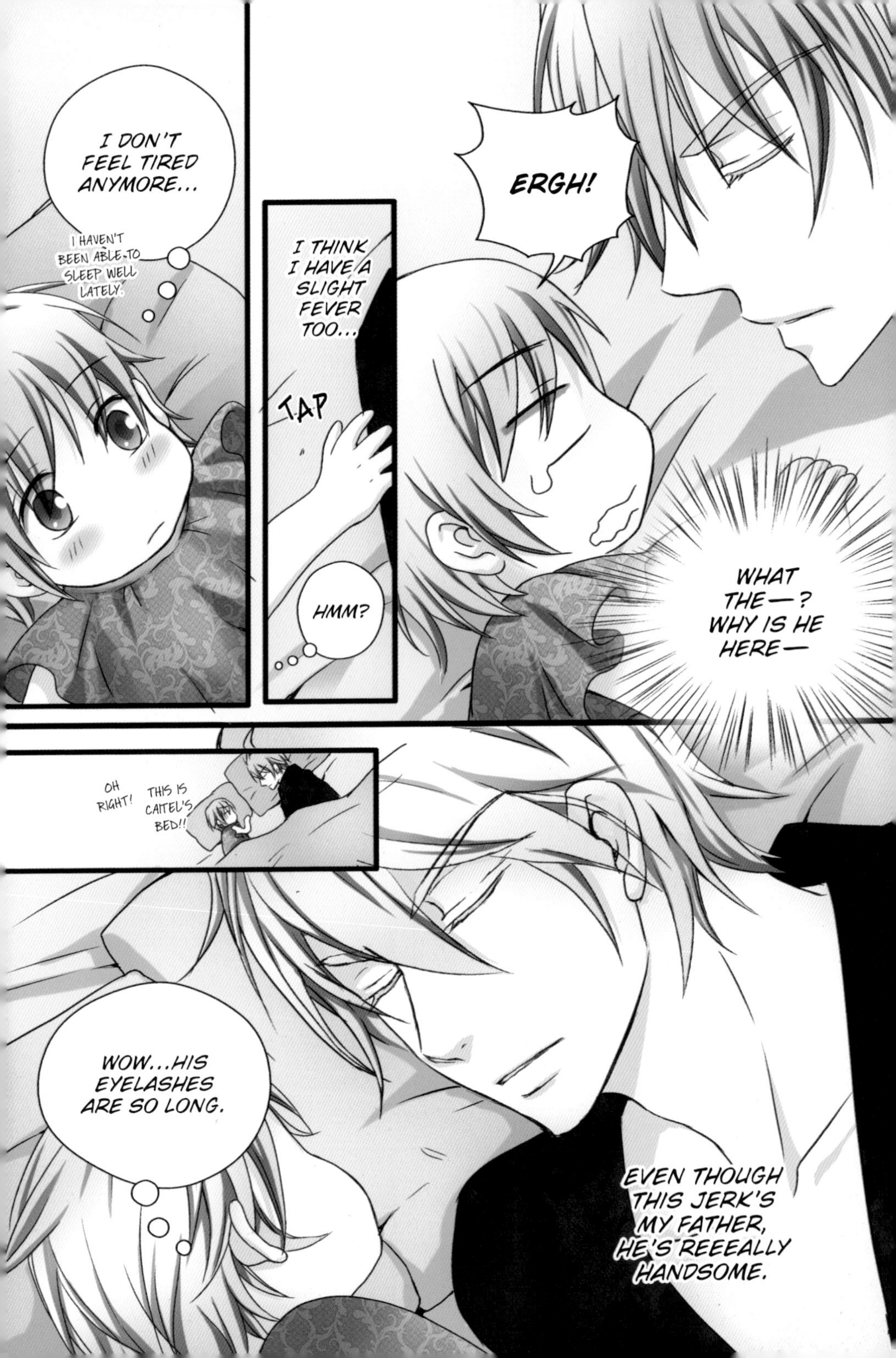
I DON'T FEEL TIRED ANYMORE...
I HAVEN'T BEEN ABLE TO SLEEP WELL LATELY.
I THINK I HAVE A SLIGHT FEVER TOO...
TAP
HMM?
ERGH!
WHAT THE—? WHY IS HE HERE—
OH RIGHT!
THIS IS CAITEL'S BED!!
WOW...HIS EYELASHES ARE SO LONG.
EVEN THOUGH THIS JERK'S MY FATHER, HE'S REEEALLY HANDSOME.

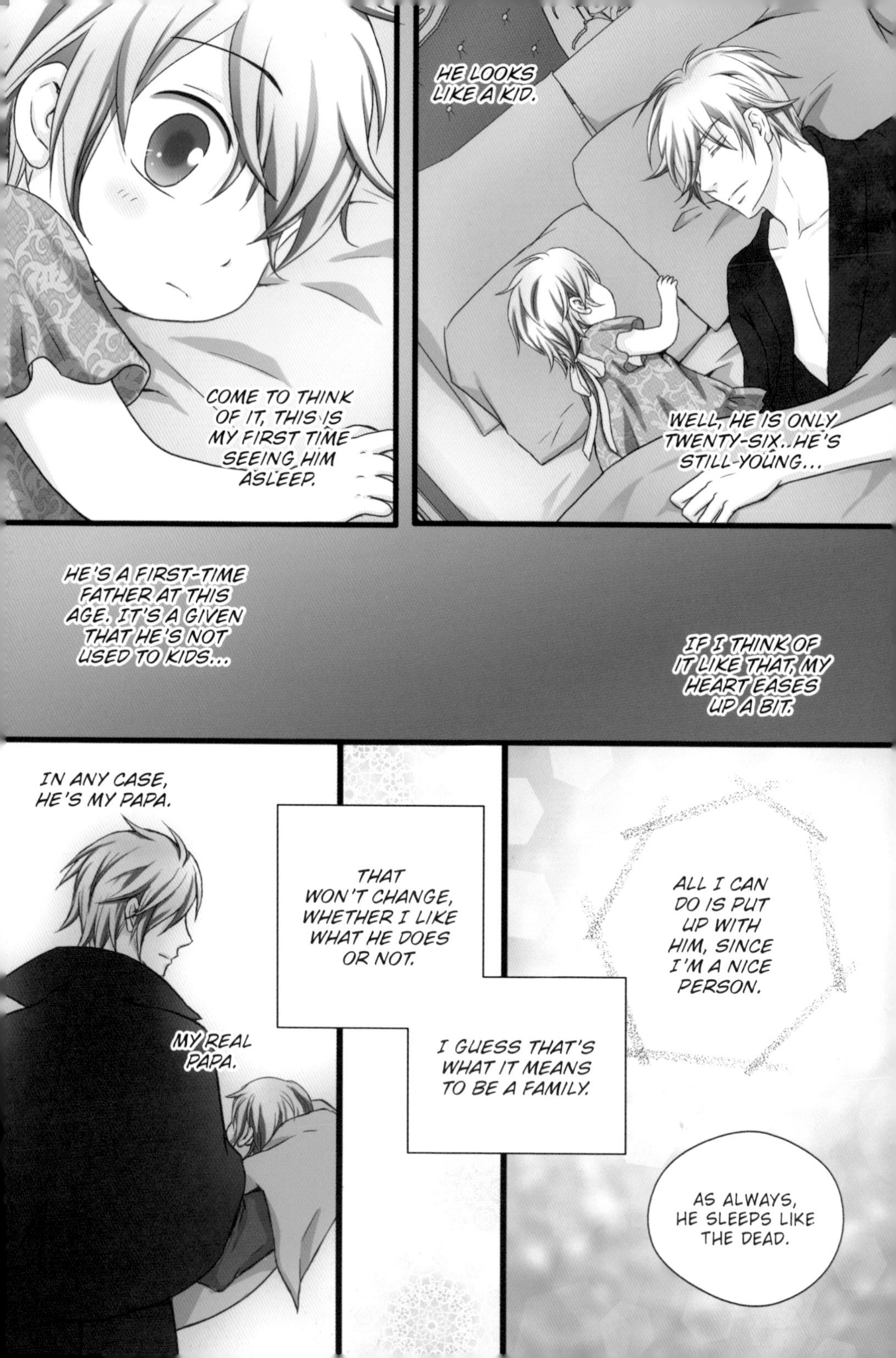
COME TO THINK OF IT, THIS IS MY FIRST TIME SEEING HIM ASLEEP.
HE LOOKS LIKE A KID.
WELL, HE IS ONLY TWENTY-SIX..HE'S STILL YOUNG...
HE'S A FIRST-TIME FATHER AT THIS AGE. IT'S A GIVEN THAT HE'S NOT USED TO KIDS...
IF I THINK OF IT LIKE THAT, MY HEART EASES UP A BIT.
IN ANY CASE, HE'S MY PAPA.
MY REAL PAPA.
THAT WON'T CHANGE, WHETHER I LIKE WHAT HE DOES OR NOT.
I GUESS THAT'S WHAT IT MEANS TO BE A FAMILY.
ALL I CAN DO IS PUT UP WITH HIM, SINCE I'M A NICE PERSON.
AS ALWAYS, HE SLEEPS LIKE THE DEAD.

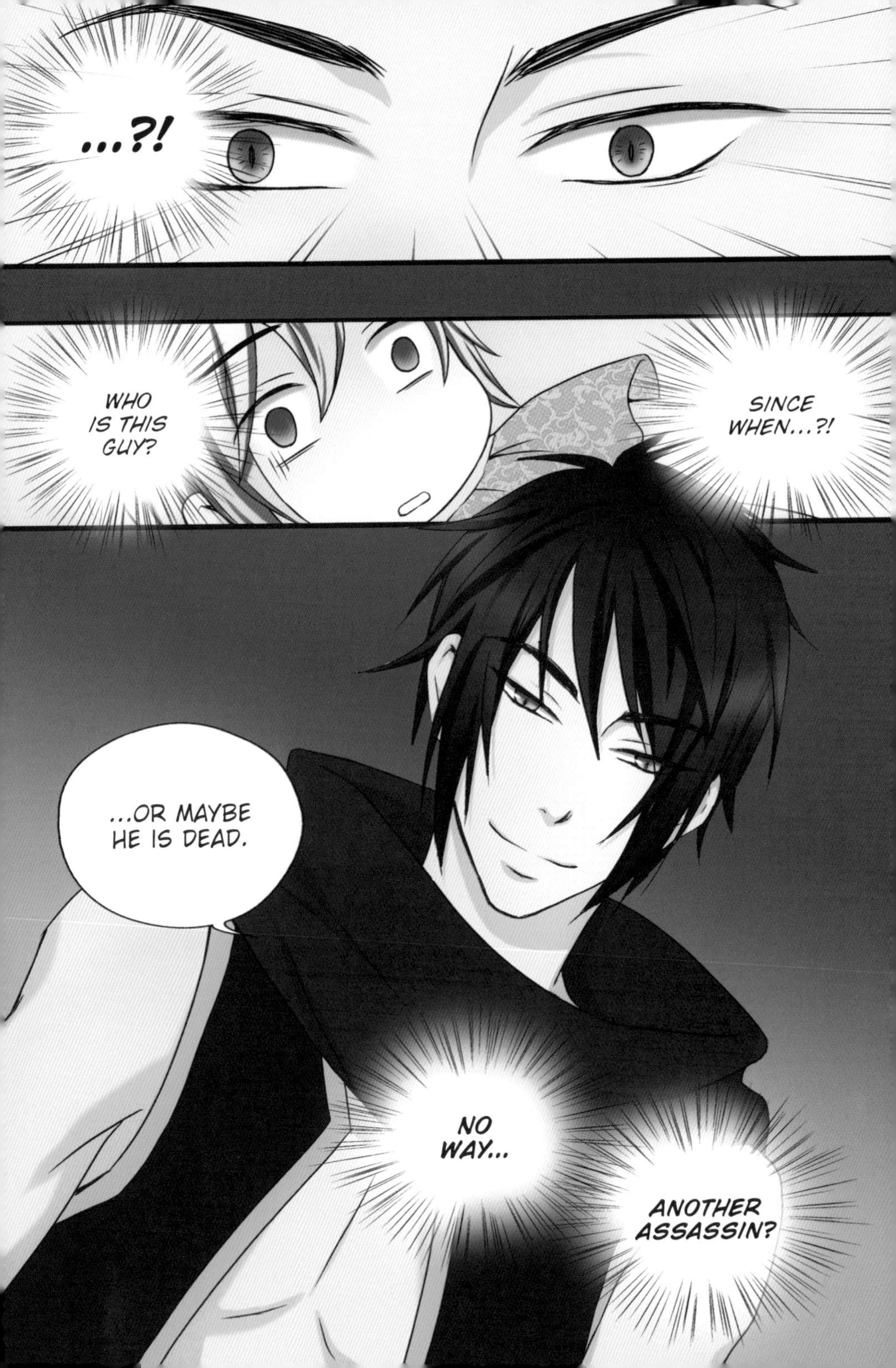
...?!
WHO IS THIS GUY?
SINCE WHEN...?!
...OR MAYBE HE IS DEAD.
NO WAY...
ANOTHER ASSASSIN?

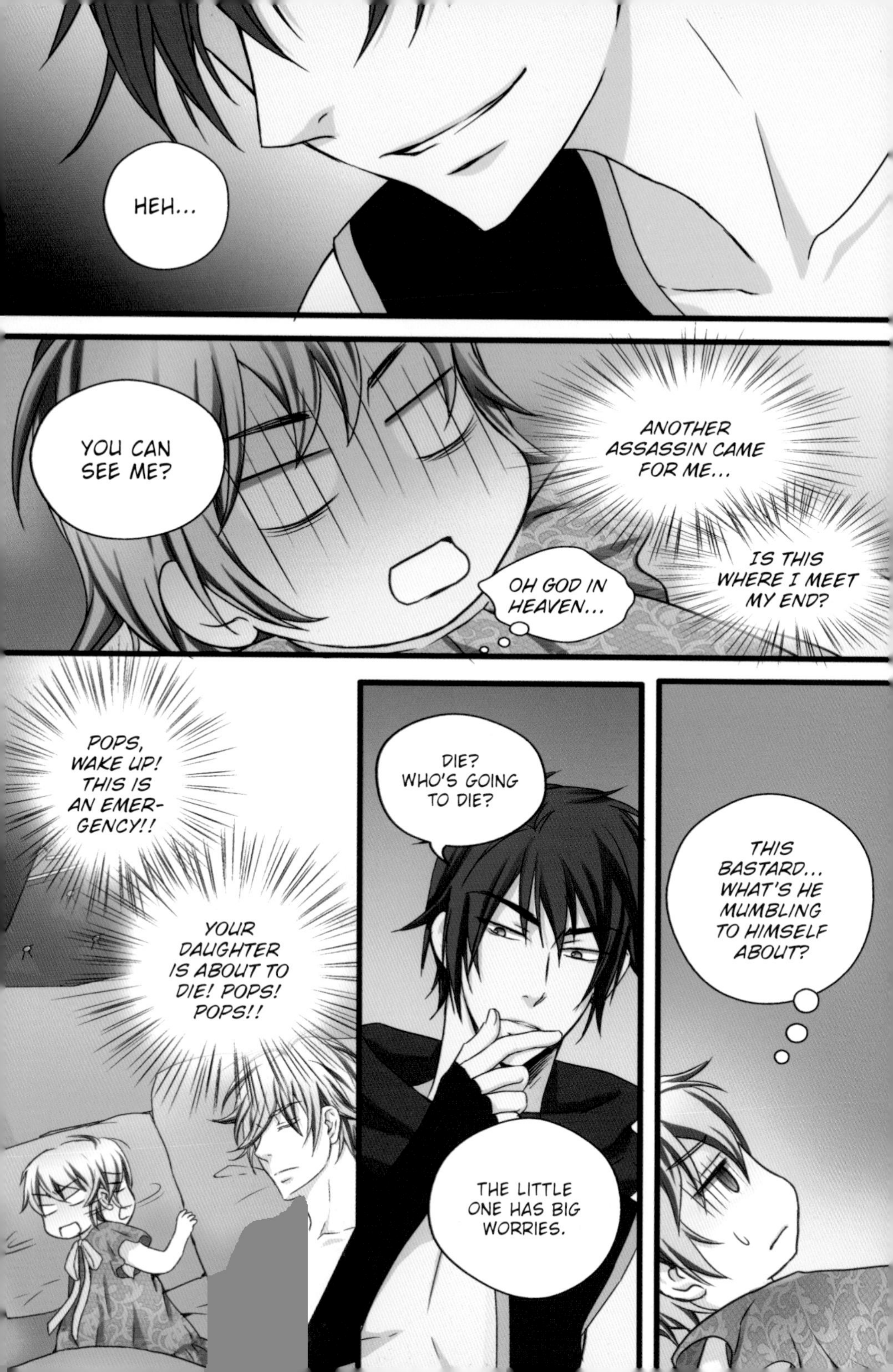
HEH...
YOU CAN SEE ME?
ANOTHER ASSASSIN CAME FOR ME...
OH GOD IN HEAVEN...
IS THIS WHERE I MEET MY END?
POPS, WAKE UP! THIS IS AN EMER-GENCY!!
YOUR DAUGHTER IS ABOUT TO DIE! POPS! POPS!!
DIE? WHO'S GOING TO DIE?
THE LITTLE ONE HAS BIG WORRIES.
THIS BASTARD... WHAT'S HE MUMBLING TO HIMSELF ABOUT?

I'M NOT TALKING TO MYSELF.

I'M HAVING A CONVERSATION WITH YOU.

HUH? I-I-I-IS HE READING MY MIND RIGHT NOW?

WH-WH-WHAT ARE YOU?!

WHY? WHAT COULD YOU EVEN DO—WARD ME OFF WITH GARLIC? POUR SALT ACROSS THE DOORWAY?

YOU ASSHOLE, THINK YOU'RE FUNNY?

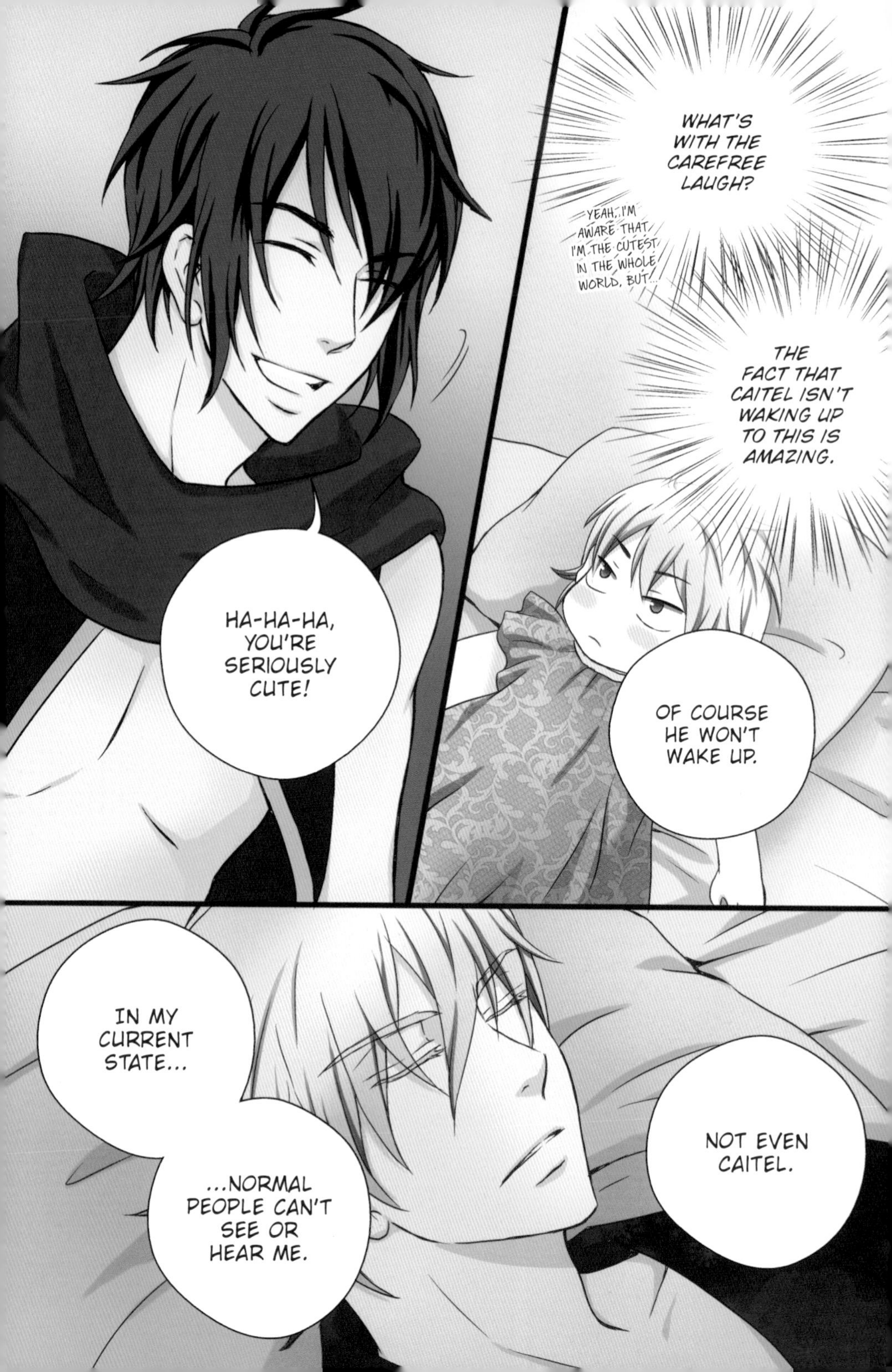
HA-HA-HA, YOU'RE SERIOUSLY CUTE!
WHAT'S WITH THE CAREFREE LAUGH?
YEAH, I'M AWARE THAT I'M THE CUTEST IN THE WHOLE WORLD, BUT...
THE FACT THAT CAITEL ISN'T WAKING UP TO THIS IS AMAZING.
OF COURSE HE WON'T WAKE UP.
IN MY CURRENT STATE...
...NORMAL PEOPLE CAN'T SEE OR HEAR ME.
NOT EVEN CAITEL.

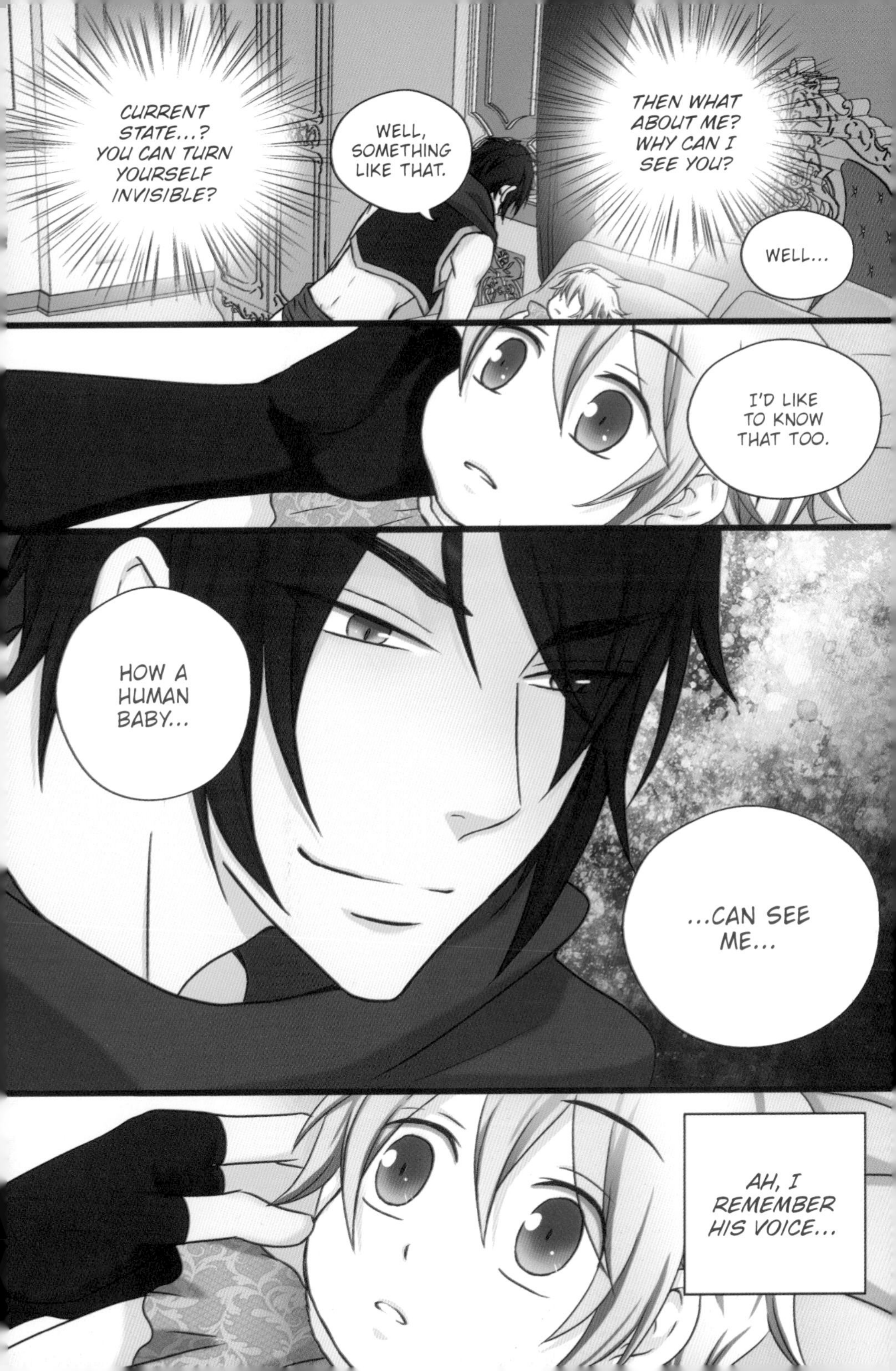
CURRENT STATE...? YOU CAN TURN YOURSELF INVISIBLE?
WELL, SOMETHING LIKE THAT.
THEN WHAT ABOUT ME? WHY CAN I SEE YOU?
WELL...
I'D LIKE TO KNOW THAT TOO.
HOW A HUMAN BABY...
...CAN SEE ME...
AH, I REMEMBER HIS VOICE...

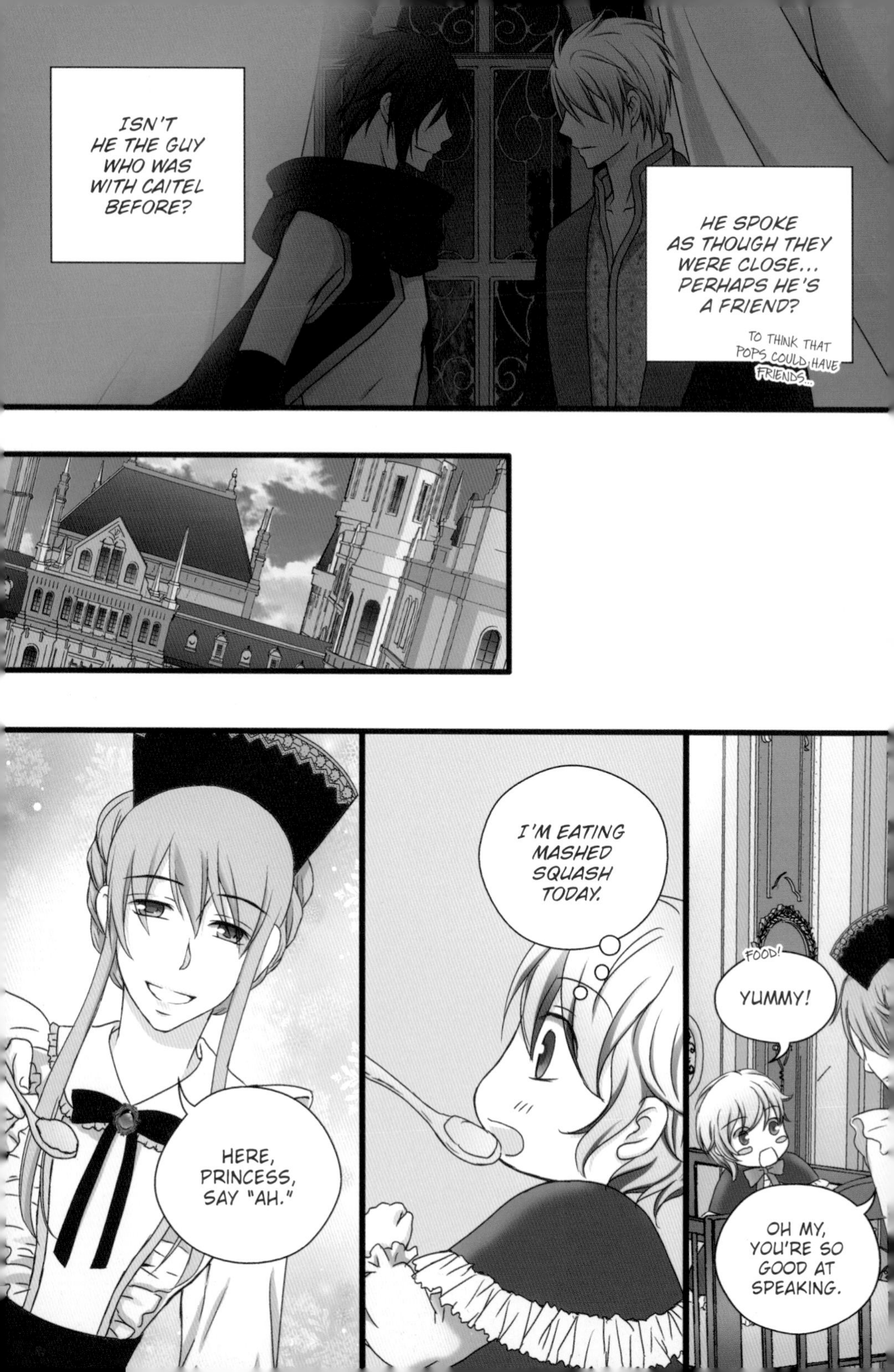
ISN'T HE THE GUY WHO WAS WITH CAITEL BEFORE?
HE SPOKE AS THOUGH THEY WERE CLOSE... PERHAPS HE'S A FRIEND?
TO THINK THAT POPS COULD HAVE FRIENDS...
HERE, PRINCESS, SAY "AH."
I'M EATING MASHED SQUASH TODAY.
FOOD!
YUMMY!
OH MY, YOU'RE SO GOOD AT SPEAKING.

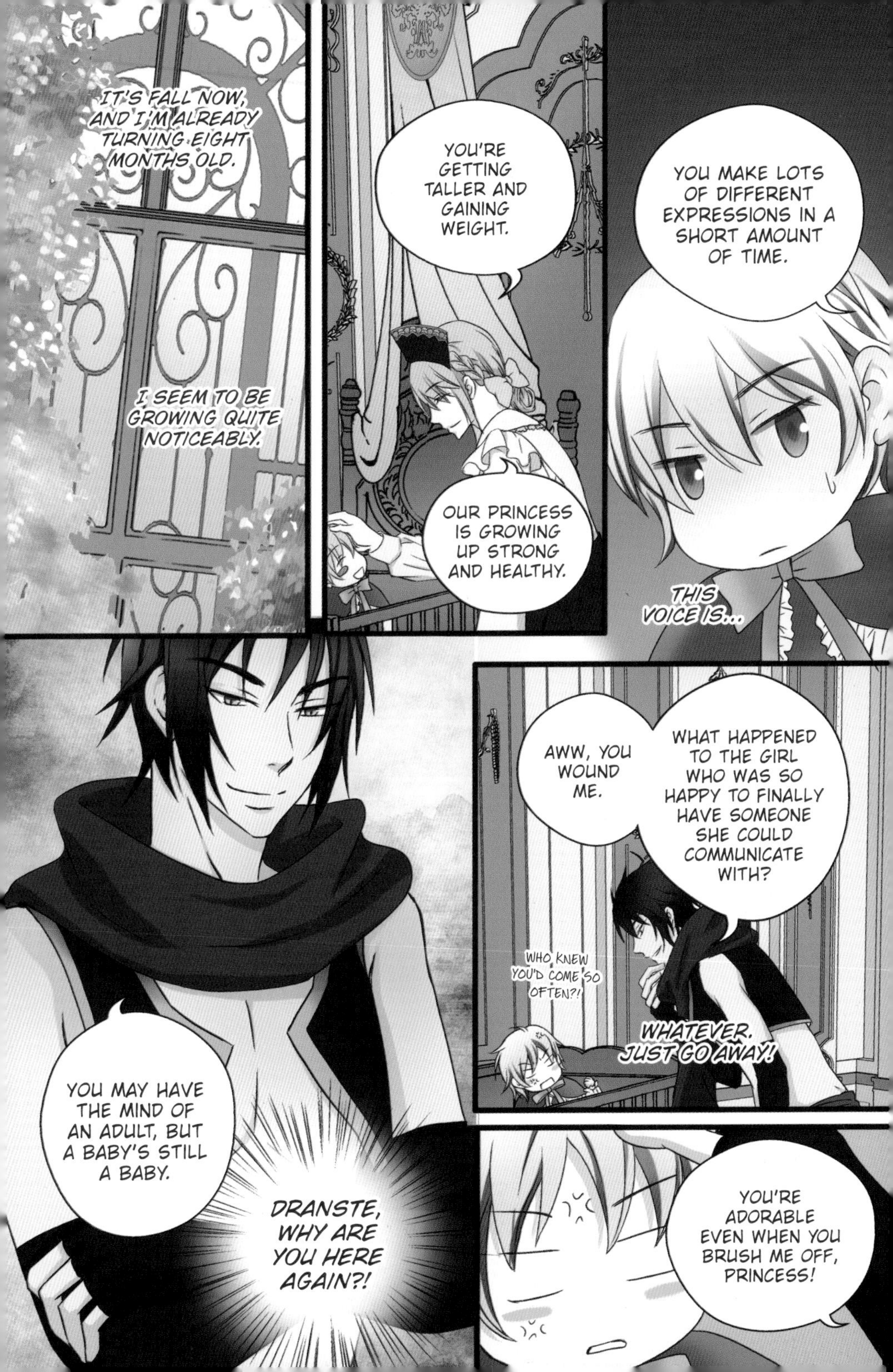
IT'S FALL NOW, AND I'M ALREADY TURNING EIGHT MONTHS OLD.
I SEEM TO BE GROWING QUITE NOTICEABLY.
YOU'RE GETTING TALLER AND GAINING WEIGHT.
OUR PRINCESS IS GROWING UP STRONG AND HEALTHY.
YOU MAKE LOTS OF DIFFERENT EXPRESSIONS IN A SHORT AMOUNT OF TIME.
THIS VOICE IS...
YOU MAY HAVE THE MIND OF AN ADULT, BUT A BABY'S STILL A BABY.
DRANSTE, WHY ARE YOU HERE AGAIN?!
AWW, YOU WOUND ME.
WHAT HAPPENED TO THE GIRL WHO WAS SO HAPPY TO FINALLY HAVE SOMEONE SHE COULD COMMUNICATE WITH?
WHO KNEW YOU'D COME SO OFTEN?!
WHATEVER. JUST GO AWAY!
YOU'RE ADORABLE EVEN WHEN YOU BRUSH ME OFF, PRINCESS!

ACCORDING TO HIM, THIS IS A TYPE OF TELEPATHY.

APPARENTLY THE REASON CAITEL OR SERIRA CAN'T HEAR HIM IS BECAUSE THEY'RE FULLY HUMAN, SO THEY'RE INCOMPATIBLE OR SOMETHING LIKE THAT.

MY THOUGHTS SCATTER AROUND ME, AND THIS PUNK CAN PICK THEM UP.

THAT'S GOOD AND ALL, BUT WHY AM I THE ONLY ONE THAT CAN SEE HIM?

I TOLD YOU BEFORE.

IT'S IN YOUR BLOOD.

AND WHAT DO YOU MEAN BY BLOOD?

I DON'T KNOW EITHER.

ARE YOU KIDDING?

IN ANY CASE, I THINK THE FACT THAT YOU'RE MORE CAPABLE THAN NORMAL BABIES IS BECAUSE OF YOUR BLOOD.

YOUR BODY IS THAT OF A BABY, BUT YOUR INTELLIGENCE AND EMOTIONAL CAPACITY HAVE PRETTY MUCH BEEN FULLY DEVELOPED, CORRECT?

ACCORDING TO HIS LOGIC, MY MEMORIES FROM MY PREVIOUS LIFE MAY HAVE TO DO WITH MY BLOOD TOO, BUT...

...DOES THIS MEAN I'M NOT A NORMAL HUMAN?

WELL, YOU'RE 98.2% HUMAN.

THEN I'M BASICALLY HUMAN!

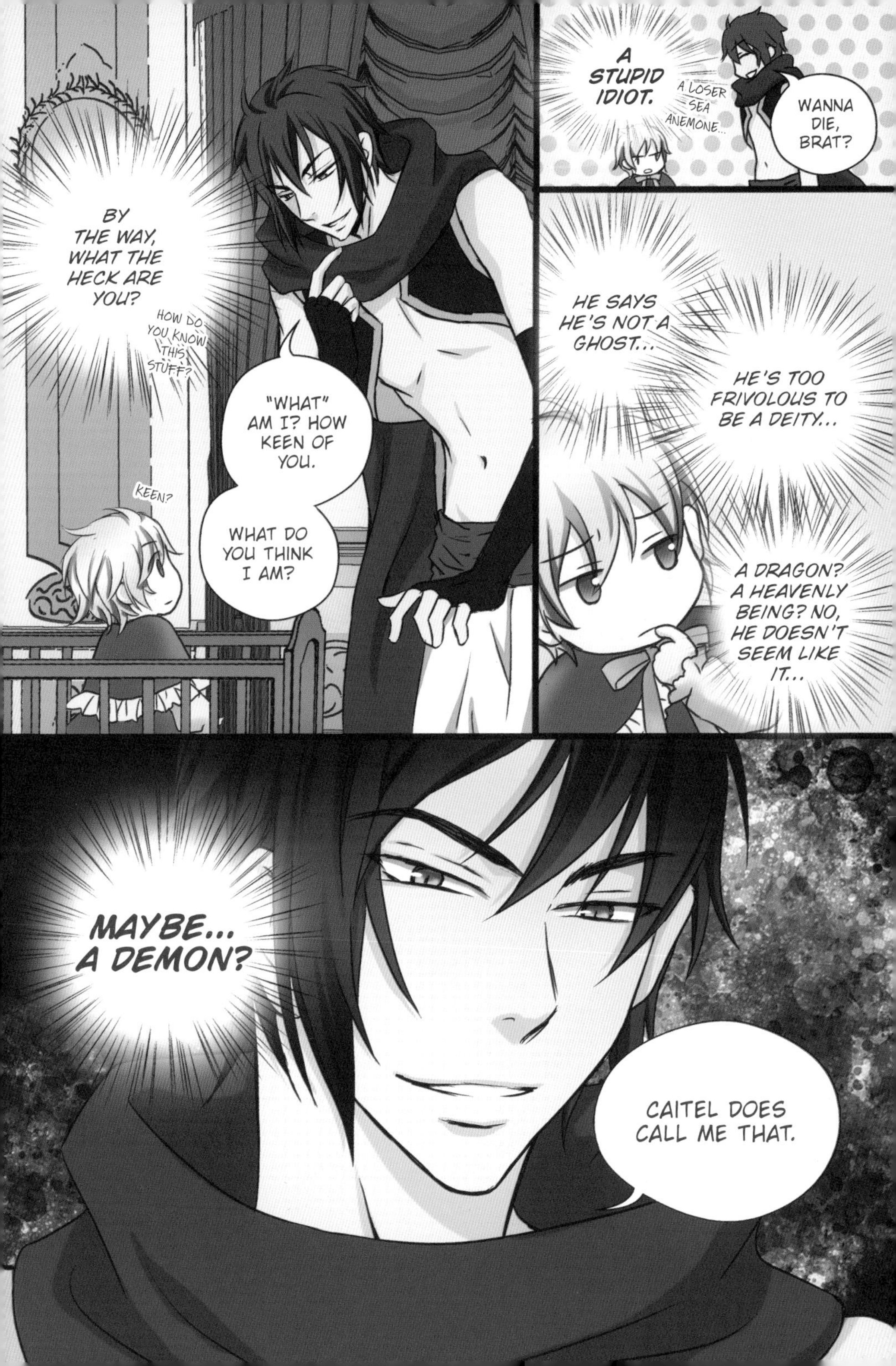
BY THE WAY, WHAT THE HECK ARE YOU?
HOW DO YOU KNOW THIS STUFF?
"WHAT" AM I? HOW KEEN OF YOU.
KEEN?
WHAT DO YOU THINK I AM?
A STUPID IDIOT.
A LOSER SEA ANEMONE...
WANNA DIE, BRAT?
HE SAYS HE'S NOT A GHOST...
HE'S TOO FRIVOLOUS TO BE A DEITY...
A DRAGON? A HEAVENLY BEING? NO, HE DOESN'T SEEM LIKE IT...
MAYBE... A DEMON?
CAITEL DOES CALL ME THAT.

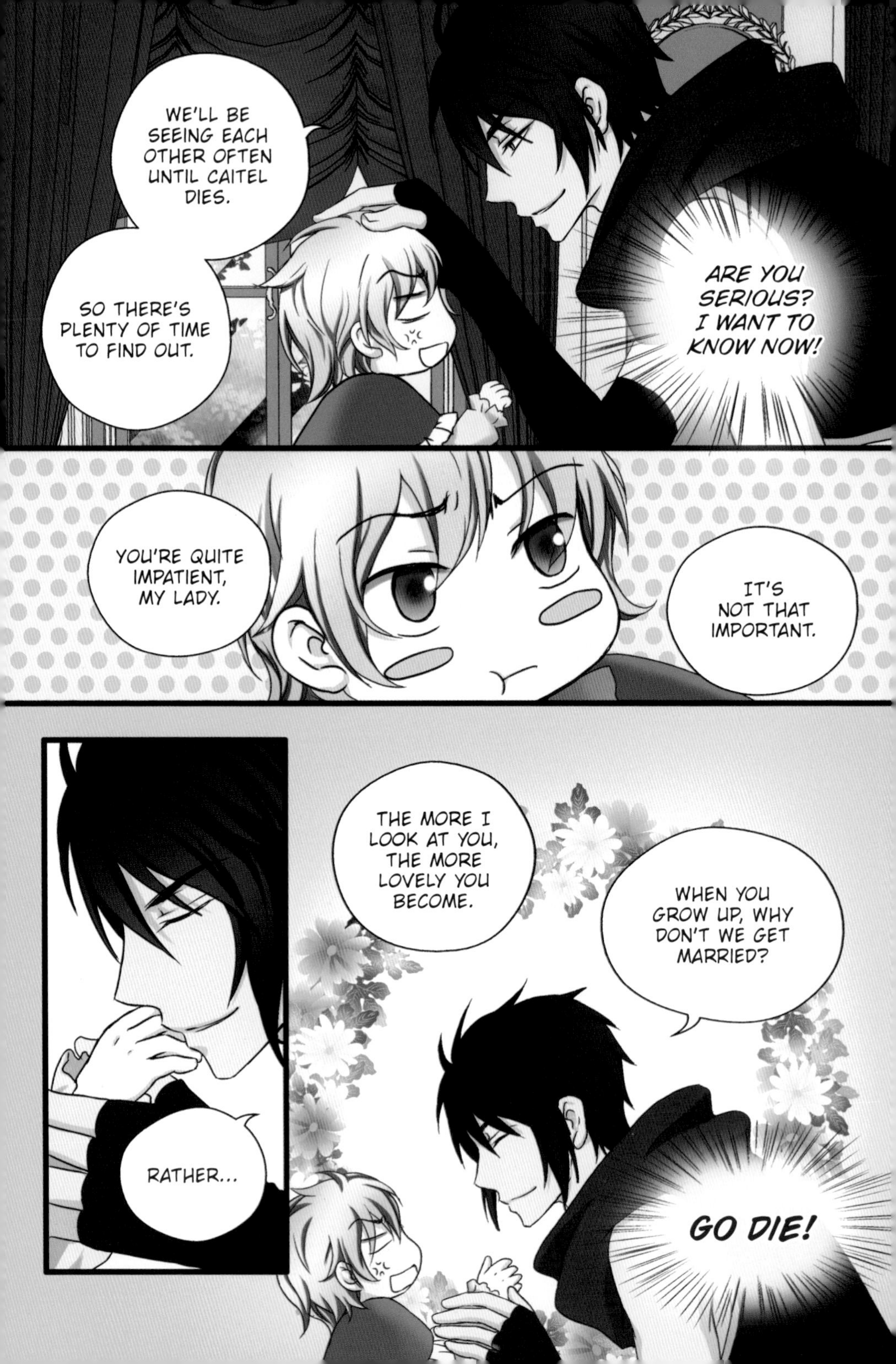
WE'LL BE SEEING EACH OTHER OFTEN UNTIL CAITEL DIES.
SO THERE'S PLENTY OF TIME TO FIND OUT.
ARE YOU SERIOUS? I WANT TO KNOW NOW!
YOU'RE QUITE IMPATIENT, MY LADY.
IT'S NOT THAT IMPORTANT.
RATHER...
THE MORE I LOOK AT YOU, THE MORE LOVELY YOU BECOME.
WHEN YOU GROW UP, WHY DON'T WE GET MARRIED?
GO DIE!

DAUGHTER
OF THE
EMPEROR

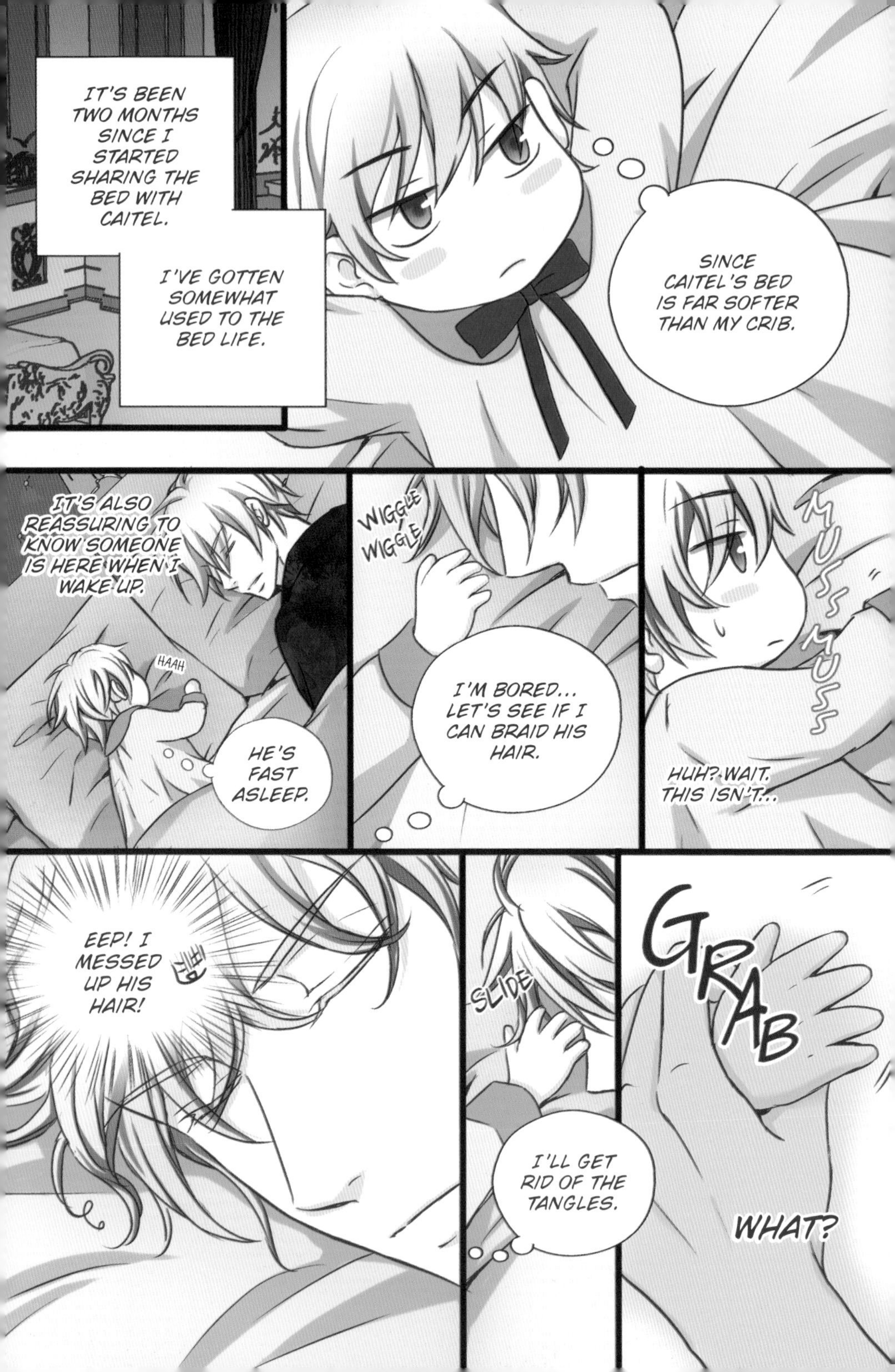
IT'S BEEN TWO MONTHS SINCE I STARTED SHARING THE BED WITH CAITEL.
I'VE GOTTEN SOMEWHAT USED TO THE BED LIFE.
SINCE CAITEL'S BED IS FAR SOFTER THAN MY CRIB.
IT'S ALSO REASSURING TO KNOW SOMEONE IS HERE WHEN I WAKE UP.
HAAH
HE'S FAST ASLEEP.
WIGGLE WIGGLE
I'M BORED... LET'S SEE IF I CAN BRAID HIS HAIR.
MUSS MUSS
HUH? WAIT. THIS ISN'T...
EEP! I MESSED UP HIS HAIR!
SLIDE
I'LL GET RID OF THE TANGLES.
GRAB
WHAT?

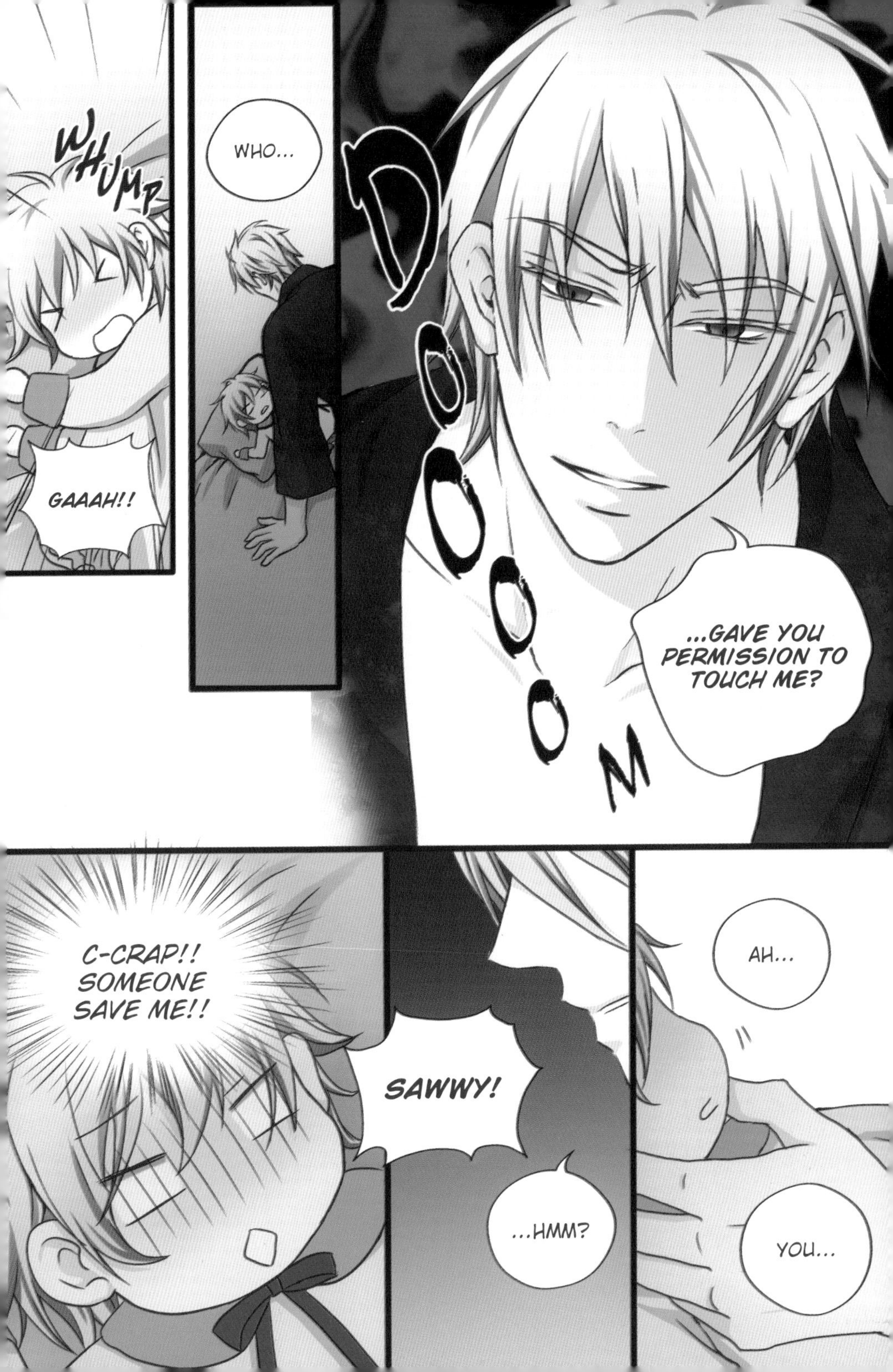
WHUMP
GAAAH!!
WHO...
DOOOOOM
...GAVE YOU PERMISSION TO TOUCH ME?
C-CRAP!! SOMEONE SAVE ME!!
SAWWY!
...HMM?
AH...
YOU...

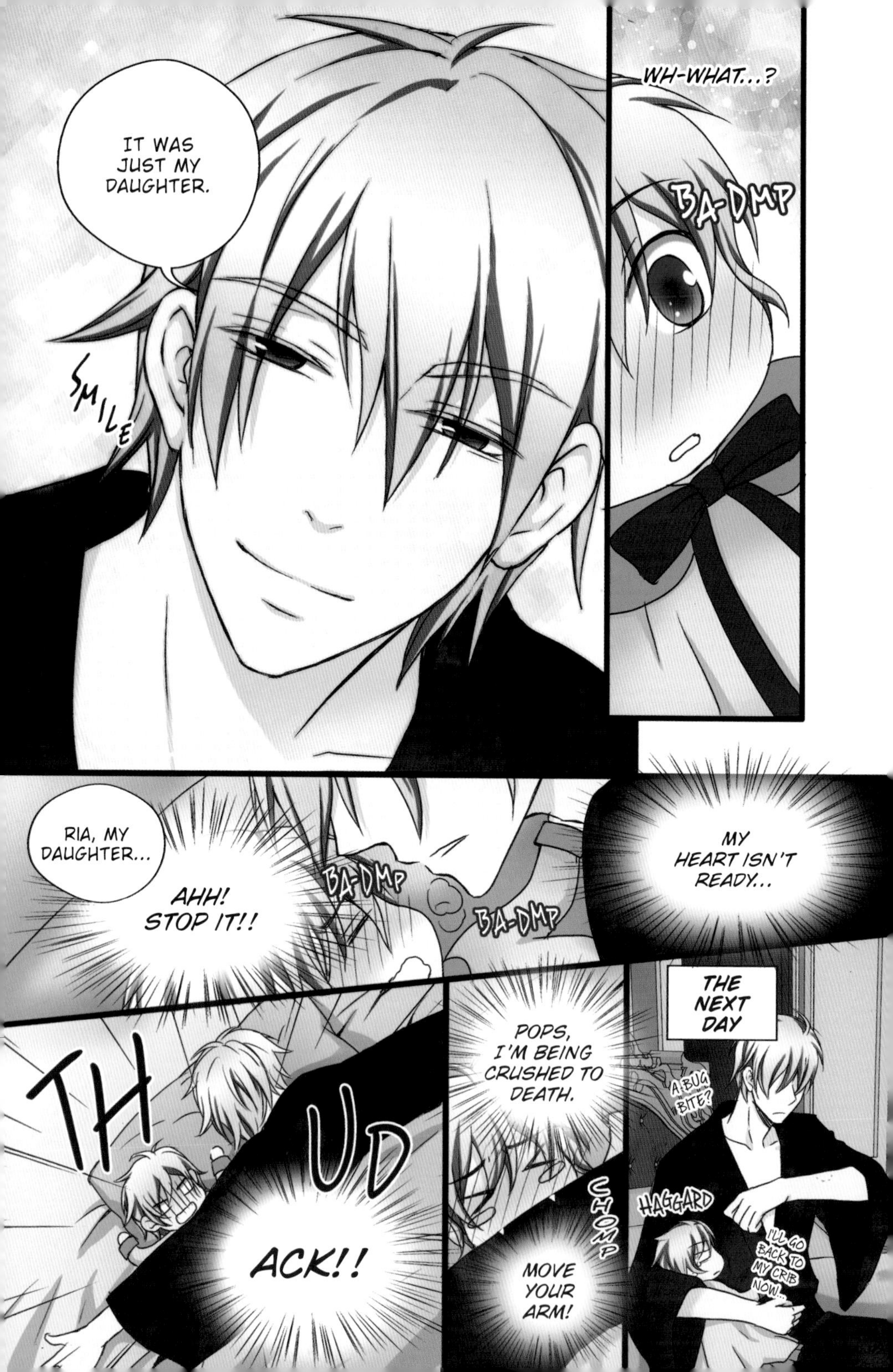
IT WAS JUST MY DAUGHTER.
SMILE
WH-WHAT...?
BA-DMP
RIA, MY DAUGHTER...
AHH! STOP IT!!
BA-DMP
BA-DMP
MY HEART ISN'T READY...
THUD
ACK!!
POPS, I'M BEING CRUSHED TO DEATH.
CHOMP
MOVE YOUR ARM!
THE NEXT DAY
A BUG BITE?
HAGGARD
I'LL GO BACK TO MY CRIB NOW...

You're My Papa! (3)

DAUGHTER
OF THE
EMPEROR

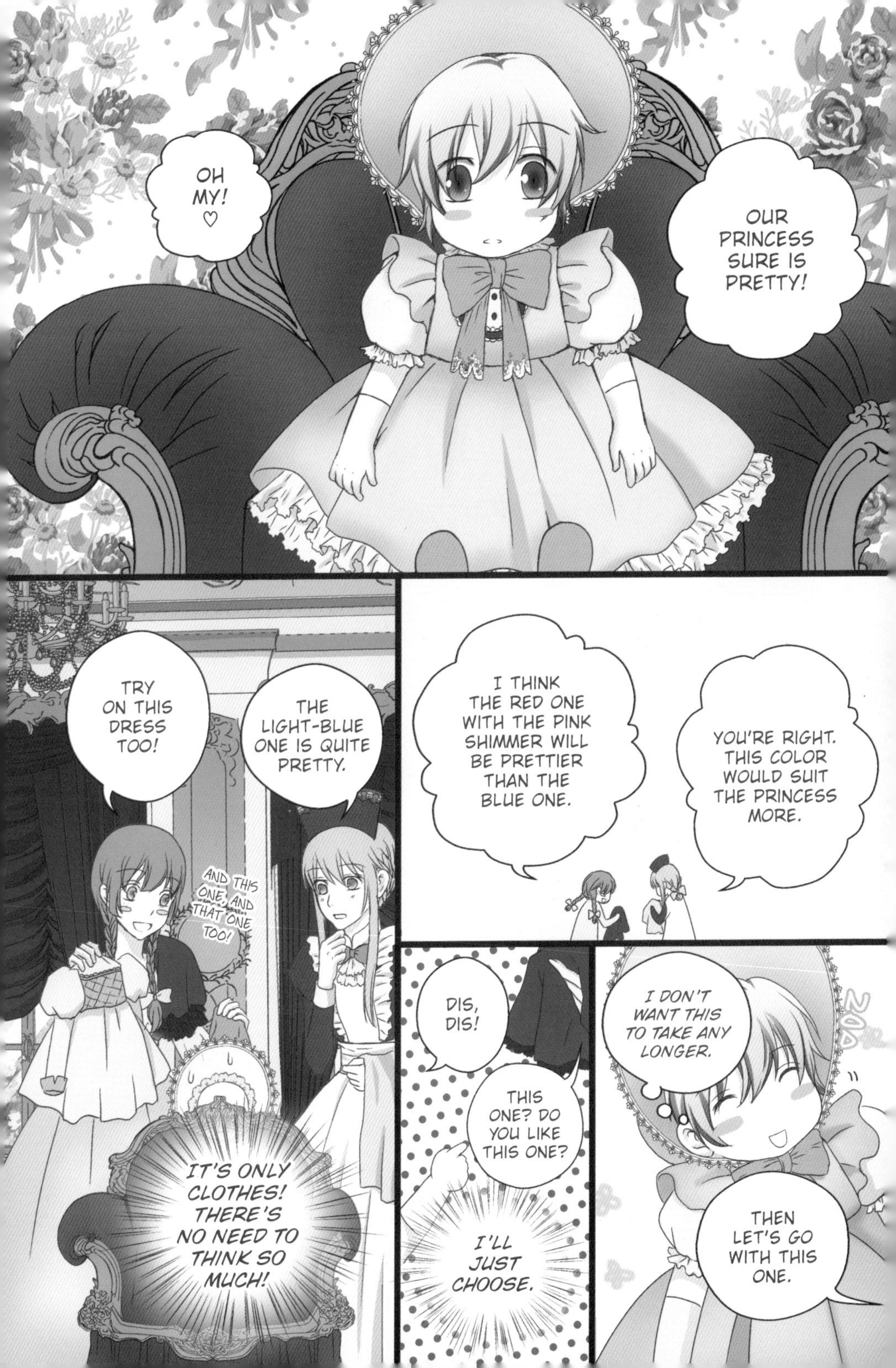
OH MY! ♡
OUR PRINCESS SURE IS PRETTY!
TRY ON THIS DRESS TOO!
THE LIGHT-BLUE ONE IS QUITE PRETTY.
AND THIS ONE, AND THAT ONE TOO!
IT'S ONLY CLOTHES! THERE'S NO NEED TO THINK SO MUCH!
I THINK THE RED ONE WITH THE PINK SHIMMER WILL BE PRETTIER THAN THE BLUE ONE.
YOU'RE RIGHT. THIS COLOR WOULD SUIT THE PRINCESS MORE.
DIS, DIS!
THIS ONE? DO YOU LIKE THIS ONE?
I'LL JUST CHOOSE.
I DON'T WANT THIS TO TAKE ANY LONGER.
THEN LET'S GO WITH THIS ONE.

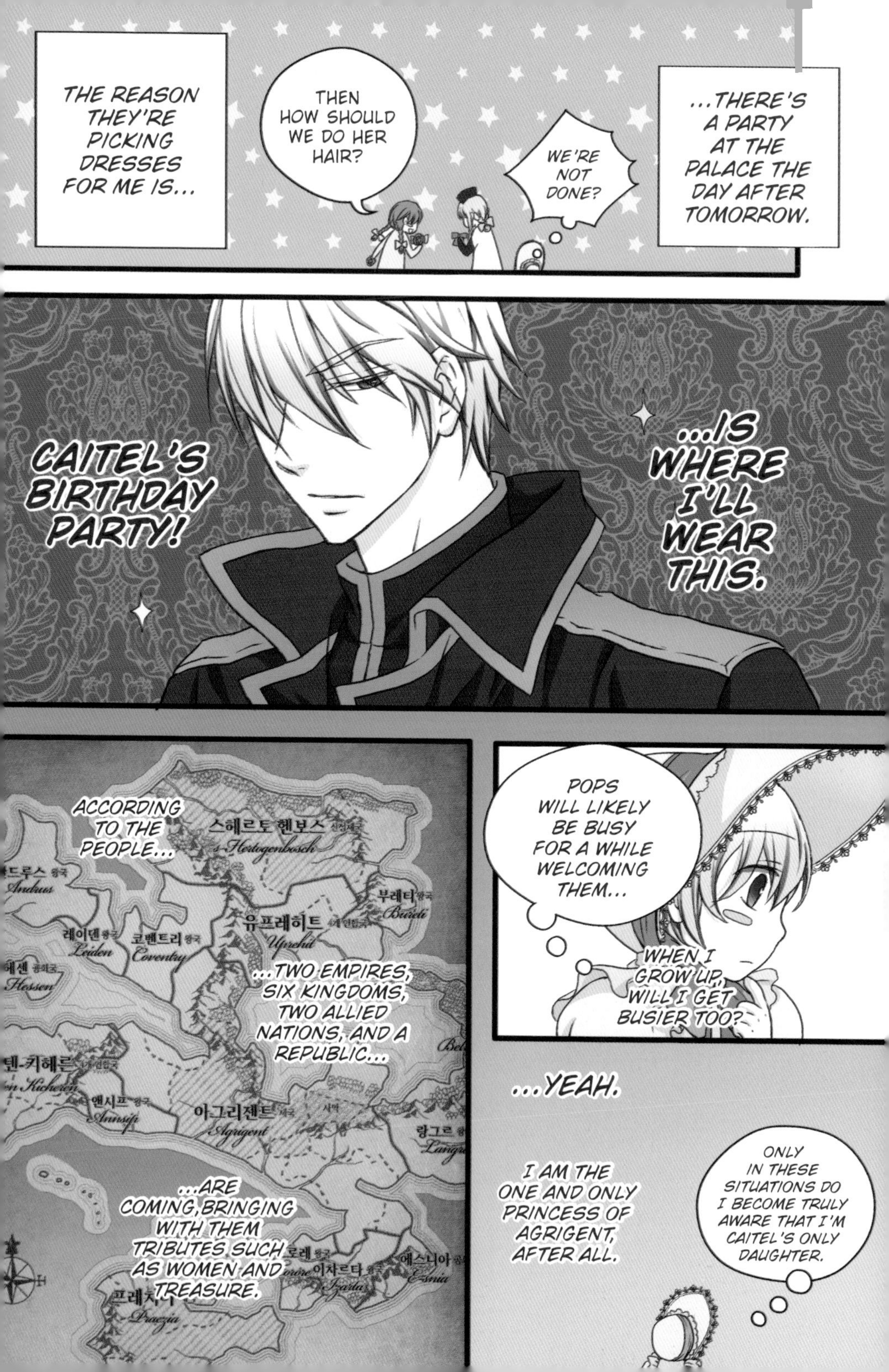
THE REASON THEY'RE PICKING DRESSES FOR ME IS...
THEN HOW SHOULD WE DO HER HAIR?
WE'RE NOT DONE?
...THERE'S A PARTY AT THE PALACE THE DAY AFTER TOMORROW.
CAITEL'S BIRTHDAY PARTY!
...IS WHERE I'LL WEAR THIS.
ACCORDING TO THE PEOPLE...
스헤르토헨보스
s-Hertogenbosch
유프레히트
Uprehit
레이덴
Leiden
코벤트리
Coventry
아그리젠트
Agrigent
...TWO EMPIRES, SIX KINGDOMS, TWO ALLIED NATIONS, AND A REPUBLIC...
...ARE COMING, BRINGING WITH THEM TRIBUTES SUCH AS WOMEN AND TREASURE.
POPS WILL LIKELY BE BUSY FOR A WHILE WELCOMING THEM...
WHEN I GROW UP, WILL I GET BUSIER TOO?
...YEAH.
I AM THE ONE AND ONLY PRINCESS OF AGRIGENT, AFTER ALL.
ONLY IN THESE SITUATIONS DO I BECOME TRULY AWARE THAT I'M CAITEL'S ONLY DAUGHTER.

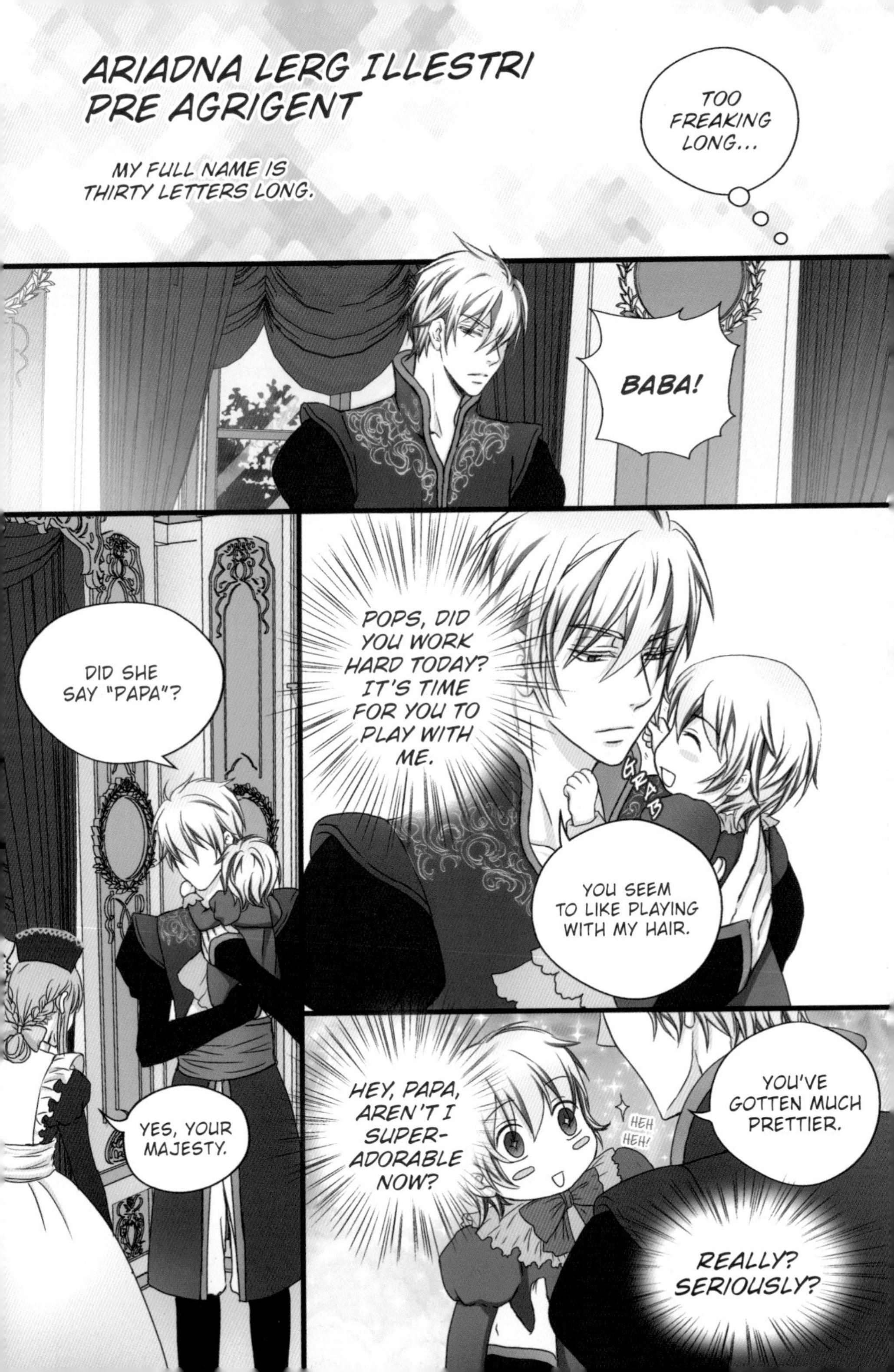
ARIADNA LERG ILLESTRI PRE AGRIGENT
MY FULL NAME IS THIRTY LETTERS LONG.
TOO FREAKING LONG...
BABA!
DID SHE SAY "PAPA"?
YES, YOUR MAJESTY.
POPS, DID YOU WORK HARD TODAY? IT'S TIME FOR YOU TO PLAY WITH ME.
GRAB
YOU SEEM TO LIKE PLAYING WITH MY HAIR.
HEY, PAPA, AREN'T I SUPER-ADORABLE NOW?
HEH HEH!
YOU'VE GOTTEN MUCH PRETTIER.
REALLY? SERIOUSLY?

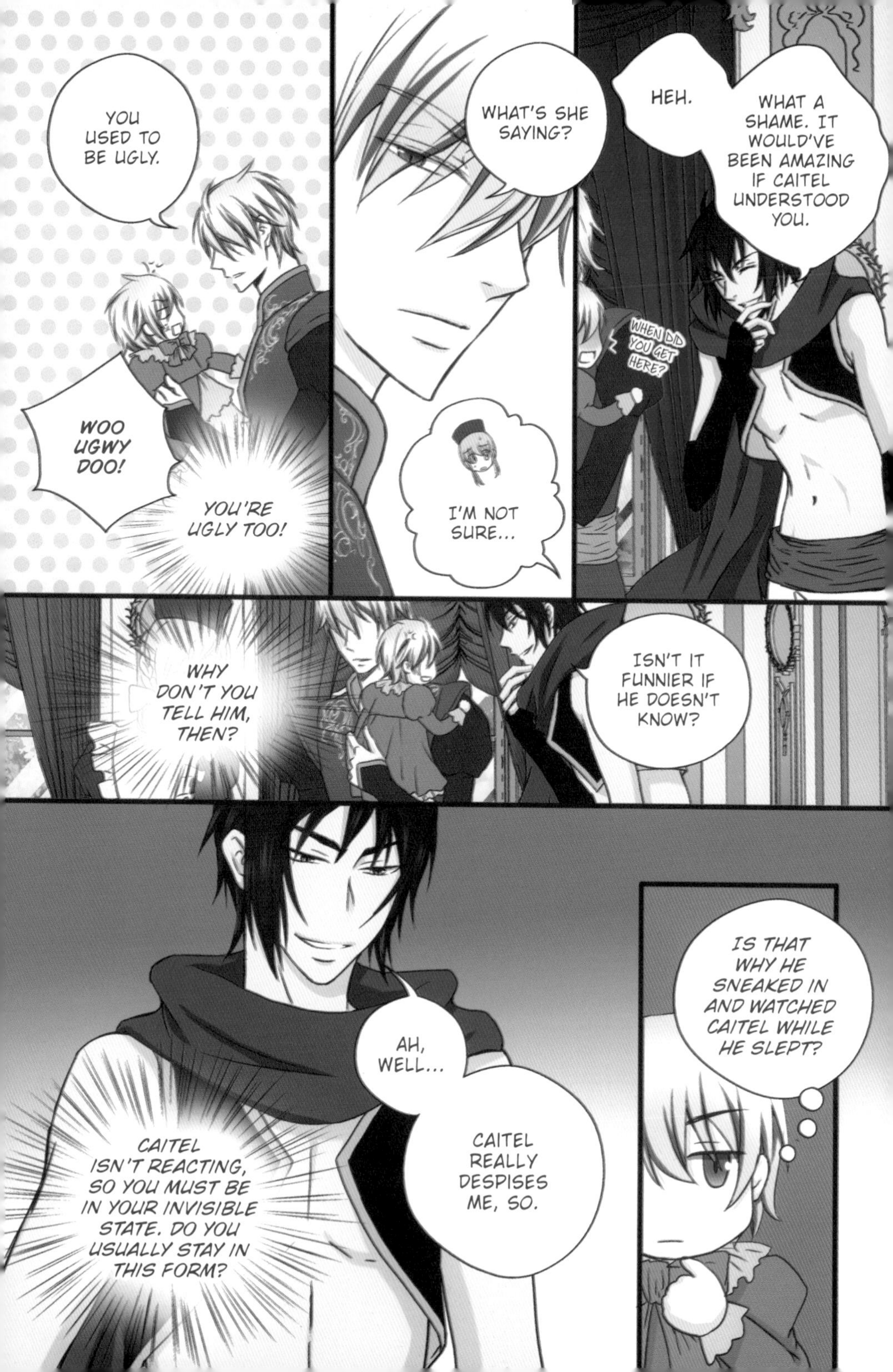
YOU USED TO BE UGLY.
WOO UGWY DOO!
YOU'RE UGLY TOO!
WHAT'S SHE SAYING?
I'M NOT SURE...
HEH.
WHAT A SHAME. IT WOULD'VE BEEN AMAZING IF CAITEL UNDERSTOOD YOU.
WHEN DID YOU GET HERE?
WHY DON'T YOU TELL HIM, THEN?
ISN'T IT FUNNIER IF HE DOESN'T KNOW?
CAITEL ISN'T REACTING, SO YOU MUST BE IN YOUR INVISIBLE STATE. DO YOU USUALLY STAY IN THIS FORM?
AH, WELL...
CAITEL REALLY DESPISES ME, SO.
IS THAT WHY HE SNEAKED IN AND WATCHED CAITEL WHILE HE SLEPT?

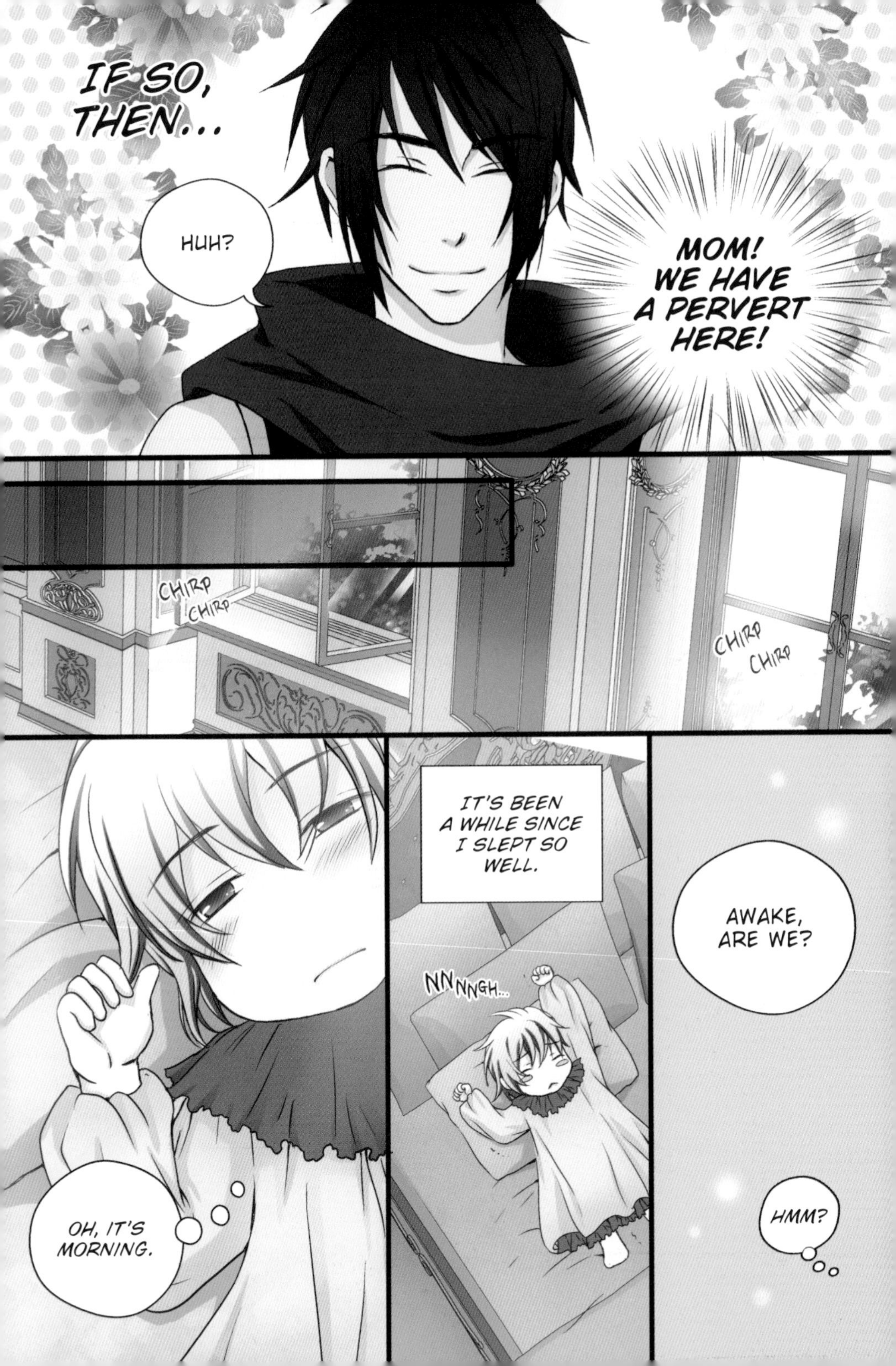
IF SO, THEN...
HUH?
MOM! WE HAVE A PERVERT HERE!
CHIRP CHIRP
CHIRP CHIRP
OH, IT'S MORNING.
IT'S BEEN A WHILE SINCE I SLEPT SO WELL.
NNNNGH...
AWAKE, ARE WE?
HMM?

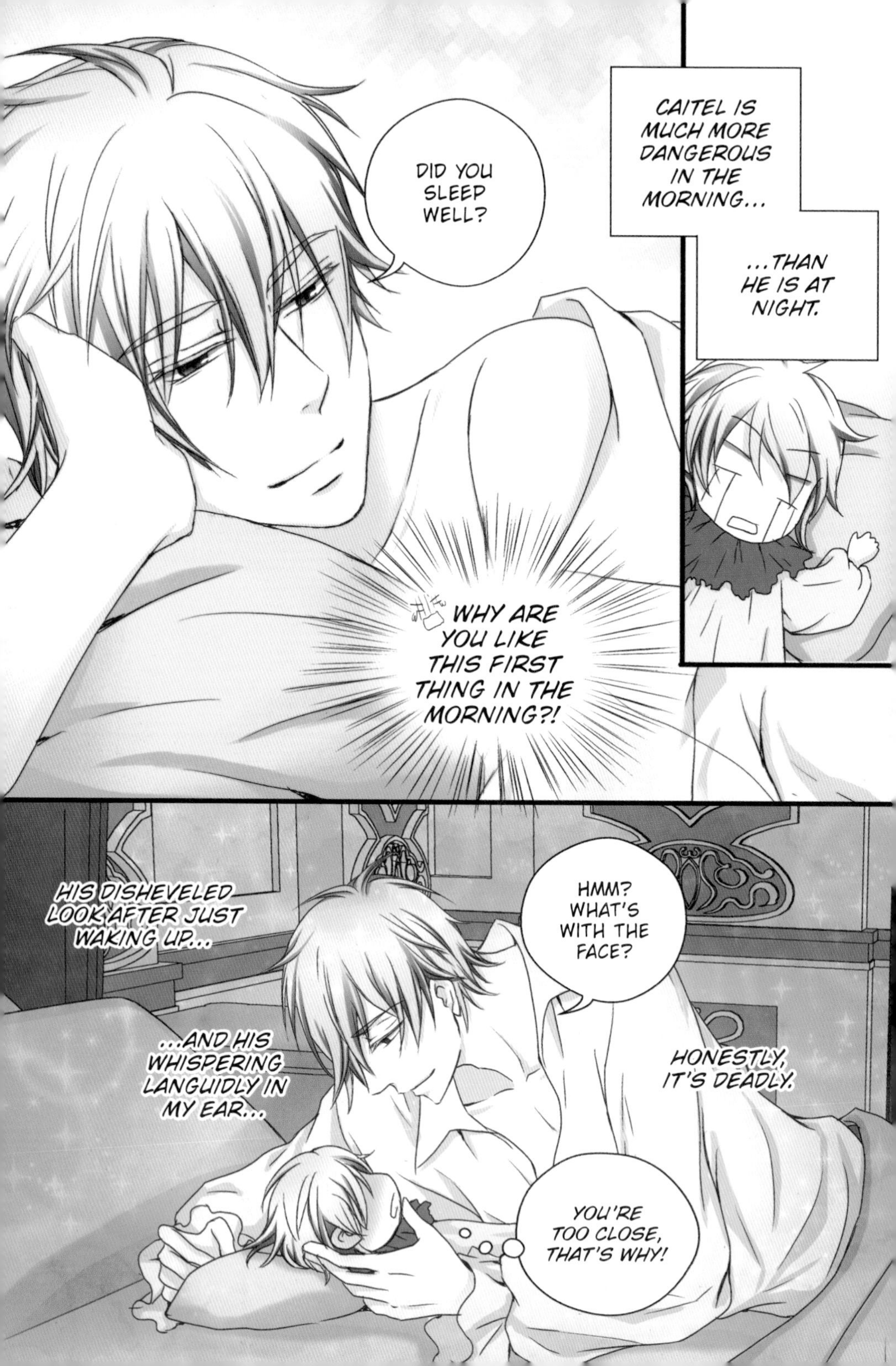
DID YOU SLEEP WELL?
WHY ARE YOU LIKE THIS FIRST THING IN THE MORNING?!
CAITEL IS MUCH MORE DANGEROUS IN THE MORNING...
...THAN HE IS AT NIGHT.
HIS DISHEVELED LOOK AFTER JUST WAKING UP...
HMM? WHAT'S WITH THE FACE?
...AND HIS WHISPERING LANGUIDLY IN MY EAR...
HONESTLY, IT'S DEADLY.
YOU'RE TOO CLOSE, THAT'S WHY!

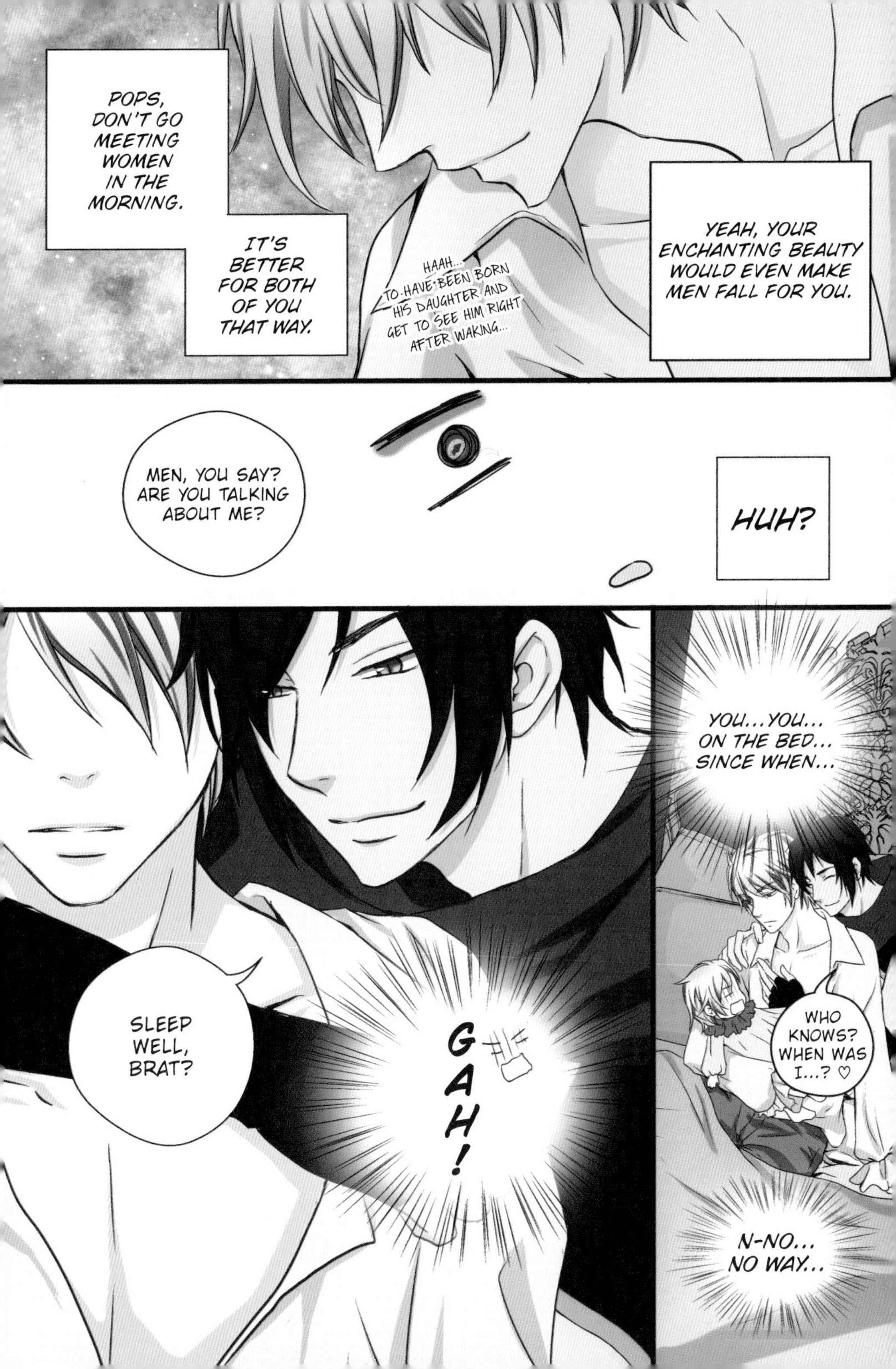
POPS, DON'T GO MEETING WOMEN IN THE MORNING.
IT'S BETTER FOR BOTH OF YOU THAT WAY.
HAAH... TO HAVE BEEN BORN HIS DAUGHTER AND GET TO SEE HIM RIGHT AFTER WAKING...
YEAH, YOUR ENCHANTING BEAUTY WOULD EVEN MAKE MEN FALL FOR YOU.
MEN, YOU SAY? ARE YOU TALKING ABOUT ME?
HUH?
SLEEP WELL, BRAT?
GAH!
YOU...YOU... ON THE BED... SINCE WHEN...
WHO KNOWS? WHEN WAS I...? ♡
N-NO... NO WAY...

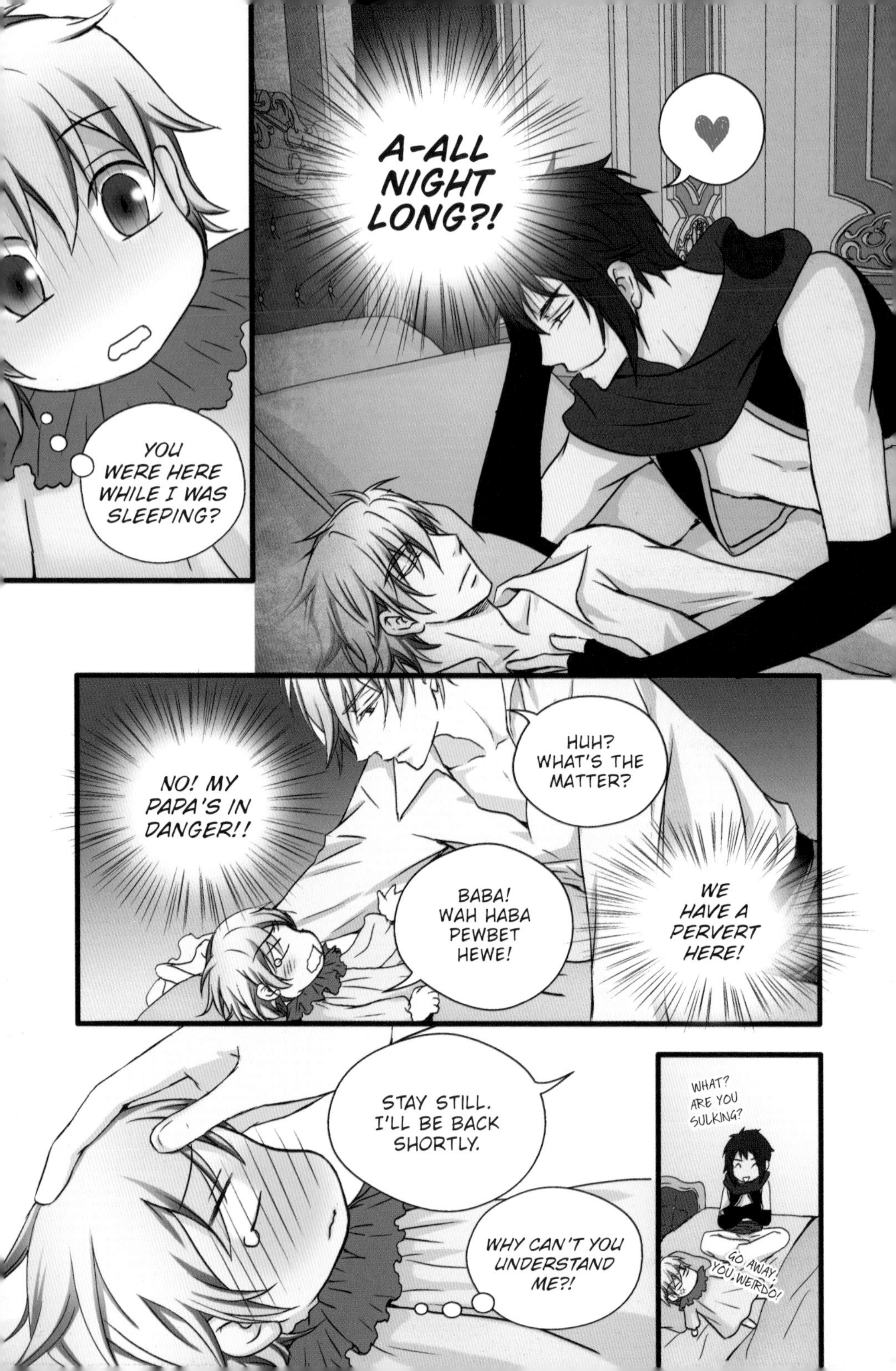
YOU WERE HERE WHILE I WAS SLEEPING?
A-ALL NIGHT LONG?!
NO! MY PAPA'S IN DANGER!!
HUH? WHAT'S THE MATTER?
BABA! WAH HABA PEWBET HEWE!
WE HAVE A PERVERT HERE!
STAY STILL. I'LL BE BACK SHORTLY.
WHY CAN'T YOU UNDERSTAND ME?!
WHAT? ARE YOU SULKING?
GO AWAY, YOU WEIRDO!

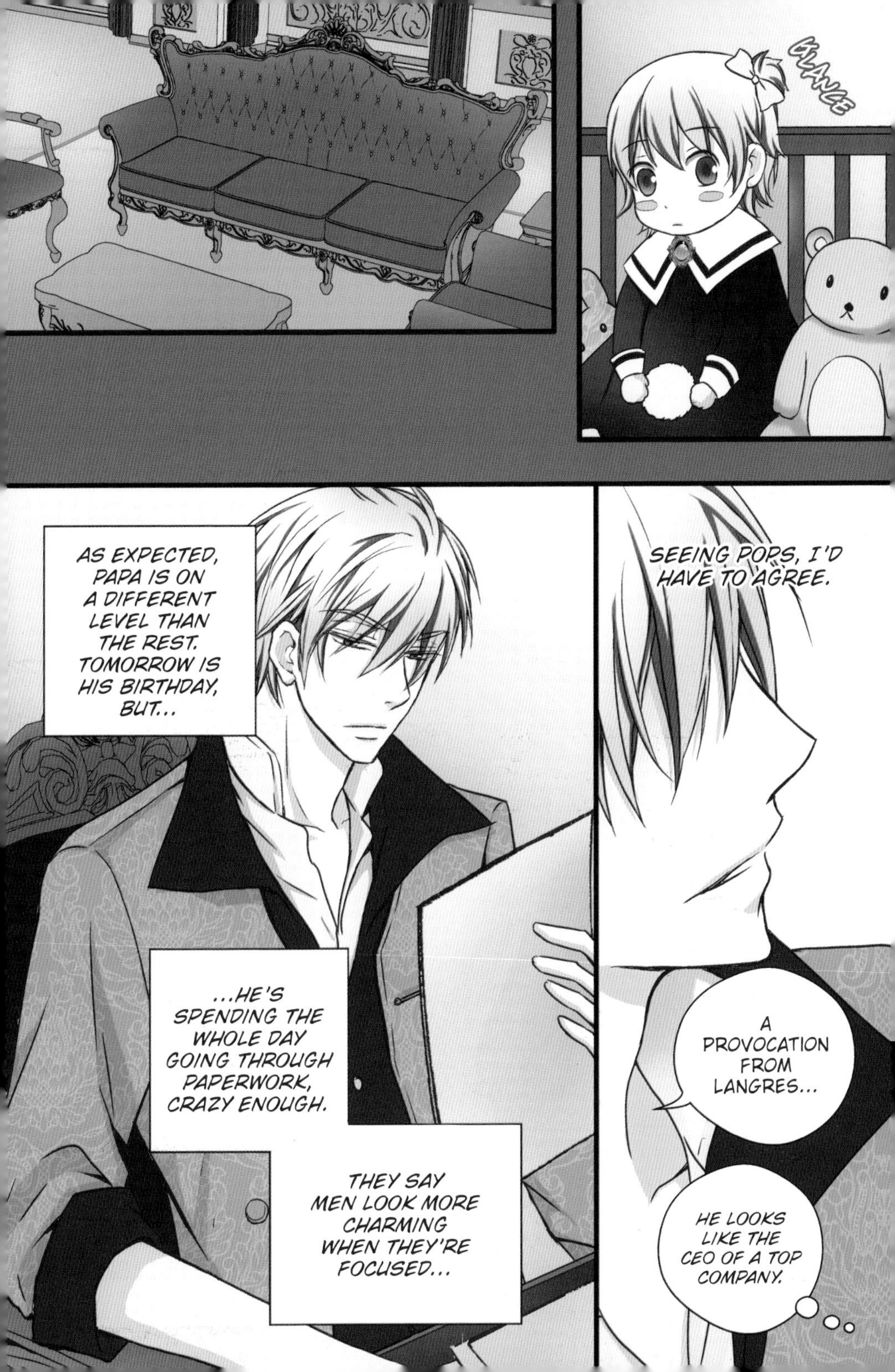
GLANCE
AS EXPECTED, PAPA IS ON A DIFFERENT LEVEL THAN THE REST. TOMORROW IS HIS BIRTHDAY, BUT...
...HE'S SPENDING THE WHOLE DAY GOING THROUGH PAPERWORK, CRAZY ENOUGH.
THEY SAY MEN LOOK MORE CHARMING WHEN THEY'RE FOCUSED...
SEEING POPS, I'D HAVE TO AGREE.
A PROVOCATION FROM LANGRES...
HE LOOKS LIKE THE CEO OF A TOP COMPANY.

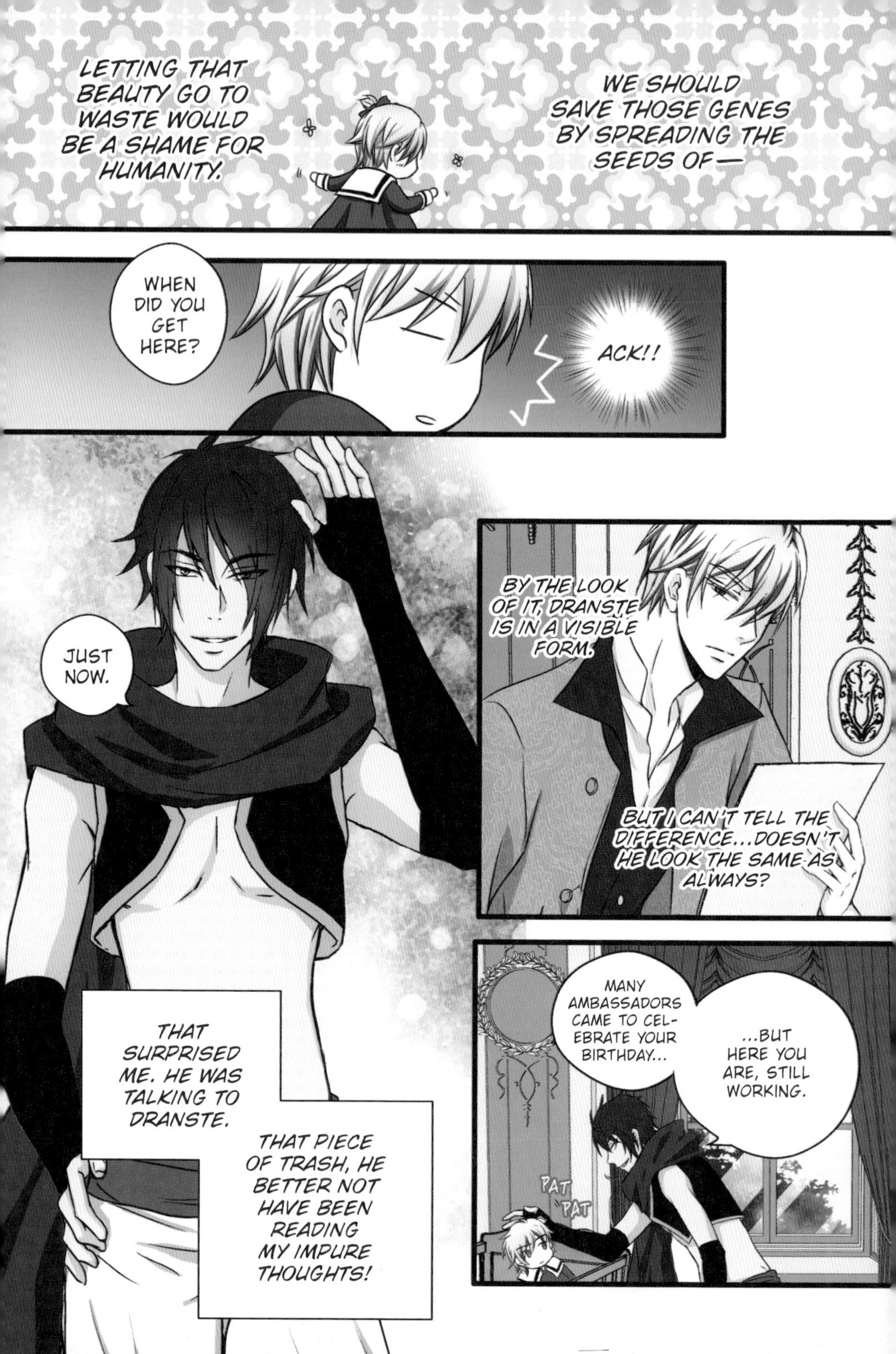
LETTING THAT BEAUTY GO TO WASTE WOULD BE A SHAME FOR HUMANITY.
WE SHOULD SAVE THOSE GENES BY SPREADING THE SEEDS OF—
WHEN DID YOU GET HERE?
ACK!!
JUST NOW.
BY THE LOOK OF IT, DRANSTE IS IN A VISIBLE FORM.
BUT I CAN'T TELL THE DIFFERENCE...DOESN'T HE LOOK THE SAME AS ALWAYS?
THAT SURPRISED ME. HE WAS TALKING TO DRANSTE.
THAT PIECE OF TRASH, HE BETTER NOT HAVE BEEN READING MY IMPURE THOUGHTS!
MANY AMBASSADORS CAME TO CEL-EBRATE YOUR BIRTHDAY...
...BUT HERE YOU ARE, STILL WORKING.
PAT PAT

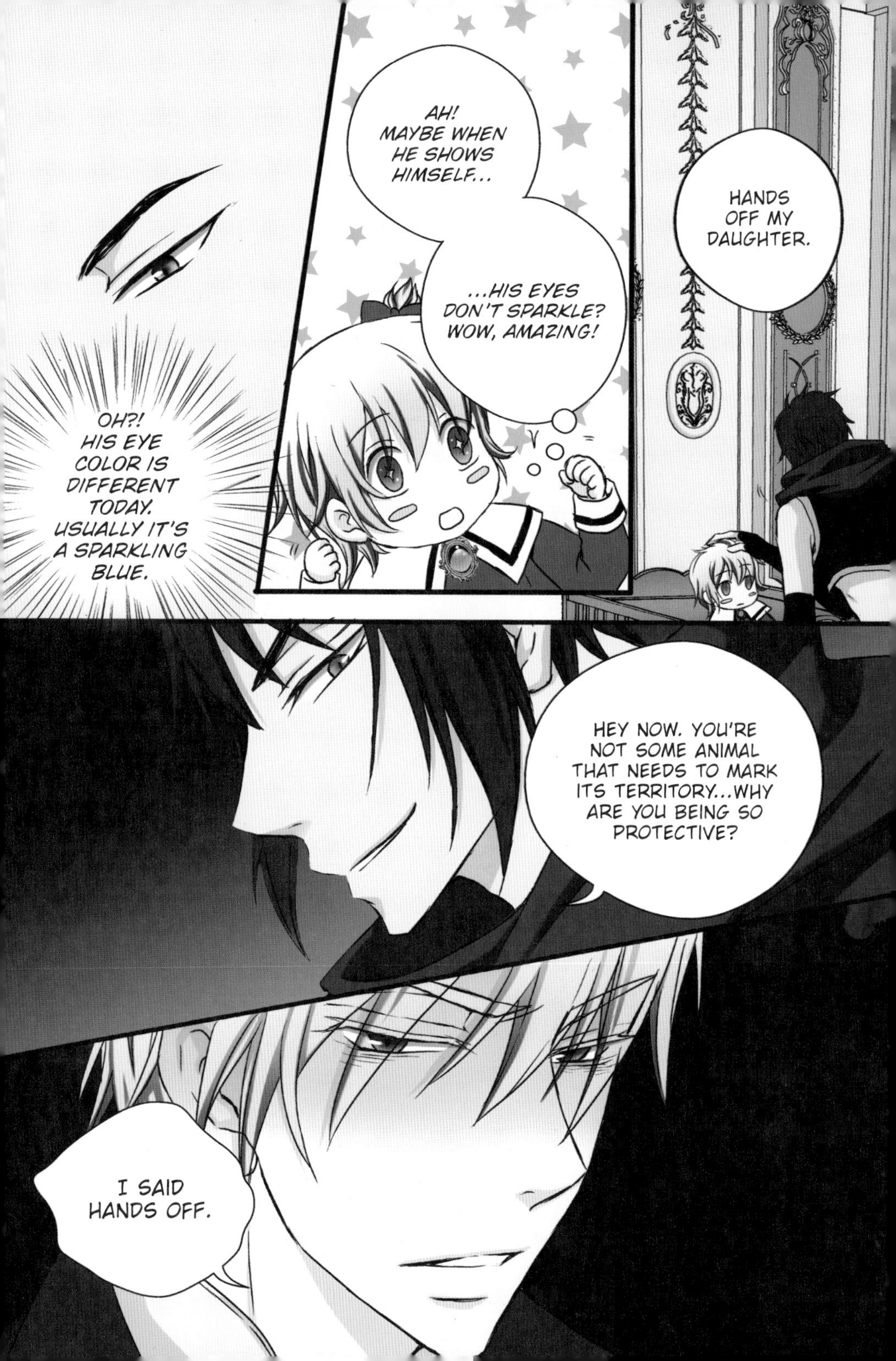
OH?! HIS EYE COLOR IS DIFFERENT TODAY. USUALLY IT'S A SPARKLING BLUE.
AH! MAYBE WHEN HE SHOWS HIMSELF...
...HIS EYES DON'T SPARKLE? WOW, AMAZING!
HANDS OFF MY DAUGHTER.
HEY NOW. YOU'RE NOT SOME ANIMAL THAT NEEDS TO MARK ITS TERRITORY...WHY ARE YOU BEING SO PROTECTIVE?
I SAID HANDS OFF.

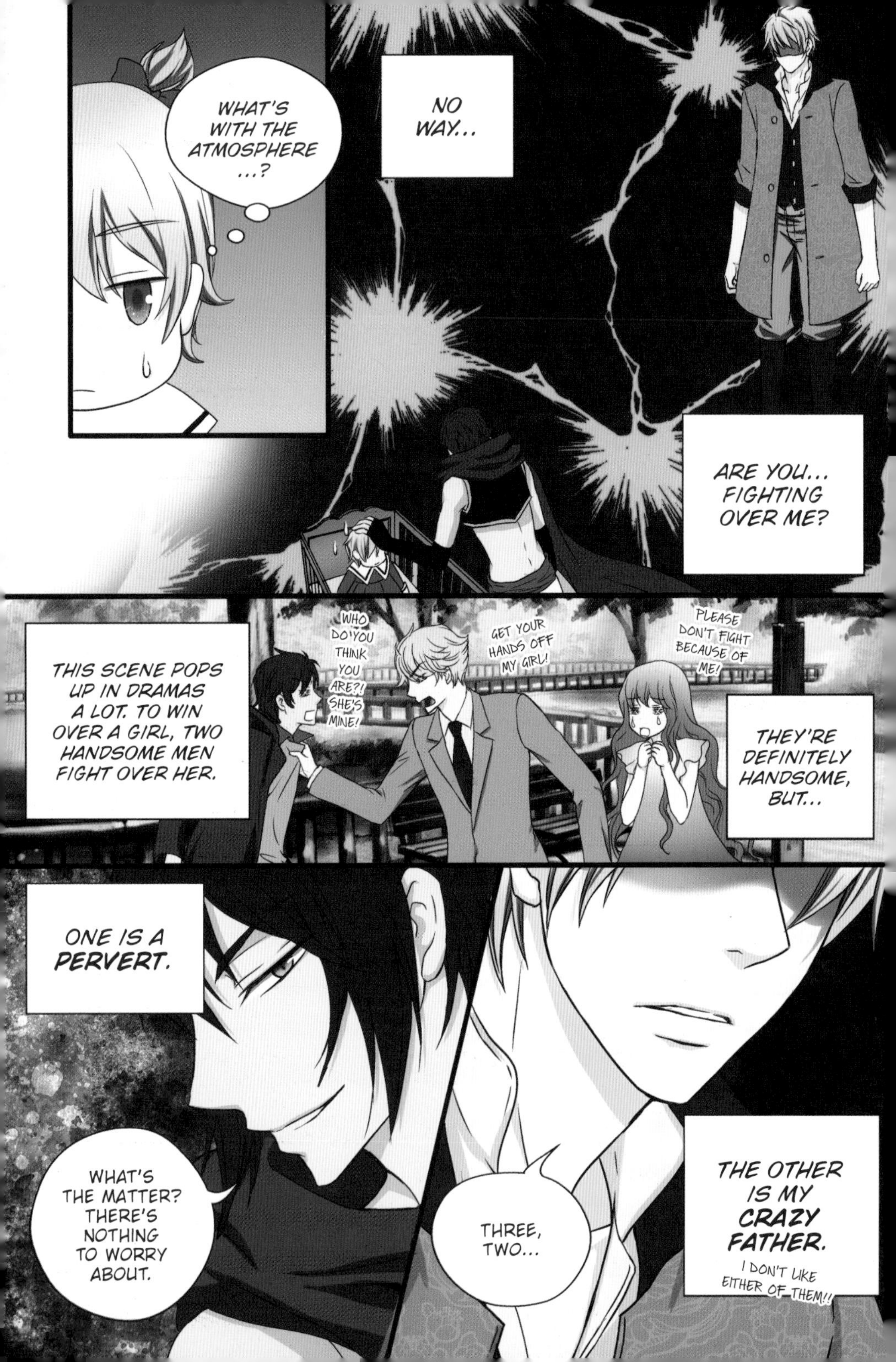
WHAT'S WITH THE ATMOSPHERE ...?
NO WAY...
ARE YOU... FIGHTING OVER ME?
THIS SCENE POPS UP IN DRAMAS A LOT. TO WIN OVER A GIRL, TWO HANDSOME MEN FIGHT OVER HER.
WHO DO YOU THINK YOU ARE?! SHE'S MINE!
GET YOUR HANDS OFF MY GIRL!
PLEASE DON'T FIGHT BECAUSE OF ME!
THEY'RE DEFINITELY HANDSOME, BUT...
ONE IS A PERVERT.
WHAT'S THE MATTER? THERE'S NOTHING TO WORRY ABOUT.
THREE, TWO...
THE OTHER IS MY CRAZY FATHER.
I DON'T LIKE EITHER OF THEM!!

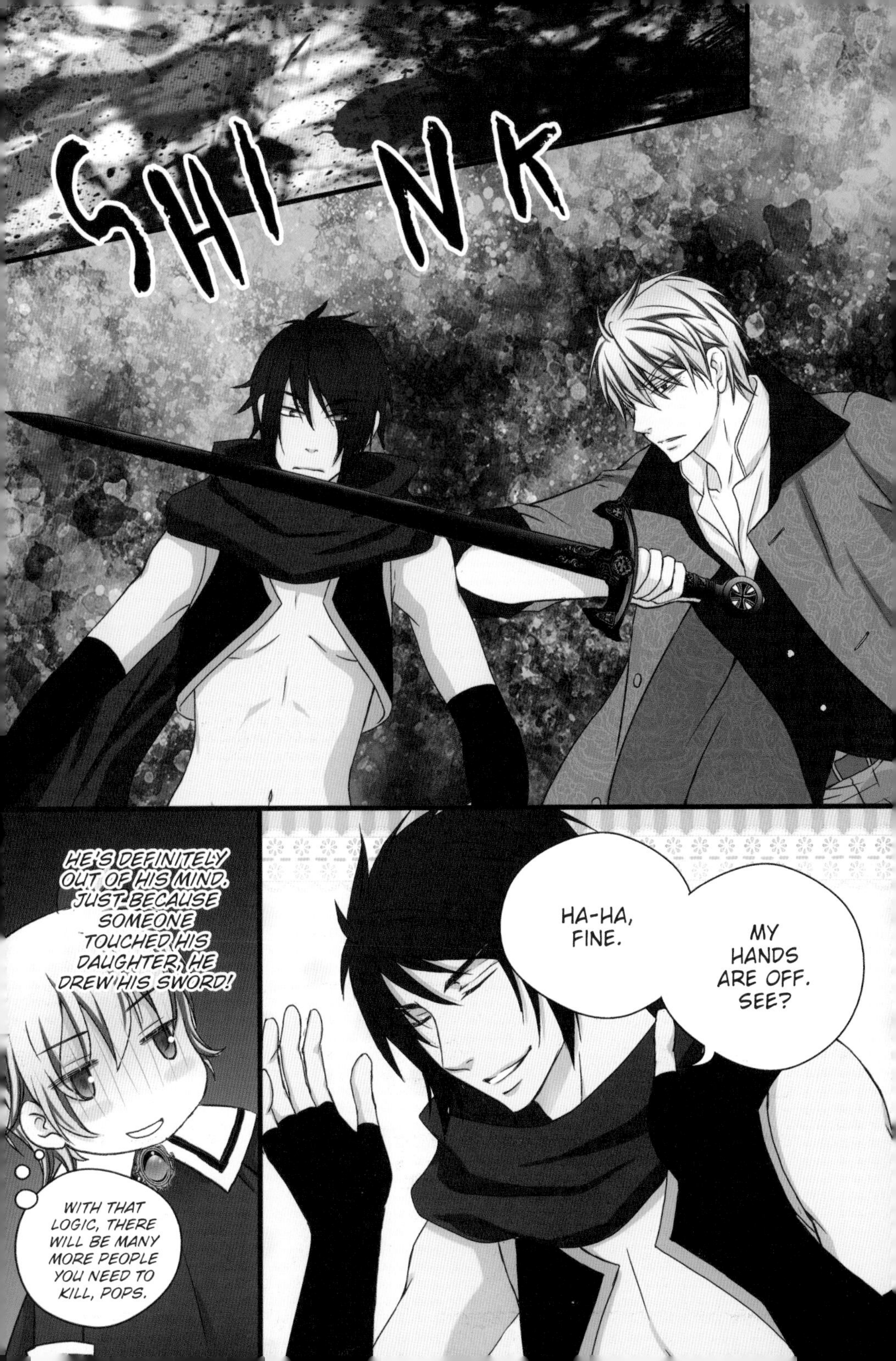
SHINK
HE'S DEFINITELY OUT OF HIS MIND. JUST BECAUSE SOMEONE TOUCHED HIS DAUGHTER, HE DREW HIS SWORD!
WITH THAT LOGIC, THERE WILL BE MANY MORE PEOPLE YOU NEED TO KILL, POPS.
HA-HA, FINE.
MY HANDS ARE OFF. SEE?

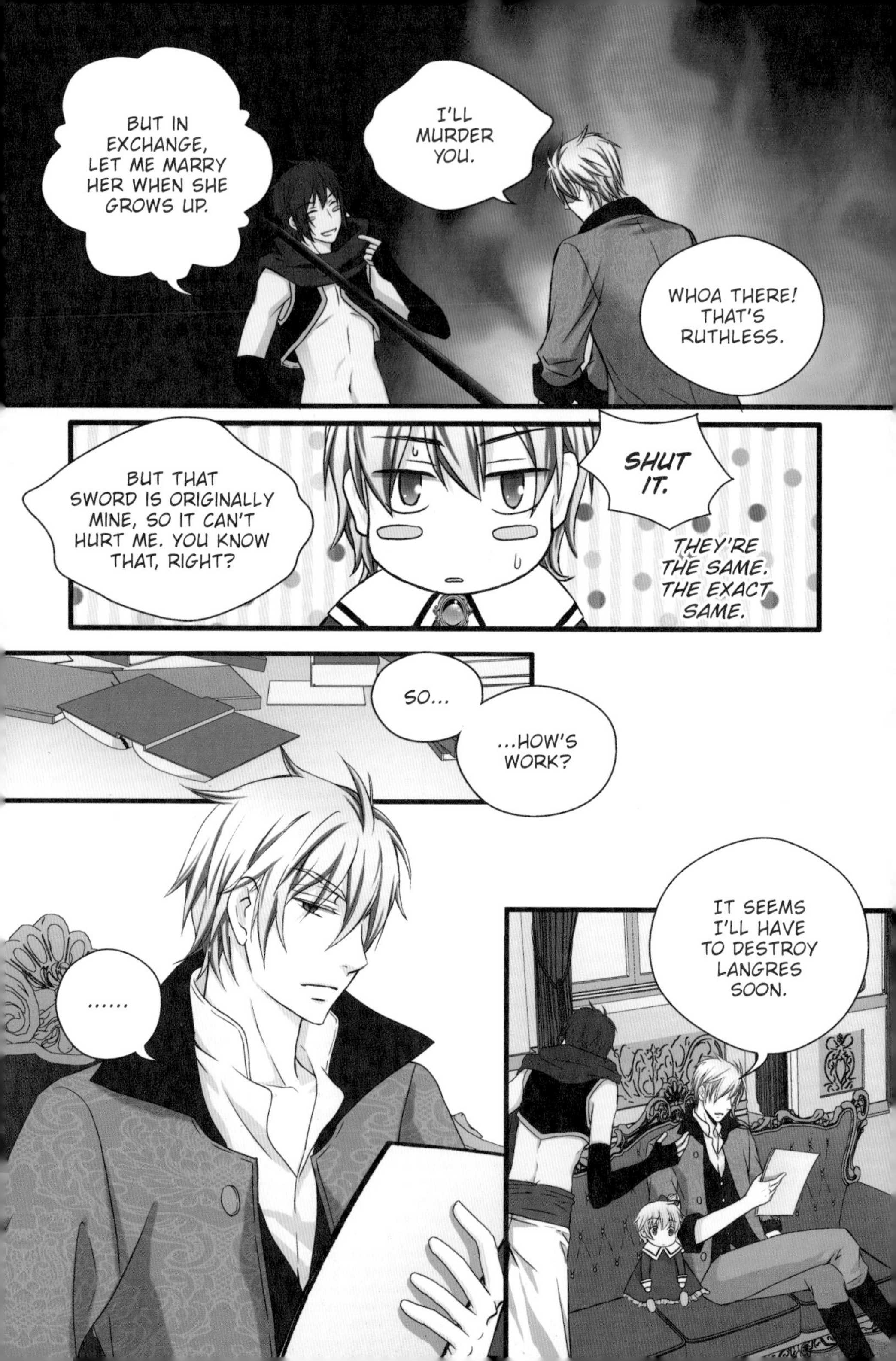

BUT IN EXCHANGE, LET ME MARRY HER WHEN SHE GROWS UP.
I'LL MURDER YOU.
WHOA THERE! THAT'S RUTHLESS.
BUT THAT SWORD IS ORIGINALLY MINE, SO IT CAN'T HURT ME. YOU KNOW THAT, RIGHT?
SHUT IT.
THEY'RE THE SAME. THE EXACT SAME.
SO...
...HOW'S WORK?
......
IT SEEMS I'LL HAVE TO DESTROY LANGRES SOON.

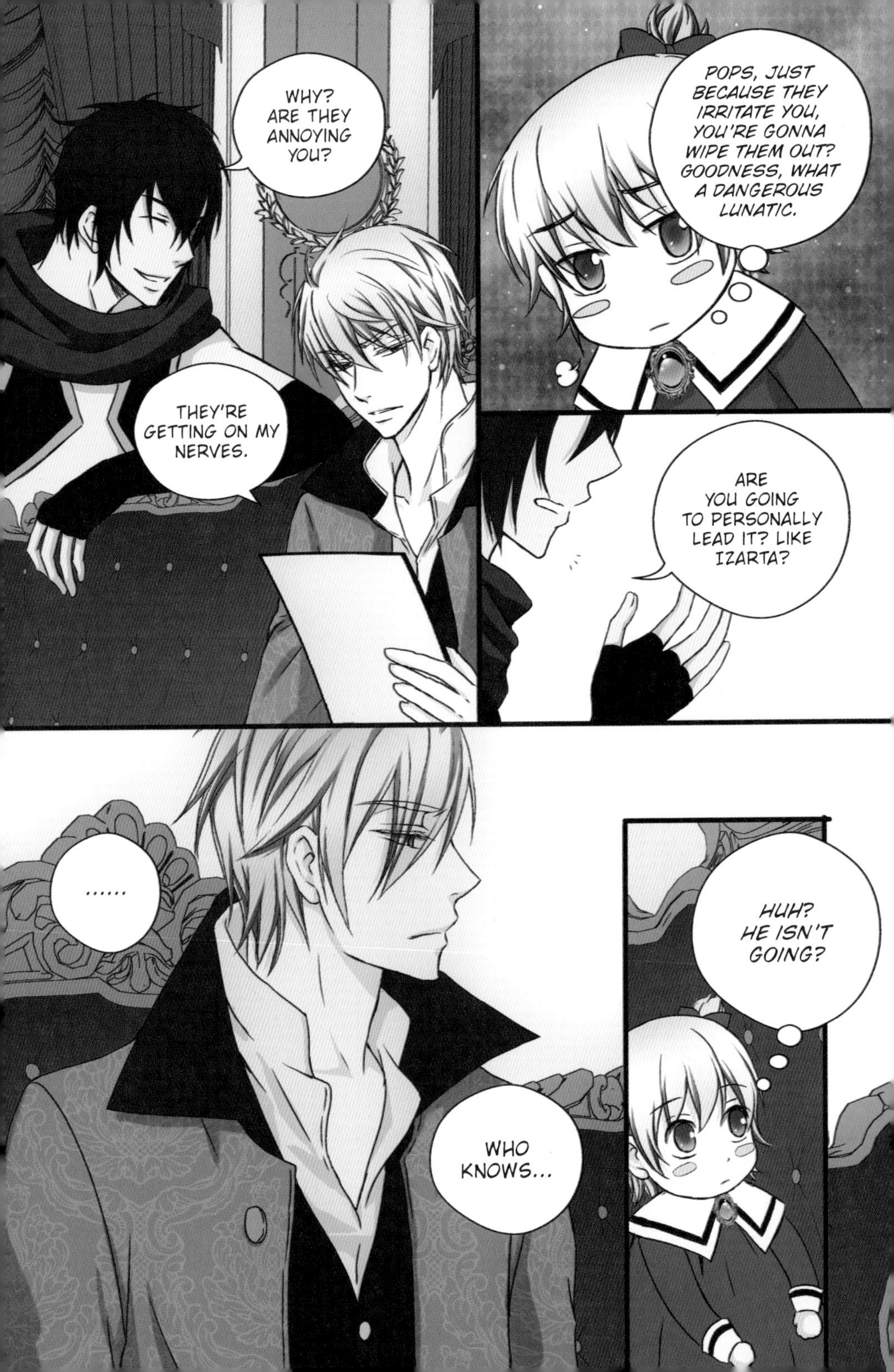
WHY? ARE THEY ANNOYING YOU?
THEY'RE GETTING ON MY NERVES.
POPS, JUST BECAUSE THEY IRRITATE YOU, YOU'RE GONNA WIPE THEM OUT? GOODNESS, WHAT A DANGEROUS LUNATIC.
ARE YOU GOING TO PERSONALLY LEAD IT? LIKE IZARTA?
......
WHO KNOWS...
HUH? HE ISN'T GOING?

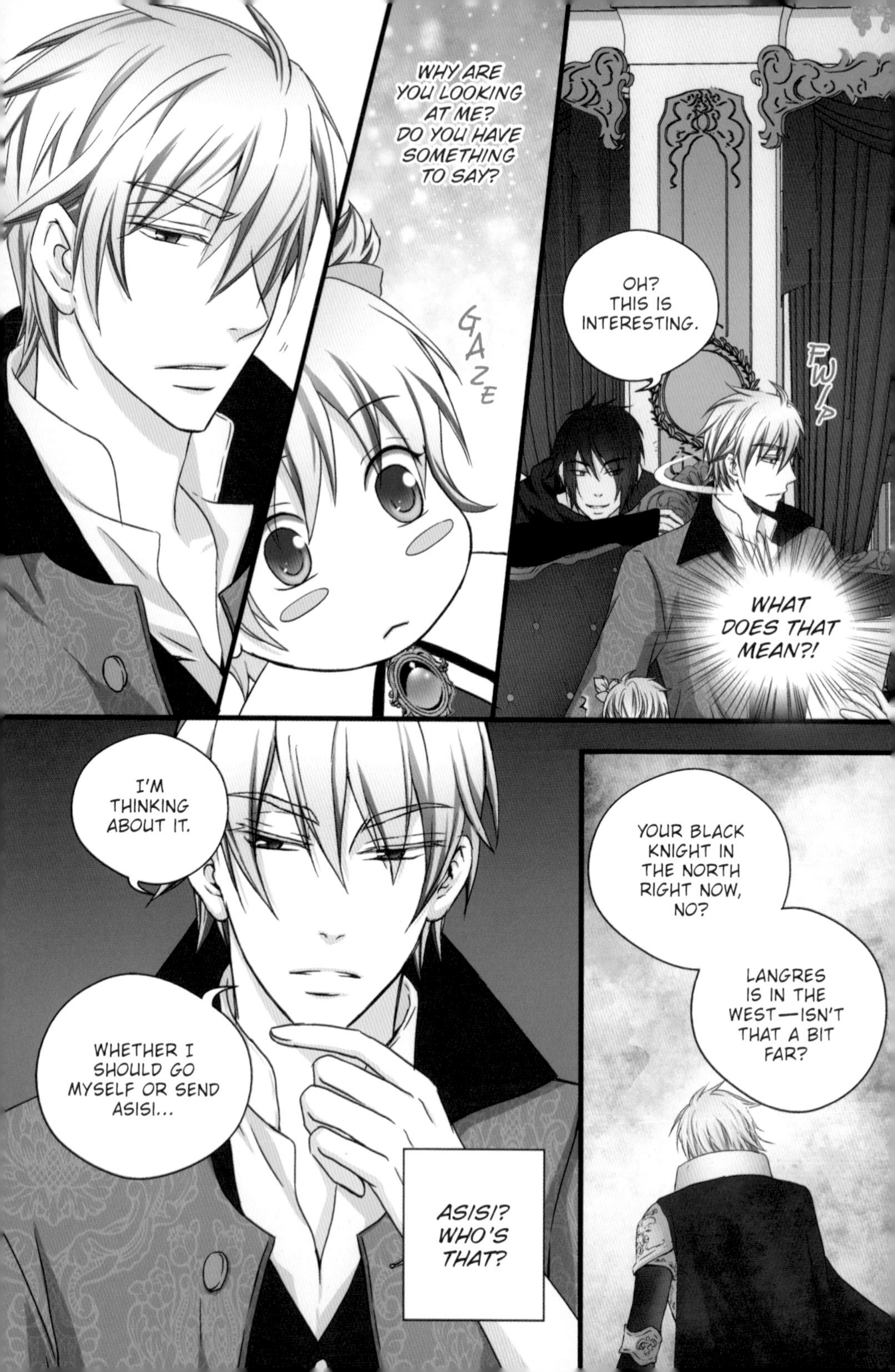
WHY ARE YOU LOOKING AT ME? DO YOU HAVE SOMETHING TO SAY?
GAZE
OH? THIS IS INTERESTING.
FWIP
WHAT DOES THAT MEAN?!
I'M THINKING ABOUT IT.
WHETHER I SHOULD GO MYSELF OR SEND ASISI...
ASISI? WHO'S THAT?
YOUR BLACK KNIGHT IN THE NORTH RIGHT NOW, NO?
LANGRES IS IN THE WEST—ISN'T THAT A BIT FAR?

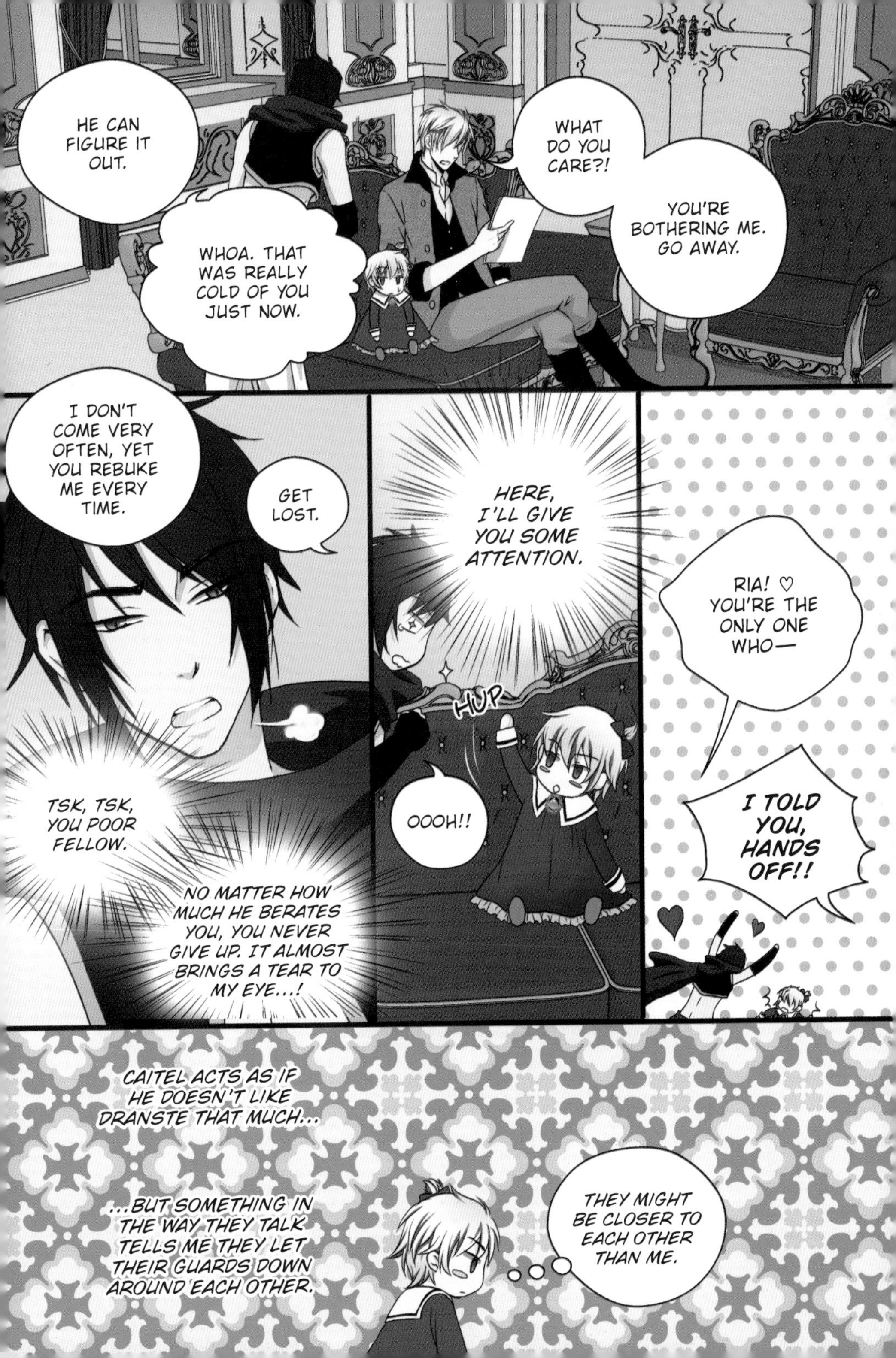
HE CAN FIGURE IT OUT.
WHOA. THAT WAS REALLY COLD OF YOU JUST NOW.
WHAT DO YOU CARE?!
YOU'RE BOTHERING ME. GO AWAY.
I DON'T COME VERY OFTEN, YET YOU REBUKE ME EVERY TIME.
GET LOST.
TSK, TSK, YOU POOR FELLOW.
NO MATTER HOW MUCH HE BERATES YOU, YOU NEVER GIVE UP. IT ALMOST BRINGS A TEAR TO MY EYE...!
HERE, I'LL GIVE YOU SOME ATTENTION.
HUP
OOOH!!
RIA! ♡ YOU'RE THE ONLY ONE WHO—
I TOLD YOU, HANDS OFF!!
CAITEL ACTS AS IF HE DOESN'T LIKE DRANSTE THAT MUCH...
...BUT SOMETHING IN THE WAY THEY TALK TELLS ME THEY LET THEIR GUARDS DOWN AROUND EACH OTHER.
THEY MIGHT BE CLOSER TO EACH OTHER THAN ME.

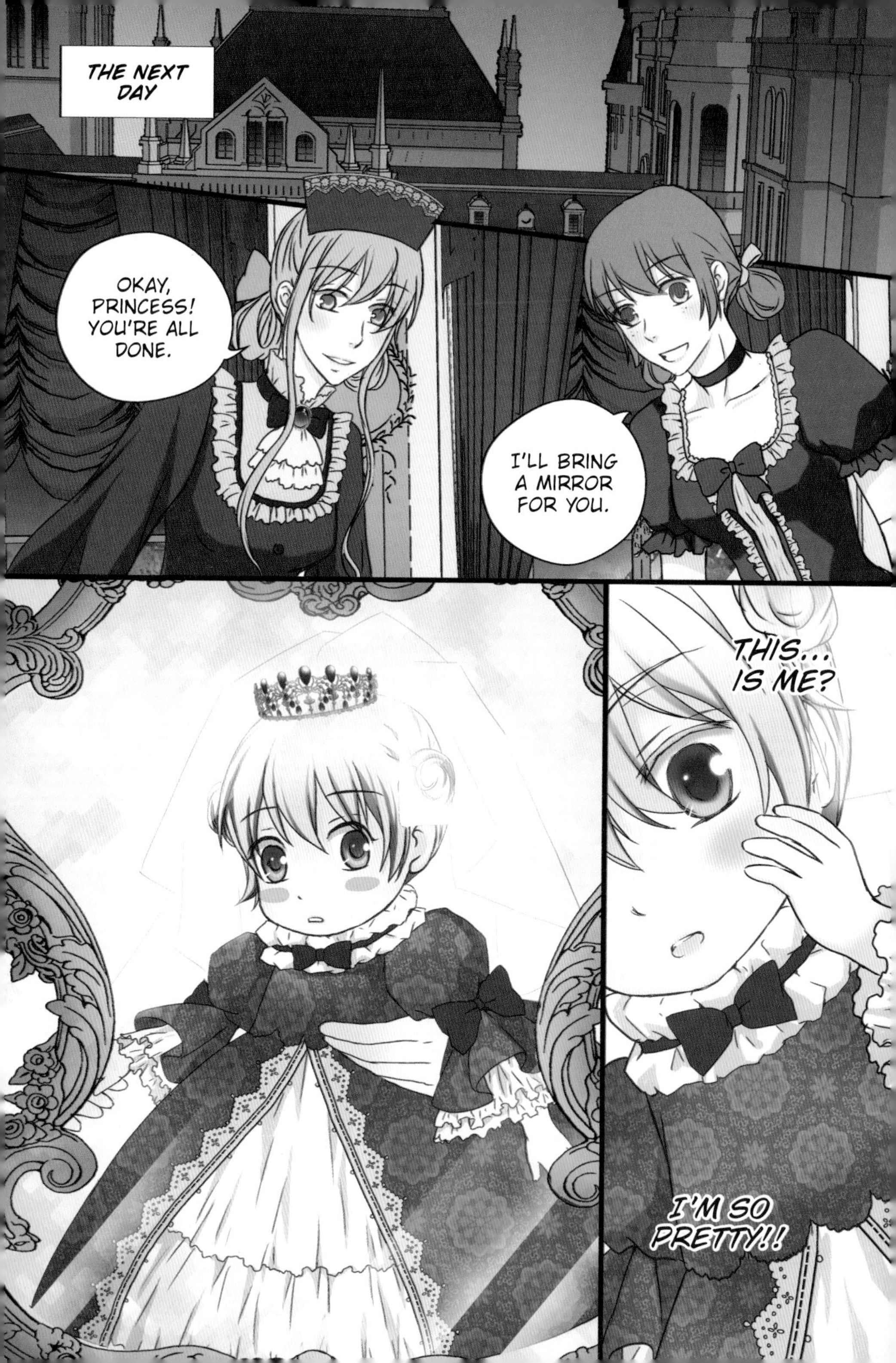
THE NEXT DAY
OKAY, PRINCESS! YOU'RE ALL DONE.
I'LL BRING A MIRROR FOR YOU.
THIS... IS ME?
I'M SO PRETTY!!

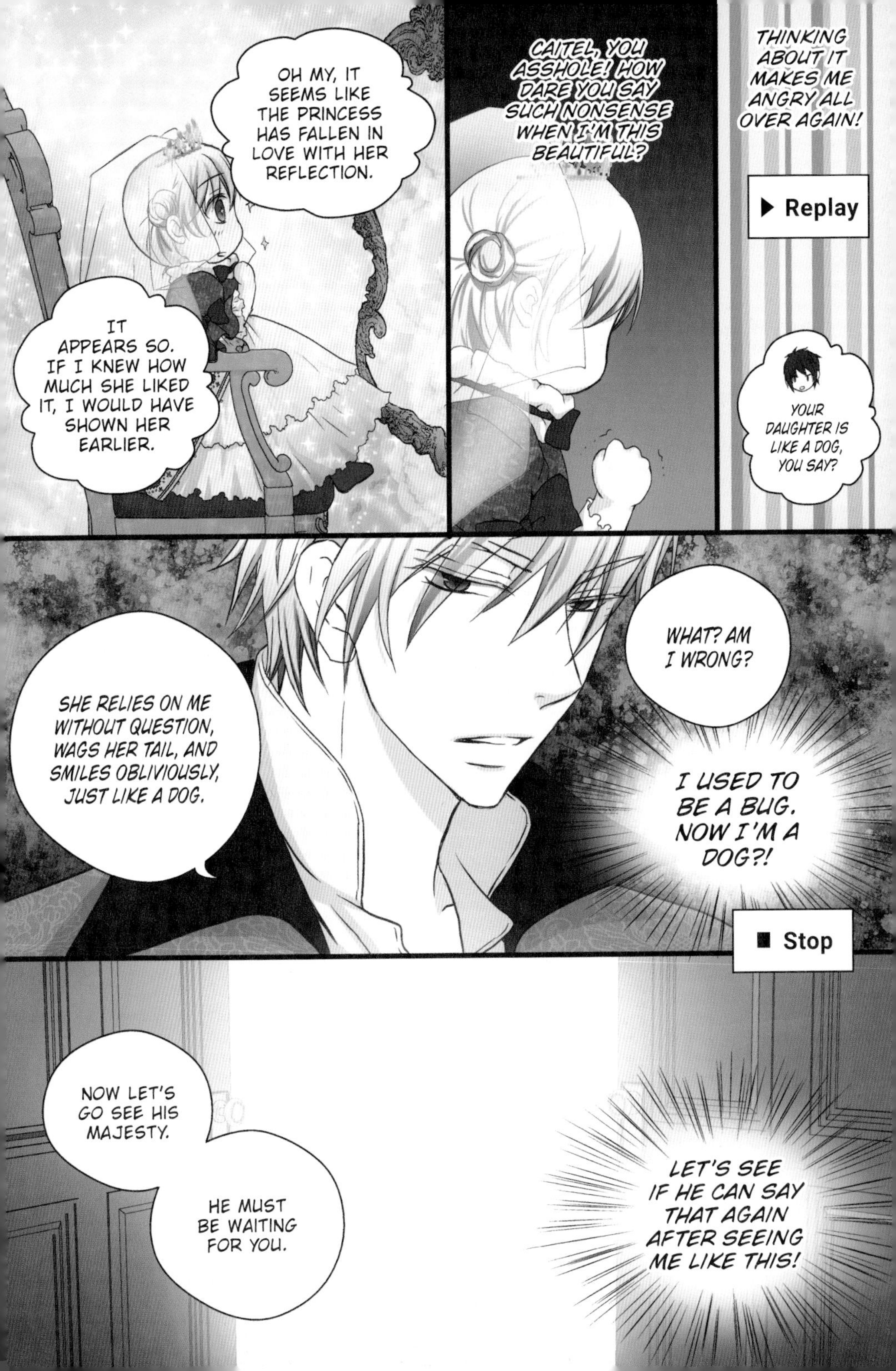
OH MY, IT SEEMS LIKE THE PRINCESS HAS FALLEN IN LOVE WITH HER REFLECTION.
IT APPEARS SO. IF I KNEW HOW MUCH SHE LIKED IT, I WOULD HAVE SHOWN HER EARLIER.
CAITEL, YOU ASSHOLE! HOW DARE YOU SAY SUCH NONSENSE WHEN I'M THIS BEAUTIFUL?
THINKING ABOUT IT MAKES ME ANGRY ALL OVER AGAIN!
▶ Replay
YOUR DAUGHTER IS LIKE A DOG, YOU SAY?
SHE RELIES ON ME WITHOUT QUESTION, WAGS HER TAIL, AND SMILES OBLIVIOUSLY, JUST LIKE A DOG.
WHAT? AM I WRONG?
I USED TO BE A BUG. NOW I'M A DOG?!
■ Stop
NOW LET'S GO SEE HIS MAJESTY.
HE MUST BE WAITING FOR YOU.
LET'S SEE IF HE CAN SAY THAT AGAIN AFTER SEEING ME LIKE THIS!

DAUGHTER OF THE EMPEROR

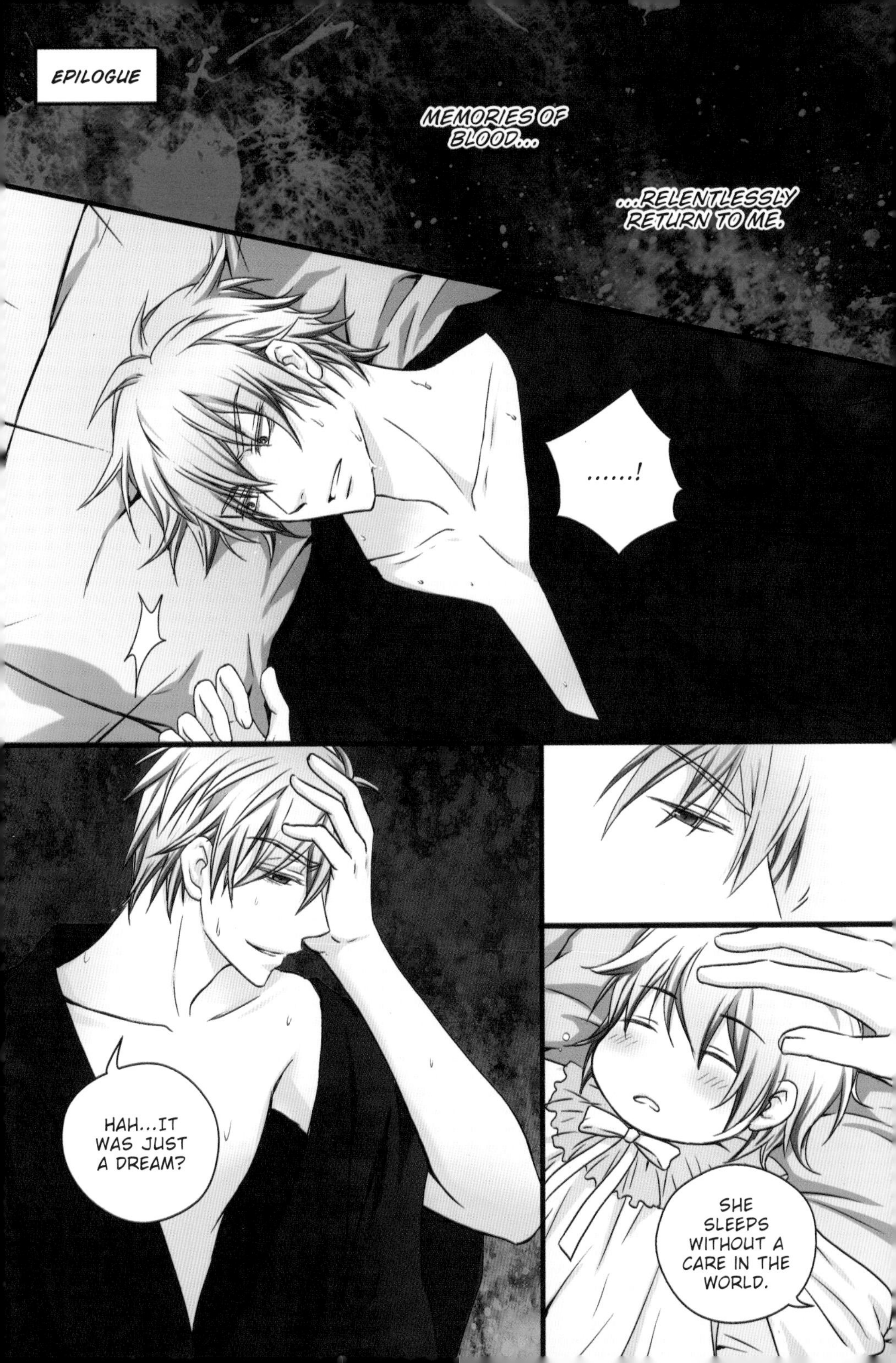
EPILOGUE
MEMORIES OF BLOOD...
...RELENTLESSLY RETURN TO ME.
......!
HAH...IT WAS JUST A DREAM?
SHE SLEEPS WITHOUT A CARE IN THE WORLD.

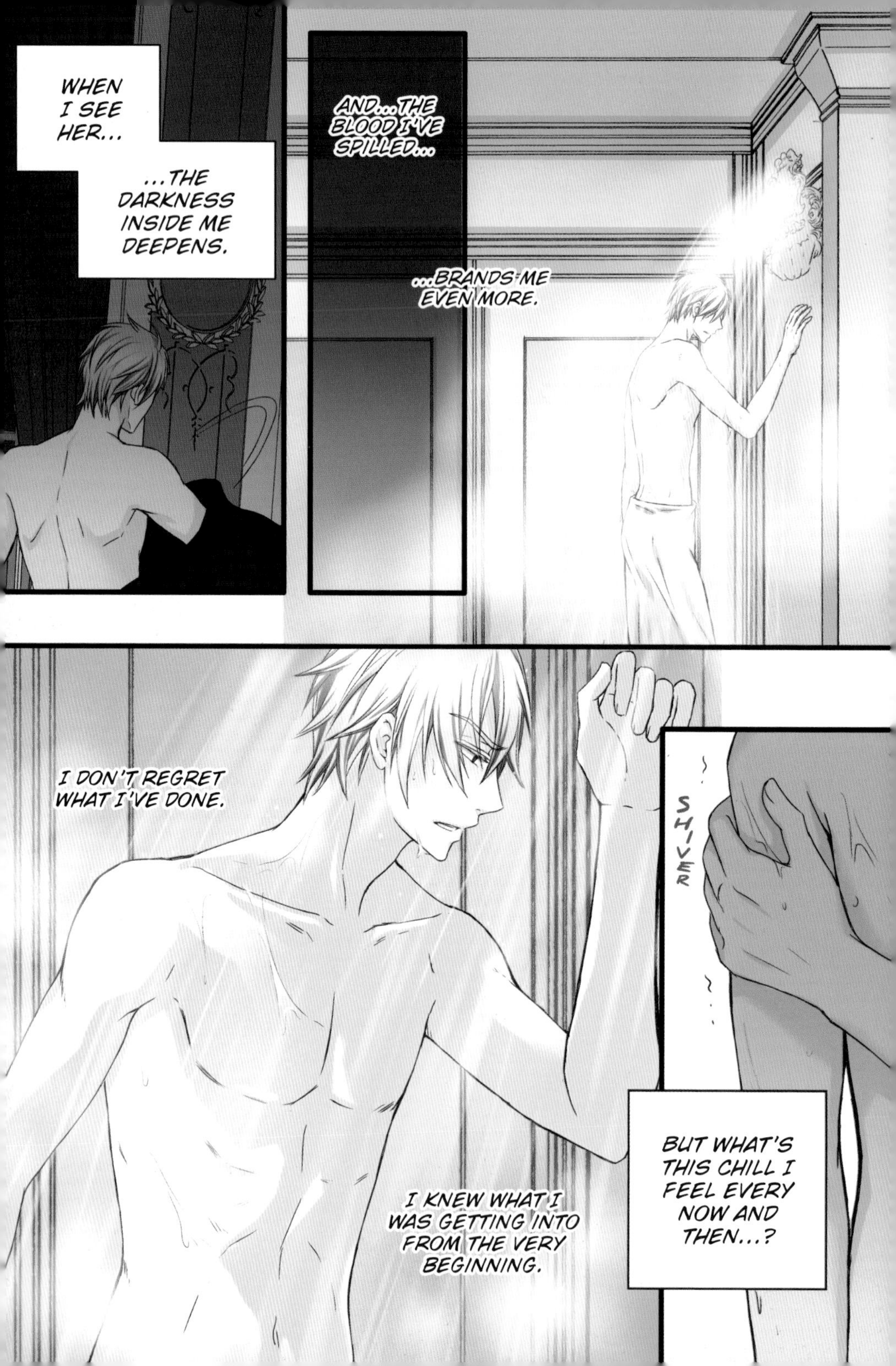
WHEN I SEE HER...
...THE DARKNESS INSIDE ME DEEPENS.
AND...THE BLOOD I'VE SPILLED...
...BRANDS ME EVEN MORE.
I DON'T REGRET WHAT I'VE DONE.
I KNEW WHAT I WAS GETTING INTO FROM THE VERY BEGINNING.
SHIVER
BUT WHAT'S THIS CHILL I FEEL EVERY NOW AND THEN...?

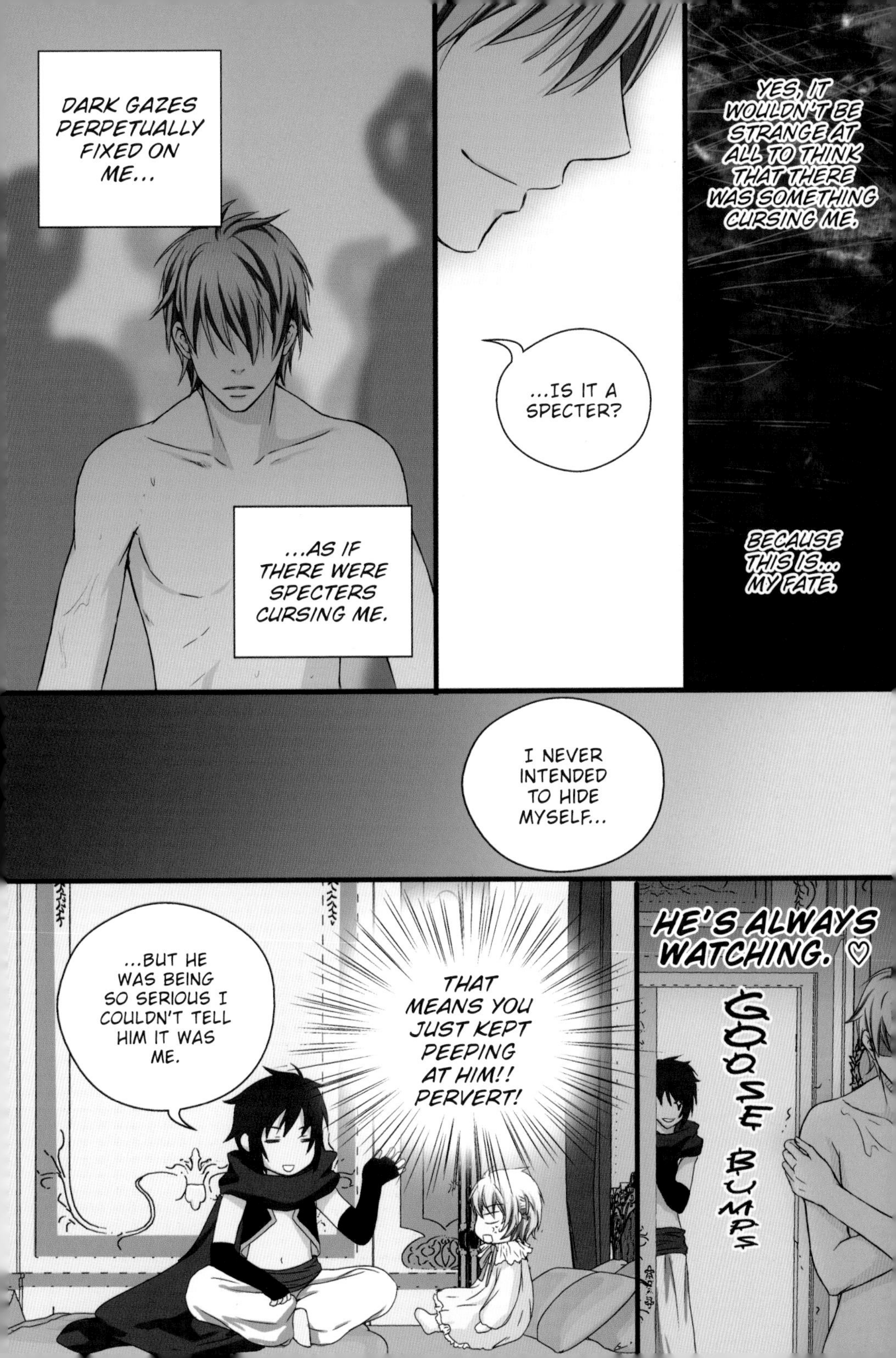
DARK GAZES PERPETUALLY FIXED ON ME...
...AS IF THERE WERE SPECTERS CURSING ME.
...IS IT A SPECTER?
YES, IT WOULDN'T BE STRANGE AT ALL TO THINK THAT THERE WAS SOMETHING CURSING ME.
BECAUSE THIS IS... MY FATE.
I NEVER INTENDED TO HIDE MYSELF...
...BUT HE WAS BEING SO SERIOUS I COULDN'T TELL HIM IT WAS ME.
THAT MEANS YOU JUST KEPT PEEPING AT HIM!! PERVERT!
HE'S ALWAYS WATCHING. ♡
GOOSE BUMPS

DAUGHTER
OF THE
EMPEROR

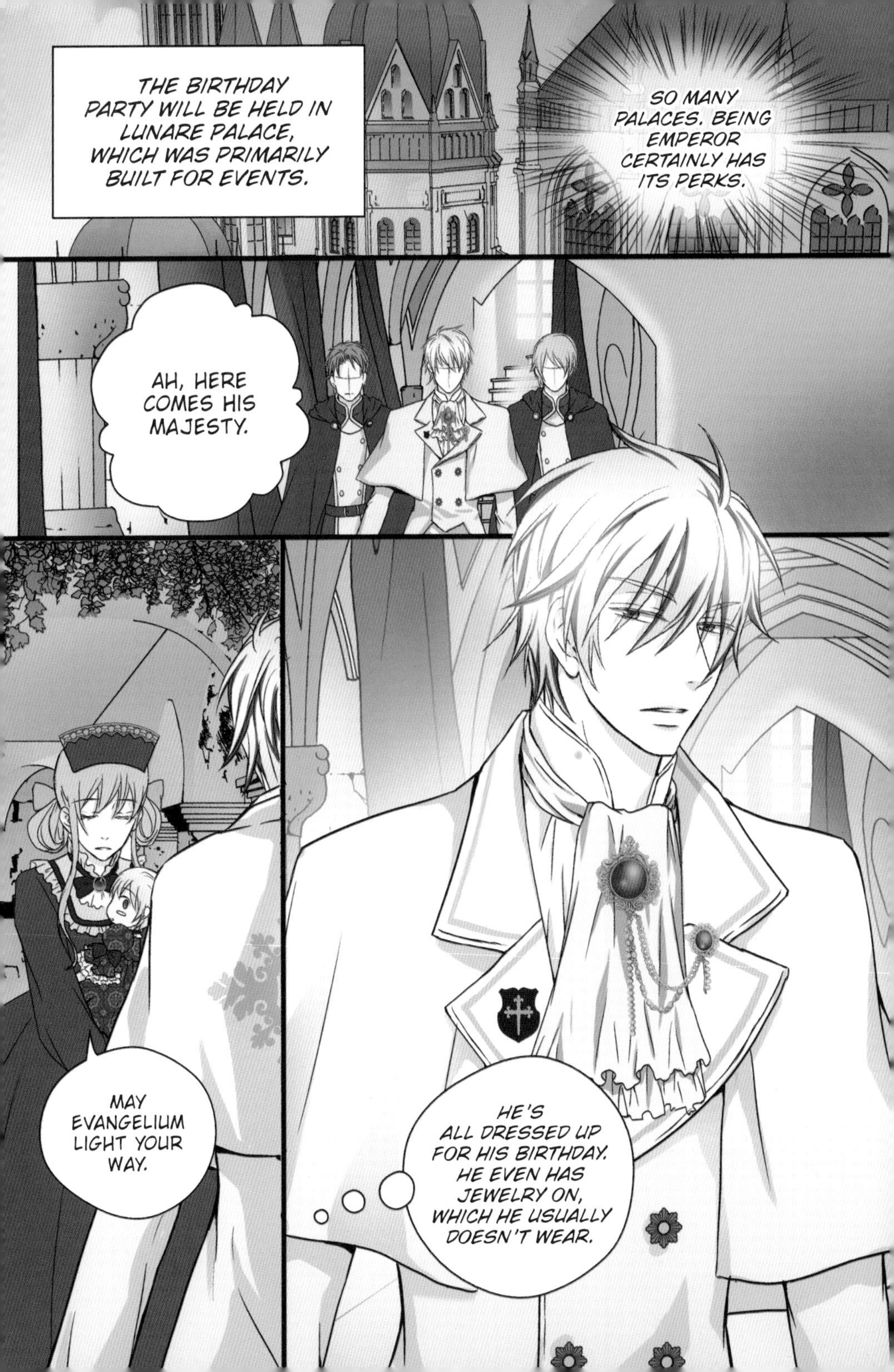
THE BIRTHDAY PARTY WILL BE HELD IN LUNARE PALACE, WHICH WAS PRIMARILY BUILT FOR EVENTS.
SO MANY PALACES. BEING EMPEROR CERTAINLY HAS ITS PERKS.
AH, HERE COMES HIS MAJESTY.
MAY EVANGELIUM LIGHT YOUR WAY.
HE'S ALL DRESSED UP FOR HIS BIRTHDAY. HE EVEN HAS JEWELRY ON, WHICH HE USUALLY DOESN'T WEAR.

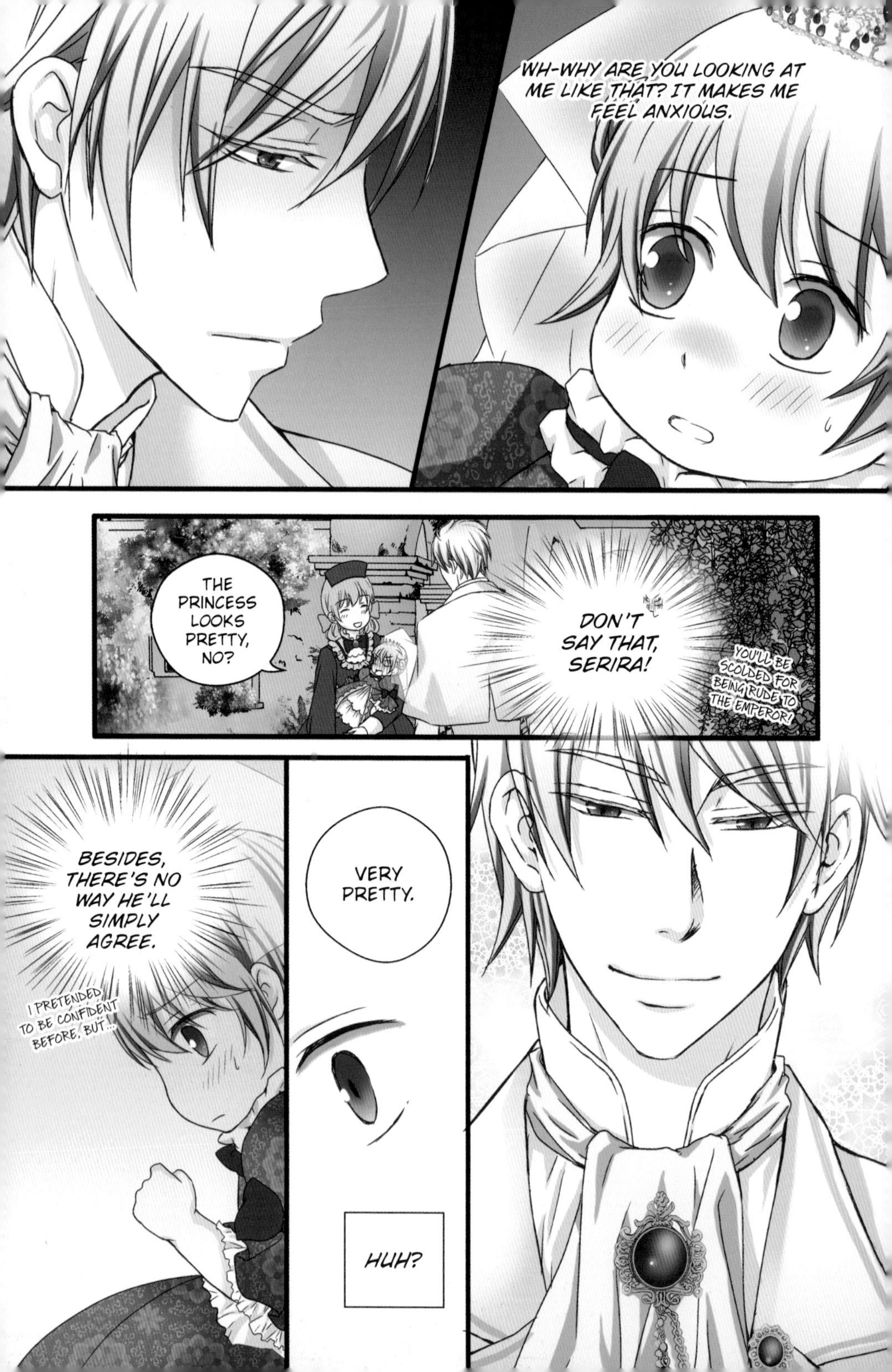
WH-WHY ARE YOU LOOKING AT ME LIKE THAT? IT MAKES ME FEEL ANXIOUS.
THE PRINCESS LOOKS PRETTY, NO?
DON'T SAY THAT, SERIRA!
YOU'LL BE SCOLDED FOR BEING RUDE TO THE EMPEROR!
BESIDES, THERE'S NO WAY HE'LL SIMPLY AGREE.
I PRETENDED TO BE CONFIDENT BEFORE, BUT...
VERY PRETTY.
HUH?

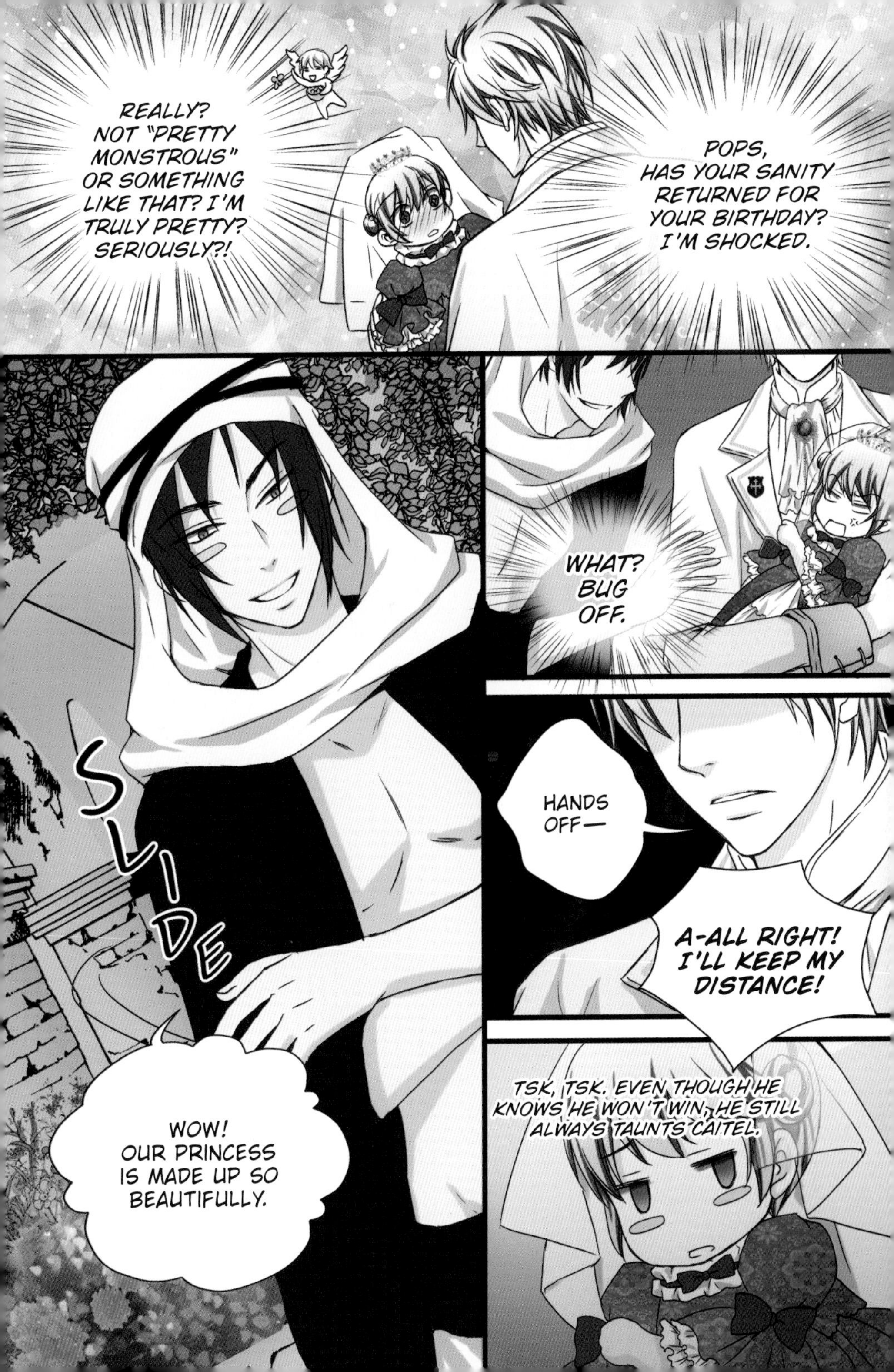
REALLY? NOT "PRETTY MONSTROUS" OR SOMETHING LIKE THAT? I'M TRULY PRETTY? SERIOUSLY?!
POPS, HAS YOUR SANITY RETURNED FOR YOUR BIRTHDAY? I'M SHOCKED.
SLIDE
WOW! OUR PRINCESS IS MADE UP SO BEAUTIFULLY.
WHAT? BUG OFF.
HANDS OFF—
A-ALL RIGHT! I'LL KEEP MY DISTANCE!
TSK, TSK. EVEN THOUGH HE KNOWS HE WON'T WIN, HE STILL ALWAYS TAUNTS CAITEL.

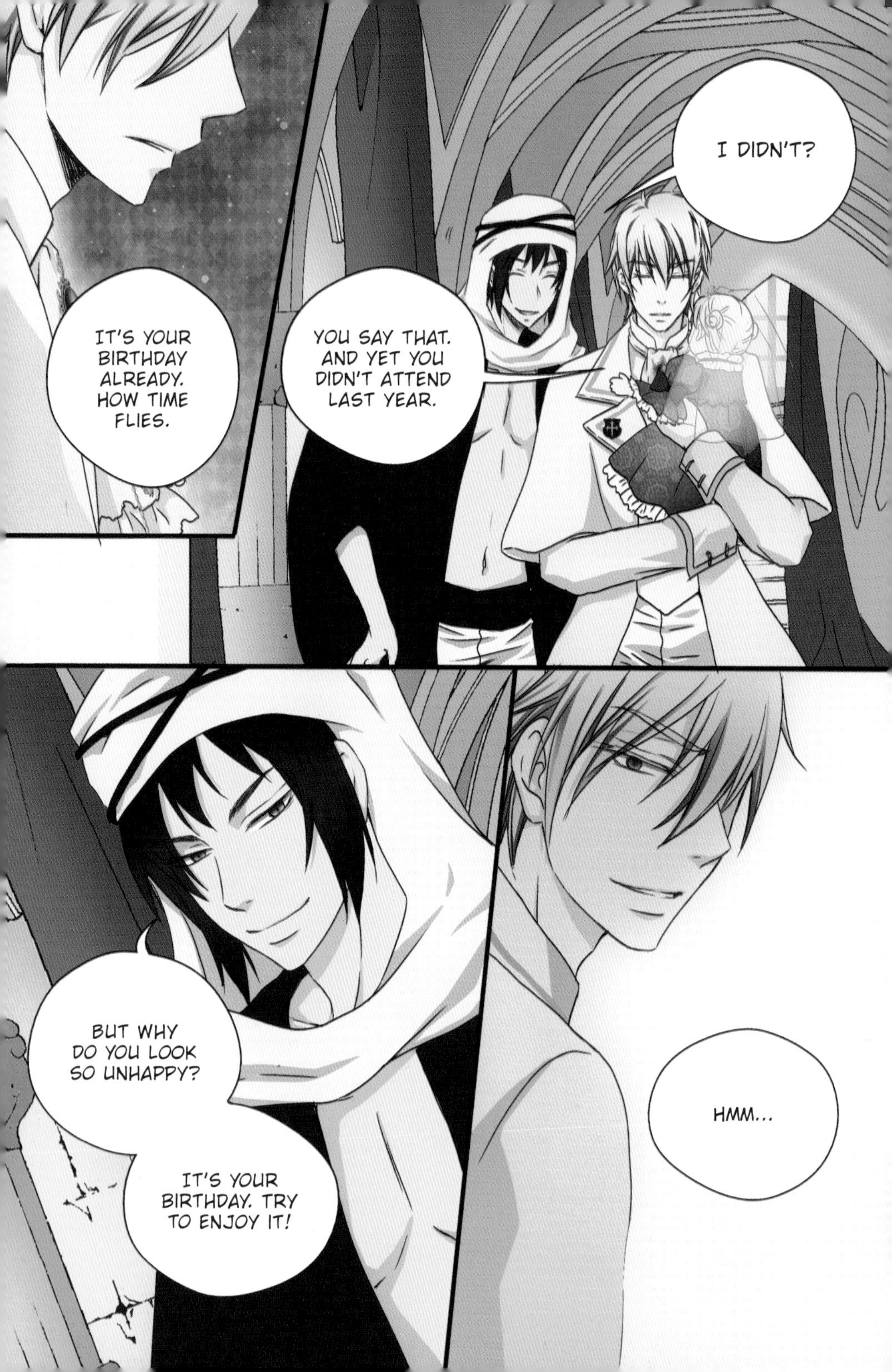
IT'S YOUR BIRTHDAY ALREADY. HOW TIME FLIES.
YOU SAY THAT. AND YET YOU DIDN'T ATTEND LAST YEAR.
I DIDN'T?
BUT WHY DO YOU LOOK SO UNHAPPY?
IT'S YOUR BIRTHDAY. TRY TO ENJOY IT!
HMM...

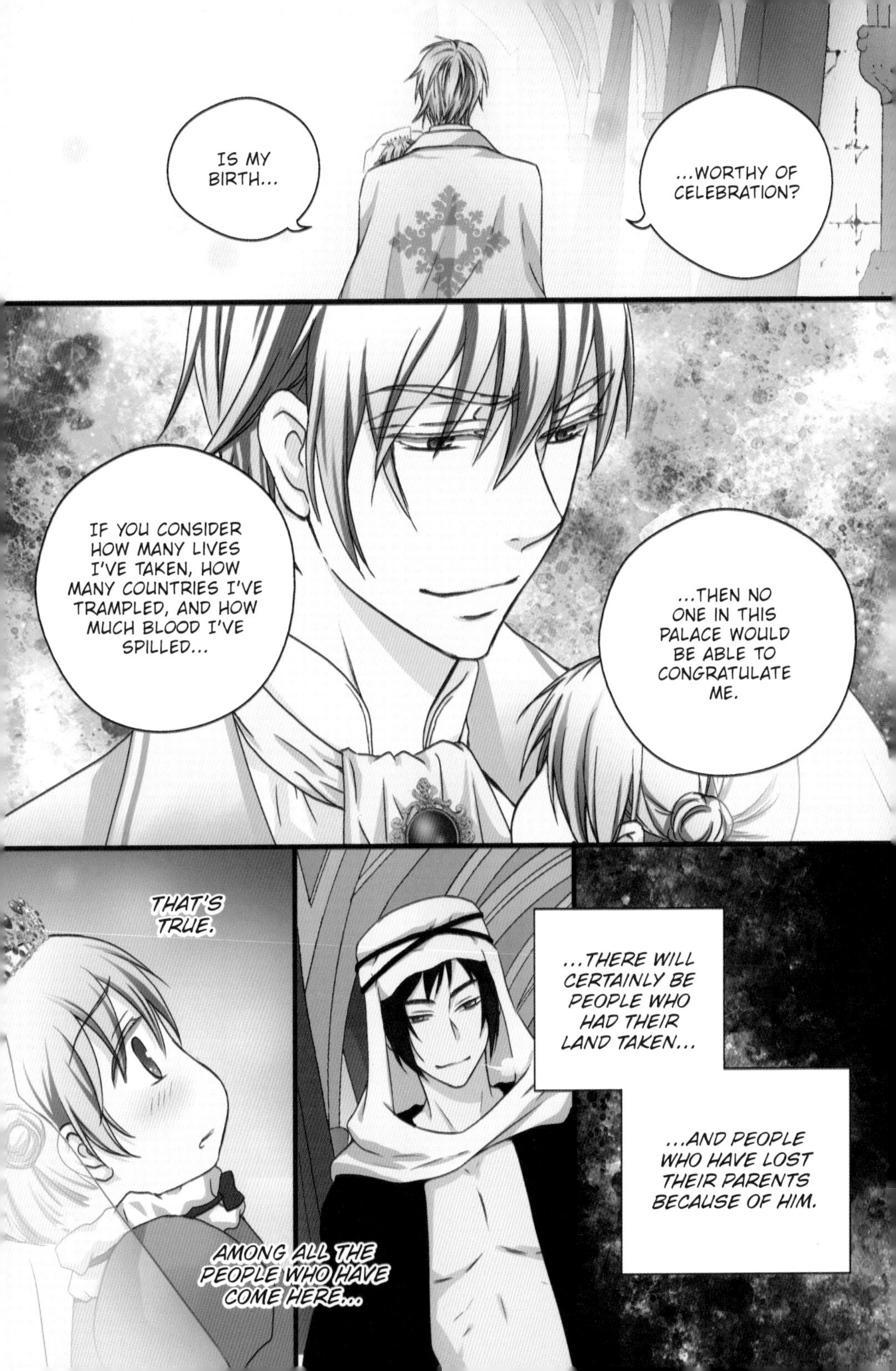
IS MY BIRTH...
...WORTHY OF CELEBRATION?
IF YOU CONSIDER HOW MANY LIVES I'VE TAKEN, HOW MANY COUNTRIES I'VE TRAMPLED, AND HOW MUCH BLOOD I'VE SPILLED...
...THEN NO ONE IN THIS PALACE WOULD BE ABLE TO CONGRATULATE ME.
THAT'S TRUE.
AMONG ALL THE PEOPLE WHO HAVE COME HERE...
...THERE WILL CERTAINLY BE PEOPLE WHO HAD THEIR LAND TAKEN...
...AND PEOPLE WHO HAVE LOST THEIR PARENTS BECAUSE OF HIM.

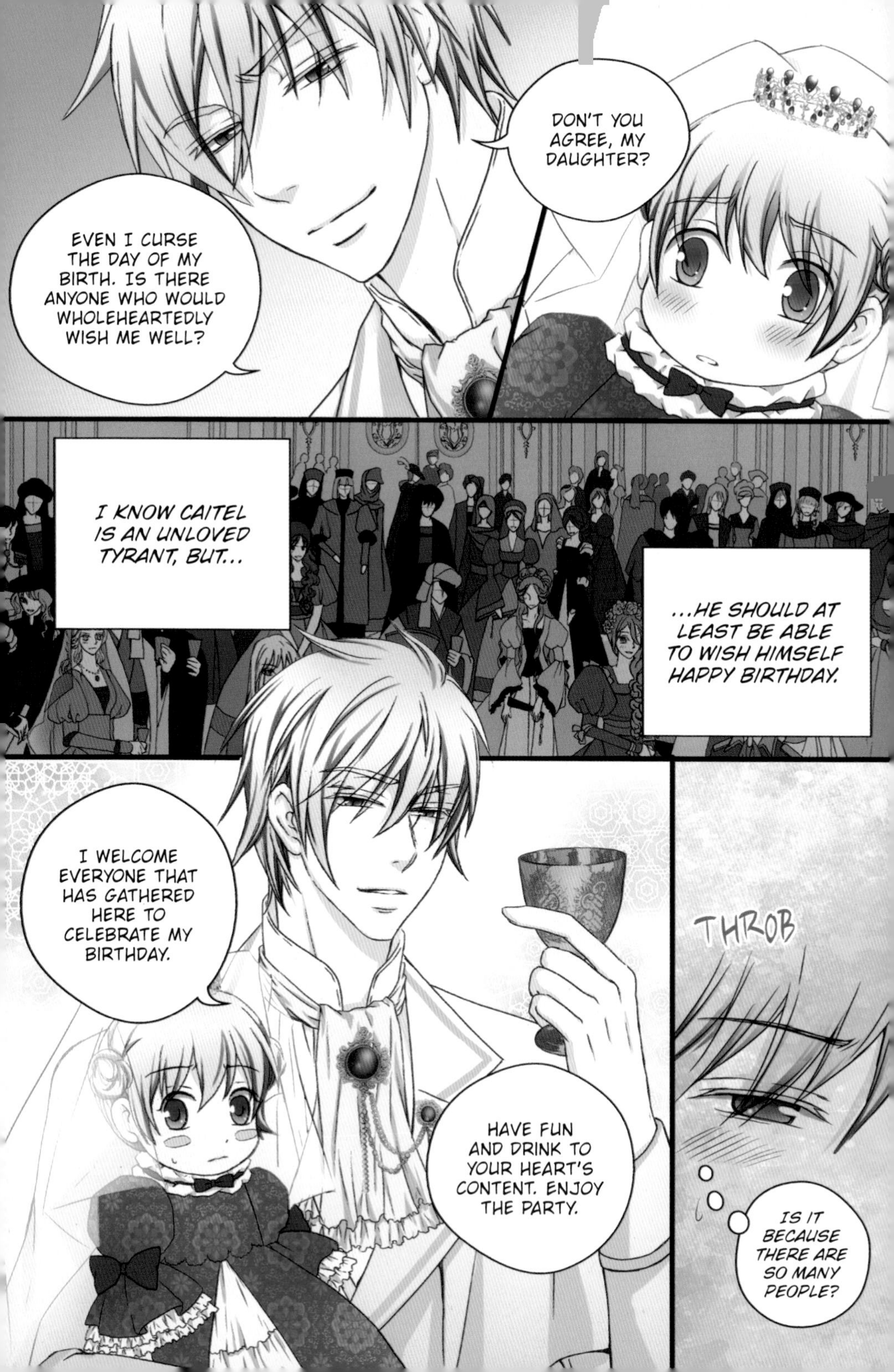
EVEN I CURSE THE DAY OF MY BIRTH. IS THERE ANYONE WHO WOULD WHOLEHEARTEDLY WISH ME WELL?
DON'T YOU AGREE, MY DAUGHTER?
I KNOW CAITEL IS AN UNLOVED TYRANT, BUT...
...HE SHOULD AT LEAST BE ABLE TO WISH HIMSELF HAPPY BIRTHDAY.
I WELCOME EVERYONE THAT HAS GATHERED HERE TO CELEBRATE MY BIRTHDAY.
HAVE FUN AND DRINK TO YOUR HEART'S CONTENT. ENJOY THE PARTY.
THROB
IS IT BECAUSE THERE ARE SO MANY PEOPLE?

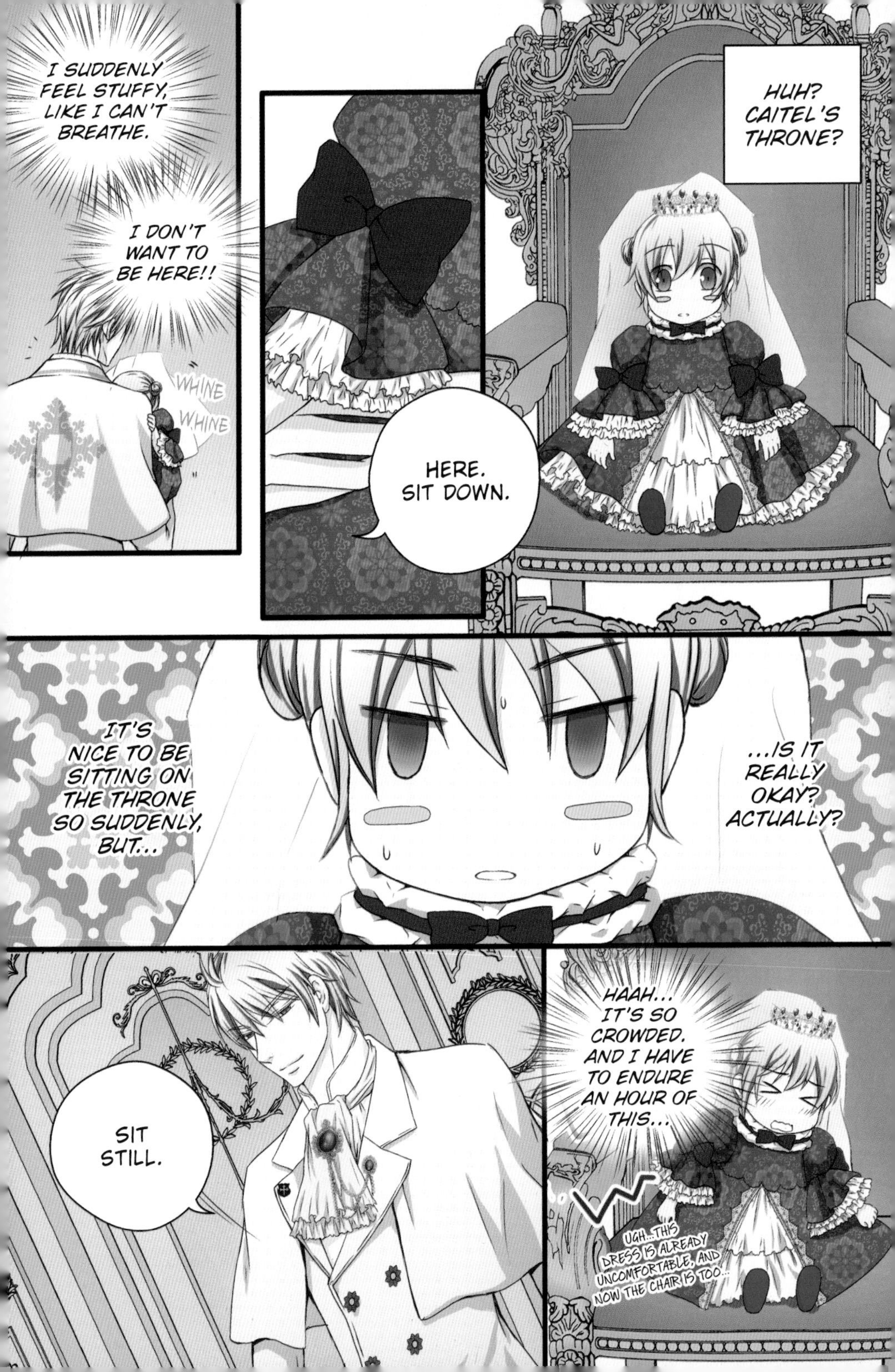
I SUDDENLY FEEL STUFFY, LIKE I CAN'T BREATHE.
I DON'T WANT TO BE HERE!!
WHINE
WHINE
HERE. SIT DOWN.
HUH? CAITEL'S THRONE?
IT'S NICE TO BE SITTING ON THE THRONE SO SUDDENLY, BUT...
...IS IT REALLY OKAY? ACTUALLY?
SIT STILL.
HAAH... IT'S SO CROWDED. AND I HAVE TO ENDURE AN HOUR OF THIS...
UGH...THIS DRESS IS ALREADY UNCOMFORTABLE, AND NOW THE CHAIR IS TOO...

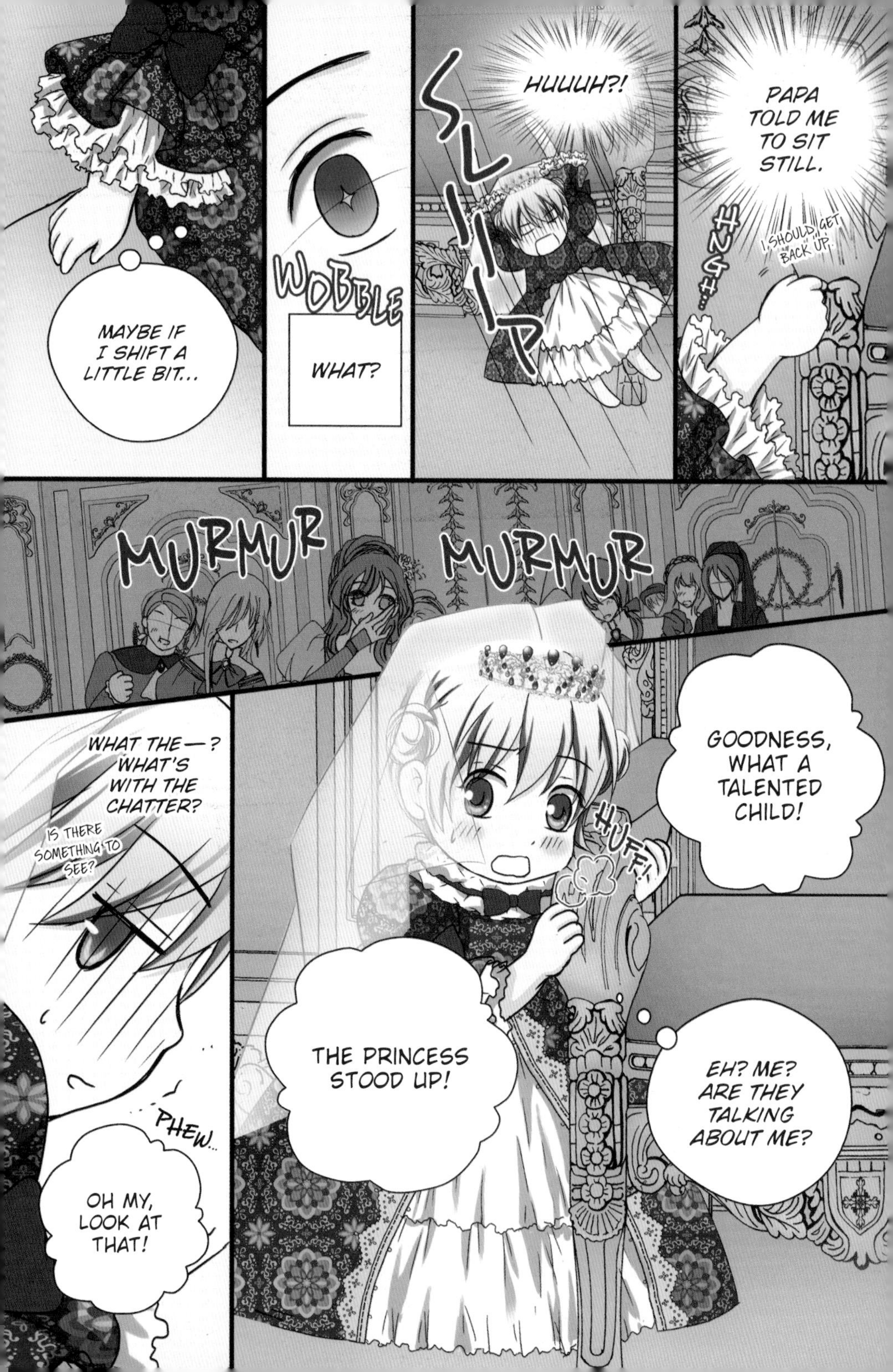
MAYBE IF I SHIFT A LITTLE BIT...
WOBBLE
WHAT?
HUUUH?!
PAPA TOLD ME TO SIT STILL.
HNGH...
I SHOULD GET BACK UP.
MURMUR
MURMUR
WHAT THE—? WHAT'S WITH THE CHATTER?
IS THERE SOMETHING TO SEE?
PHEW...
OH MY, LOOK AT THAT!
HUFF!
GOODNESS, WHAT A TALENTED CHILD!
THE PRINCESS STOOD UP!
EH? ME? ARE THEY TALKING ABOUT ME?

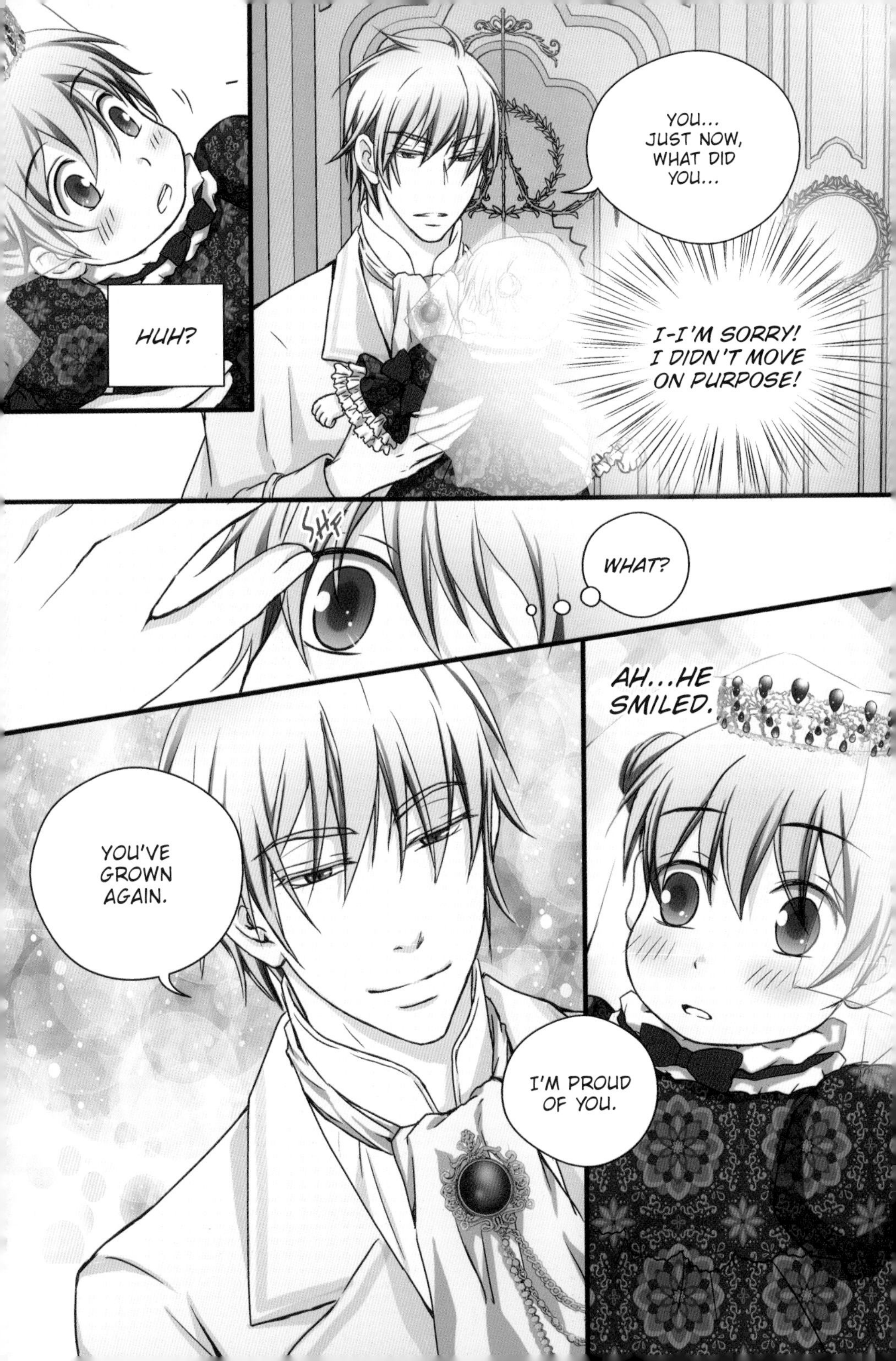
HUH?
YOU... JUST NOW, WHAT DID YOU...
I-I'M SORRY! I DIDN'T MOVE ON PURPOSE!
SHF
WHAT?
YOU'VE GROWN AGAIN.
AH...HE SMILED.
I'M PROUD OF YOU.

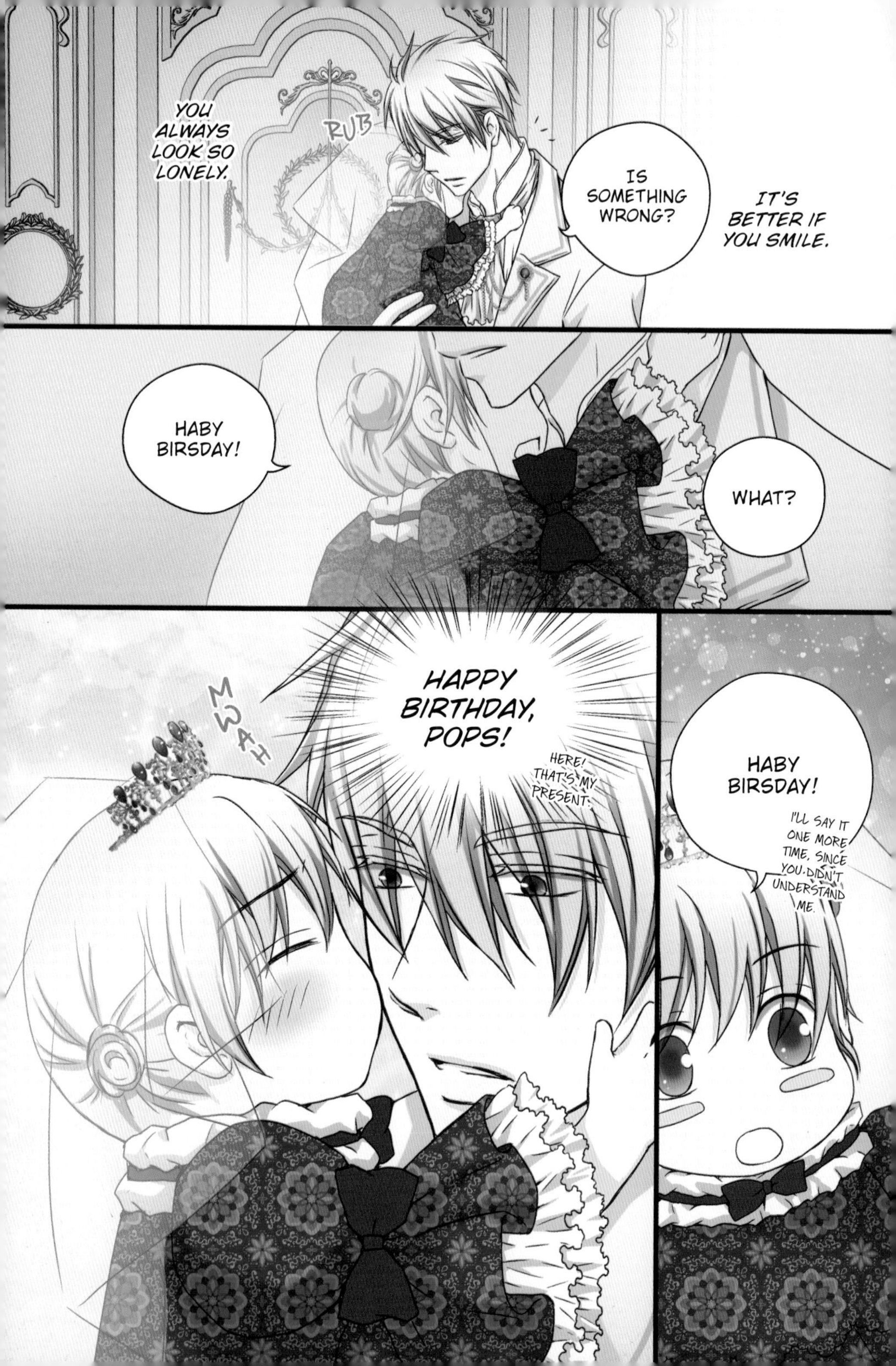
YOU ALWAYS LOOK SO LONELY.
RUB
IS SOMETHING WRONG?
IT'S BETTER IF YOU SMILE.
HABY BIRSDAY!
WHAT?
MWAH
HAPPY BIRTHDAY, POPS!
HERE! THAT'S MY PRESENT.
HABY BIRSDAY!
I'LL SAY IT ONE MORE TIME, SINCE YOU DIDN'T UNDERSTAND ME.

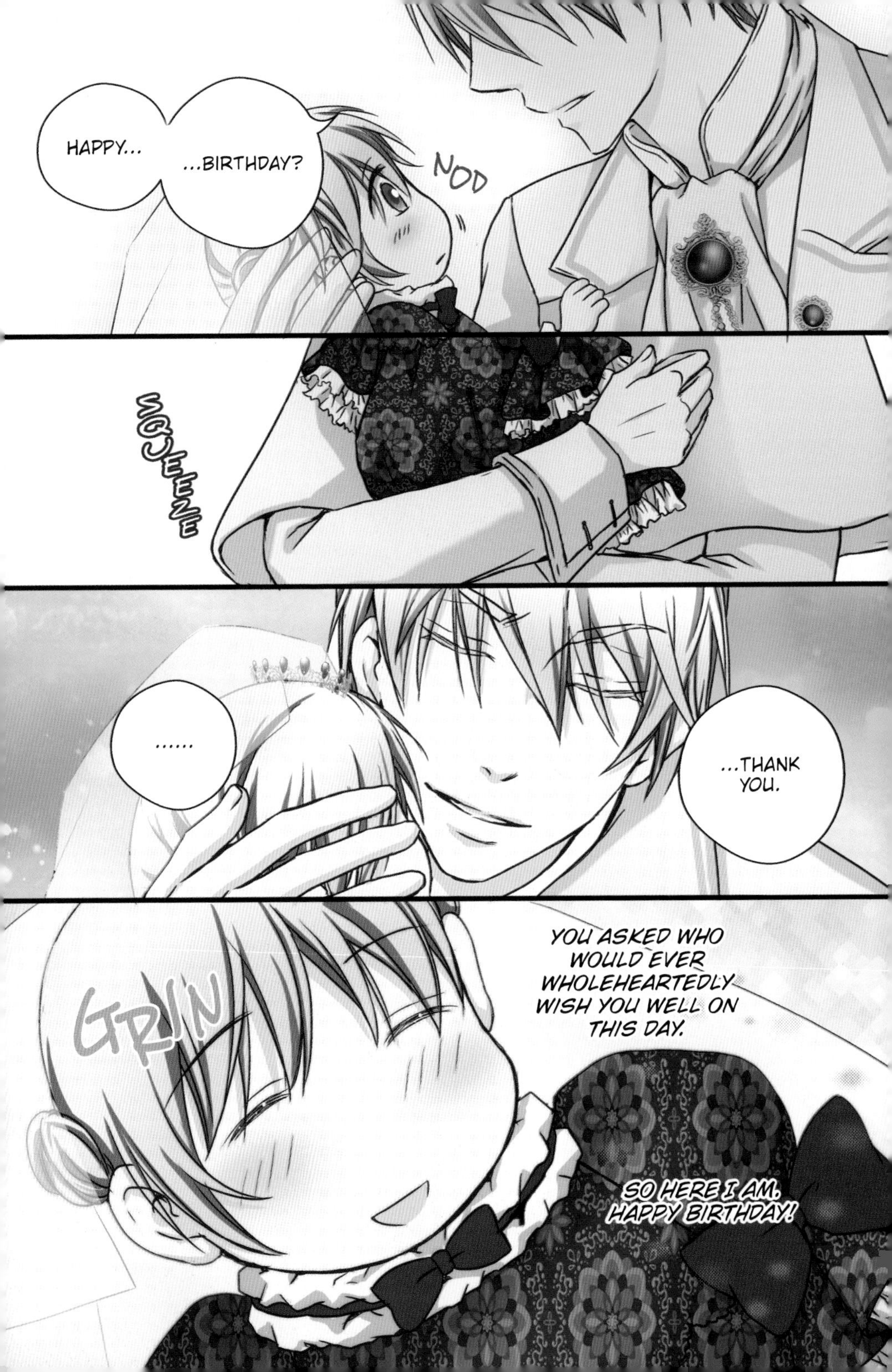
HAPPY...
...BIRTHDAY?
NOD
SQUEEZE
......
...THANK YOU.
GRIN
YOU ASKED WHO WOULD EVER WHOLEHEARTEDLY WISH YOU WELL ON THIS DAY.
SO HERE I AM. HAPPY BIRTHDAY!

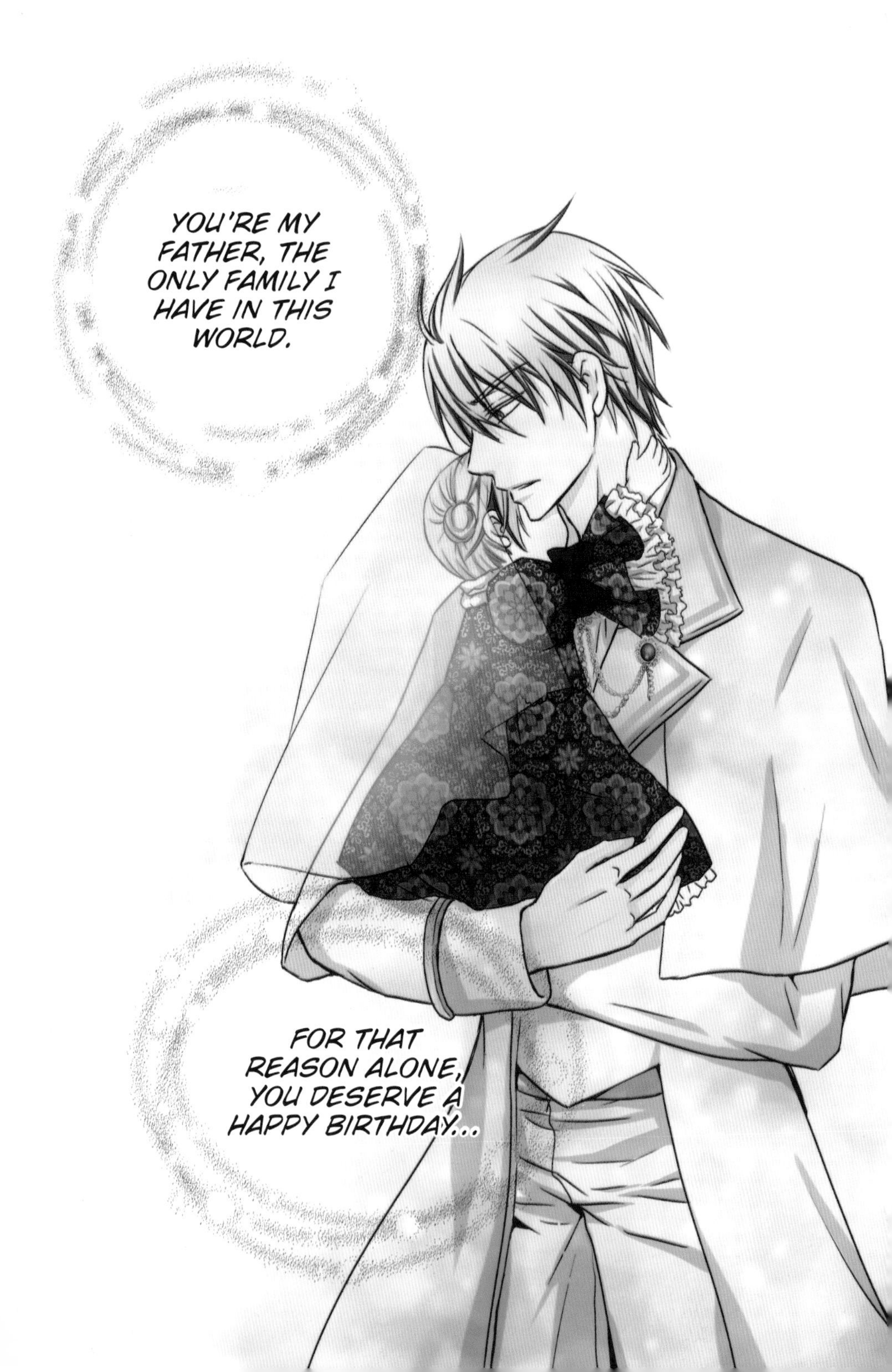
YOU'RE MY FATHER, THE ONLY FAMILY I HAVE IN THIS WORLD.
FOR THAT REASON ALONE, YOU DESERVE A HAPPY BIRTHDAY...

DAUGHTER
OF THE
EMPEROR

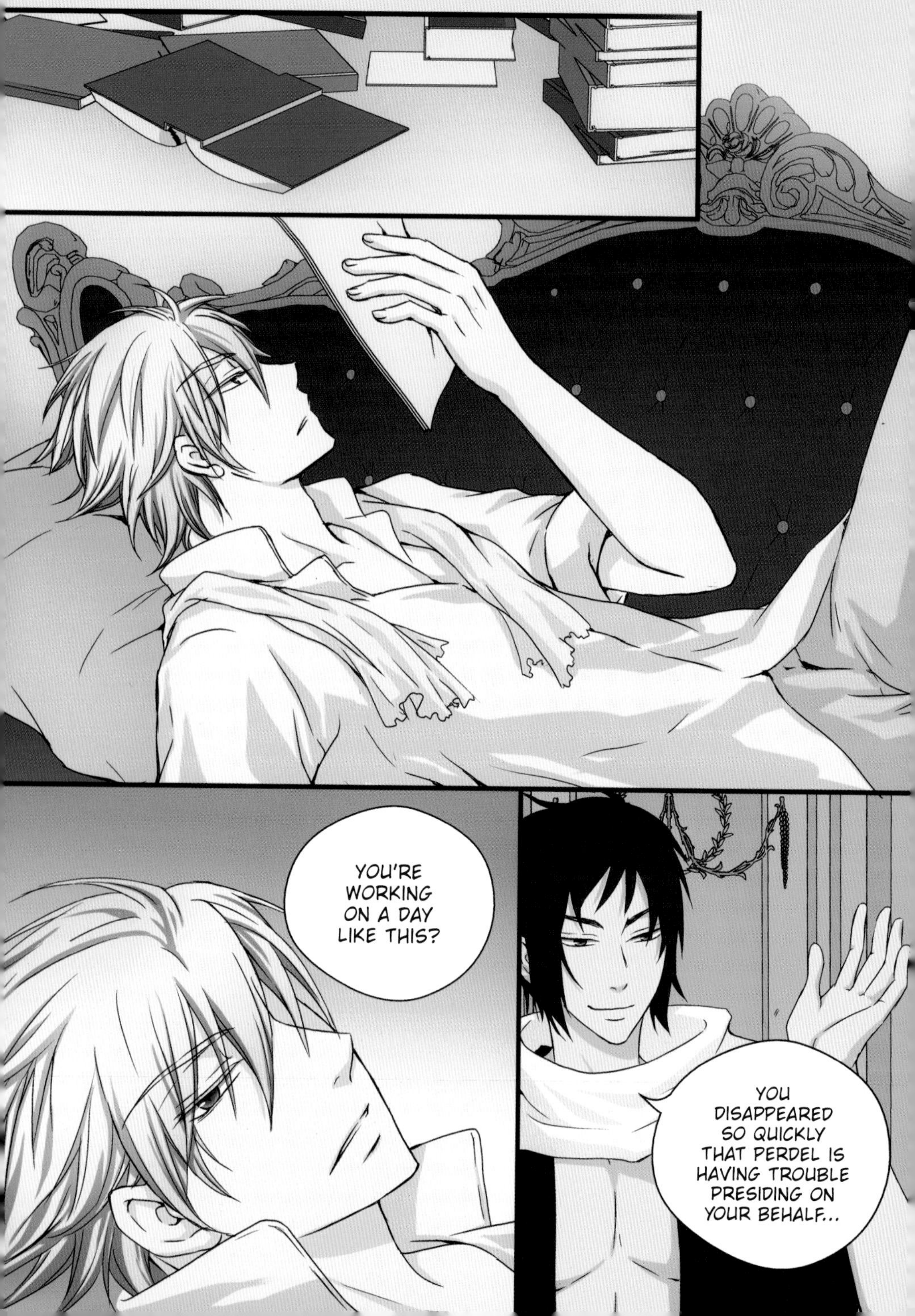
YOU'RE WORKING ON A DAY LIKE THIS?
YOU DISAPPEARED SO QUICKLY THAT PERDEL IS HAVING TROUBLE PRESIDING ON YOUR BEHALF...

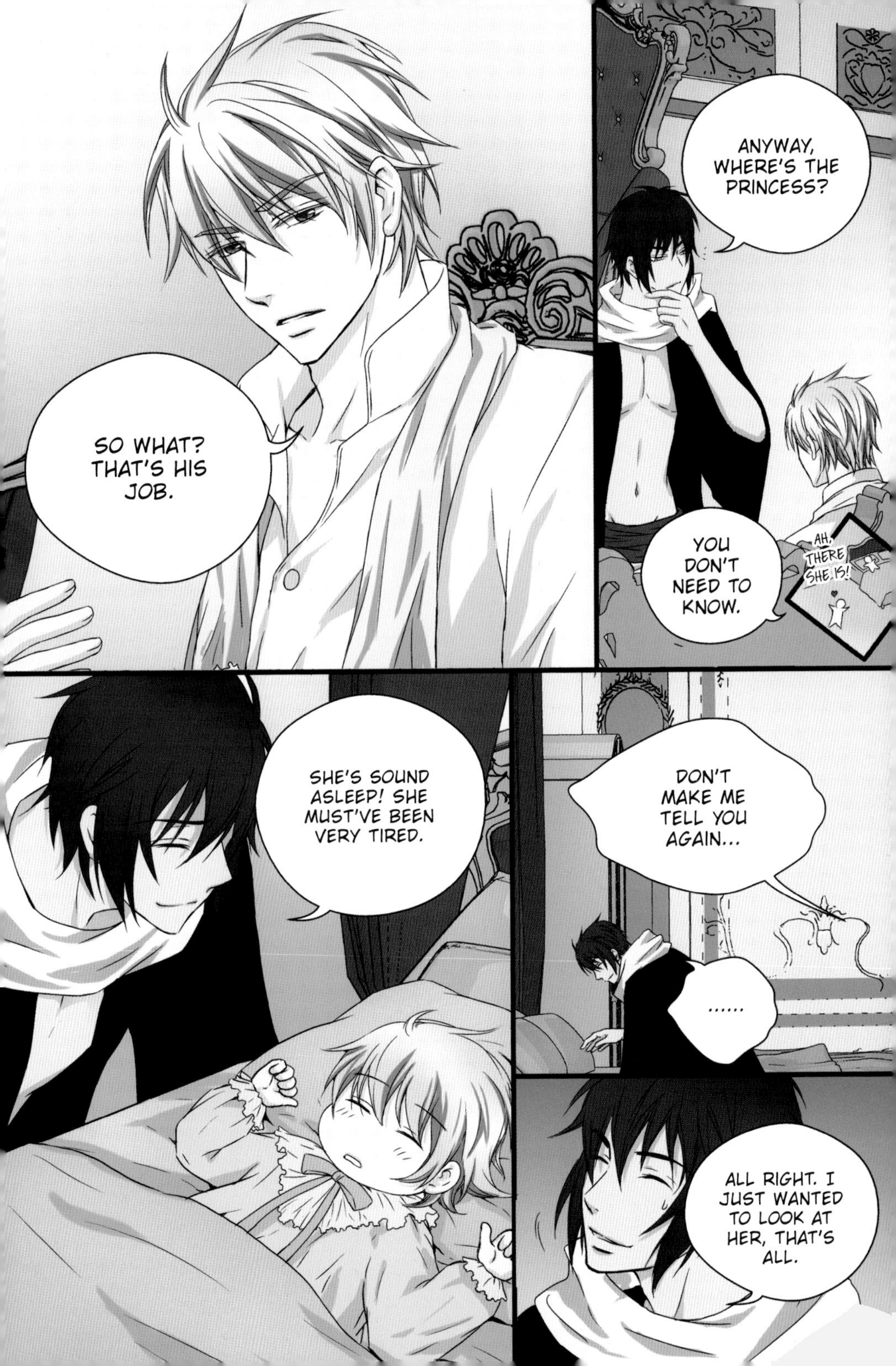
SO WHAT? THAT'S HIS JOB.
ANYWAY, WHERE'S THE PRINCESS?
YOU DON'T NEED TO KNOW.
AH, THERE SHE IS!
SHE'S SOUND ASLEEP! SHE MUST'VE BEEN VERY TIRED.
DON'T MAKE ME TELL YOU AGAIN...
......
ALL RIGHT. I JUST WANTED TO LOOK AT HER, THAT'S ALL.

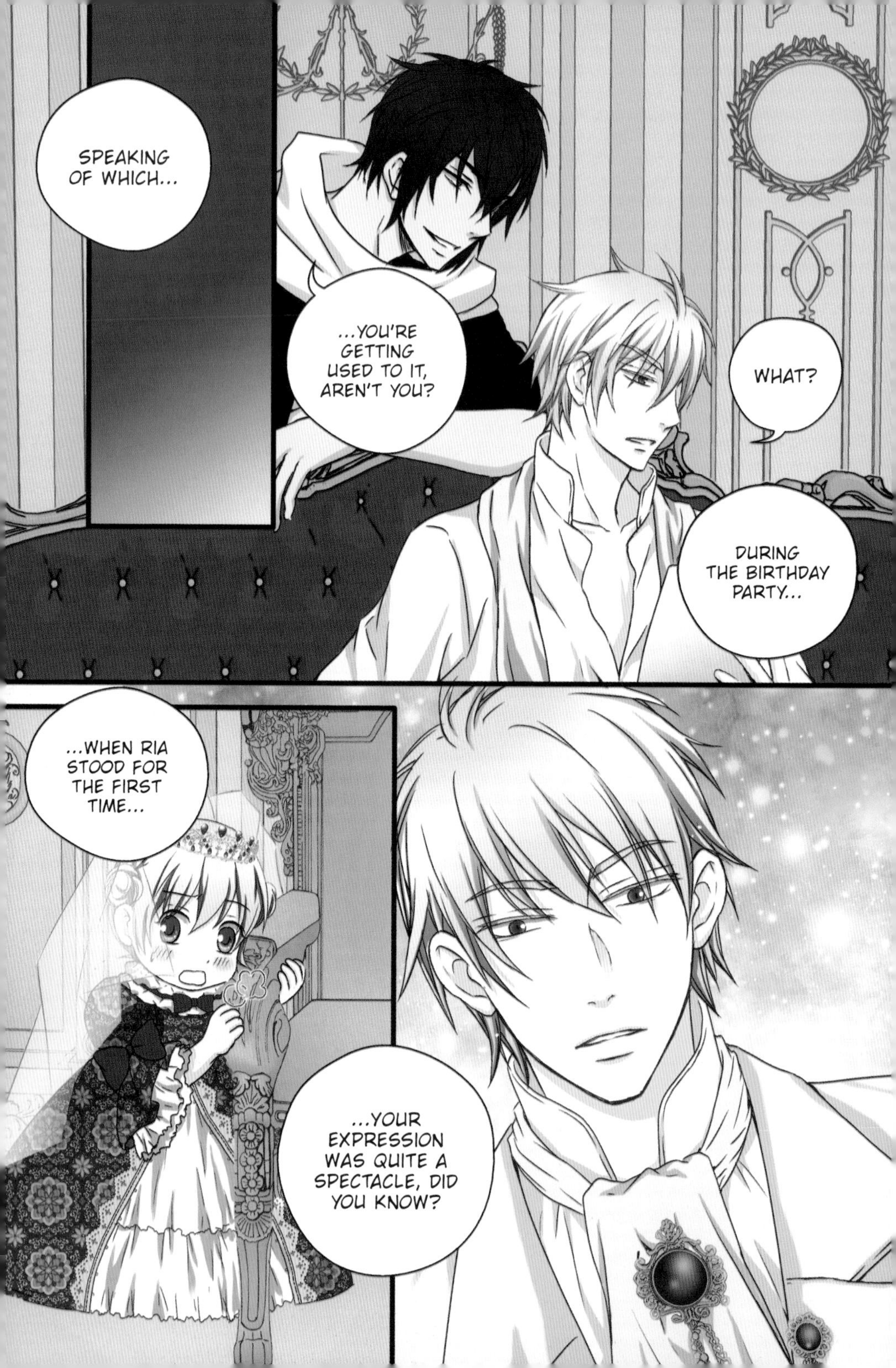
SPEAKING OF WHICH...
...YOU'RE GETTING USED TO IT, AREN'T YOU?
WHAT?
DURING THE BIRTHDAY PARTY...
...WHEN RIA STOOD FOR THE FIRST TIME...
...YOUR EXPRESSION WAS QUITE A SPECTACLE, DID YOU KNOW?

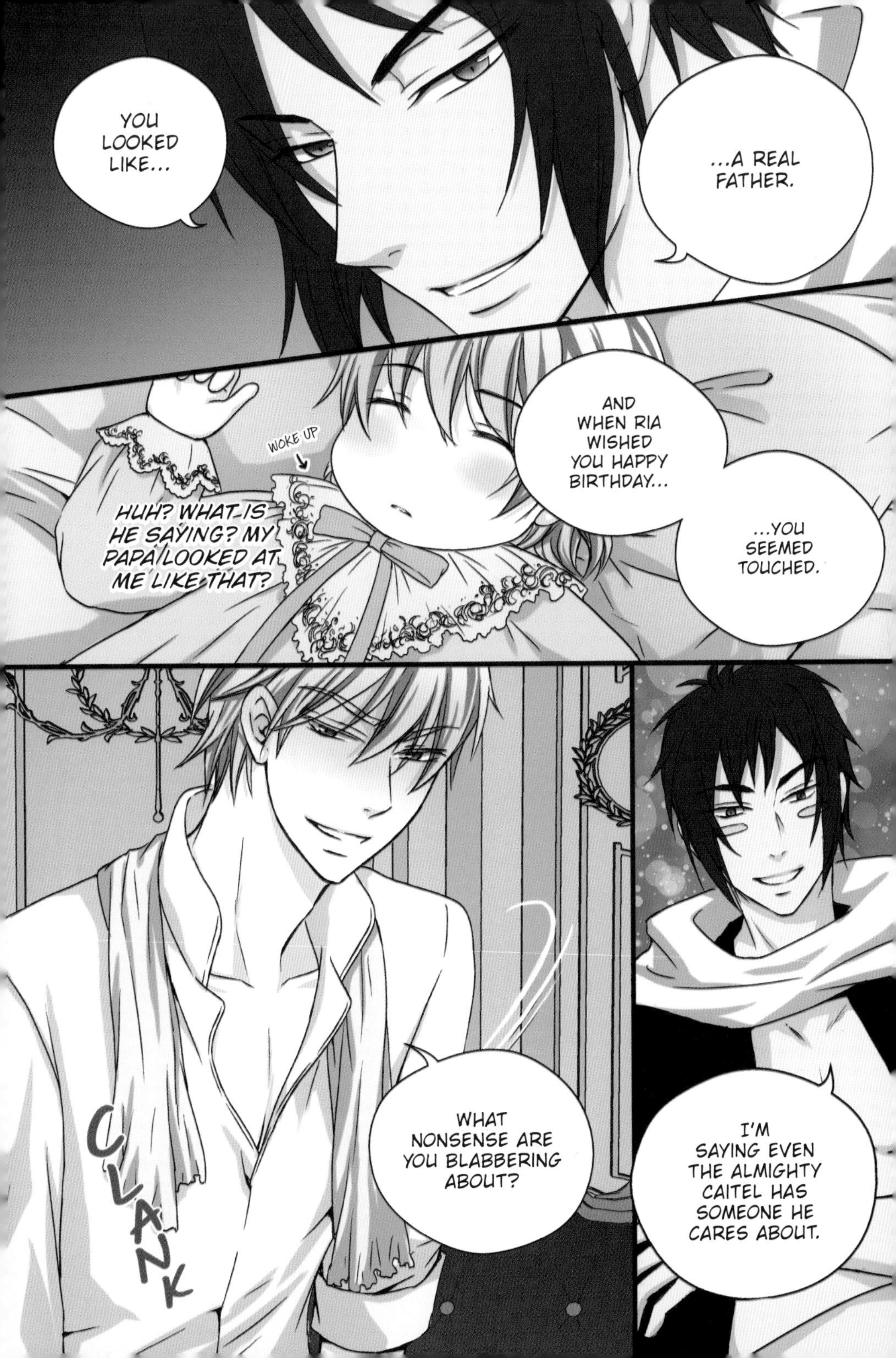
YOU LOOKED LIKE...
...A REAL FATHER.
WOKE UP
HUH? WHAT IS HE SAYING? MY PAPA LOOKED AT ME LIKE THAT?
AND WHEN RIA WISHED YOU HAPPY BIRTHDAY...
...YOU SEEMED TOUCHED.
CLANK
WHAT NONSENSE ARE YOU BLABBERING ABOUT?
I'M SAYING EVEN THE ALMIGHTY CAITEL HAS SOMEONE HE CARES ABOUT.

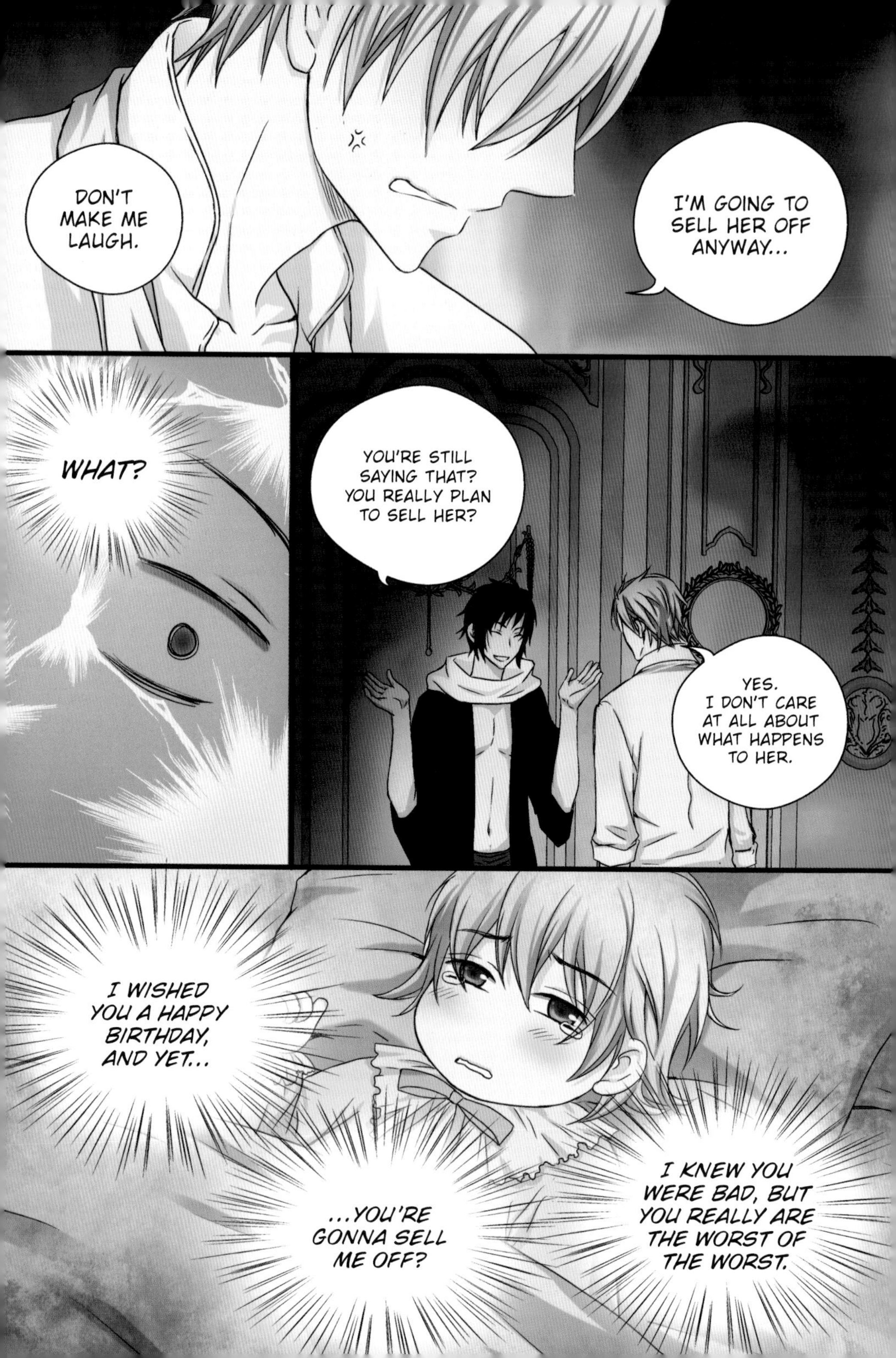

DON'T MAKE ME LAUGH.
I'M GOING TO SELL HER OFF ANYWAY...
WHAT?
YOU'RE STILL SAYING THAT? YOU REALLY PLAN TO SELL HER?
YES. I DON'T CARE AT ALL ABOUT WHAT HAPPENS TO HER.
I WISHED YOU A HAPPY BIRTHDAY, AND YET...
...YOU'RE GONNA SELL ME OFF?
I KNEW YOU WERE BAD, BUT YOU REALLY ARE THE WORST OF THE WORST.

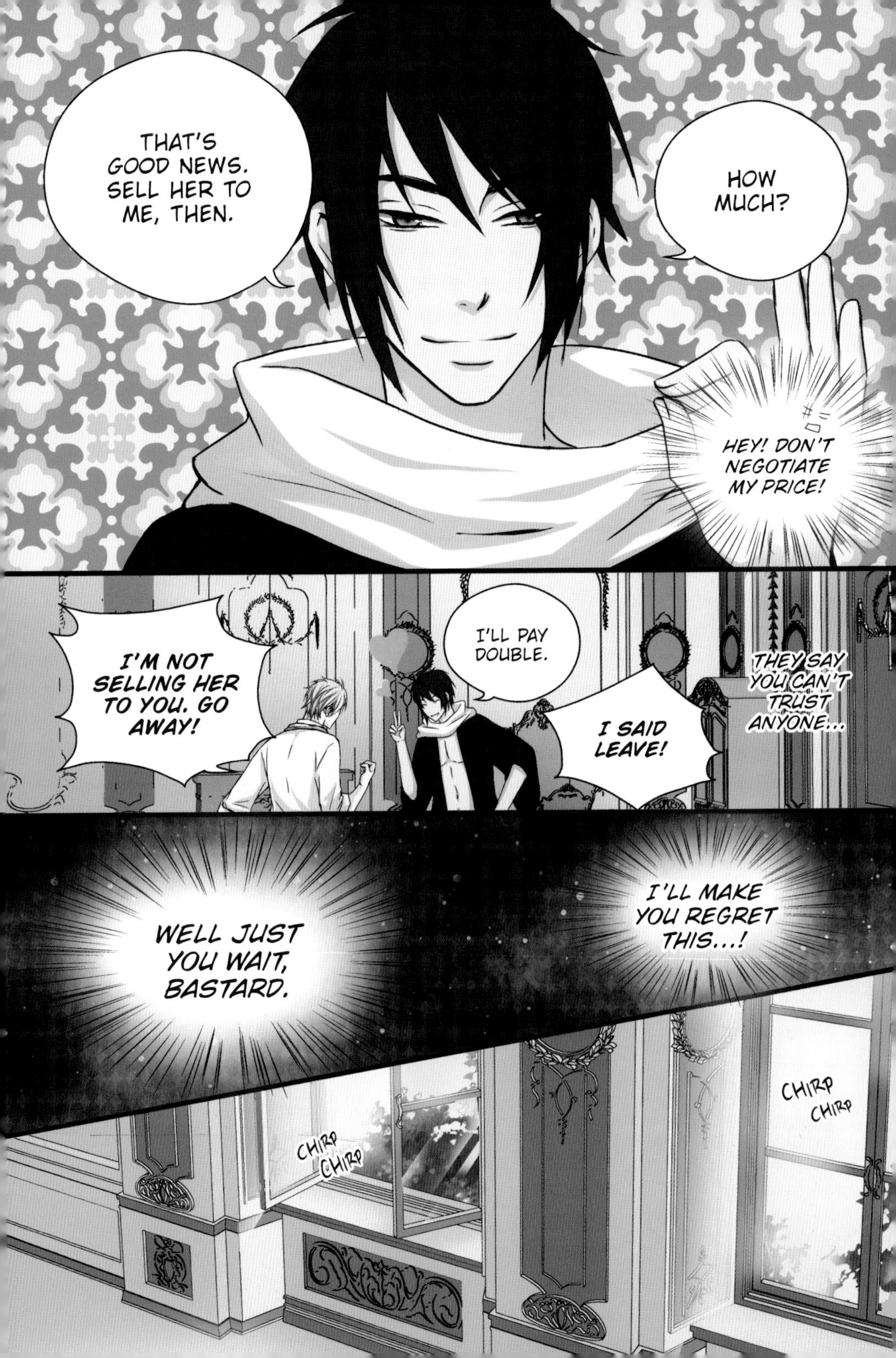
THAT'S GOOD NEWS. SELL HER TO ME, THEN.
HOW MUCH?
HEY! DON'T NEGOTIATE MY PRICE!
I'M NOT SELLING HER TO YOU. GO AWAY!
I'LL PAY DOUBLE.
I SAID LEAVE!
THEY SAY YOU CAN'T TRUST ANYONE...
WELL JUST YOU WAIT, BASTARD.
I'LL MAKE YOU REGRET THIS...!
CHIRP CHIRP
CHIRP CHIRP

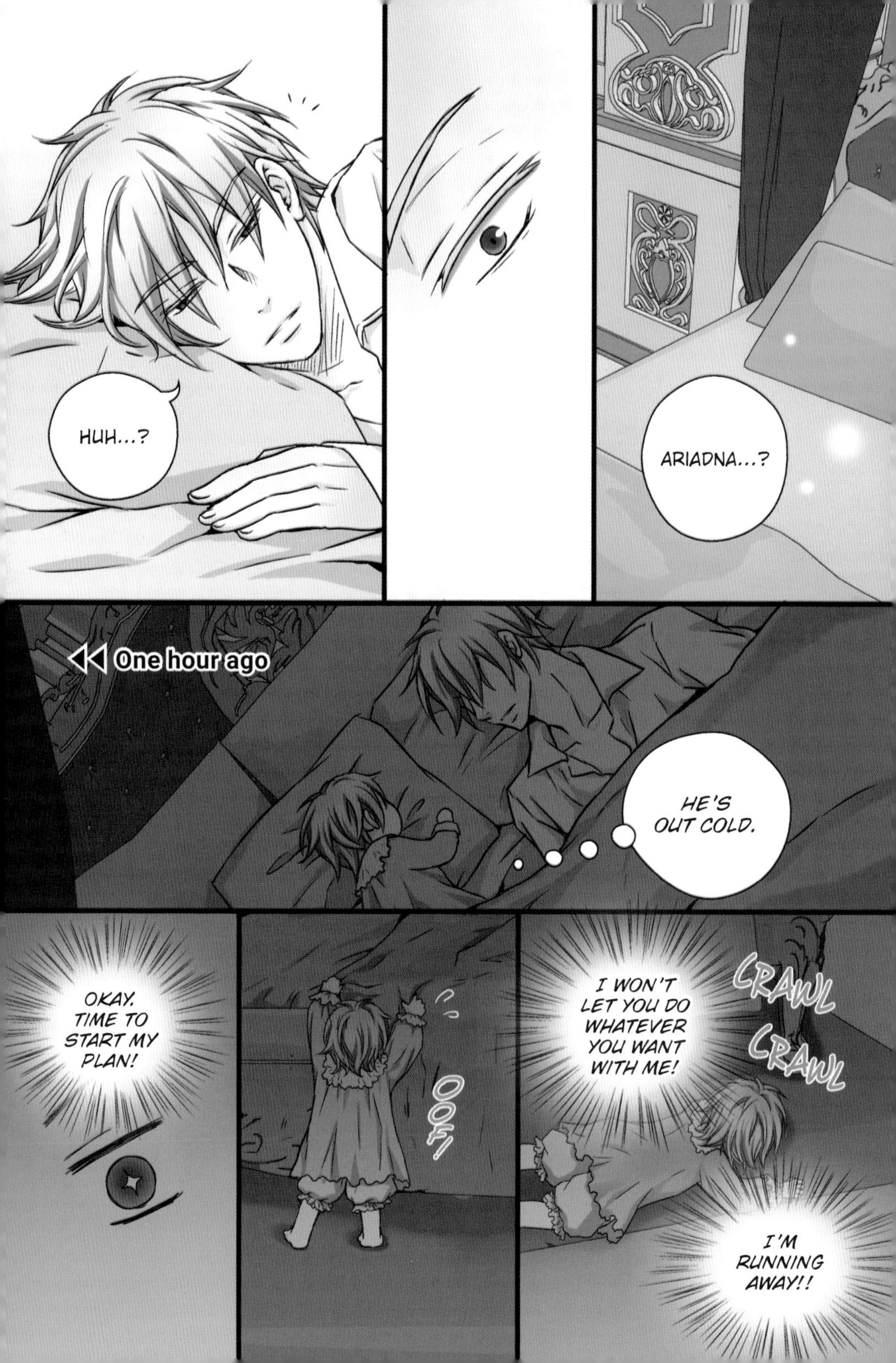
HUH...?
ARIADNA...?
One hour ago
HE'S OUT COLD.
OKAY. TIME TO START MY PLAN!
OOF!
I WON'T LET YOU DO WHATEVER YOU WANT WITH ME!
CRAWL CRAWL
I'M RUNNING AWAY!!

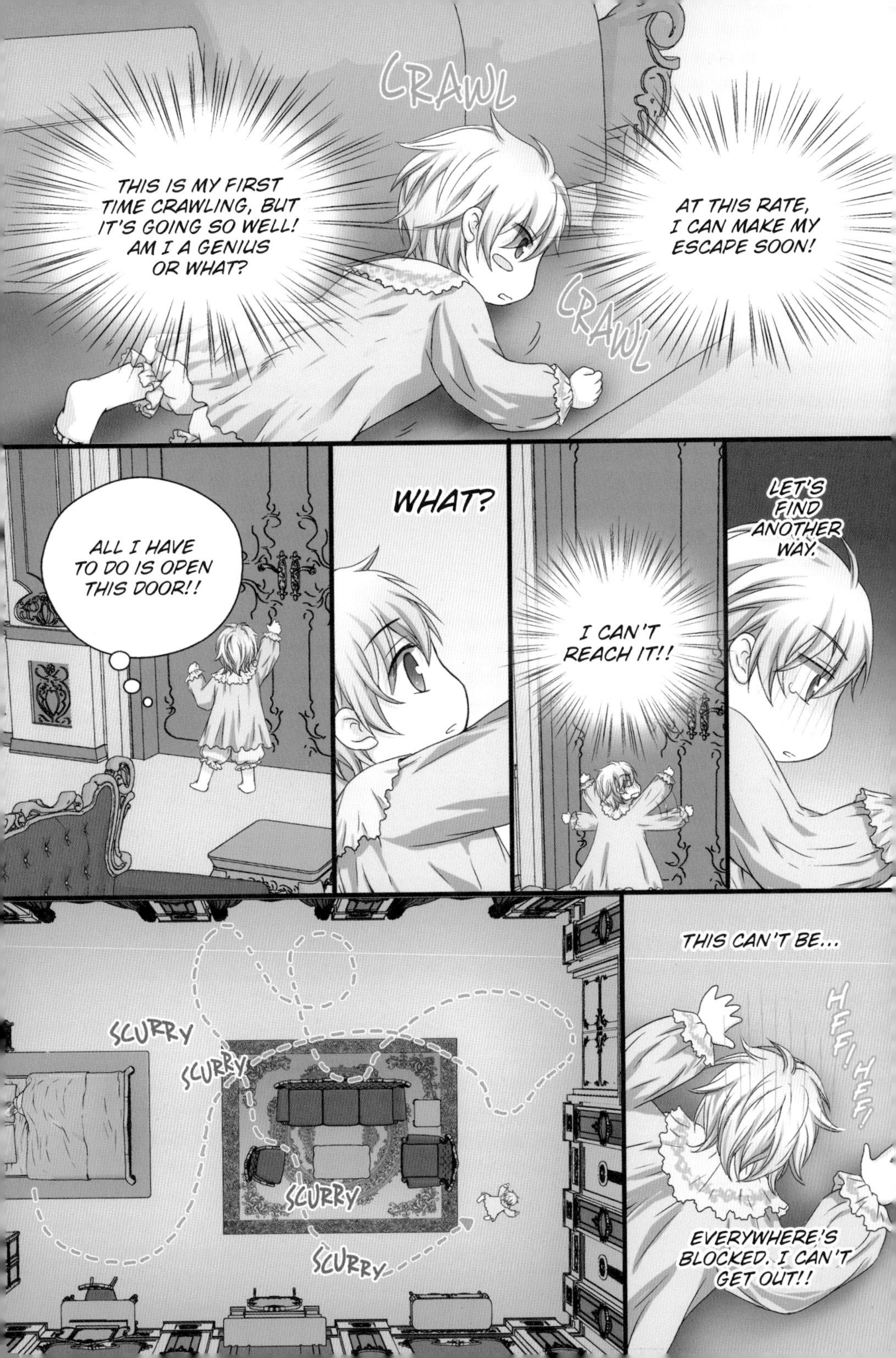
CRAWL
THIS IS MY FIRST TIME CRAWLING, BUT IT'S GOING SO WELL! AM I A GENIUS OR WHAT?
CRAWL
AT THIS RATE, I CAN MAKE MY ESCAPE SOON!
ALL I HAVE TO DO IS OPEN THIS DOOR!!
WHAT?
I CAN'T REACH IT!!
LET'S FIND ANOTHER WAY.
SCURRY
SCURRY
SCURRY
SCURRY
THIS CAN'T BE...
HFF! HFF!
EVERYWHERE'S BLOCKED. I CAN'T GET OUT!!

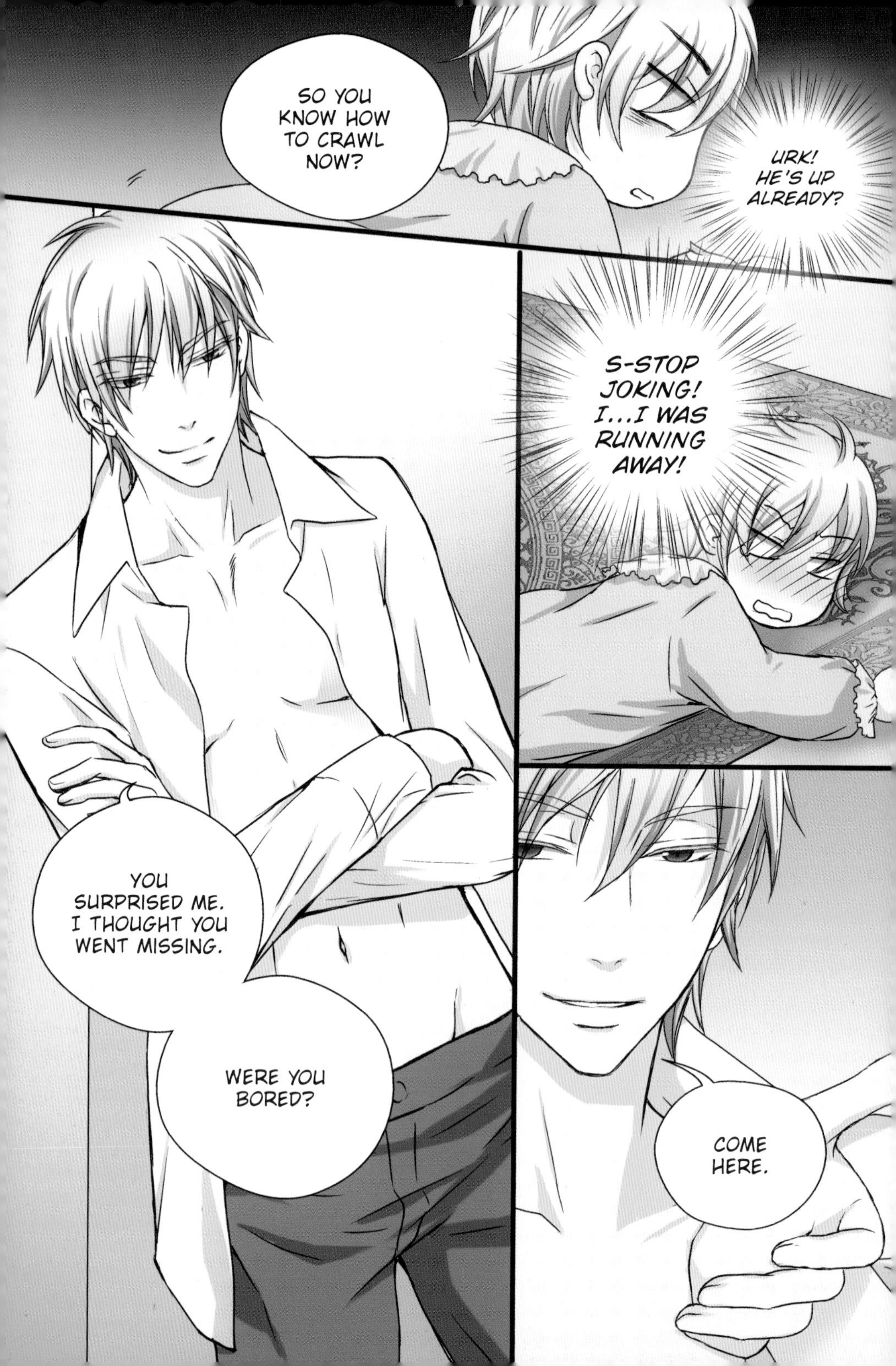
SO YOU KNOW HOW TO CRAWL NOW?
URK! HE'S UP ALREADY?
YOU SURPRISED ME. I THOUGHT YOU WENT MISSING.
WERE YOU BORED?
S-STOP JOKING! I...I WAS RUNNING AWAY!
COME HERE.

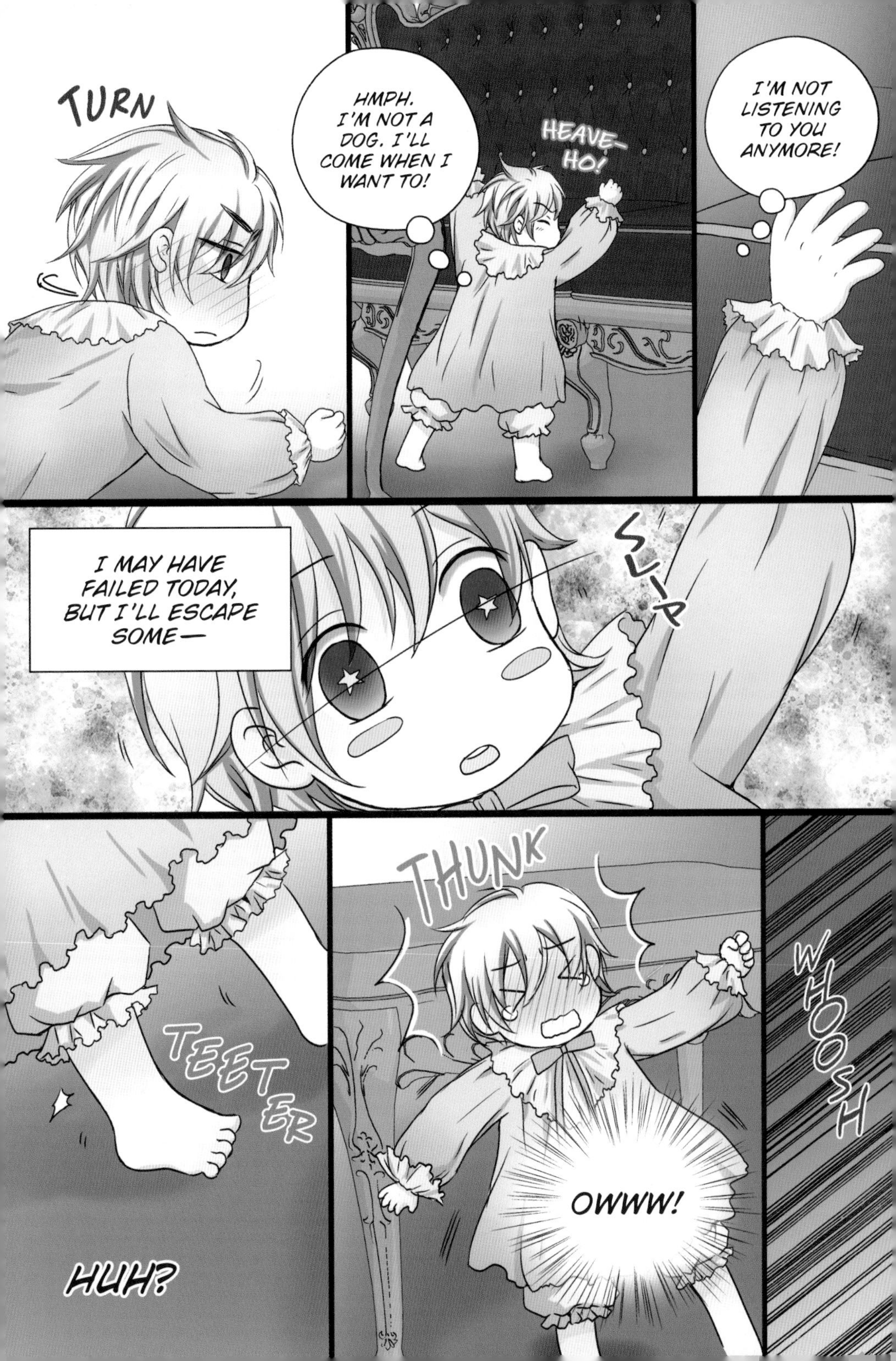
TURN
HMPH. I'M NOT A DOG. I'LL COME WHEN I WANT TO!
HEAVE-HO!
I'M NOT LISTENING TO YOU ANYMORE!
I MAY HAVE FAILED TODAY, BUT I'LL ESCAPE SOME—
SLIP
TEETER
HUH?
THUNK
OWWW!
WHOOSH

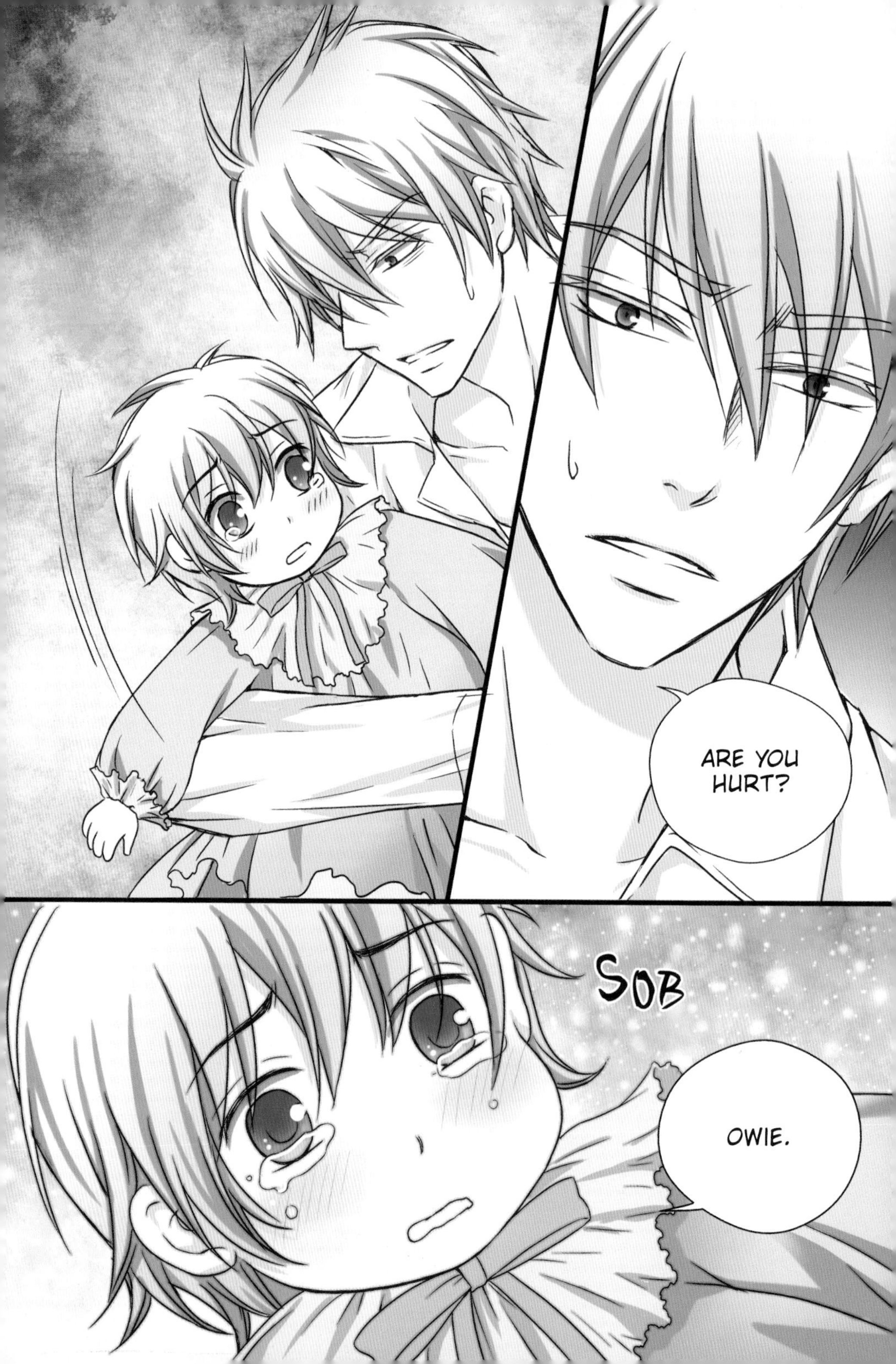
ARE YOU HURT?
SOB
OWIE.

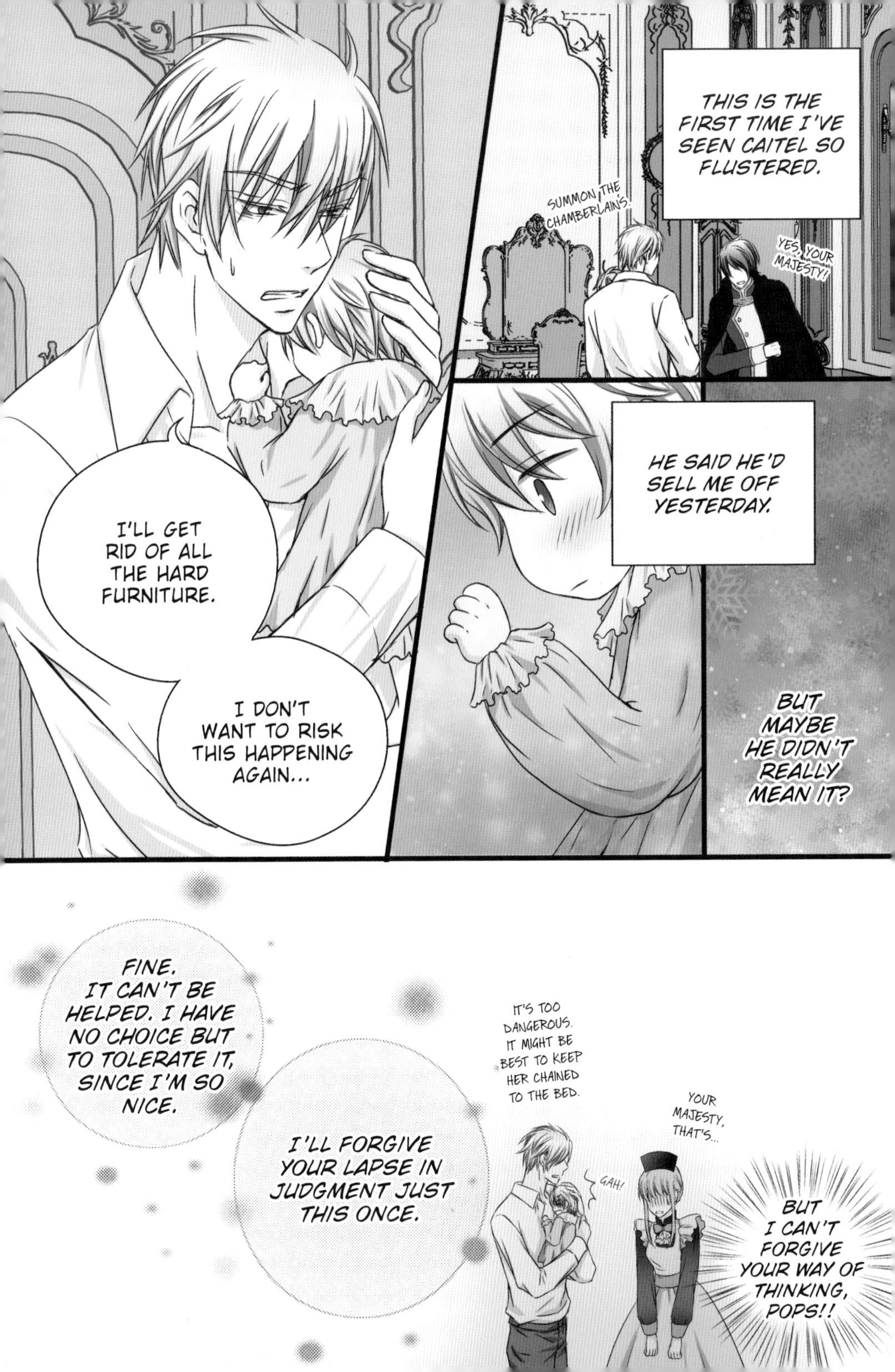

I'LL GET RID OF ALL THE HARD FURNITURE.
I DON'T WANT TO RISK THIS HAPPENING AGAIN...
THIS IS THE FIRST TIME I'VE SEEN CAITEL SO FLUSTERED.
SUMMON THE CHAMBERLAIN'S.
YES, YOUR MAJESTY!
HE SAID HE'D SELL ME OFF YESTERDAY.
BUT MAYBE HE DIDN'T REALLY MEAN IT?
FINE. IT CAN'T BE HELPED. I HAVE NO CHOICE BUT TO TOLERATE IT, SINCE I'M SO NICE.
I'LL FORGIVE YOUR LAPSE IN JUDGMENT JUST THIS ONCE.
IT'S TOO DANGEROUS. IT MIGHT BE BEST TO KEEP HER CHAINED TO THE BED.
YOUR MAJESTY, THAT'S...
GAH!
BUT I CAN'T FORGIVE YOUR WAY OF THINKING, POPS!!

DAUGHTER
OF THE
EMPEROR
To be continued...

Bonus

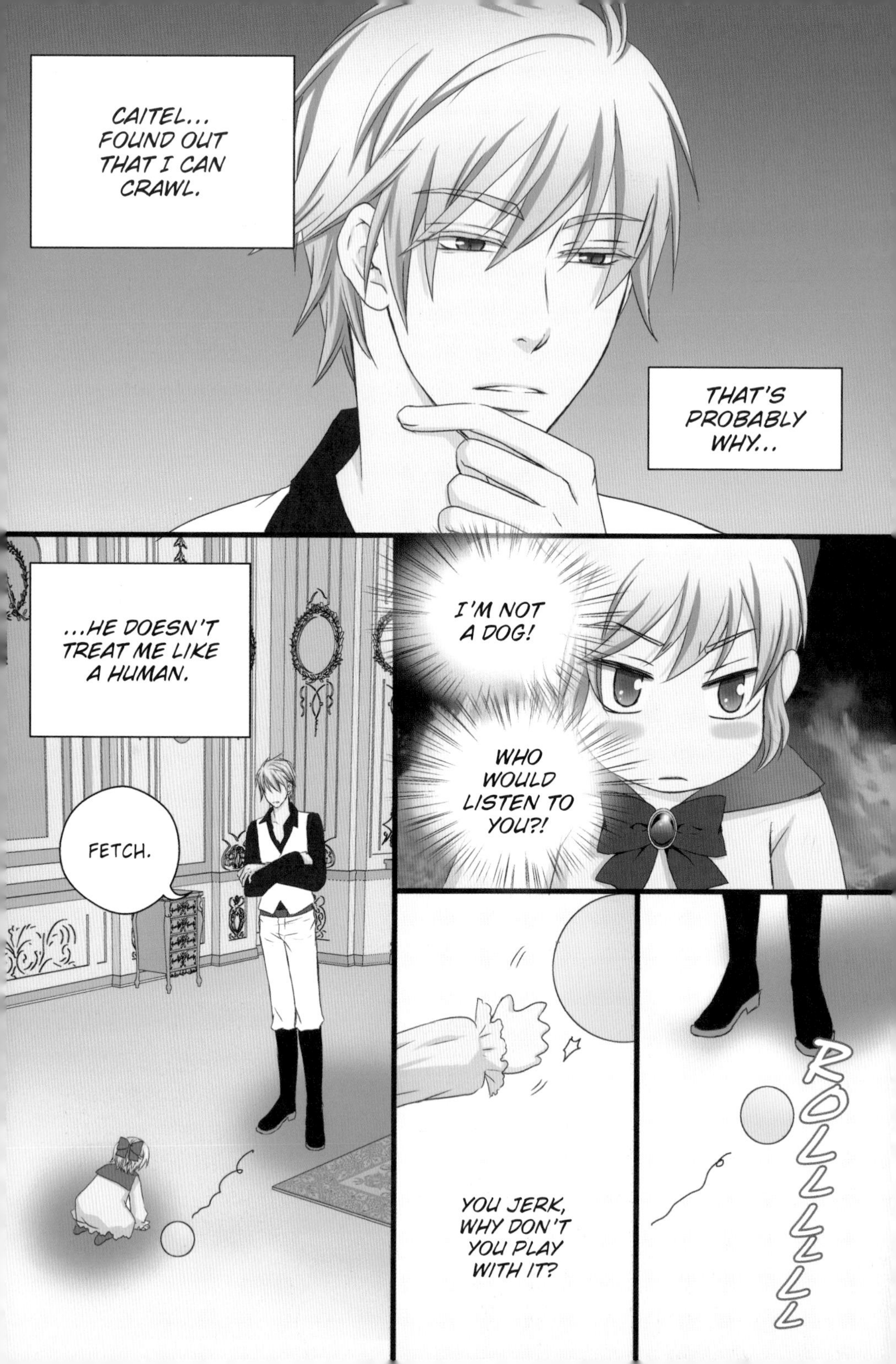
CAITEL... FOUND OUT THAT I CAN CRAWL.
THAT'S PROBABLY WHY...
...HE DOESN'T TREAT ME LIKE A HUMAN.
FETCH.
I'M NOT A DOG!
WHO WOULD LISTEN TO YOU?!
YOU JERK, WHY DON'T YOU PLAY WITH IT?
ROLLLLLL

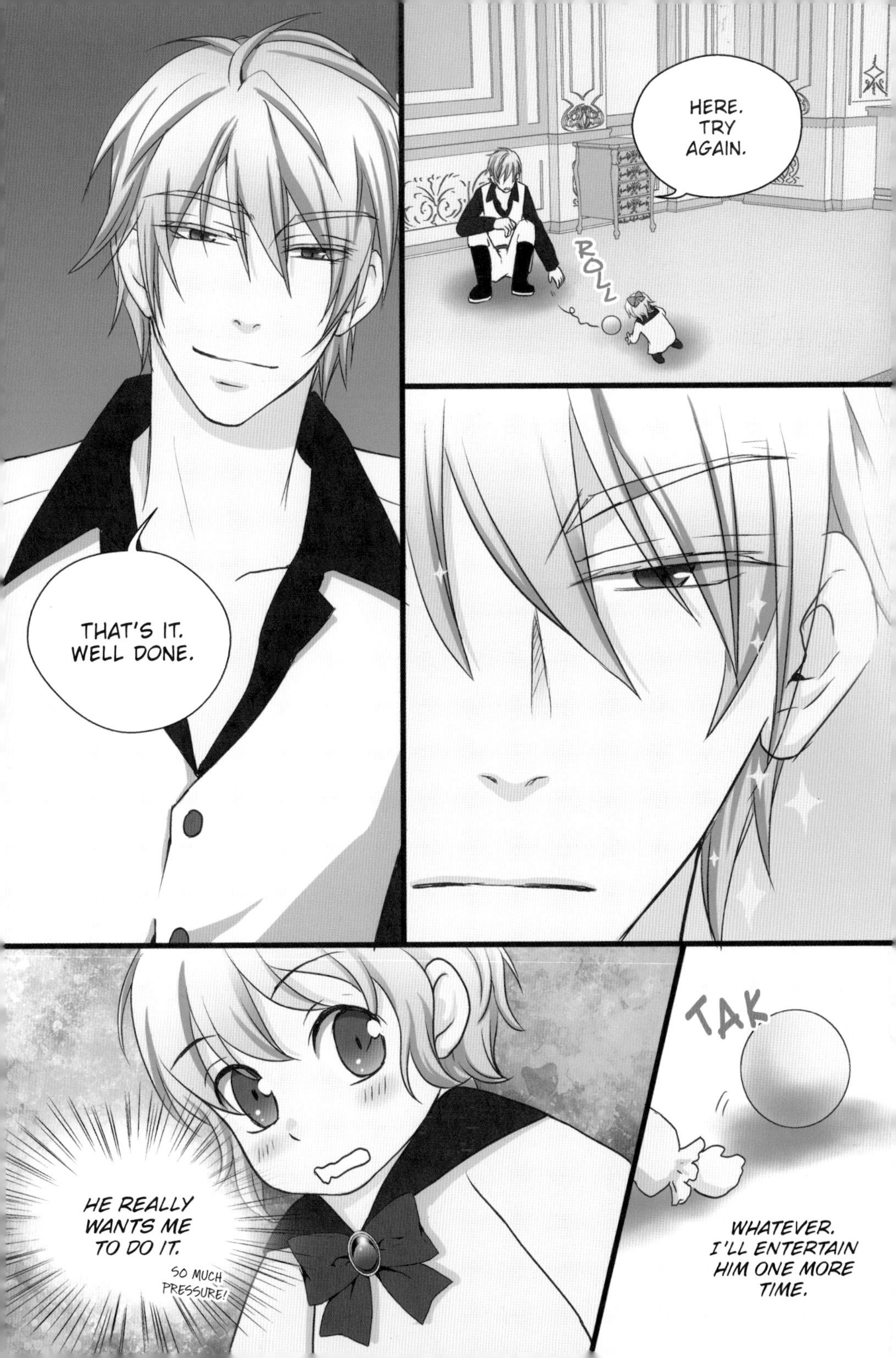
THAT'S IT. WELL DONE.
HERE. TRY AGAIN.
ROLL
HE REALLY WANTS ME TO DO IT.
SO MUCH PRESSURE!
TAK
WHATEVER. I'LL ENTERTAIN HIM ONE MORE TIME.

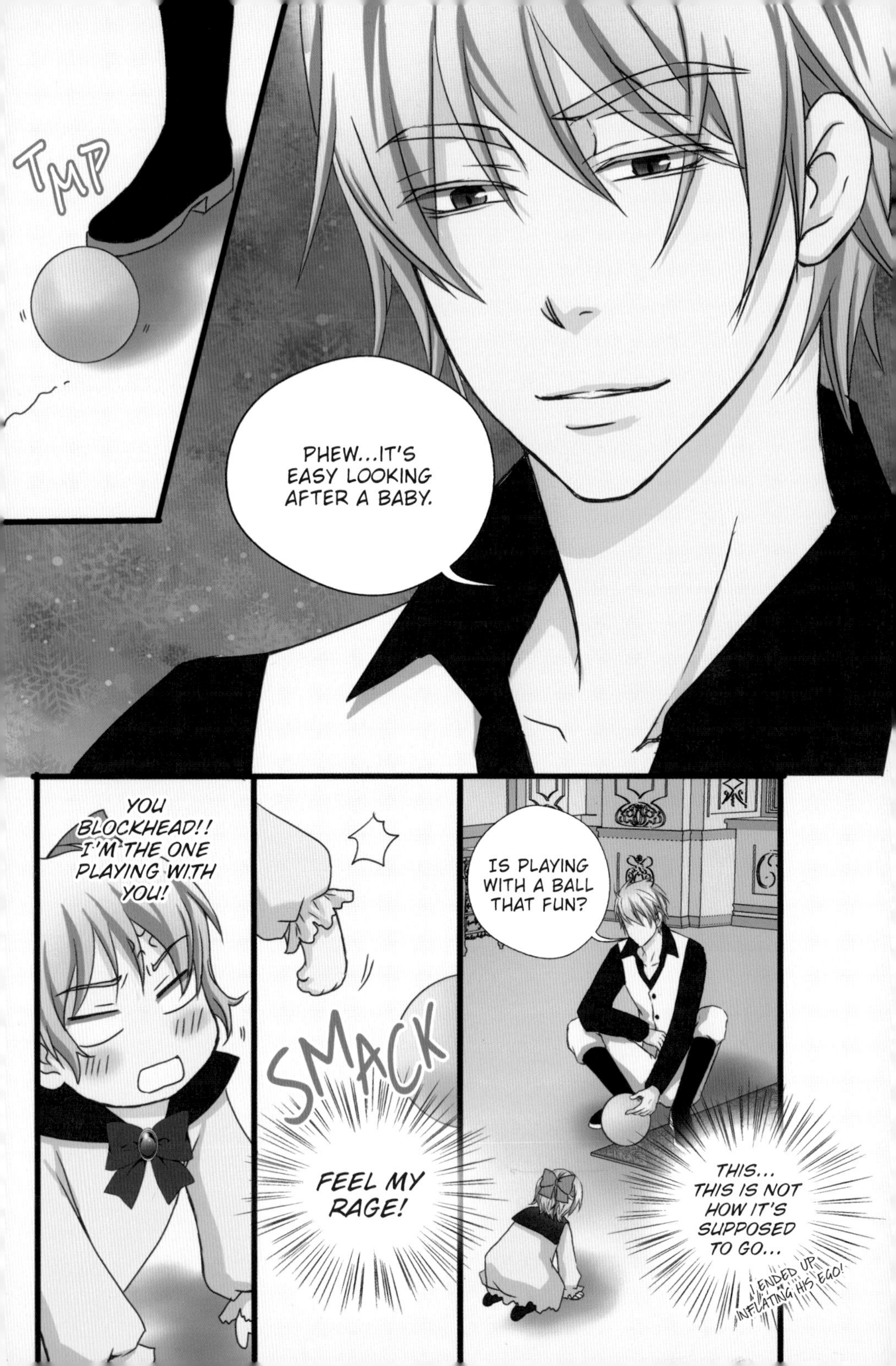
TMP
PHEW...IT'S EASY LOOKING AFTER A BABY.
YOU BLOCKHEAD!! I'M THE ONE PLAYING WITH YOU!
SMACK
FEEL MY RAGE!
IS PLAYING WITH A BALL THAT FUN?
THIS... THIS IS NOT HOW IT'S SUPPOSED TO GO...
I ENDED UP INFLATING HIS EGO!

Afterword

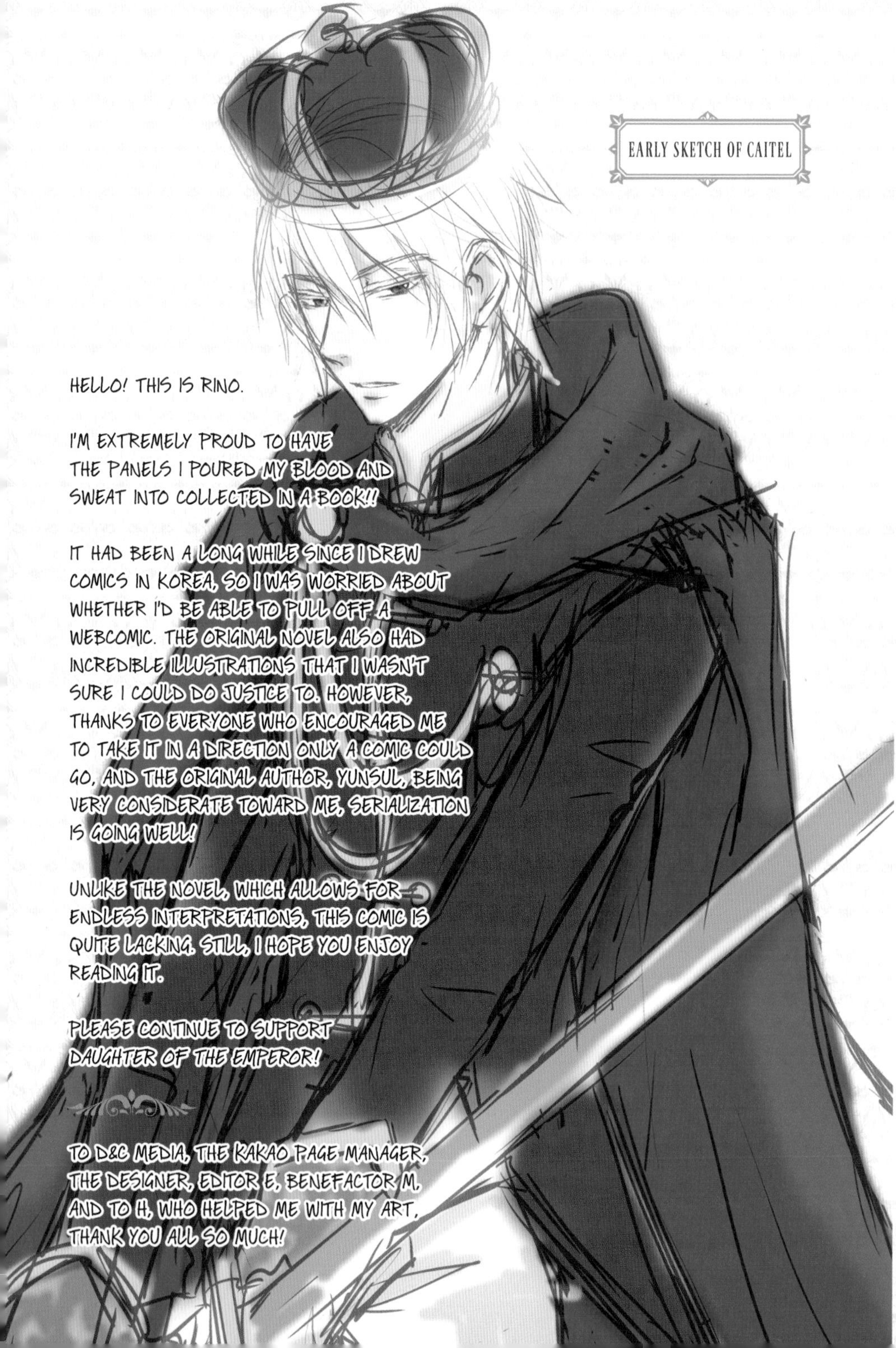

EARLY SKETCH OF CAITEL

HELLO! THIS IS RINO.

I'M EXTREMELY PROUD TO HAVE THE PANELS I POURED MY BLOOD AND SWEAT INTO COLLECTED IN A BOOK!!

IT HAD BEEN A LONG WHILE SINCE I DREW COMICS IN KOREA, SO I WAS WORRIED ABOUT WHETHER I'D BE ABLE TO PULL OFF A WEBCOMIC. THE ORIGINAL NOVEL ALSO HAD INCREDIBLE ILLUSTRATIONS THAT I WASN'T SURE I COULD DO JUSTICE TO. HOWEVER, THANKS TO EVERYONE WHO ENCOURAGED ME TO TAKE IT IN A DIRECTION ONLY A COMIC COULD GO, AND THE ORIGINAL AUTHOR, YUNSUL, BEING VERY CONSIDERATE TOWARD ME, SERIALIZATION IS GOING WELL!

UNLIKE THE NOVEL, WHICH ALLOWS FOR ENDLESS INTERPRETATIONS, THIS COMIC IS QUITE LACKING. STILL, I HOPE YOU ENJOY READING IT.

PLEASE CONTINUE TO SUPPORT DAUGHTER OF THE EMPEROR!

TO D&C MEDIA, THE KAKAO PAGE MANAGER, THE DESIGNER, EDITOR E, BENEFACTOR M, AND TO H, WHO HELPED ME WITH MY ART, THANK YOU ALL SO MUCH!

DAUGHTER
OF THE
EMPEROR

VOLUME 2 PREVIEW

THE MASTERMIND IS FINALLY EXPOSED!

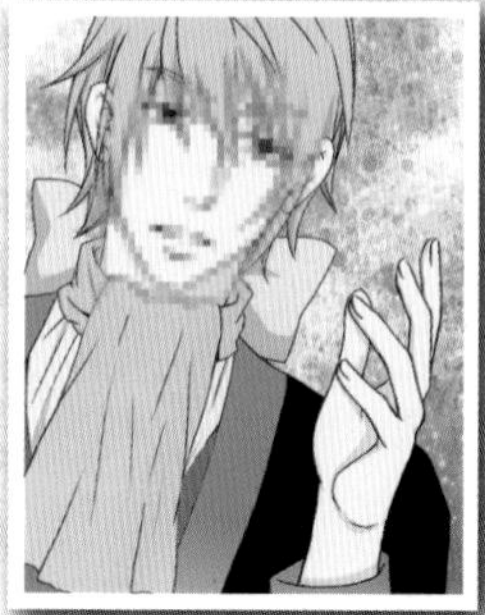

THIS GUY

THIS GUY!

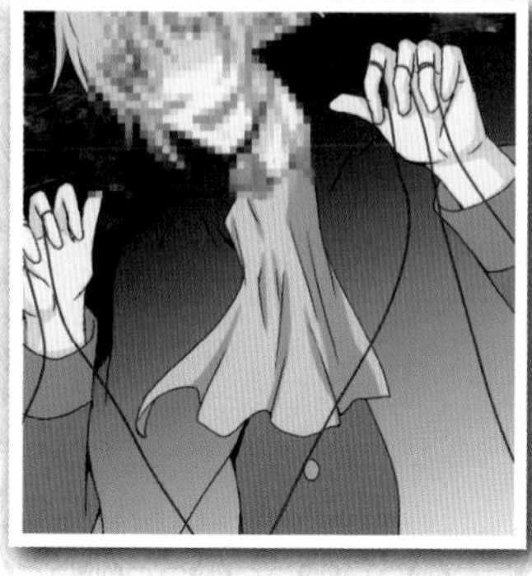

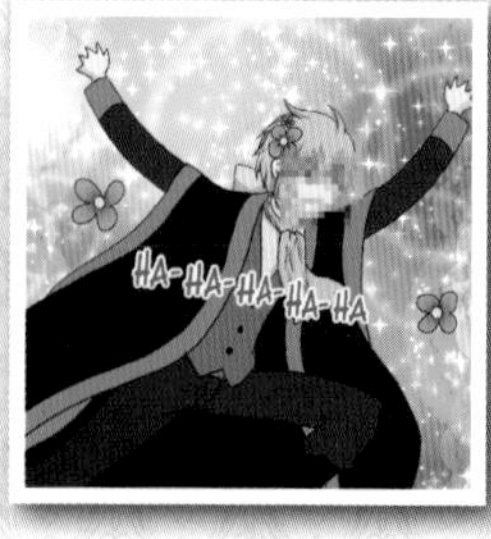
HA-HA-HA-HA-HA

THIS GUY??

THEY'RE ALL THE SAME PERSON?!

EEK!

HAPPY DAYS WITH PAPA ♡

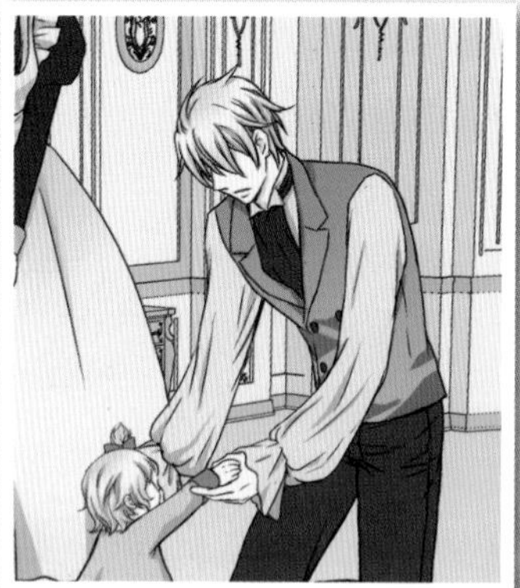

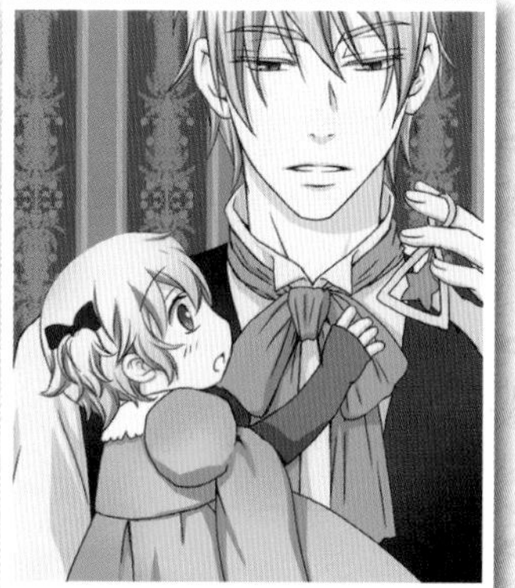

I want to switch places with Ria ♡_♡

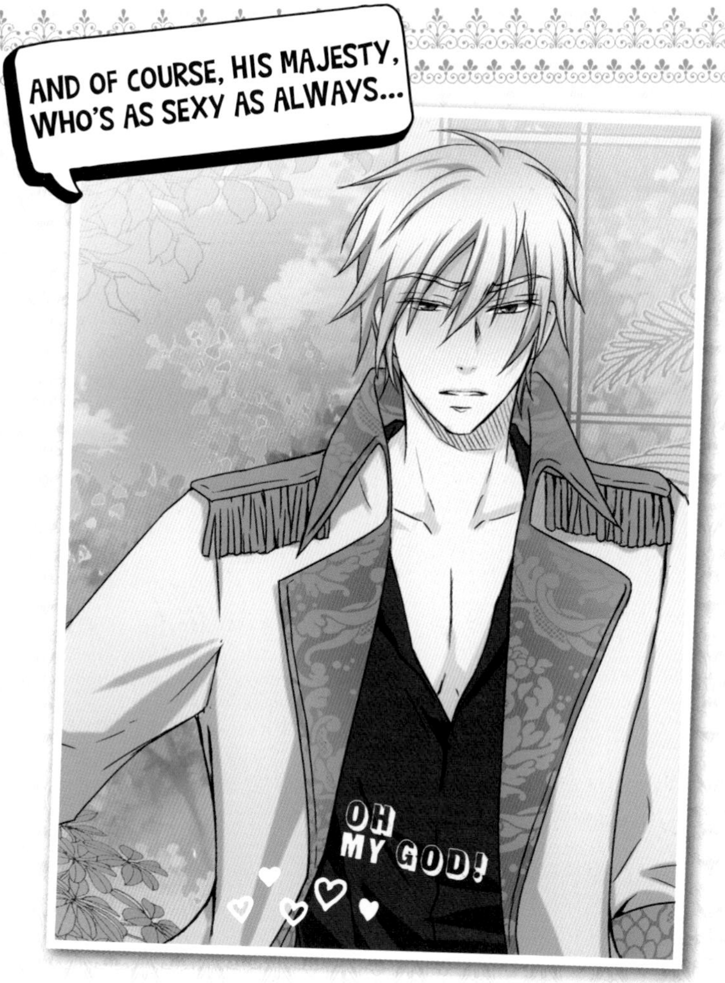
AND OF COURSE, HIS MAJESTY, WHO'S AS SEXY AS ALWAYS...
OH MY GOD!

ALL THIS AND MORE IN...

DAUGHTER OF THE EMPEROR

RINO 1 Original story by YUNSUL

Translation: MICAH KIM   Lettering: BIANCA PISTILLO

Daughter of the Emperor Volume 1
© RINO, YUNSUL 2015 / D&C WEBTOON Biz
All rights reserved.
First published in Korea in 2015 by D&C WEBTOON Biz Co., Ltd.

English translation © 2022 by Yen Press, LLC

Yen Press
150 West 30th Street, 19th Floor
New York, NY 10001

Visit us at yenpress.com ⊙ facebook.com/yenpress
twitter.com/yenpress ⊙ yenpress.tumblr.com ⊙ instagram.com/yenpress

First Yen Press Edition: May 2022

Yen Press is an imprint of Yen Press, LLC.
The Yen Press name and logo are trademarks of Yen Press, LLC.

Library of Congress Control Number: 2022931225

ISBNs: 978-1-9753-4092-6 (paperback)
978-1-9753-4093-3 (ebook)

10 9 8 7 6 5 4 3 2 1

TPA

Printed in South Korea